General History of the Caribbean

TITLES IN THE SERIES

Volume I   Autochthonous Societies

Volume II   New Societies: The Caribbean in the Long Sixteenth Century

Volume III   The Slave Societies of the Caribbean

Volume IV   The Long Nineteenth Century: Nineteenth-Century Transformations

Volume V   The Caribbean in the Twentieth Century

Volume VI   Methodology and Historiography of the Caribbean

General History

of the

Caribbean

Volume II

New societies: The Caribbean in the

long sixteenth century

Editor: Pieter C. Emmer
Co-editor: German Carrera Damas

CARIBBEAN

UNESCO Publishing

First published 1999

Published jointly by
UNESCO PUBLISHING/MACMILLAN EDUCATION LTD
London and Basingstoke
Companies and representatives throughout the world.

UNESCO ISBN 92-3-103357-3
Macmillan ISBN 0-333-72455-0 PBK
                0-333-72454-2 Hbk

Printed in Hong Kong

A catalogue record for this book is available from the British Library.

Acknowledgements

The cover photograph is taken from a painting titled 'Father Bartolomé de Las Casas explains Christianity to
the Cacique Henry', anonymous, Haiti. Photograph © Michel Claude, UNESCO collection.

The authors and publishers wish to acknowledge, with thanks, the following photographic sources:

The Barbados Museum, Plate 17
Biblioteca Nacional, Madrid, Plates 7, 13, 14 and 15
Bibliothèque Nationale de France, Plates 1, 4, 5, 6, 8 and 11
Bibliothèque Ste Genevieve, Paris, Plate 12
British Library, London, Plate 10
Cuban National Library, Plates 3 and 16
Museo Naval, Madrid, Plate 9
The Newberry Library, Plate 2

The publishers have made every effort to trace the copyright holders, but if they have inadvertently
overlooked any, they will be pleased to make the necessary arrangements at the first opportunity.

CONTENTS

Preface *Federico Mayor, Director-General of UNESCO* vi

Description of the Project *Professor Sir Roy Augier* ix

List of Contributors xii

List of tables xv

Plates xvi

Map: The Caribbean xvii

Introduction: The creation of a new Caribbean society, 1492–1650
  Horst Pietschmann and *Pieter C. Emmer* 1

1 The Caribbean environment and early settlement
  David Watts 29

2 The initial linkage with America: a general framework
  Ruggiero Romano 43

3 The establishment of primary centres and primary plantations
  Frank Moya Pons 62

4 Spanish expansion in America, 1492 to c. 1580
  Horst Pietschmann 79

5 French, English and Dutch in the Lesser Antilles: from privateering
  to planting, c. 1550–c. 1650
  Anne Pérotin-Dumon 114

6 Forced African settlement. The basis of forced settlement: Africa and
  its trading conditions
  Enriqueta Vilá Vilar with *Wim Klooster* 159

7 Native society and the European occupation of the Caribbean
  islands and coastal *Tierra Firme*, 1492–1650
  Neil L. Whitehead 180

8 The city in the Hispanic Caribbean, 1492–1650
  Alfredo Castillero-Calvo 201

9 Intellectual, artistic and ideological aspects of cultures in the New World
  Gustavo Martin-Fragachan 247

10 The cartography of the Caribbean, 1500–1650
  David Buisseret 308

Bibliography 319

Index 334

PREFACE

Federico Mayor
Director-General of UNESCO

How should the Caribbean be defined? It is here understood as encompassing not only the islands but also the coastal part of South America, from Colombia to the Guyanas and the riverine zones of Central America, in so far as these parts of the mainland were the homes of people engaged from time to time in activities which linked their lives with those of people in the islands. Despite the varieties of languages and customs resulting from the convergence there – by choice or constraint – of peoples of diverse cultures, the Caribbean has many cultural commonalities deriving from the shared history and experience of its inhabitants. In this region, endowed with exceptionally beautiful landscapes and still undiscovered ocean resources, there grew up from the sixteenth century onwards a completely new society, which has in our own time distinguished itself by producing a relatively large number of internationally recognized personalities in many fields – poets, novelists, painters, dancers, designers, musicians, sportsmen, jurists, historians, politicians.

In seeking to promote the preservation of cultural identities and greater understanding among peoples through the exchange of cultural information, UNESCO has found it important to facilitate the writing of a new history of this region. I call this history 'new' because until quite recently Caribbean histories were more about exploits of European nation states in the Caribbean – histories of war and trade in the islands and the mainland. Such histories of the individual islands as were published before this time tended to be written from the standpoint of resident Europeans. It was the movement for political autonomy, and the broadening of historiography in the European and American universities in the first half of the century, that led initially to changes of emphasis in the study of the history of single islands, and later to histories of topics which linked the islands, notably the sugar industry, slavery, slave laws and Asian immigration.

In the established universities of Havana and Puerto Rico and in new ones such as the University of the West Indies, departments of Caribbean studies were opened with the aim of undertaking teaching and research on Caribbean literature, history, culture and society, the better to understand forces that had shaped the region and to identify the many elements which constitute Caribbean culture. The main findings of the scholars since then are reflected in the six volumes of this

vi

history, thereby presenting a more regional account than before of the Caribbean past and of the people who have constituted Caribbean society.

This history traces the development of the region starting with the autochthonous peoples of the Caribbean. This includes the hunters and the gatherers as well as the incipient cultivators associated with the beginnings of village life. Situated as they were at what had become the gateway to the New World, these populations were the first to be enslaved. The inhabitants of the Greater Antilles were decimated by acts of excessive inhumanity and disease. The Caribs survived longer through their well-honed fighting skills, but their numbers dwindled nevertheless and in the eighteenth century those who still resisted were transported to the coast of Belize where they established communities that exist to this day and from where they now return to teach their native language – 'Garifuna' – to the few Caribs who remain in Dominica and in St Vincent. The story of these early societies is told in the first two volumes.

Volume III of this history (The Slave Societies) will constitute a central point of reference. In examining the creation of new societies, full account is taken of slavery, the terrible toll of human life and suffering it exacted and its pervasive impact on the psyche of the Caribbean people, both white and black. Resistance to slavery took many forms, of which marronnage in Haiti, Jamaica and Suriname, where the numbers were large, has received the most attention. Revolts and rebellions persisted throughout the region from the seventeenth century, although the best known is understandably that which led to Haiti's independence at the beginning of the nineteenth century. The abolition of the British slave trade left slavery itself intact, until it gradually succumbed in the decades of the nineteenth century, first to the creed of the French Revolution, then to the combination of slave rebellions in the islands and the determined protestations of humanitarians and free traders in Europe.

By the middle of the nineteenth century the disputes between estate owners and the emancipated field labourers, referred to in Volumes I and IV, opened the way for the influx of people from Asia, predominantly from India, thus adding a new element to the Creole societies which had gradually been formed since the sixteenth century. To avoid this supply of new labour for sugar estates becoming the restoration of slavery in a new guise, the recruitment of the labourers and their condition of work in the islands were regulated by law. Nevertheless, the constraints of indenture and the indignities attendant on being estate labourers affected the way in which Creole societies developed in the twentieth century. Undoubtedly, slavery and indenture have influenced the social and economic relations of societies in the circum-Caribbean in ways productive of ethnic and class conflict. Yet they have not only been the sources of cruelty and injustice, of acts remembered and resented. By persistent resistance to these oppressive regimes, these societies have also endowed themselves with the dignity and self-confidence of free men.

During the latter part of the nineteenth century, the impulse towards autonomy which was felt by some of the propertied and educated élites was frustrated by international, political and economic circumstances outside their control. The production of sugar from cane continued to dominate the Caribbean economies, with oil, minerals and tourism becoming important items in the twentieth century. The influx of

American capital and the gradual diminution of European interests in the Caribbean led to the expansion of American influence in the region from the turn of the century onwards, notably in Cuba, Haiti and Santo Domingo. This was the context in which the movements for self-determination worked, complicated everywhere by racial prejudice and disparities in the ownership of property.

In the years following the Second World War, examined in Volume V, the islands and their immediate mainland neighbours have sought a variety of solutions to the problems which arise from societies asserting political autonomy while possessing economies dependent on overseas markets where their goods are protected from competition. Puerto Rico became the 'Estado Libre', a Commonwealth; the French-speaking islands became departments of France; the Dutch-speaking islands, prior to the independence of Suriname, all became part of the Kingdom of the Netherlands; the British islands first flirted with a Federation, then became independent states separately; other states, following periods of military dictatorship, have pursued the path of socialist revolution. Currently, both in the islands and on the continent, there is a growing tendency for policy to be guided by regionalism, by the impulse towards association and co-operation, towards the formation of trading blocs, initially prompted by geographical propinquity.

These subregions have recently begun concerted efforts towards recognizing and confirming that their mutual interests will be served by closer association. It is therefore appropriate that the two UNESCO projects of the *General History of the Caribbean* and the *General History of Latin America* are being undertaken simultaneously. The two histories should be read together as distinct parts of a unified whole, as an element in UNESCO's contribution to regional development through mutual understanding and cultural integration. Every effort will be made for both histories to reach as wide a public as possible in the major languages of the region, through the universities, through the schools by means of specially adapted versions (textbooks and children's books), and eventually through radio and television, plays and films.

I wish, in conclusion, to extend my sincere thanks to the Chairman, Rapporteur and members of the International Scientific Committee and to the editors and authors of the various volumes who have come together to participate in this significant enterprise. My thanks also go to the governments and universities which have supported the project and to the Association of Caribbean Historians, so many of whose members have contributed generously to the creation of this work.

Description of the Project

Professor Sir Roy Augier
Chairman of the Drafting Committee for
the *General History of the Caribbean*

The decision to commission a UNESCO General History of the Caribbean, taken by the twenty-first session of the General Conference of UNESCO (1980), was an instance of the change in cultural policy which resulted in a shift in emphasis from the 'common heritage of all mankind' to acknowledging the 'diversity of cultures' and commissioning the histories of Africa, Central Asia, Latin America and the Caribbean, as well as a revision of the *History of Mankind*. In all these cases, the brief of the Director-General was for a history observed from inside the region not from the outside, as if from the ports and capitals of European colonizers. Cultural identity, unity in diversity, and therefore the cultural heritages of the regions, were to inform the themes chosen for the history, giving prominence to those groups, persons and cultures hitherto either excluded from historical narratives, or treated more as objects than as actors in the description of events.

By December 1981, when the Working Group for the Preparation of a General History of the Caribbean met in Paris, the ideas and aims expressed by the UNESCO General Conferences of 1978 and 1980 were widely shared by the twenty scholars, Caribbean and European, whom the Director-General had invited in their personal capacity to break ground for the project. The aspirations of the ground-breakers embraced geography, anthropology, archaeology, ethnography, demography, society, religion, politics, ethnicity, culture, rituals, customs, socio-linguistics, music, dance, festivals, oral tradition, historiography, and cartography. One is tempted to conclude *etcetera*, and rightly so, because their successors noticed that, in 1981, the Working Group had overlooked gender and the environment. The inclusiveness of their vision of the history of the Caribbean was, no doubt, due to the desire of the twenty scholars that the history of its people and their habitat should be written as if observed from inside the region.

How was this vision to be made concrete in a few volumes, limited to twenty chapters each? How, within that general framework, to deal adequately with the wide diversity of size, ancestry, religion, language, custom, politics? How to set the chronological limits to volumes without cutting off themes artificially? How to integrate the material into a Caribbean narrative and avoid writing history as merely summary accounts of the larger islands?

The task was given to the Drafting Committee which first met in Kingston in April 1983. Of its nineteen members, twelve were from the Caribbean and seven from Africa, India, Europe and the Americas. At first, the Committee used the text of the

Report of the Working Group (1981) to elicit the themes significant for Caribbean history. But in the discussion which followed, the form of organization proposed by the Working Group was abandoned and replaced by five themes which would make for a coherent history of the Caribbean region while being consonant with the UNESCO guidelines.

These were Autochthonous Societies, New Societies: The Long Sixteenth Century, Slave Societies, The Long Nineteenth Century, The Caribbean in the Twentieth Century, and they became, with slight elaboration, the titles for the first five volumes of the history. The Drafting Committee also promised to consider adding an annexe containing maps and statistics, and this in time became the sixth volume, Methodology and Historiography of the Caribbean.

Volume I – Autochthonous Societies
This volume relates the history of the origins of the earliest Caribbean peoples, and analyses their various political, social, cultural and economic organizations over time, in and around the Caribbean region.

Volume II – New Societies: The Caribbean in the Long Sixteenth Century
The subject of this volume is the evolution of Caribbean society through the intrusion of Europeans, and it examines the dramatic changes in politics, society and culture which occurred until 1680. These changes are studied in conjunction with the rapidly dwindling presence of the Amerindians and the increasing numbers of Spanish, English, French and Dutch settlers.

Volume III – Slave Societies of the Caribbean
The slave societies were more than societies with enslaved Africans, so this volume examines the demographic and economic as well as social and cultural aspects of all those communities which resulted from the establishment of the Caribbean slave systems.

Volume IV – The Long Nineteenth Century: Nineteenth-Century Transformations
Emphasizing themes rather than chronology, this volume covers the period from the end of slavery (although this varies in time from territory to territory) to the twentieth century. Its major themes are dependent labour groups, especially emigrants from Asia, the development and diversification of local economies, and the emergence throughout the region of varying degrees of national consciousness as well as forms of government.

Volume V – The Caribbean in the Twentieth Century
The prevalence and persistence of the plantation, the ubiquity of underemployment, the vulnerability of dependent Caribbean economies, popular and labour protests, decolonization and neo-colonialism are all considered in this volume. It also explores the effects of migration, mass communications and modernization on the cultures of local societies.

Volume VI – Methodology and Historiography of the Caribbean
This volume has three sections. The first examines sources of historical evidence and the techniques used to study them for the purpose of writing Caribbean history. In

the second, the historiography of the region is treated thematically, tracing the changes in the interpretation of the past. The third is devoted to the historiography of particular territories and history-writing in all its branches.

At its first meeting, the Drafting Committee also made three decisions which should be noticed here: it appointed editors for the five volumes and the proposed annexe; it decided that since it had provided in some detail the contents of Volumes II and III, the editors could complete work on the contents of their volumes and name the authors by the end of 1983; it acknowledged that the contents of Volume I needed detailed elaboration and agreed that the editor should have the help of a workshop of specialists to provide the details. Nevertheless, the Committee proposed that Volumes I, II and III should be published first and together and set July 1986 as the date for the final submission of manuscripts to UNESCO.

Provisional calendars for producing histories in several volumes and with chapters from scores of authors are not dates that are likely to be met. As has been the case with other multi-volume histories, inviting the most competent historians to be editors and authors has also meant taking the risk that the publication of the work will be long-delayed, since such persons normally have many other commitments. The estimates made in April of 1983 were soon wildly out. The first meeting of the Bureau of the Drafting Committee scheduled for September 1984 was held in May 1985. The new date proposed for the submission of manuscripts of Volumes I, II and III was December 1987. Volume III, which was published in 1997, was submitted in 1992.

When the General History of the Caribbean was first proposed, there were just enough historians who had researched their topics across the barriers of language. Since then the existence of the Association of Caribbean Historians has made possible a substantial increase of our comparative knowledge of the region's past. At its meetings, papers on similar topics and related themes pertaining to different territories, are presented in the languages of the Caribbean, thus giving historians access to the results of research done across the barriers of language. To that extent these six volumes can be said to be a work in progress, a marker towards a fully integrated Caribbean history.

List of Contributors

David Buisseret (USA) is Jenkins and Virginia Garrett Professor of History at the University of Texas, Arlington, USA. He was director of the Smith Center for the History of Cartography in the Newberry Library, Chicago. Previously he had been Professor of History at the University of the West Indies, Mona and editor of *The Jamaican Historical Review*. In 1979 he was awarded the Centennial medal of the Institute of Jamaica. He is the author of several publications including *Historic Architecture of the Caribbean* (1980/83).

Alfredo Castillero Calvo (Panamá) received his Ph.D. in *Historia de América* at the University of Madrid. He has held Visiting Professorships at the Universities of Yale, Stanford and Costa Rica and is currently Professor of Panamanian and Latin American History at the University of Panama. His publications include *Arquitectura, Urbanismo y Sociedad. La Vivienda Colonial en Panamá. Historia de un Sueño* (1994), *Conquista, Evangelización y Resistencia* (1995) and *La Ciudad Imaginada. El Casco Viejo de Panamá* (1999).

Pieter Emmer (The Netherlands) has been Professor of History of European Expansion in the University of Leiden, The Netherlands since 1989. He was a visiting fellow commoner at Churchill College, Cambridge, UK and Visiting Professor at the Universities of Bamberg, Texas, USA and Hamburg, Germany. He has published *The Dutch in the Atlantic Economy, 1580–1880. Trade, Slavery and Emancipation* (1998) and with Magnus Moerner has edited *European Expansion and Migration: Essays on the Intercontinental Migration from Africa, Asia and Europe* (1992).

Wim Klooster (The Netherlands) has been Assistant Professor of History at the University of Southern Maine, USA since 1998. He received his Ph.D. at the University of Leiden, The Netherlands in 1995 and subsequently became a visiting fellow at the John Carter Brown Library, Providence, USA and the Charles Warren Center, Harvard University, USA. His publications include *The Dutch in the Americas, 1600–1800: A Rare Narrative History with the Catalogue of an Exhibition of Rare Prints, Maps and Illustrated Books from the John Carter Brown Library* (1997) and *Illicit Riches: Dutch Trade in the Caribbean, 1648–1795* (1998).

Gustavo Martin-Fragachan (Venezuela). Formerly Associated Researcher at the University of California, Berkeley, USA, he is currently Professor at the Central University of Venezuela. He has published *Magic and Religion in Contemporary Venezuela* (1983), *Theory of Magic and Religion* (1983), *Essays in Political Anthropology* (1984), *Homologies: Writing on Rationality* (1991) and *Social Sciences: Between Epistemology and Deconstruction* (1995).

Frank Moya Pons (Dominican Republic) is the author of twenty books and more than fifty scholarly articles. He has taught Latin American and Caribbean history at Columbia University and the University of Florida, USA, and has lectured extensively throughout the world. He is currently a Visiting Research Professor at the City College of the The City University of New York (CUNY), USA, and works as a consultant and development specialist in the Dominican Republic.

Anne Pérotin-Dumon (France) holds a Ph.D. in History from the University of Paris, Sorbonne, France. Following a career at the French Ministry of Culture as curator of archives, she taught at Kent State University and the University of Virginia (USA). At present, she is Professor of History at the Catholic University of Chile, Santiago, and a contributing editor of the *Handbook of Latin American Studies (History of the Caribbean and the Guyanas)*. Her many publications include *Etre patriote sous les tropiques: La Guadeloupe, la colonisation et la revolution 1789–1794* (1985), *La ville aux iles, la ville dans l'ile: Basseterre et Pointe-à-Pitre, Guadeloupe 1650–1820* (1999).

Horst Pietschmann (Germany) is Professor of Latin American History at the University of Hamburg, Germany. He has been Secretary-General and later President of the European Association of Latin Americanist Historians (AHILA). He has published extensively, including *El Estado y su evolución al principio de la colonización española de América* (1989), *La introducción de las intendencias en Nueva España* (1996). He co-edited *Mittel-, Südamerika und die Karibik bis 1760, Handbuch der Gesichte Lateinamerikas, vol. 1* (1994) and has been chief editor of *Jahrbuch für Gesichte von Staat, Wirtschaft und Gesellschaft Lateinamerikas* since 1995.

Ruggiero Romano (Italy) gained his Ph.D. at the University of Naples. He has taught in universities in Europe and Latin America, has Honorary Doctorates from the Universities of Buenos Aires and Cordoba, Argentina, Lima, Peru and Camerino, Italy and is an Honorary Professor at the University of Ayacucho, Peru. He was visiting Professor at the Colegio de México, 1992–5.

ENRIQUETA VILÁ VILAR (Spain) received a doctorate in history from Escuela de estudios Hispano-Americanos. She is at present Director of *Historigrafía y Bibliografía Americanistas* and sits on the Consejo Asesor Anvario de estudios Americanos. Specializing in the sixteenth and seventeenth centuries, she has published *Historia de Puerto Rico, 1600–1650* and *Hispanoamérica y la trata esclavista.*

DAVID WATTS (UK) is currently Reader in Geography at the University of Hull, UK. He was founder-editor and is now senior editor of the *Journal of Biogeography.* Among his many publications are *Man's impact on the vegetation of Barbados, 1627–1800* (1966), *Principles of biogeography* (1971), *Third directory of biogeographers* (1981), *The West Indies: patterns of development, culture and environmental change since 1492* (1987/90), *Los indias occidentales* (1992) and *Population density, the water resource and land degradation in the eastern Caribbean* (1996).

NEIL L. WHITEHEAD (UK) received his D.Phil. in Social Anthropology from Oxford University, UK. He is currently an Associate Professor of Anthropology at the University of Wisconsin, Madison, USA. His major publications include *Lords of the Tiger Spirit – A History of the Caribs* (1988), with P. Hulme, *Wild Majesty – Encounters with Caribs from Columbus to the Present Day* (1992), with R.B. Ferguson, *War in the Tribal Zone, Expanding States and Indigenous Warfare* (1992), and *Wolves from the Sea – Readings in the Anthropology of the Native Caribbean* (1995) and *The Discoverie of the Large, Rich and Bewtiful Empyre of Guiana by Walter Ralegh* (1998).

TRANSLATORS Part One of the Introduction and Chapter 4 were translated from the German by Ann Richner and UNESCO Translation Services respectively. Chapter 2 was translated from the Italian by UNESCO Translation Services. Chapter 6 was translated from the Spanish by NIHERST School of Languages and Chapters 8 and 9 from the Spanish by Andrew Hurley.

List of Tables

Table 3.1   Sugar production in Española and Puerto Rico, 1568–1607   72

Table 3.2   Ginger exports and prices, 1581–1615   74
            (in quintales and maravedies)

Appendix tables Chapter 6:

African slaves taken to Caribbean ports (1595–1601)   172

African slaves arriving in Cartagena and Veracruz in the first half of the
seventeenth century   173

African slaves arriving in other Caribbean ports in the first half of the
seventeenth century   174

PLATES

1 A Carib man and woman from J.B. Du Tertre, *Histoire Generale des Antilles*, Paris, 1667

2 Amerindians using tobacco from Girolamo Benzoni, *La historia del mondo nuevo*, Venice, 1565

3 Havana, a famous port in North America, on the island of Cuba, by Peter Shank

4 Fort and Bourg of Magdelaine, Guadeloupe from J.B. Du Tertre, *Histoire Generale des Antilles*, Paris, 1667

5 A young negro paddling a canoe made out of a single tree trunk, from Theodor de Bry, *Americae*, Frankfurt, 1590–1643

6 A female mulatto slave, dressed in the local fashion, smoking a pipe, from Theodor de Bry, *Americae*, Frankfurt, 1590–1643

7 Islas de los Canibales y de San Juan (The Islands of the Cannibals and San Juan) c. 1621

8 Sugar canes and the method of producing sugar

9 Detail from the world map by Juan de La Cosa, c. 1500

10 Detail from the world map by Giovanni Matteo Contarini, 1505

11 Detail of the Caribbean from the map of the Atlantic Ocean in the 'Miller' Atlas, c. 1519

12 Map showing the Audiencia of Española, from the *Decadas* of Antonio Herrera, Madrid, 1601–1615

13 Cuba, from the *Islario General* of Alonso de Santa Cruz, c. 1546

14 Barbados, from the *Descripcion geographica* of Nicolás de Cardona, 1592

15 Plan of Santo Domingo by Bautista Antonelli, 1592

16 A plan of Havana by Cristobal de Rojas, c. 1603

17 A new and accurate map of Barbados by John Ogilby, cartographer to the King

The Caribbean

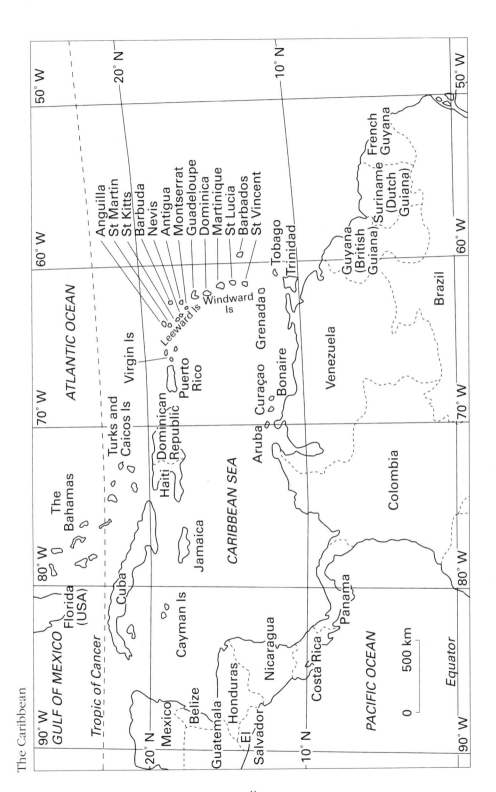

Introduction: The Creation of a New Caribbean Society, 1492–1650

PART ONE

Horst Pietschmann

In the context of a history of the Caribbean, 12 October 1492, the day on which Christopher Columbus landed on one of the islands in the region, was one of the most decisive, if not the most decisive point in a long-term historical perspective. This date marked the end of the biological isolation of the American continent, the consequences of which were vividly revealed by A. Crosby.[1] On this date, the pandemics of the Old World spread to the New World, unleashing a demographic catastrophe among the native inhabitants of the Americas and causing the Europeans to alter the composition of the region's inhabitants in so permanent a manner as to initially turn the Caribbean into a universal melting pot for humanity. Indo-Americans, Europeans, black Africans and Asians ended up, sometimes voluntarily, sometimes forcibly, in the region. They brought with them diverse biological, cultural and historical legacies, establishing contacts with each other and gradually interbreeding. There has hardly been a process, in a period capable of reconstruction by historians from literary sources, which has unfolded in such a decisive manner and which is associated with such dramatic changes as the one which continued to unfold in the Caribbean after the above date. This volume will analyse the historical background of Indo-Americans, black Africans and Asians elsewhere, but how should we assess the Caribbean's European legacy during the early stages of this 'cultural clash'? Why did the Spaniards come in the first place? What part did the Iberian peninsula play in that period of European history? What political, religious, social, economic and other legacies did the Spaniards and their European successors bring with them to the Caribbean?

These questions are generally answered only briefly by some sections of more recent historiography from the perspective of European history and with reference to the concrete epochal context. The 'discovery of the

Americas' by Columbus, which marked the changeover from the Middle Ages to the Modern Age, is characterized in this context as a significant event. Historiography, arguing more from a Spanish viewpoint, against the backdrop of the start of a new epoch, thus characterizes radical changes in that epoch on the Iberian peninsula, such as the union between Aragón and Castille under Ferdinand and Isabella and the end of the *Reconquista* signalled by the conquest of the last Moorish Kingdom of Granada in 1492. It briefly outlines religious developments, referring to the expulsion of the Jews from Spain which also took place in 1492, and analyses economic and social transformations, before turning to the Spanish conquest of the Americas. In this historiographical line, the Caribbean is usually viewed as a kind of intermediate station prior to the conquest of the large American Indian mainland empire and culture, assuming the character of a 'laboratory' in which the mechanism used in the conquest and colonization of the mainland was developed. With its reference to Columbus, this historical movement usually makes only cursory mention of Portuguese expansion in the Atlantic and the role played by the Italians in this trend, and frequently fails to make any mention whatsoever of the Canary Islands or refers to them only as a relay station for Spanish shipping bound for America.[2]

The association with Portugal, Italy and the Canary Islands can, of course, be traced back even further, to late medieval Europe. Appropriately there is also an historiographical school which takes a broader view of these difficult issues, namely the historiography of the history of European expansion. After the Second World War this branch of history aligned itself to the older tradition of 'the history of European discoveries and conquests', firmly adopting the European colonization process outside Europe as the subject of its research and therefore quickly developing the new term 'the history of European expansion', in order to express the opinion that the consequences of European expansion to other continents should now also be the subject of research interest. This historiographical tradition wasted no time in alluding to late medieval forerunners of the expansion process in areas outside Europe. The thirteenth century, and the radical changes which it brought to Europe, formed the starting point of the evaluation. The adoption of Aristotle into European intellectual life, with its leaning toward empirical science, technical innovation, the development of modern commercial, economic and banking methods, demographic growth, and the extension of urban life produced by it, together with contemporary theological debate on the treatment of non-Christians and the universal role of the Papacy, formed both the background and starting point for this evaluation of the expansion process. Using historical events as a reference point, its course can be traced as follows: the advance of the Iberian *Reconquista* into the straits of Gibraltar; the dispatch of the Italian merchant fleet through the straits of Gibraltar into the North Sea region; the poorly-documented voyage of the Vivaldi brothers from Genoa through the same straits southwards along the African coast; the rediscovery of the Canary Islands at the beginning of the fourteenth century by Lancellotto Malcocello, followed by the early attempts of Béthencourt and LaSalle from Normandy to conquer and colonize the Canary Islands at the start of the fourteenth century, concluding with Henry the Navigator and his efforts to reconnoitre the West African coast. The Mediterranean region is the dynamic factor in this historiographical line thrusting outward into the Atlantic, with first Portugal and then Spain taking the lead in the fifteenth century as territorial states consolidated at an early stage due to their geographical location, creating the first early contemporary overseas empires. In this strongly Eurocentric history of expansion, the history of expansion in the European Mediterranean for the area bordering the process extended well beyond the first line with its orientation, in terms of national history, towards Portugal and Spain, due not least to the Turkish advance into the Eastern Mediterranean. From this perspective, the central arena for the historical process was initially the mid and southern Atlantic and, since the second half of the sixteenth century, the entire region. The historian who embodies the whole of its historiographical tradition most clearly is probably Charles Verlinden with his history of Atlantic civilization. Viewed from this broader perspective the Caribbean is quickly transformed into an 'American Mediterranean'.[3] While, in the earlier mentioned historiographical tradition, the Caribbean is of significance rather more as a transit region for the Spanish conquest of the American mainland and then in relation to the links between Spain and its colonial empire, it began to assume its own historical identity more forcefully in this latter tradition, with the name 'American Mediterranean'. This lent it an important, historically active role, a role which admittedly increased in importance only after the remaining European colonial powers had advanced into the region. The 'American Mediterranean' has so far been only very inadequately defined in historical terms and is still waiting for its own Fernand Braudel.

But even this historical school can only be used to a limited extent to outline fully the European legacy of the Caribbean during this early phase in its history, even if the French historian, Pierre Chaunu postulates this so conclusively in his apodictic 'Tout commence au XIIIe siècle', for which he gives a detailed substantiation.[4] This most recent reference by contemporary historians to the late European Middle Ages overlooks the fact that, within medieval history, a line of research exists which claims that Europe, or in any event the heart of early medieval Europe, always was expansive. The conquest and conversion to Christianity of medieval European frontiers started in very early times in Slav areas of eastern and south-eastern Europe, Scandinavia, Scotland, Ireland and the Iberian peninsula. The standards set by theological and legal standards justifying this colonization process, the methods and institutions which it employed, the treatment of those conquered or newly converted to Christianity, etc., needed to be linked to the relevant processes taking place in the Atlantic region, in order to clarify the question of continuity and lack of continuity in this connection. This link also helps to answer the question as to what the Iberian or Mediterranean legacy really was and whether the Caribbean was in fact just a 'laboratory' for the colonization of America, or if it was already part of a fully developed pan-European expansion and colonization tradition. The institution of '*encomienda/ repartimiento*' introduced by the Spaniards in the Caribbean as a system of obtaining dues from the natives or recruiting workers is generally defined in literature as an Iberian legacy from the *Reconquista* era, even though the German Order of Knights also used the institution of *encomienda* in the colonization of the Baltic. However, no comparative study currently exists between the Ibero-Caribbean and Baltic *encomienda*. General accounts of the medieval European expansion process, such as that presented by James Muldoon, would need to be considered here at the very least.[5]

The reference to the *encomienda* of the German Order of Knights in the Baltic may appear exotic in the context of a history of the Caribbean but it leads us to the more general issue of whether the Mediterranean legacy of this expansion process was not over-emphasized when the history of European expansion in the Atlantic was written. The Polish humanist, Johannes Dantiscus, who spent a long period at the Court of Charles V in Spain and wrote innumerable letters which Polish historiography has only recently started to evaluate, forms a bridge between the Baltic and the Atlantic.[6] Although we are very well informed on Italian merchants in the Iberian peninsula, especially in Spain, and their role in the expansion process, not least due to works by Ruth Pike and Enrique Otte, we know very little of the role of merchants from the North Sea region at this time. It is known that, in addition to Martin Behaim, between 100 and 200 merchants from the North Sea region were already plying their trade in Lisbon in Columbus's day, and a certain Fernâo Olmos or Ferdinand van Ulmen, apparently from Flanders, undertook a legendary journey westwards from the Azores before Columbus started his. However, little is known apart from this, of the role played by traders from the North Sea in the expansion process. This is due not least to the fact that fundamental reference material was destroyed by the great Lisbon earthquake of the eighteenth century. In any event, Flemish entrepreneurs were already in evidence in Madeira during the last thirty years of the fifteenth century, shipping sugar from there to Flanders. In addition to Italian merchants and financiers, German mining entrepreneurs were, for example, also to be found very early on in the

Caribbean, in particular the famous Welser company from Upper Germany in Venezuela.[8]

This information on trading is not significant in terms of the national prestige of individual European nations, in the context of 'we were there too', but because it places a different slant on expansion history at the start of the modern era. This is due not only to the possibly stronger influence of the North Sea region in the expansion process than was previously thought, but also because the European legacy of the Caribbean region may need to be reassessed on this information, perhaps going as far back as the transition from the fifteenth to the sixteenth century. The massive presence of merchants from the Mediterranean and North Sea regions in the Iberian peninsula around 1500 could indicate that expansion into the Atlantic, and the European occupation of the Caribbean was, right from the start, a much more powerful pan-European undertaking than so far suggested, in particular, in the historiographical tradition initially mentioned. Therefore, on this basis, assessments of the early adoption of the Caribbean as a new phenomenon and possibly also of its nature should be different. Not least the fact that, early in the sixteenth century, cartographic records of the Caribbean region would confirm this as they were much more advanced in northern Europe than on the Iberian peninsula or in Italy.

Admittedly the research trends outlined above by no means solve the problems of historiographical focus on the Caribbean. Thus epochal accounts of the history of the Renaissance refer, of course, also to the expansion process, taking account of numerous problems of that phase of expansion history even if, in this context, the Atlantic and the Caribbean are treated more as a phenomenon on the margins of the 'known world'. At an early stage one also encounters the Caribbean region in European cultural history as the supplier of 'exotic' products and phenomena ranging from sea monsters to cannibalism, from parrots to pharmaceutical and medicinal plants and finally well-known European luxury products from the developing plantation economy of the region.[9] In this historiographical tradition, the Caribbean frequently takes on a completely different form in European consciousness than that found in historical records dealing directly with it. In addition, other historiographical European traditions, such as the history of capitalism, the history of work and other sections of historiography, communicate views, in varying degrees of detail, and often one-sidedly, on the region's development which extended its influence into the region itself – a topic also still in need of thorough historiographical reappraisal.

One line of research, to be viewed at least as a partial offshoot of European expansion history, was of greater significance when documenting the history of the region – namely independent colonial history.[10] Based to a degree on political developments in the post-Second World War period, this independent colonial history became a sub-discipline which actually developed its research interest only from the point of view of Europe or European colonial powers, increasingly questioning the formative influences on this now independent group of states on the basis of their respective colonial pasts. Thus, in this research tradition, more emphasis was placed on questions concerning historical origins using subsequent political, economic, social and other problems of the independent state as a starting point – a research topic which very quickly linked up with the more recent political and sociological development debate.[11] Although this new historiography produced much more powerful links to the present, it also produced more pronounced individualization – with the individual independent states in this region, and no longer the Caribbean region as a whole, forming the reference framework for a now very wide-ranging research tradition. Admittedly, in this tradition, the states formed in the Greater Antilles, i.e. Cuba, Haiti, and Puerto Rico with its special relationship to the USA, did of course dominate. They were the only ones to have at their disposal broader general historical literature and a large number of studies on historical trends during specific epochs or on central tropics, even though frequently written by foreigners. Only a few of the English, French and Dutch-speaking island societies, whose political status *vis-à-vis* their respective European mother countries sometimes differs, have at their disposal intensive historiographical research traditions comparable to those of the Spanish-speaking states of the region and Haiti. It is therefore often easier to obtain information on the history of the Caribbean in libraries outside the region, such as in the USA, England or the Netherlands, than in the individual countries themselves, especially when related to the low institutional grading of research and educational establishments in the region, with the exception of Cuba and Puerto Rico. Even CARIFTA and CARICOM, the two integration schemes in existence in the Caribbean post-Second World War, have not produced a knock-on effect to overcome this educational deficit with its consequences for the identity-awareness of the region. In 1992, with the celebration of the 500th anniversary of Columbus' voyage, major efforts were made for the first time to preserve, reconstruct and research major historical landmarks and monuments in the Caribbean.[12]

The fact that the Spanish-speaking Caribbean and Haiti demonstrate a significantly better developed historical tradition than the remainder of the region is the result of the wide-reaching effect of one aspect of the association between the pre-European history of the Caribbean, with its European legacy and Spanish colonization at the start of the sixteenth century, to which the name of the region itself refers. Before the arrival of the Spanish the warring Caribs reached out from the South American mainland across the

Lesser Antilles, carrying out successful raids against the more developed civilization of the Taínos living principally in the Greater Antilles. Information provided by the Taínos about their enemies must also have contributed to the belief, which rapidly spread among the Spanish, that the Caribs were cannibals. This tradition, which the first indigenous natives to encounter Europeans attributed to their neighbours, either to keep the new arrivals off their backs or to find favour with them, is clearly documented time and again in reference material.[13] The general belief in medieval Europe that cannibals could be enslaved was an association which referred back to the etymological relationship of the word 'slave' and 'Slav' in all the major western and middle-European languages of Europe. As the indigenous Indian population, first of Haiti and Puerto Rico and then of Cuba, rapidly fell victim to biological disease and numerous attacks by the Spanish and then decreased in number, bordering islands and mainland areas became, for the Spaniards, a reservoir for capturing slaves, since they declared them putatively or intentionally to be inhabited by cannibals. At the same time a debate was raging among the Spaniards over two colonization models. One, rather more peaceful, involved the integration of the indigenous population into an inclusive rural, agrarian-urban, global patriarchal hierarchy, in the tradition of the Spanish *Reconquista*, and a strongly urban-capitalistically oriented model with powerful Italian-Mediterranean influences which, at the same time, represented differing European traditions. The second model was in a rather more hierarchical medieval tradition which treated the indigenous, generally rural, populations in a less caring manner and was a movement aimed at a general *'mise en valuer'*, with the population concerned being used only as a workforce, a movement interested more in short-term profit than in long-term development.

The ideologies of the 1960s and 1970s led large sections of the historiography dealing with these processes to attempt to prove that all expansion was influenced either by 'medieval feudalism' or 'modern capitalism'. In so doing, they overlooked that both lines of tradition, with their differing social concepts, were involved in Spanish expansion and the violent clashes between *conquistadores* and colonists, frequently characterized by historiography as rivalries between individual personalities or clans, often involving disputes over the implementation of these different social models. The latter of these two movements prevailed in the Antilles due to the discovery of gold on Haiti and Cuba. This led, as a result of slave-hunting, to the depopulation of the Lesser Antilles, which caused a crisis for Spanish colonization of the Greater Antilles when gold supplies were exhausted and economic alternatives, in the form of a plantation economy, could not be developed quickly enough due to a lack of workers and capital. Thus the division of the

Caribbean region into two areas, one under Spanish influence and the other as a number of uninhabited islands or coastal strips, later invaded by other European powers, was predetermined in the sixteenth century.

Moreover attacks in this region by other European naval powers from the late sixteenth century took advantage of the fact that supporters of the late medieval hierarchical model, who had migrated westwards to the American mainland, succeeded in gradually establishing this type of hierarchical order there, supported by the differentiated and highly-developed indigenous population whose subjugation had been swiftly achieved, thanks to compatriots from their homeland. This order not only produced agrarian surpluses but also allowed them to set up and politically control[14] a complex precious-metal mining industry, from silver deposits found principally in the border areas of this colonization region. These surpluses, when transported to Europe, were the main attraction which encouraged other European naval powers to enter and subsequently settle in the region.

It was possible to draw these fundamental lines on which the development of Spanish colonization are based only after the disappearance of ideological dividing lines. Some of their aspects can be identified in works of classic art and cultural history by Erwin Walter Palm and Luis Weckmann.[15] Of course, in numerous details they still require differentiated historical reconstruction from a historical perspective which looks, in its historical dynamics, at the complete process of Spanish expansion and colonization in America in the sixteenth century in the Caribbean and bordering mainland area. This process is influenced far more strongly by the differing levels of civilization of the American population at the time of the arrival of the Europeans, on the one hand, and by the internal contradictions involved in the break-up of European society, principally in western and southern Europe and the Iberian peninsula, in particular. These different elements affected one another in turn, at various times in the development process, in such a way as to produce phenomena and causal clusters with longer term effects. The latter initially facilitated and/or triggered or brought about later developments in terms of historical dynamics in distant regions, that is in Europe and America. In this context the Caribbean was initially, in any event, the scene of historical processes. However its role as a 'laboratory' for the advance of historical development was, from the beginning of the colonization process, also an historic one, thanks to its geography, nature, flora and fauna and, not least its people. Much remains to be discovered and researched for large areas of the historical development of the past five hundred years.

PART TWO

The creation of a second expansion system

Pieter C. Emmer

After 1600 the process of the expansion of Europe received a new impetus, since the nations of north-western Europe, France, England and the Netherlands were able to broaden their attack on the Hapsburg empire to include the non-European world. After a period of internal strife, the new European nations had developed enough maritime power to allow them to explore the sea routes to Asia, Africa and the New World and to take on the Spanish and Portuguese as adversaries in those parts.

How had this new maritime power been achieved? The answer is simple: by developing a more efficient shipbuilding industry, and by creating more institutions to finance trade and overseas settlements than the Iberians had done. In addition, the nations of north-western Europe could command many more unskilled, young, unmarried, landless youths for manning their navies, merchant marines and trading posts and for peopling their overseas settlements than Spain. It would go well beyond the scope of this introductory chapter to look into all these matters separately and to discuss the demographic changes within France, England and the Netherlands. It will be sufficient to note that these three 'new' European powers had larger populations than Spain at this time, as well as more ships employed in European waters. What the nations of north-western Europe lacked during the sixteenth century was the organization to bring together investments of a size which allowed for sustained inter-continental trade and for settlement overseas.[16]

However, this situation changed at the very end of the sixteenth century. Slowly, the trading companies from north-western Europe started to send ships on voyages to Asia, Africa and the New World. Once they had started to explore, trade and settle the world outside Europe, the speed, magnitude and effects of this process very quickly surpassed anything the Iberian expansion had been able to produce.

The reasons for this unrivalled dynamism were many. First of all, it should be noted that the Spanish expansion outside of Europe had not grown as a branch of a much more extensive Spanish trade within Europe. For the French, English and Dutch the intra-European trade had been developed first and it always remained much more important than their intercontinental commerce. Consequently, the countries of north-western Europe could switch ships, men and capital more easily than the Spanish from employment within to that outside of Europe. This explains why in developing lucrative shipping routes and attractive settlement ventures the nations of north-western Europe could provide cheap, reliable transport in a volume and with a flexibility unknown to the Iberian world.[17]

Secondly, the amount of investments available for overseas ventures was much larger in north-western Europe than in the Iberian peninsula. Many of the Iberian commercial ventures had been financed with money from foreign, Italian investors. In France, England and the Dutch Republic the development of agriculture as well as that of national and international trade and manufacturing had created – in addition to the nobility – considerable groups of propertied people both in cities and in the country, who could be induced to invest their money in trade and overseas settlement. In order to make it attractive to invest at a limited risk, commercial circles in north-western Europe created shareholding companies. These institutions constituted a breakthrough in national and international financing and it explains why the overseas expansion of France, England and the Netherlands was backed by much more investment capital than the non-European ventures of the Spanish.[18]

The third explanation of the unrivalled speed at which the overseas expansion of the countries from north-western Europe took place can be found in the social composition of the population of these countries. Only in north-western Europe and nowhere else were there so many poor, unmarried males ready to migrate. In addition to this group the countries of north-western Europe also saw the rise of a group of merchants, farmers, professionals and landed gentry, who not only had money available to invest internationally, but also the entrepreneurial skills to establish themselves overseas, setting up plantations, farms and trading firms. The existence of these two social groups explains why the overseas expansion of England, France and the Dutch Republic could result in the rapid creation of so many plantation colonies as well as of large immigrant-populated settlement colonies.[19]

Last, but not least, the religious differences between the Iberian countries and north-western Europe should be considered. Was Protestantism, the new Christian ideology, enabling England and the Dutch Republic to develop a new kind of individual capitalism, while Portugal and Spain remained under the influence of Catholicism with its preference for medieval, communal economic values such as limited profits and 'just prices'? Unfortunately, modern research provides us with a much more complex historical reality than Max Weber would have it. In fact, it was not Protestantism, but rather the relatively liberal religious attitudes of local governments in England, the Netherlands and France, which allowed the development of business communities of mixed religious persuasions. Of course, in England some groups of Protestant and Catholic dissenters were driven into exile during the seventeenth century and so were the French Huguenots after 1685. Relatively speaking, however, none of the countries of north-western Europe experienced such severe religious persecutions as did Spain.[20] The exodus of non-Catholics from the Iberian peninsula greatly aided the transfer of commercial experience to north-western Europe. France, England and the Netherlands might have possessed the men, the ships and the money to embark on commercial expansion outside of Europe, but the start of the second expansion system was considerably aided by the expertise of the Sephardic Jews from Spain and Portugal, who had settled in northern Europe.[21]

The subsequent clash between the first expansion system of Spain and Portugal on one side and the second system of France, England and the Netherlands on the other has been called the first global war. Around 1650 the geographical contours of both systems were already more or less fixed. In Asia, Spain and Portugal were pushed into a marginal position, while the merchants of the countries of north-western Europe became important participants in the inter-Asian trade as well as the major carriers and traders of Asian products outside of Asia. In Africa the two competing European expansion systems managed to divide the trading contacts between them, which was also done in the New World, where the two systems carved out separate spheres of influence and settlement. The defeat of the Dutch in Brazil showed that the balance between the two systems was situated in the Caribbean and not on the mainland of South America.[22]

The maritime penetration and settlement

For more than a century after Columbus, the Caribbean basin had remained an area where the rapidly declining autochthonous population, mainly Caribs and Arawaks, were trying to come to grips with the incoming Spanish settlers and their African slaves. No other nation from expanding Western Europe had succeeded in establishing a settlement of its own, despite the fact that English, French and Dutch ships intruded from time to time in the Caribbean region during the course of the sixteenth century.[23]

These French, English and Dutch maritime incursions into the Caribbean changed little in the political and socioeconomic structures of the region. In fact, Amerindians as well as the Spanish settler communities came to use the new penetrators as alternative links with the outside world. It had become obvious that the policymakers in Lisbon, Madrid and Seville gave preference to developing economic ties with the promising mainland areas of north-eastern Brazil, Peru and Mexico. Thus the Iberian economic interests in the Caribbean declined during the course of the sixteenth century.[24]

No doubt it was partly due to the weakness of the Spanish commercial and political presence in most of the Caribbean region which stimulated the ships of other European nations to come into the area. In the first place, the regular shipments of the valuable export products of Spanish America to Spain attracted many pirates and privateers into the Caribbean, where the *flotas* assembled before their departure to Europe.[25] In addition to the ships of the *flota*, the Spanish inter-settlement trade within the region also provided an attraction, albeit a limited one: the hides, sugar and ginger produced in the Caribbean only had a comparatively low value in comparison to the precious metals and the plantation products which reached the Caribbean from the South American mainland in transit for Europe.[26]

Over time, there were several products which caused the French, English and Dutch to develop regular trading with the Caribbean in spite of Spanish attempts at stopping these intrusions: pearls, dyewood, tobacco and salt. Tobacco was grown both by the Spanish and Amerindian communities in the Caribbean. Saltpans were present in several locations in the region. Dyewood and pearls were offered for trade by the Amerindians. For tobacco and salt there existed a rapidly rising demand in Europe. It has been calculated that around the turn of the sixteenth century the majority of the tobacco imported into England and the major share of Caribbean salt imported into the Netherlands as a preservative for food and fish had been shipped directly from the Caribbean.[27]

It took a long time before the English, the Dutch and the French settled in the Caribbean. Once they had started, however, the speed with which these settlements increased, as well as the size of their populations, was many times greater than those of the previous Spanish settlements. In contrast to the Spanish experience, the new Europeans created small communities of buccaneers which preceded and subsequently existed alongside the much larger population settlements. These small 'amphibious' societies came into existence after 1550 when the English, French and Dutch ships came to penetrate the Caribbean in order to hunt the rich Spanish *flotas* or to trade in hides and tobacco with the Spanish colonists.

Originally, the intruders from north-western Europe pursued an internationally legalized business: capturing enemy ships. However, illegal prize-taking in time of peace soon became common practice. Many sailors deserted the ships on which they had arrived in the Caribbean, formed small groups, obtained small ships and started to raid Spanish settlements and Spanish ships. They usually settled on the small islands in the vicinity of the larger Spanish islands.[28] These settlements should, however, not be confused with the population settlements, which were much larger and which were set up in order to exploit the tropical environment of the Caribbean.

There is no single explanation for the reason why the maritime penetration of the English, French and Dutch changed to settlement during the second and third decades of the seventeenth century. There had been various attempts before, most of them on the 'Wild Coast', the coastal area on the South American mainland between the mouths of the Orinoco and Amazon rivers.[29] Few of these settlements met with success; it seemed impossible to overcome the difficulties which presented themselves to the 'new' Europeans as soon as they got off their ships: to keep healthy, to develop the vital exchange relationship with the Amerindians, to develop a defence against the Spanish and against other competing groups of Europeans and – last but not least – to speedily develop an agricultural output which would feed the new settlers and could be used as an export crop in order to pay for further imports.[30]

It was not until 1624 that the first non-Spanish settlers in the Caribbean islands were there to stay, at the island of St Kitts (St Christopher), quickly migrating from there to Nevis, Antigua, Montserrat, Guadaloupe, Martinique and the Bahamas. In addition, a group of settlers from the coast of Guyana settled on Barbados, while the Dutch occupied some small islands to be used as trading stations: Curaçao (and from there Aruba and Bonaire) as well as St Martin, Saba and St Eustatius.[31]

What made these new European settlements permanent? Firstly, the absence of a sizeable Spanish and Amerindian population on these islands should be mentioned. The Spanish presence was mostly limited to the larger islands in the Caribbean, and their military chance of retaliation on the smaller islands in the Eastern Caribbean was virtually absent. On some of the smaller islands the position of the Amerindians prevented conquest and on some islands the intruding Europeans managed to conquer enough land to settle while establishing an uneasy balance with the autochthonous population.[32]

A second reason for the concerted efforts of the new intruders to break through the 'anti-settlement barrier' in the Caribbean was of a political-commercial kind. During the first two decades of the seventeenth century the anti-Hapsburg wars in Europe had abated. The Iberian ports were open again to English, French and Dutch ships, allowing them to take in American produce such as salt and tobacco. At the same time, the Spanish authorities in the Caribbean region clamped down on the illicit smuggling trade with the non-Iberian ships. New fortifications were built in order to protect the saltpans, and the cultivation of tobacco was no longer allowed to the Spanish colonists. The renewed hostilities with Spain in Europe stimulated the merchant houses and shipping firms in England, France and the Netherlands to switch from buying Caribbean products in Spain to the creation of new centres of settlement and production in the Caribbean under their own flags, in spite of the increased Spanish resistance.[33]

The third reason for the success of the new settlements in the Caribbean was their financial backing, which was different from that of the Spanish colonies in the region. Some settlements were created by 'Lords Proprietors'. These were wealthy merchants or noblemen, who hoped to increase their income and wealth by creating a settlement in the New World. A second possibility of financing a venture overseas was the creation of a joint-stock company. This institution allowed the landed classes, as well as merchants and shipping firms in England, France and the Netherlands, to bring together the capital for establishing a settlement or a trading post. The joint stock company enabled the investors to buy just a few shares and thus to limit the amount of their capital at risk.[34]

Unfortunately, there are no figures available to demonstrate the difference in the amounts of overseas investments between that of the Iberians and of the nations from north-western Europe. The difference must have been considerable. In addition to the larger investments from north-western Europe recent research has shown that the buccaneers also made an important financial contribution to the economy of the early settlements in the English and French Caribbean. Once regular settlement colonies had been established, the buccaneers increased in numbers by accommodating indentured servants, who had escaped the appalling living and working conditions in the Caribbean or who had fulfilled their contracts, in addition to sailors who had jumped ship.

It has always been assumed that the increasing activities of the buccaneers actually had impeded the growth of a regular export economy in the Caribbean. Why were the buccaneers otherwise forced to disappear at the end of the seventeenth century? It was when international cooperation between the colonial powers in the Caribbean ended the maritime anarchy in the region. During most of the seventeenth century, however, buccaneers and regular settlements had co-existed side by side. Recent research has shown that the buccaneers did not damage the economic growth of these colonies, but in fact stimulated economic growth by investing part of their spoils in the new plantations. Later on, investors from Europe took over.[35]

The Amerindians, the 'new' Europeans and the Africans

There is no doubt that the Amerindians in the Caribbean were as vital to the creation of the new English, French and Dutch settlements as to those of the Spanish during the previous century. All Europeans were quite helpless in coping with their new surroundings, at least during the initial stages. The Amerindians taught the incoming groups of new settlers how to use the Caribbean environment to their advantage. In addition, the Amerindians warned the newcomers against the forthcoming attacks of hurricanes and of the Spanish. In the Guianas they considered the Dutch and English to be more friendly than the Spaniards since these nations were only there to trade while the Iberians had enslaved many Amerindians. Thus the Caribs came to the aid of the Dutch in their attacks on Spanish Trinidad.[36]

In spite of these friendly relations, the connections between Amerindians and the new group of Europeans on several Caribbean islands very quickly ended with the extinction or expulsion of the Amerindians. In fact, the French and English settlers on St Kitts, the very first island of settlement, cooperated in killing all the autochthonous inhabitants of the islands five years after their arrival. Of course, the Amerindian presence in the larger Caribbean islands such as Guadaloupe and Martinique, remained important until well after 1650. On both islands there existed a frontier between Europeans and Caribs. Also, several of the smaller islands, such as St Vincent and Dominica, were not settled by Europeans because of the fierce opposition by the Amerindians.[37]

However, the relative speed with which the French, British and Dutch severed the originally friendly ties with the Amerindian population already indicated long before 1650 that the newly-arrived penetrators from Europe were willing to allot only a marginal place to the autochthonous population of the West Indies, if any at all. Unlike the situation in the Spanish Caribbean, the Amerindians were not used as slaves on the plantations of the newly-settled islands. Only on the plantations of the Guianas some 'red slaves' appear to have acted as hunters or fishermen. The first reason to explain this difference would be the rapidly declining number of Amerindians: by the time of the arrival of the British, French and Dutch the number of Amerindians on the islands in the Eastern Caribbean was much reduced. On Barbados there were no Amerindians at all. Also, the Caribs of the Eastern Caribbean were able to fend off the Europeans much longer than the Arawaks living on the larger islands. The absence of Amerindians on the first European plantations in the Guianas could be explained by the military weakness of the new European enclaves.[38]

There are several reasons why the newly-arrived settlers from Western Europe felt no great urge to integrate the Amerindian population into their

newly-founded societies. Unlike the Spanish, the new settlers were not interested in employing the Amerindians in economic activities after the first years
of settlement had passed. In contrast to the more or less self-sufficient
Spanish settlements, the English, French and Dutch implantations in the
Caribbean remained closely connected to their respective mother countries
and continued to receive large numbers of immigrants. In the beginning all
new settlements could operate with almost exclusively European labour. In
addition, the new settlers had little interest in missionary activities, which
made them also differ from the Spanish.[39]

How many new settlers from Europe did arrive? It has been calculated
that in 1650, 56900 Europeans lived in the British Caribbean and around
15000 in the French and Dutch Antilles. This meant that on average around
2000 to 3000 Europeans per year came into the Caribbean during the period
1624–50. Natural increase could almost be ignored, as will be explained
below. These regular, massive immigrations from Europe created a drastic
change from the previous situation; the sparsely-populated Spanish
Caribbean counted perhaps one European to 10 square miles; around 1650
the islands of the English Caribbean had become one of the heaviest populated areas in the world, with more than 50 Europeans per square mile.[40]

The reason for the rapid increase in population lay in the large supply
of young, unmarried, male labourers which existed in northern France, the
Low Countries and in several parts of England, Scotland and Ireland. These
young men were very mobile: they took up long-term employment far away
from home as farmhands, sailors in the Navy and in the merchant marine or
as apprentices in the manufacturing industries. This source of labour was
tapped by the first planter-colonists, who went back themselves to hire
labour or asked their family or agents to do so.[41]

The majority of the Europeans coming into the Caribbean were bound
by contract either to their future employer or to the captain of the ship on
which they had made the crossing. In the latter case the captain had the right
to 'sell' his indentured labourer or *engagé* to the highest bidding employer.
This system enabled many poor young workers to make the trans-Atlantic
crossing without any previous savings. In addition to these contracts of
indenture, the regular arrival of new settlers was further assured by 'mate-
ships' between captains and planters by which captains on emigrant vessels
operated as recruiting agents in Europe on behalf of certain West Indian
planters.[42]

After 1660, however, the immigration of Europeans into the Caribbean
declined. Slowly, but gradually, the truth about the wretched conditions for
indentured servants in the West Indies had travelled back to Europe and
subsequently changed the minds of many emigrants. Rather than facing the
tropical heat, the high death rate and bad treatment young men from north-

western Europe preferred to sign contracts of indenture for North America, where conditions were said to be much better. In addition, a decline in the selling prices of tobacco, by then the major export crop of the Caribbean, had reduced the possibilities of the employers in the Caribbean to pay more than employers elsewhere.[43]

Between 1630 and 1640 the economies of the new Caribbean were in decline and the European and Amerindian societies were shrinking because of the high mortality, stagnating immigration, and emigration out of the region. In many ways the newly-implanted British, French and Dutch societies were embarking on a pattern which would make them resemble the previously established societies in the region under Spanish domination.[44]

Instead, after 1640, the British and French Caribbean embarked upon a new economic course in which the production of sugar for export became the dominant activity. In its wake the Dutch trading establishments in the Caribbean also got a new lease of life. The manpower to produce this export commodity was mainly made up of slaves brought over from Africa.[45]

Both sugar and African slaves had been part and parcel of the economy and society of the Spanish Caribbean during the sixteenth century. The Arawaks of the Guianas are known to have grown sugar cane and this product was also grown in the Spanish settlements, in addition to tobacco. Also, the Spanish had brought slaves from Africa to all of their settlements of the New World in order to complement Amerindian and European labour which was in short supply. The British, Dutch, and in particular the French, had done the same, again since the supply of labourers from Europe had not been sufficient or was decreasing.[46]

All this was not enough to create a large-scale sugar export industry. In order to export sugar, the juice from the sugar cane had to be processed in a special way, allowing for further refining in Europe. The new technology to achieve this was brought to the Caribbean by the Dutch, who had in turn acquired their skills from the Portuguese sugar planters in Brazil. Also, sugar planting in Brazil had shown that large groups of African slaves were able to perform the special, almost industrial type of agricultural labour required for the strictly regimented sugar plantations.[47]

However, the rapid increase in the number of Africans in the new Caribbean during the decade between 1640 and 1650 could be attributed to several factors and not only to the changeover from tobacco to sugar. As has been mentioned above, the price of indentured servants from Europe was already rising dramatically during the 1640s and their supply decreased even more because of the rise in wages in those areas in Europe where these emigrants came from. During the 1640s and 1650s the number of indentured servants did not decline because prisoners from the Civil War and from Ireland were deported to the West Indies. After 1660, however, there was no escape from importing slaves. Slaves were the only alternative as providers of manpower for any economic activity in the Caribbean and the demand for slaves increased accordingly.[48] After 1645 the supply of slaves from Africa to the Caribbean increased because the Dutch had shifted their large slave supply network from Brazil to the Caribbean.[49] In addition, the mortality rate among the inhabitants of the newly-implanted societies in the Caribbean had declined somewhat, which made the hiring of the indentured labour more expensive and the purchase of slave labour cheaper. The explanation for these divergent tendencies in the case of indentured labour can be derived from the contracts of indenture, in which the indentured labourer usually was promised a sum of money, agricultural utensils and… a piece of land. During the first decade of the newly-implanted societies, most indentured labourers did not live long enough to see their contracts expire. However, the declining mortality, in addition to contracts with a shorter period of indenture, made more labourers survive their period of indenture and sub-sequently their employers had to supply more land, which was expensive. In the case of buying African slaves, the declining mortality in the Caribbean also affected its cost-benefit analysis: the longer the slave lived, the more labour the slave could give for the same purchasing price. In addition to this explanation, it has been pointed out that the almost industrial organization of labour gangs on the sugar plantations could only be forced upon the slaves and not on indentured labourers from Europe.[50]

Sugar and slaves were to mould most of the societies in the French, British and Dutch Caribbean, in which there was almost no room for the Amerindians and only a limited demand for Europeans. By 1650, however, this development had only started in Barbados, while the other British islands, as well as the French and Dutch possessions, still had a more diversified economy and society than the one in Barbados. By that year 12 000 to 13 000 slaves or only one-fifth of all new arrivals in the new Caribbean had come from Africa. However, the African presence in the French, British and Dutch possessions in the region was to grow more rapidly than any other.[51]

Incomplete societies and the 'new environment' in the Caribbean

In many ways, the new implantations in the Caribbean as described above have been labelled as 'incomplete societies'. The new settlements were incomplete, since their inhabitants declined in numbers without constant immigration from Europe and Africa. And indeed, every ethnic group in these societies could be qualified as such. The Amerindians, of course, were rapidly declining in numbers because of the contacts with the European and African diseases, as had been the case in all other areas of the New World.[52]

The second ethnic group which could not sustain itself was that of the newly-arrived Europeans. Their number had to be supplemented every year by new emigrants from Europe. The first reason for their demographic decline could be found in difficulties in their adaptation to the Caribbean environment. The new Europeans from north-western Europe were slow in changing their hygienic customs to adapt to the demands of the tropics. Also, their eating and drinking habits, which were geared to the temperate climate of Western Europe, were hardly suitable in the Caribbean. Tropical diseases, such as yellow fever and malaria, played havoc among the new arrivals. To all this, the Iberians seemed to have come better prepared. The first houses built by the new settlers were not adequate for the tropical conditions and not designed to take advantage of the cool trade winds blowing constantly in many parts of the region. After the first decade of settlement had stimulated the adaptive activities of the European settlers (as had been the case in the Spanish Caribbean) some of these problems could be overcome. However, when this initial, precarious period of settlement had passed, the second, structural reason for the demographic decline of the European settler community began to dominate: the disparity between the sexes. Right from the start, the new incoming shiploads of European immigrants were mainly made up of young, unmarried males. In spite of the subsequent arrival of some European women as wives of the more well-to-do planters, this imbalance between the sexes remained unchanged. This situation precluded the growth towards a self-contained, creole society of expatriate Europeans which was so typical of the Spanish Caribbean.[53]

The same situation applied to the third ethnic group which made up the incomplete social fabric of the 'New Caribbean': the Africans. Again, the majority of the African slaves brought to the French, Dutch and British colonies were young males, who came to be used in an agro-industrial labour system that was unknown in West Africa. In spite of their greater physical adaptability to the Caribbean tropics than that of the Europeans, their number had to be supplemented year after year by new imports from Africa in order to avoid demographic decline.[54]

In many respects the early Dutch, English and French participation in the Atlantic slave trade followed the Portuguese example. However, the geographical origin of the 10 000 to 12 000 slaves imported into the British and French Caribbean up to 1650 differed from those brought to Brazil. By far the largest share came from the Guinea coast. Only the Dutch brought in some slaves from their newly-conquered slaving station at Sao Paulo de Luanda in Angola. The total number of slaves shipped from Africa to the New World did not change during the period 1625–50. The additional activities by the English, Dutch and French slavers replaced some of the Portuguese slaving activities directed at exportation to Spanish America.[55]

Also, the slaving techniques used by the Portuguese were copied by the new slave-trading nations. As the Portuguese had done before, the English, French and Dutch all established trading forts along the Guinea coast. In fact Elmina, the main Dutch station on the Gold Coast had been taken from the Portuguese in 1637.[56]

By 1650 a new man-made Caribbean environment had come into existence, which differed greatly from the remaining Spanish colonies in the region.

The first, and certainly most visible, 'new environment' had been created in agriculture. All newly-implanted communities in the Caribbean had only been able to survive by first depleting the existing Caribbean flora and fauna. As a consequence of these new implantations the affected regions were faced by a massive deforestation as well as by a sharp reduction in the numbers of wild hogs and turtles. After the first few years of settlement the new settlers made progress in incorporating the gifts of Caribbean nature into their new ecology: they started to grow and eat some Caribbean foodstuffs. However, this development was arrested by the growing cultivation of cash crops for export. Slowly, the remaining settlers as well as the new arrivals managed to divorce their agriculture and livestock almost completely from what the Caribbean had to offer. In the end only the Caribbean soil and climate were valued by the Europeans. Food was imported from outside. The remnants of the Caribbean flora and fauna were left to the African slaves and Maroons, who blended them with some African agricultural foods. However, some slave food was also imported from North America.[57]

The second 'new environment' created in the new Caribbean was the economic environment. Indeed, the new Caribbean was one of the few regions in the Atlantic world which could only exist and develop by the constant importation of management, capital and labour and by producing exports to pay for this. In spite of this dependence on the outside world, all commercial ties with the new Caribbean were dominated by outside firms and companies situated in North America and Europe.[58]

A similar development took place in the creation of a new cultural environment in the British, French and Dutch Caribbean. The constant importations of Europeans and Africans precluded a situation in which attempts could have been made at integration of all these incoming elements. Thus, the barriers between the different groups remained phenomenal. In addition, cultural barriers were at the same time also social and ethnic barriers. In addition, the Europeans of the new Caribbean, unlike the Spanish, made few attempts at imposing their language and religion on the

Amerindians and Africans. No doubt one of the reasons for this was that – again unlike the Spanish – the Europeans of English, Irish, Scottish, Dutch, German, Scandinavian and French origin already displayed large differences between each other in language and religion.[59]

All these 'new environments' and all these elements of incompleteness made the British, French and Dutch Caribbean stand out among the other parts of the region. Already by 1650 the new Caribbean had shown a potential for rapid economic development and would continue to grow into a unique, semi-industrial agricultural area. The society that came into existence in the 'New Caribbean' differed widely from all the other societies in the Atlantic, and even from the societies that had come into existence in the Spanish Caribbean, in that most of the British, French, Danish and Dutch areas remained pioneer societies with a constantly changing immigrant population with a very high turnover, and with an almost impregnable barrier between the élite and the lower class consisting solely of black African slaves.

NOTES

1   Alfred W. Crosby, *The Columbian Exchange, Biological and Cultural Consequences of 1492* (Westport, Conn. 1972); a comprehensive older work handling the subject from a broader perspective by the same author, *Ecological Imperialism. The Biological Expansion of Europe, 900–1900* (Cambridge, New York, 1986) etc.; also, as a historiographical precursor for the Caribbean, Francisco Guerra. The Influence of Disease on Race, Logistics and Colonization in the Antilles, in *Journal of Tropical Medicine and Hygiene,* No. 69, February 1966, pp. 23–35; cf. a more recent general work on the subject Sheldon Watts, *Epidemics and History. Disease, Power and Imperialism* (New Haven-London, 1997); cf. also William M. Denevan (ed.) *The Native Population of the Americas in 1492* (Madison-London, 1976).

2   The line, chiefly extending from Spain, principally includes works dealing with the creation of the 'Spanish Empire', cf. for example, Richard Konetzke, *Das spanische Weltreich* (Grundlagen und Entstehung, Munich, 1943); John Horace Parry, *The Spanish Seaborne Empire* (London, 1966) and, in addition, numerous Spanish textbooks and general accounts. Authors concentrating on 'voyages of discovery' in the narrower sense of the term, generally include the Canary Islands in greater detail in their research, cf. for example, numerous works by historians like Alfonso Garcia-Gallo, Demetrio Ramos Pérez or Antonio Rumeu de Armas; in addition a series of investigations are available which concentrate exclusively on the Canary Islands, for example, most recently in a broader context Felipe Fernández Armesto, *The Canary Islands after the Conquest. The Making of a Colonial Society in the Early Sixteenth Century* (Oxford, 1982).

3   Particularly historians specializing in discovery and expansion stress the Mediterranean perspective, cf. for example, Charles Verlinden in *Les origines de la civilisation atlantique. De la Renaissance à l'age des Lumières* (Neuchatel-Paris, 1966); Pierre Chaunu, *L'expansion européenne du XIIIe au XVe siècle*

21

(Paris, 1969); and by the same author, *Conquête et exploitation des nouveaux modes* (Paris, 1969), who questioned the hypothesis of the Caribbean as a Mediterranean laboratory probably the most determinedly, even though Carl Ortwin Sauer focused clearly on the early history of this region in *The Early Spanish Main* (Berkelcy, Los Angeles, 1966), 4th edition with a new foreword by Anthony Pagden, Berkeley, Los Angeles, 1992 and, in doing so, dispensed with references to early European history to the greatest degree, whilst still acknowledging it in his account. Francisco Morales Padrón, *Historia del descubrimiento y conquista de América* (Madrid, 1981), plus numerous later new editions; and, in a dedicated volume, John H. Parry, *The Age of Reconaissance* (London, 1963), afforded more attention to medieval forerunners and the Mediterranean region, also considering, as an approach, the association between the North Sea region and the expansion process in the Atlantic in addition to frequent references to the Vikings. Even though Samuel Eliot Morison in *The European Discovery of America. The Southern Voyages, AD 1492–1616* (Oxford, 1974), defined this expansion as a pan-European phenomenon confining himself, in a second volume, which is scarcely of interest in this context, on the 'Northern Voyages' only, to a geographical division along northern and southern traditional lines in his rather more stock-taking account. The extent to which this occurred is open to question, bearing in mind the intensified North-South discourse which was taking place at that particular time.

4   Pierre Chaunu, *L'expansion*, cf. note 3, p. 55.

5   Cf. James Muldoon, *Popes, lawyers and infidels: the church and the non-Christian World, 1250–1550* (Philadelphia, 1979); James Muldoon (ed.) *The Expansion of Europe: the first phase* (Philadelphia, 1977); the same author (ed.) *Varieties of religious conversion in the Middle Ages* (Gainesville, 1997); James Muldoon, *Canon law, the expansion of Europe, and world order* (Ashgate, 1998); also on these issues cf. Joseph Höffner, *La ética colonial española del siglo de oro* (Madrid, 1957); Paulino Castañeda Delgado, *La teocracia pontifical en las controversias sobre el nuevo mundo* (México, 1996); Pedro Borges, *Misión y civilización en América* (Madrid, 1986); Josep-Ignasi Saranyana *et al.*, *Historia de la teologia latinoamericana. Primera parte: siglos XVI y XVII* (Pamplona, 1996); Johannes Meier, *Die Anfänge der Kirche auf den Karibischen Inseln. Die Geschichte der Bistümer Santo Domingo, Concepción de la Vega, San Juan de Puerto Rico und Santiago de Cuba von ihrer Entstehung (1511/22) bis zur Mitte des 17. Jahrhunderts* (Immensee, 1991); cf. also Jean-Paul Roux (Lyon, 1989); Charles Verlinden and Eberhard Schmitt (eds) *Die mittelalterlichen Ursprünge der europäischen Expansion. Dokumente zur Geschichte der europäischen Expansion*, (ed.) Eberhard Schmitt, Bd. 1 (Munich, 1986). Literature relating to the individual medieval colonization processes cannot be listed here. We refer you to important general works on the history of the Middle Ages containing an abundance of bibliographical references.

6   Cf. Ryszard Stemplowski, 'Joannes Dantiscus en la España de Carlos V. Un informe sobre las investigaciones en curso', in P.M. Piñero Ramirez and Chr. Wentzlaff-Eggebert, (eds) *Sevilla en el imperio de Carlos V. Encrucijada entre dos mundos y dos épocas* (Seville, 1991), pp. 131–8.

7   Enrique Otte, *Sevilla y sus mercaderes a fines de la Edad Media. Edicion e introducción Antonio-Miguel Bernal, Antonio Collantes de Terán* (Seville 1996); by the same author, 'Das genuesische Unternehmertum und Amerika unter den

Katholischen Königen' in *Jahrbuch für Geschichte von Staat, Wirtschaft und Gesellschaft Lateinamerikas*, vol. 2, 1965, pp. 30–74; the same author, 'Die Negersklavenlizenz des Laurent de Gorrevod. Kastilisch-genueische Wirtschafts- und Finanzinteressen bei der Einführung der Negersklaverei in Amerika', in *Spanische Forschungen der Görresgesellschaft*, First series, vol. 22 (Münster, 1965), pp. 283–320; by the same author, *Las perlas del Caribe: Nueva Cádiz de Cubagua* (Caracas, 1977); Ruth Pike, *Enterprise and Adventure.The Genoese in Sevilla and the Opening of the New World* (Ithaca, NY, 1966); Hermann Kellenbenz (ed.) *Fremde Kaufleute auf der Iberischen Halbinsel. Kölner Kolloquien zur internationalen Sozial- und Wirtschaftsgeschichte*, vol. 1 (Cologne-Vienna, 1970); in many of his works H. Kellenbenz focuses on inter- national trade links at the end of the Middle Ages, beginning of the modern era, and during the modern era, particularly in connection with the Caribbean, cf. Hermann Kellenbenz, *Kleine Schriften. Vierteljahrschrift für Sozial- und Wirtschaftsgeschichte*, Supplements 92–94, 3 vols (Stuttgart, 1991); also cf. J.N. Ball, *Merchants and Merchandise. The Expansion of trade in Europe (1500–1630)* (London, 1977); John Everaert, 'Marchands flamands à Lisbonne et l'exportation du sucre de Madère (1480–1530)' in *Actas do I colóquio interna- cional de historia da Madeira (1986)* (Funchal, 1989), p. 451 ff.; Virginia Rau, 'Les marchands-banquiers étrangers au Portugal sous le régne de Joâo III (1521–1527)' in *Les aspects internationaux de la découverte océanique aux XVe et XVIe siècles* (Paris, 1966); for general background cf. also Jean Favier, *De l'or et des épices. Naissance de l'homme d'affaires au Moyen Age* (Paris 1987); Simonetta Cavaciocchi, a cura di, *Prodotti e tecniche d'oltremare nelle economie europee secc. XII–XVIII, Atti della 'Ventinovesima Settimana di Studi'*, 14–19 aprile, 1997, Istituto Internazionale di Storia Economica 'F. Datini', Prato Series II-Atti delle 'Settimane di Studi' e altri convegni, vol. 29 (Florence, 1998). Santiago Olmedo Bernal, *El dominio del Atlántico en la baja Edad Media. Los titulos juridicos de la expansión peninsular hasta el Tratado de Tordesillas* (Salamanca, 1995); Ana Maria Carabias Torres (ed.) *Las relaciones entre Portugal y Castilla en la época de los descubrimientos y las expansión colonial* (Salamanca, 1994); Luis Adão da Fonseca and José Manuel Ruiz Asencio (eds) *Corpus documental del Tratado de Tordesillas* (Valladolid, 1995); Jesús Varela Marcos (ed.) *El Tratado de Tordesillas en la Cartografia Histórica* (Valladolid, 1994); Demetrios Ramos, *Audacia, negocios y politica en los viajes españoles, de 'descubrimiento y rescate'* (Valladolid, 1981) and, by the same author, *Genocidio y conquista: viejos mitos que siguen en pie* (Madrid, 1998), are fundamental for the period immediately following the advance into the Caribbean.

8   Cf. the collection of publications, quoted in footnote 7, by H. Kellenbenz and his work on the Fuggers: Hermann Kellenbenz, *Die Fugger in Spain and Portugal up to 1560*, 3 vols (Munich, 1990); Juan Friede, *Los Welser en la conquista de Venezuela* (Caracas-Madrid, 1961); Eberhard Schmitt and Friedrich Karl von Hutten (eds) *Das Gold der Neuen Welt. Die Papiere des Welser- Konquistadors und Generalkapitäns von Venezuela Philipp von Hutten 1534–1541* (Hildburghausen, 1996) (first of 3 announced vols).

9   Cf. for example, Detlef Heikamp, *Mexico and the Medici* (Florence, 1972); Dieter Harlfinger, *Die Wiedergeburt der Antike und die Auffindung Amerikas. 2000 Jahre Wegbereitung einer Entdeckung* (Hamburg, 1992); Urs Bitterli, *Die 'Wilden' und die 'Zivilisierten'. Grundzüge einer Geistes- und Kulturgeschichte der*

europäische-überseeischen Begegnung, Second revised and extended edition (Munich, 1991); Jean-Paul Duviols, *L'Amérique espagnole vue et rêvée. Les livres de voyages de Christophe Colomb à Bougainville* (Paris, 1985); John H. Elliott (ed.) *The Hispanic World, Civilization and Empire, Europe and the Americas, Past and Present* (London, 1991); Allain Cabantous, *Le ciel dans la mer. Christianisme et civilisation maritime XVIe–XIXe siècle* (Paris, 1990); Jörg Fisch, *Krieg und Frieden im Friedensvertrag. Eine universalgeschichtliche Studie über Grundlagen und Formelemente des Friedensschlusses* (Stuttgart, 1979); by the same author, *Die europäische Expansion und das Volkerrecht. Die Auseinandersetzung um den Status der überseeischen Gebiete vom 15. Jahrhundert bis zur Gegenwart* (Stuttgart, 1984); Heinz Gollwitzer, *Geschichte des weltpolitischen Denkens,* 2 vols (Göttingen 1972–1982); Horst Gründer, Welteroberung und Christentum. Ein Handbuch zur Geschichte der Neuzeit (Gütersloh, 1992). Sir Charles Oman, *A History of the Art of War in the Sixteenth Century,* reprint (London, 1991); Marc Ferro, *Histoire des colonisations. Des Conquêtes aux Indépendances, XIIIe-XXe siècle* (Paris, 1994); Sidney W. Mintz, *Sweetness and Power: The Place of Sugar in Modern World History* (New York, 1985); Jonathan I. Israel, *European Jewry in the Age of Mercantilism 1550–1750* (Berkeley, 1991); Fernand Braudel, *Civilisation matérielle et capitalisme,* 3 vols (Paris, 1967); John Thornton, *Africa and the Making of the Atlantic World, 1400–1680* (Cambridge, 1992). References to the Caribbean appear in all the works mentioned. As can already be seen from some titles this admittedly has something to do with the more recent trend toward the development of global history which extends beyond national borders, looking at large sections of history and their correlation and interchangeability. Following on from the trend in the 1960s and 1970s towards detailed small-scale empire research, broader bases are becoming dominant again, cf. in connection with the latter aspect Horst Pietschmann, *Geschichte des atlantischen Systems, 1580–1830. A historical experiment outside the boundaries of national historical perspectives,* Berichte aus den Sitzungen der JOACHIM JUNGIUS-GESELLSCHAFT DER WISSENSCHAFTEN E.V., Hamburg, volume 16, number 2, 1998.

10 On this subject cf. in greater detail the histories of Horst Pietschmann, quoted in footnote 9. These historiographies on the history of the colonial past of European colonial powers can be divided, if not clearly classified, into studies which grew out of expansion history and are still linked with it and investigations which, since the 1970s, increasingly look at the colonial past of later independent states in order to extract associations with and origins of subsequent emancipation movements and the processes involved in the creation of states and nations. Of particular importance in this respect for Hispanoamerica and the Caribbean is the Americanist-Sevillan school, whose own line of research on the history of the Caribbean region has been in evidence since the 1940s. It is strongly influenced by the historian Francisco Morales Padrón who, as a professor of discovery history, not only wrote important general accounts, cf. his *Historia del descubrimiento* quoted in footnote 2, but also organized over many years a series of congresses on the history of the Canary Islands and the Americas and who, in addition to his monographs on the history of the Caribbean, instigated countless dissertations on the region. First initiatives to intensify collaboration between Latinamerican historians can be traced back to him; cf. also his work Francisco Morales Padrón, *Jamaica española* (Seville,

1952); cf. on the history of this school José Antonio Calderón Quijano, *El Americansimo en Sevilla, 1900–1980* (Seville, 1987), with a bibliographical summary. The Madrid school, on the other hand, was associated rather more with Spain's early discovery history. With their own institutes financed by the 'Consejo Superior de Investigaciones Cientificas' each school possessed a research-oriented institutional base – the 'Escuelo de Estudios. Hispano-americanos', Sevilla and the 'Instituto Gonzalo Fernández de Oviedo', Madrid and published for decades a plethora of studies on the history of the Caribbean region in the two journals *Anuario de Estudios Americanos* and *Revista de Indias*, the majority of which were based on the extensive reference material available in Spain. The reference editions on the history of the Spanish Caribbean were also based mainly on Spanish archives, irrespective of whether they were maintained by Spanish researchers or historians from the Caribbean. Unfortunately, to date no fairly systematic bibliographical summary exists of the plethora of historical contributions – books, journal articles, published documents – on the colonial history of the Caribbean originating from this reference material and from schools which have directly influenced almost all historians working on colonial Hispanoamerica to a greater or lesser extent.

11 Cf. for example, David Watts, *The West Indies: Patterns of Development, Culture and Environmental Change since 1492*, Cambridge (New York, 1987); Helmut Blume, *Die Westindischen Inseln*, 2nd edition (Braunschweig, 1973), although both works attempt to confirm the uniform character of the region. In addition, a plethora of publications on individual states and islands in the region are available.

12 Cf. Horst Pietschmann, 'Das 500. Jubiläum der Kolumbusfahrt aus der Perspektive der Organisation Amerikanischer Staaten (OAS/OEA)' in Gerhard Wawor and Titus Heydenreich (eds) *Columbus 1892/1992. Heldenverehrung und Heldendemontage* (Frankfurt/M., 1995), p. 123 ff.

13 Cf. Bitterli, *Die 'Wilden*, quoted in footnote 9; also Jean Paul Duviols, *L'Amérique*, quoted *ibid*; Emma Martinell Gifre, *La comunicacion entre españoles e indios: Palabras y gestos* (Madrid, 1992); in a broader context also Fredi Chiapelli (ed.) *First Images of America: The Impact of the New World on the Old*, 2 vols (Berkeley, 1976); F. Jennings, *The Invasion of America: Indians, Colonialism and the Cant of Conquest* (Chapel Hill, 1978); Juan Gil, *Mitos y utopias del descubrimiento*, 3 vols (Madrid, 1989); Anthony Pagden, *European Encounters with the New World. From Renaissance to Romanticism* (New Haven and London, 1993).

14 On the significance of both social models in Spanish expansion cf. Horst Pietschmann, 'La resistencia española al imperio: Las Indias en los años iniciales del reinade de Carlos V' in Universidad Complutense de Madrid (ed.) *Estudios de Historia del Derecho Europeo. Homenaje al Prof. G. Martinez Diez*, 2 vols (Madrid), vol. 2, p. 13 ff; by the same author, '500 años de historia iberoameri-cana. Variantes ejemplares del desarrollo histórico', in AA. VV., *El Reino de Granada y el Neuvo Mundo*, V. Congreso Internacional de Historia de América, Mayo de 1992, 3 vols (Granada, 1994), vol. 3, p. 75 ff.; and by the same author, 'Die iberische Expansion im Atlantik und di kastilisch-spanische Entdeckung und Eroberung Amerikas', in Walther L. Bernecker, Raymond Th. Buve, John R. Fisher, Horst Pietschmann and Hans-Werner Tobler (eds) *Handbuch der Geschichte Lateinamerikas*, 3 vols (Stuttgart, 1992–1996), vol. 1., p. 23 ff.

15 Erwin Walter Palm, *Los Monumentos Arquitectónicos de La Española* (Santo Domingo, 1984); Luis Weckmann, *La herencia medieval de México*, 2 vols (Mexico, 1984).

16 Immanuel Wallerstein, *The Modern World System, Capitalist Agriculture and the Origins of the European World-Economy in the Sixteenth Century* (New York, 1974) pp. 165–221.

17 G.V. Scammell, *The World Encompassed; The First European Maritime Empires, c.800–1500* (London, 1981), p. 373 (The Netherlands), p. 436, (France) pp. 460–5 (England).

18 P.W. Klein, 'The Origins of Trading Companies' in L. Blussé and F. Gaastra (eds) *Companies and Trade; Essays on Overseas Trading Companies during the Ancien Régime* (The Hague, 1981), pp. 17–28.

19 P.C. Emmer (ed.) *Colonialism and Migration; Indentured Labour Before and After Slavery* (Dordrecht, 1986), pp. 19–124 (Essays by B.H. Slicher van Bath, Henry A. Gemery, Ernst van den Boogaart, Frédéric Mauro and Günter Moltmann); Renate Pieper, 'Die demographische Entwicklung', in H. Pietschmann (ed.) *Handbuch der Geschichte Lateinamerikas, 1, Mittel-, Südamerika und die Karibik bis 1760* (Stuttgart, 1994), pp. 313–28; Ida Altman and James Horn, 'Introduction', in Ida Altman and James Hord (eds) *To Make America's Emigration in the Early Modern Period* (Berkeley, 1991), pp. 3, 4, and Bernard Bailyn, *Voyagers to the West: A Passage in the Peopling of America on the Eve of Revolution* (New York, 1986), p. 24.

20 Lyle N. McAlister, *Spain and Portugal in the New World, 1492–1700* (Oxford, 1984), p. 294 mentions 275 000 *moriscos* being expelled from Spain.

21 Jonathan I. Israel, *Dutch Primacy in World Trade, 1585–1740* (Oxford, 1989), pp. 42, 74.

22 K.G. Davies, *The North Atlantic World in the Seventeenth Century* (Oxford, 1974), p. 290.

23 Kenneth R. Andrews, *Trade, Plunder and Settlement; Maritime Enterprise and the Genesis of the British Empire, 1480–1630* (Cambridge, 1984); and Cornelis Ch. Goslinga, *The Dutch in the Caribbean and on the Wild Coast, 1580–1680* (Gainesville, 1971).

24 M. Devèze, *Antilles, Guyanes, la mer des Caraïbes de 1492 à 1789* (Paris, 1977), ch. IV.

25 McAlister, *Spain and Portugal in the New World*, pp. 201–3.

26 David Watts, *The West Indies; Patterns of Development, Culture and environmental Change since 1492* (Cambridge, 1987), p. 129; K.R. Andrews, 'The English in the Caribbean, 1560–1620', in K.R. Andrews, N.P. Canny and P.E.H. Hair (eds) *The Westward Enterprise; English Activities in Ireland, the Atlantic and America, 1480–1650* (Liverpool, 1978), pp. 103–9.

27 Joyce Lorimer, 'The English Contraband Tobacco Trade in Trinidad and Guiana', in Andrews, Canny and Hair (eds) *The Westward Enterprise*, p. 136; J.G. van Dillen, *Van Rijkdom en Regenten; Handboek tot de Economische en Sociale Geschiedenis van Nederland tijdens de Republiek* ('s-Gravenhage, 1970), p. 141; and Goslinga, *The Dutch in the Caribbean and on the Wild Coast*, p. 132.

28 Ward, *The West Indies*, pp. 132–5.

29 Kenneth R. Andrews, *The Spanish Caribbean; Trade and Plunder, 1530–1630* (New Haven/London, 1978), pp. 224–34.

30   Carl and Roberta Bridenbaugh, *No Peace Beyond the Line; the English in the Caribbean, 1624–1690* (New York, 1972), pp. 35–68.

31   Devèze, *Antilles, Guyanes*, pp. 131–52.

32   Bridenbaugh, *No Peace Beyond the Line*, pp. 29–32.

33   Andrews, *The Spanish Caribbean*, pp. 250–5.

34   Richard Pares, *Merchants and Planters* (Cambridge, 1960), pp. 1–6.

35   Theodore K. Rabb, *Enterprise and Empire; Merchant and Gentry Investment in the Expansion of England, 1575–1640* (Harvard, 1967), pp. 55–89; Nuala Zehedieh, 'Trade, Plunder, and Economic Development in Early English America, 1655–1689', *Economic History Review*, 2nd series, vol. XXXIV/2 (May, 1986), pp. 205–22.

36   Goslinga, *The Dutch in the Caribbean and on the Wild Coast*, p. 81 and Lorimer, 'The English contraband tobacco trade in Trinidad and Guiana, 1590–1617', pp. 147–9; Jean-Pierre Moreau, 'Navigation européenne dans les Petites Antilles aux XVIe et début du XVIIe siècles. Sources documentaires, approche archéologique', *Revue francaise d'histoire d'outre-mer*, vol. LXXIV/275, pp. 129–47.

37   Richard S. Dunn, *Sugar and Slaves; the Rise of the Planter Class in the English West Indies, 1624–1713* (New York, 1973), pp. 18, 19; and Devèze, *Antilles, Guyanes*, p. 150.

38   Dunn, *Sugar and Slaves*, pp. 269, 270; Jean-Marcel Hurault, *Francais et Indiens en Guyane, 1604–1972* (Paris, 1972), p. 81; and Neil L. Whitehead, *Lords of the Tiger Spirit; A History of the Caribs in Colonial Venezuela and Guyana, 1498–1820* (Dordrecht, 1988), pp. 184–8.

39   Davies, *The North Atlantic World*, pp. 267–9.

40   Figures from Watts, *The West Indies*, p. 151.

41   Richard S. Dunn, 'Servants and Slaves: the Recruitment and Employment of Labor', in Jack P. Greene and J.R. Pole, *Colonial British America; Essays in the New History of the Early Modern Era* (Baltimore/London, 1984), pp. 157–64; P. Butel, 'Le temps des fondations: les Antilles avant Colbert', in P. Pluchon (ed.), *Histoire des Antilles et de la Guyane* (Toulouse, 1982), pp. 69–75 and Henry A. Gemery, 'Markets for Migrants, English Indentured Servitude and Emigration in the Seventeenth and Eighteenth Centuries', in P. Emmer (ed.) *Colonialism and Migration*, pp. 45–8.

42   Carl Bridenbaugh, *Vexed and Troubled Englishmen, 1590–1642* (London, 1974), pp. 394–433.

43   Richard N. Bean and Robert P. Thomas, 'The Adoption of Slave Labor in British America', in Henry A. Gemery and Jan S. Hogendorn (eds) *The Uncommon Market; Essays in the Economic History of the Atlantic Slave Trade* (New York, 1979), pp. 377–98; David Galenson, *White Servitude in Colonial America; An Economic Analysis* (Cambridge, 1981), pp. 82–96 and Hilary McD. Beckles, *White Servitude and Black Slavery in Barbados, 1627–1715* (Knoxville, 1989).

44   Bridenbaugh, *No Peace Beyond the Line,* pp. 23–6.

45   Robert Carlyle Batie 'Why Sugar? Economic Cycles and the Changing of Staples on the English and French Antilles, 1624–1654', in *Journal of Caribbean History*, vol. 8 (1976), pp. 1–41 and Jacques Petit Jean Roget, *La société d'habitation à la Martinique, 1635–1685* (Lille/Paris, 1980), vol. II, pp. 1153–4; William A. Green, 'Supply versus Demand in the Barbadian Revolution', *Journal of Interdisciplinary History*, XVIII/3 (Winter 1988), pp. 403–18.

46   James A. Rawley, *The Trans-Atlantic Slave Trade* (New York/London, 1981), pp. 55, 62, 108, 101, 112, and Ernst van den Boogaart and Pieter C. Emmer, 'The Dutch Participation in the Atlantic Slave Trade, 1596–1650', in Gemery and Hogendorn (eds) *The Uncommon Market*, pp. 371–5.

47   Watts, *The West Indies*, pp. 177–84.

48   H.A. Gemery and J.S. Hogendorn, 'Elasticity of Slave Labor Supply and the Development of Slave Economies in the British Caribbean: the Seventeenth Century Experience', in Vera Rubin and Arthur Tuden (eds) *Comparative Perspectives on Slavery in New World Plantation Societies* (New York, 1977), pp. 72–83; John J. McCusker and Russel R. Menard, *The Economy of British America, 1607–1789* (Chapel Hill/London, 1985), pp. 148–55.

49   Van den Boogaart and Emmer, 'The Dutch Participation in the Atlantic Slave Trade, 1596–1650', pp. 371–5.

50   Barbara L. Solow, 'The Transition to Plantation Slavery; the Case of the British West Indies', in Serge Daget (ed.) *De la traite à l'esclavage; Actes du colloque international sur la traite des Noirs, Nantes 1985* (Nantes/Paris, 1988), vol. I, pp. 89–113.

51   Bridenbaugh, *No Peace Beyond the Line*, p. 13, and Dunn, *Sugar and Slaves*, pp. 67–74.

52   Of course, the Guianas should always be excepted. M. Mattioni, 'Le crépuscule indien' in P. Pluchon (ed.) *Histoire des Antilles et de la Guyane* (Toulouse, 1982), pp. 41–8.

53   Kenneth F. Kiple, *The Caribbean Slave; a Biological History* (Cambridge, 1984), pp. 7–9, and Henry A. Gemery, 'Markets for Migrants: English Indentured Servitude and Emigration in the Seventeenth and Eighteenth Centuries', in Emmer, *Colonialism and Migration*, pp. 39, 40.

54   Robert William Fogel and Stanley L. Engerman, *Time on the Cross; the Economics of American Negro Slavery* (London, 1974), pp. 13–20.

55   Richard Nelson Bean, *The British Trans-Atlantic Slave Trade, 1650–1675* (New York, 1975), pp. 35–9, and Philip D. Curtin, *The Atlantic Slave Trade; A Census* (Madison, 1969), p. 119, and John Thornton, *Africa and Africans in the Making of the Atlantic World, 1400–1680* (Cambridge, 1992), pp. 141–51.

56   Van den Boogaart and Emmer, 'The Dutch Participation in the Atlantic Slave Trade, 1596–1650', p. 374.

57   Watts, *The West Indies*, p. 173, and Richard N. Bean, 'Food Imports into the British West Indies, 1680–1845', in Rubin and Tuden (eds) *Comparative Perspectives on Slavery*, pp. 581–91.

58   Pares, *Merchants and Planters*, pp. 1–6.

59   T.H. Breen, 'Creative Adaptations; Peoples and Cultures', in Jack P. Greene and J.R. Pole (eds) *Colonial British America; Essays in the New History of the Early Modern Era* (Baltimore/London, 1984), pp. 195–232.

1

THE CARIBBEAN ENVIRONMENT AND EARLY SETTLEMENT

David Watts

Introduction: the natural environment and the first settlers

The very first settlers who arrived in the island Caribbean from either Central or South America, around 5000 BC or slightly later, were of Amerindian stock. They were technologically primitive, though capable of travel across oceanic waters by means of timber rafts, with mat sails. Although together they have been accorded the group name of '*palaeo-Indians*', it is as yet uncertain whether there were any major cultural differences between them in their main foci of settlement within Trinidad, Cuba and Española. It is likely that their numbers were always small. Preferred sites for settlement were usually close to sea level, on favoured coasts. Those in Trinidad were easily reached by migrants from adjacent South America, across the narrow Gulf of Paria; while the longer journey from the Mexican and Central American eastern coastlines, and especially from the vicinity of Cap Gracias a Dios, to settlements in Cuba and Española, was made easier by favourable seasonal conditions of winds and currents. Such peoples possessed a stone-, or more commonly a shell-tool technology, and were well adapted to seashore living. Also derived from their mainland areas of origin, were skills they had developed for the capture of large land mammals, or sea mammals such as the manatee, for food. Although some medium-sized land mammals were present in Trinidad at the time of this early settlement, none, other than the iguana, were to be found elsewhere in the island Caribbean. There the main food resources for established palaeo-Indian groups quickly came to be the manatee, along with possibly the green turtle, a variety of shellfish, sea fish and a range of plant foods.

It is known that, at about 5000 BC, sea levels were some 2.5 to 5 m higher than today,[1] which meant that the coastal mangrove areas, in which oysters and other shellfish, and to some extent the manatee, resided, were on a larger scale than at present, and this probably facilitated settlement. Due to the paucity of good pollen or diatom data from the island Caribbean, little else is known of the general environment there at that time. However, a recent, high-resolution[2] study of the balance between oxygen-isotope ratios among fossil ostracod shells in Lake Miragoane, southern Haiti, (which is quite close to many of the southern Española palaeo-Indian sites), has not only confirmed the high sea levels of around 5000 BC, but also the existence then of a lowland climate which was much wetter than that of today, and the development of mesic tropical forest inland. The same study has further indicated that these conditions prevailed until about 1600–1700 BC, when a sudden climatic change to much drier conditions took place, accompanied by a loss of forest in the drier parts of Española and its replacement by more open, and in places desert-like vegetation. Archaeological evidence further suggests that sea level began to fall at the same time, bringing a severe restriction of the littoral zone and its rich food resources. Present sea levels were reached some 500 years later. Along with the change of climate and the associated curtailment of sea coast food resources, factors which one can assume were not local but covered the entire island Caribbean region, many long-standing palaeo-Indian settlements in Cuba and Española were abandoned, though not necessarily permanently. It is clear that one of the major features of climates during the second half of the second millennium BC was an inbuilt instability. Although generally more arid than formerly, the climate was punctuated by the sudden onset of temporary, wetter phases, in which rainfall totals rose substantially, sea level again increased, and the littoral zone was also extended. During these phases, new settlements of palaeo-Indians came to be established, as instanced by the presence of newer shell midden sites at Mayaro in Trinidad, and in Cuba and Española, but these were abandoned again whenever the climate reverted once more to its drier state.[3]

Environments and climates stabilized at close to their present conditions shortly after 1000 BC, with littoral zones relatively restricted compared to formerly, and coastlands much drier (though with wetter forests inland). Under these new conditions more culturally-advanced groups of settlers, termed *meso-Indians*, began to invade the island Caribbean from South America, first in Trinidad (from about 800 BC), and on the islands north of the Venezuelan coast, and later (from the beginning of the Christian era) in the Greater Antilles. It is likely that the Lesser Antilles were left alone by these groups. It is probable that overall numbers of meso-Indian settlers were never large, though they appear to have been skilled sailors and navigators. Like their predecessors, they lacked agricultural knowledge; but unlike their forbears they could produce crude pottery, the stylistic derivation of which, in the Greater Antilles at least, points towards Colombia as a source area.[4]

Their food resources were similar to those of the palaeo-Indians, and included a wide range of fish and shellfish, turtle, manatee and wild plant foods. Their chosen settlement sites, however, were different, being by preference on the tops of dunes, or on mounds within marshland.

A few meso-Indians were still present in the western-most extremities of Española and Cuba when Columbus first discovered these islands. Their numbers then were few, and the Spanish found out little about them. Those in Cuba had the tribal name of Guanahacibibe, lived in rough rock shelters or small caves, and possessed good-quality stone or flint tools with which they were able to fashion quality dug-out canoes. They were noticeably wary of contact with others. They were reported[5] as living 'like savages, and they have no relations with others of the island, nor do they have houses, nor village quarters, nor fields, but they live in caves, except when they go out to fish'. Those in south-western Española lived some distance away from the coast, perhaps having been forced inland by advancing Arawak Indian groups (see below). These too were wary of strangers, running away from contact and being 'as fleet as deer' – the Spanish could not catch them. None of these groups survived the Hispanic intrusion for longer than a year or two, and their numbers are likely to have been insufficient to modify the environment in any meaningful way.

Indians and their environments at the time of Hispanic contact

Other than the two small groups of meso-Indians described above, the whole of the island Caribbean at the time of Hispanic contact was occupied by peoples of a later derivation, with a considerably more advanced technological and cultural status. These people are termed *neo-Indians*. Unlike earlier groups, they used agriculture for part of their food resource in addition to the familiar earlier methods of fishing, the culling of wild animals and the collecting and gathering of wild plant materials.[6] They could also produce a wide range of pottery, and they were exceptionally skilful mariners. They lived in large, and at least in the Greater Antilles, numerous and well-organized villages, of 1000 to 2000 people. The villages usually consisted of 20 to 50 multi-family houses, presided over in their day-to-day affairs by a local chieftain, or *cacique*.[7] On a wider scale the main tribal communities, arising from allegiances of groups of villages, were ruled over by more important *caciques*. Inheritance of the role of *cacique* often followed a matrilineal line, which led to a rather complex social life, the intricacies of which varied from place to place. Thus in the Greater Antilles, five major *caciques* controlled Española in 1492, but much less clearly-defined chieftainships were found in the subsidiary territories of Puerto Rico, Jamaica, Cuba and the Bahamas. The situation is more uncertain in the numerous islands of the Lesser Antilles. In the Greater Antilles, too, judicial authority was placed in the hands of the *caciques*, except possibly in Trinidad. In all territories, a complex religious life, in which many gods were worshipped and invoked, was led by shamans. Day-to-day diversions included ball games and dancing.

Indian villages at this time were of a size that normally could easily be supported by local food resources, and no evidence exists that the population was anything other than well fed and healthy, except for the presence of a very mild form of endemic syphilis. Within the villages, individual houses tended to be arranged around a central square, in which most daytime activity took place. Because of the difficulty of clearing well-developed tropical rain forest, most villages tended to be located in or near more open forest (where in any case the soil was often more fertile than under true rain forest), and away from the coast, where vegetation again was often extremely difficult to remove, especially in mangrove terrain.[8] Individual houses were usually simple but sturdy, constructed of walls of good timber planking (e.g. mahogany in the Bahamas, silk-cotton more widely), made rainproof by a plaster of hardened mud, and a palm thatch roof. Most residential houses were circular in design, with a conical roof, though those of *caciques* were frequently more complex, often being rectangular and gabled.

Inter-community and inter-island contact for trade was encouraged, notably for the purpose of acquiring quality products which were not universally obtainable at a local level. Among these were stone celts, and various cotton products such as hammocks and particular items of clothing. Trade links to South America and, to a much lesser extent, Central America, were set up from time to time, though there were none to North America.[9] One particular skill found in the Greater Antilles was the fabrication of gold ornaments from soft gold nuggets picked up from river beds. As far as is known these ornaments never entered inter-island trade, being retained for personal use by *caciques* and their relatives. The mere existence of such ornaments, and the presence of gold *per se*, were, of course, to accentuate the possibility for conflict between Indians and Spanish, and eventually, though indirectly, hasten the downfall of Indian societies in this region.

Traditionally, the view is that, on the basis of language, two groups of neo-Indians occupied the island Caribbean, one of which spoke Arawakan, and the other Cariban, both of which are common among Indian groups in the north and north-east of South America, and which clearly are the areas of their derivation. The former were by far the earliest arrivals, reaching Trinidad from the adjacent mainland around 300 BC, and bringing with them a sub-culture termed Saladoid, with a distinctive white-on-red decorative pottery style. A second sub-culture, without this pottery style, reached Trinidad somewhat later, and was termed Barrancoid. But within the island Caribbean, the former was always more dominant, both in terms of influence and numbers, and it was they who migrated exceptionally quickly, either along the Lesser Antillean chain of islands, or more likely directly northwards across the Caribbean Sea, to reach the Greater Antilles at about AD 250. Once installed, their main centre of activity there was always Española, their 'mother island', but substantial populations also developed in Cuba, Jamaica, Puerto Rico and (after about AD 1000) the Bahamas/Lucaya.[10] From about AD 650, the Saladoid pottery style was replaced in the four large islands of the Greater Antilles by another, without the white-on-red decoration, but with increasingly complicated designs. Whether this was an endemic development, or introduced by later migrants directly from Venezuelan coastlands, is not yet clear. All these Arawakan groups came eventually to be termed 'island Arawak', or 'Taíno'.[11]

By 1492 some sections of the island Arawak population, notably in Puerto Rico and possibly also in the Samana peninsula of Española, were beginning to be forced to defend territory against other neo-Indian peoples, who spoke Cariban, and who had advanced northwards through the Lesser Antilles during the first half of the second millennium AD. Although their numbers were much smaller than those of the island Arawak, they were constantly seeking new lands in which to settle. Although they had the same basic culture as the island Arawak, they also had the reputation of being much more fierce and warlike. While this may have been the case during their expansionist phases, it is, however, unlikely to have been so for all of the time, for they were known also to have been good agriculturists, raising not only a wide range of food crops, but also high-quality cotton and tobacco.[12] Early Spanish colonizers also accorded to them the practice of cannibalism, although it must be said that the evidence for this is scanty at best, and the notion may have owed more to European mythologies of the time, which frequently ascribed cannibalism to newly-discovered peoples who were perceived to constitute a threat, than to any substantive observation of the practice. Nevertheless, this concept remained unchallenged until quite recently, not least in the group name 'Carib' granted to these Indians. It is also present in the long-held view that there were in the New World 'good' Indians (i.e. the peaceful Arawak) and 'bad' Indians (i.e. the fighting Carib), which permeated Hispanic thinking during the fifteenth and sixteenth centuries and which subsequently led to some severe misconceptions as to how they should be treated (see below). Within the last few years, Hulme and Whitehead and others[13] have strongly discounted the idea of Carib cannibalism, emphasizing instead the similarities of culture between island Arawak and Carib, and suggesting that both should now be regarded as being part of one major island Caribbean culture group rather than as separate cultural and/or linguistic entities.

To the earliest Spanish visitors and settlers, the environments which these Indian groups inhabited were green, lush and beneficent on a scale never encountered before. Vegetation was diverse, as also was the bird life, which included 'flocks of parrots which blotted out the sun'.[14] The tropical, trade wind climate was regarded as being one of perpetual spring, both gentler and warmer than that of southern Spain from whence they came, and the adequate rainfall allowed many crops to grow well. Not until 1496 were the first indications of climatic problems encountered, in the form of a hurricane. In fact, island Caribbean climates are both variable and seasonal, with a range of disadvantages which were not at first apparent. Throughout the region temperatures have no restrictive effect on plant growth, except in those few highland areas which lie over 3000 m above sea level, where frosts may occasionally occur. On the other hand, the amount of effective moisture available for plant growth can vary locationally, annually and seasonally.

Locationally, most coastlands have been relatively dry since about 1000 BC, and this is especially true of those on the leeward side of islands: those to the windward are slightly wetter. Then, the amount of received precipitation rises quite substantially as one moves upslope, so that there is, for example, very little annual water deficit for crop growth at heights of 300 m and above. This increase is due to the north-east trade winds being forced to shed their moisture as they rise to cross the higher ground. In between the sea coast and 300 m, the climate is often strongly variable.

Thus there are seasonal effects on most Caribbean islands, in which there is commonly an exceptionally arid dry season for three to four months during the first half of the year, while from June or July to November which is the warmest part of the year, a strikingly wet season occurs. The heavy rains of the wet season are derived from convectional activity including thunderstorms, from low-pressure areas which move in a westerly direction across the southern North Atlantic, and from the occasional hurricane. In addition, there is a strong general annual cyclicity in Caribbean climates, in which a series of dry years may develop every 25 to 30 years or so, during which rainfall is particularly low. All this means that crop plants in the region, which are grown mainly below 300 m in altitude, must be capable of withstanding periods of water shortage, either seasonally, or annually, while at the same time maintaining their yields. They must also be capable of surviving much wetter years, with the occasional hurricane. Most are well able to do so.

Except in Cuba there are few major areas of flat land, with most of the islands being hilly or mountainous. Vegetation and soil patterns often follow the climatic patterns closely, except where the soils are new, as in the case of recent volcanic eruptions. On coastlands, the land is often dry enough for desert shrubs and cacti, and soils are poorly developed. At altitudes above 300 m, under natural conditions, tropical rainforest is most common, giving rise to very deep though frequently very infertile soils, which hold few mineral nutrients. The best-yielding soils for crops are often found on the lower slopes of hills, between 50–250 m above sea level. Here the seasonality of climate is accentuated, with a distinct dry season, and the natural vegetation is a 'seasonal' rainforest.[15] This seasonal forest has always been easier to clear than true rainforest, and so was favoured for settlement and cultivation, both in Indian times and later. In Cuba, savannah grassland extended widely on the flat land, while along the littoral generally, most islands held a thin fringe of mangroves in which many shellfish, the manatee and some fish flourished and maintained their importance as food commodities.

Quite how neo-Indian groups perceived these environments is difficult to know, for most records pertaining to this have largely been lost. Those that do remain all reflect Spanish interpretations of Indian views. However, it is likely that districts in the seasonal rainforests were the preferred choice for settlement and cultivation, for these were relatively easy to fire or clear, and soils were more fertile than elsewhere. If such districts were also close to coastlands, with their rich animal foodstuff resources, so much the better. But it is also the case that in the more densely settled islands, such as Española, Indian groups established villages in true rainforest as well. The only areas regarded by Indians as being useless either for settlement or cultivation seem to have been savannah grasslands on open terrain. Here defence was difficult and the soils exceptionally infertile. They were, however, valued extensively for rapid travel on foot.[16]

Just how many Indians were present in the island Caribbean in 1492 remains a matter for skilful conjecture. Bartolomé de Las Casas, who probably knew Española better than any other settler, was in no doubt that in the early days of settlement and away from the Spanish, Indian populations appeared to be numerically stable. Individuals were healthy and lived to an advanced age, women bearing three to five children on average. He estimated that the population at the time of European contact of Española alone was between three and four million. But there are no population censuses to confirm or deny this. The first census, produced by Bartolomeo Columbus in 1496, determined that there were then close to one million Indians on the island, but that was subsequent to a particularly severe population decline in 1494–5.[17] The decline continued exponentially thereafter, so that by 1508–10 only 60 000 Indians remained. But it is the rate of decline in the first years of

Hispanic settlement which is especially difficult to evaluate, and which still prejudices attempts to arrive at a reasoned and generally acceptable view of the size of the native population in 1492.

One possible way to overcome this is to consider the carrying capacity of the land in respect of its ability to provide food resources for human populations. Most recent demographers have included an estimate of this in their deliberations.[18] These resources included not only the wild foodstuffs such as shellfish, sea fish, sea mammals, land animals and plants also used by their predecessors, and which provided the main protein resource, but also the small, shifting agricultural plots from which roots such as cassava, sweet potato, American yams, zanthosoma and others produced the substantive calorie-rich, carbohydrate foods on which their existence depended, under a production system termed *conuco*. There is little doubt that the combination of wild foodstuffs and *conuco* crops gave rise to a well-balanced diet which was easily maintainable, even in times of drought (the *conuco* crops were all drought-resistant).[19] Most modern analysts agree that such a food-producing system could support a large population, in a sustainable way, for many years. Using the carrying capacity methodology, Denevan has argued that a total population of about six million for all the island Caribbean in 1492 could have been about the right number, with a population density of about 25 per square kilometres generally, and much more in Española.[20]

Whether such a large population would have modified the natural environment other than in the short term is also open to question. It is probable that the cull of fish, marine mammals and land plants and animals would have been relatively small each year, and the use of such resources took place only at certain times of the year, so that such populations were not endangered and their natural balance was maintained. The traditional view also is that though *conuco* plots lost most of their inherent fertility even on good soils after three to five years, and then were left in fallow to recover while other plots were cleared, *conuco* agriculture of itself did not damage the environment in the long term. In time, and once nutrient levels had recovered, the same plots could be used again. This system of cultivation was thus inherently self-sustaining. There is nothing in the official records to challenge this view. However, some recent archaeological work has begun to question these notions, with the discovery of evidence for soil erosion in aboriginal times in two localities: parts of the Barbados south coast and Española.[21] The assumption is that these areas were overpopulated, or at the very least sites in which soil resources were being utilized too intensively, or unwisely, at particular times. There is, however, no indication at present as to whether these instances were purely isolated cases, or whether they might reflect a more common misuse of the land in some Indian communities than was previously thought.

The effect of Spanish intrusion on environments

The exploratory excursion of Columbus in 1492, and the arrival of Hispanic colonists one year later, set in train a course of events which was to rapidly change island Caribbean environments, both natural and socioeconomic, on a major scale and for ever. The nature of these changes was stimulated by three parallel sequences of events arising from Spanish settlement, namely the decline of indigenous populations and their agricultural systems, Spanish economic enterprise, and the intermingling of Old and New World disease organisms. These gave rise to a curious mixture of passive-active disturbances to the environment – passive, in terms of the increasing absence of the Indians from the region in view of their decline in numbers, and active, arising directly out of the activities of the newcomers. Their immense consequences for the subsequent history of the region are surprising not least because, at best, the population of the Spanish during the first century of colonization in these islands remained small, at no more than 10 000.[22]

With the discovery of gold ornaments in Española, the major primary aim of the Spanish was to secure for themselves as many of the ornaments and as much of the ore as possible. At the same time, new and local food sources were needed to replace those brought out from the Mediterranean, all of which had conspicuously failed to succeed in the new tropical environment.[23] Columbus' solution to these challenges was to direct Indian populations to help in the production of both. From 1495 all Indians between the ages of 14 and 70 years living in gold-producing areas, were required to produce a tribute in gold at three-month intervals. Elsewhere, tributes of spices and cotton were demanded. Foodstuffs were to be raised from Indian *conucos*. In fact, little gold was produced, the Indians claiming that they were 'ignorant of the means of mining it'.[24] To escape tribute payments, the Indians also preferred to desert their villages in large numbers. This in turn resulted in enormous social dislocation among their communities, with increased general mortality rates, some suicide, and reduced birth rates caused by an inhibition of ovulation, the consequence both of substantial and growing malnutrition, and traumas caused by the frequently violent nature of contact with the Spanish, who used dogs to enforcedly enslave them where they could.

One other consequence was that, since no Indians were left to look after them, *conucos* were abandoned and quickly reverted to weeds and secondary growth, so that aboriginal food supplies also rapidly diminished on an exponential scale. Indeed, famine came to be widespread in the central part of Española as early as 1496. These conditions were soon to spread to all other parts of that island.

All this encouraged the decline of the Indian population in Española at a staggering rate. Las Casas has suggested that between 1494 and 1508, more than three million Indians died in that island alone,[25] while at the same time very little gold, and a minimal amount of foodstuffs had been produced. As a result, from 1509 adjacent islands began to be raided for Indian labour, which was sent back to Española under conditions of slavery to work in the few gold placers which had been discovered, as well as on *conuco* land. Thus, by 1514 the Bahamas had been depopulated, and Puerto Rico had been emptied of Indians some five years later. By 1519, too, all the Indians from Jamaica had been killed, or transferred to Española, apart from some small groups who retreated to the interior mountains. In Cuba, where a few further gold placers were discovered, most Indians had been removed by the same year. By 1520, therefore, virtually all native peoples had been taken from the northern Leeward islands between the Virgins and Barbuda, excepting St Kitts and Nevis which were 'Carib' strongholds, from St Lucia, Tobago and Barbados to the south, and from most of the islands to the north of the Venezuelan coast, including Curaçao, Bonaire and Aruba. Except for additional 'Carib' groups living in the more mountainous, volcanic islands of the Lesser Antilles, virtually the whole neo-Indian population of the island Caribbean, along with the remnants of the meso-Indians, had been rendered extinct within 30 years of Spanish contact. Very little of this demographic disaster can be ascribed to the effects of European diseases introduced to populations which had little resistance to them, as was the case later in Central and South America.[26]

One of the ironies of this massive Indian depopulation is that, after the discovery of the riches in Mexico by Cortez in 1519, the Spanish themselves lost interest in the island Caribbean at an official level for almost a century, except in so far as the islands themselves provided a military buffer zone which served to protect Spanish interests on the Central and South American mainland. Elsewhere, at the local scale, small groups of settlers attempted to make profits out of tiny sugar estates set up on the arid coastlands of southern Española in the vicinity of Azua. But, using primitive technology and costly irrigation, these were never particularly successful, though they certainly produced some sugar for export for a while. In Española and Puerto Rico, European and other commercial crops were brought into the region from the Mediterranean, including several species of citrus (sweet and sour oranges, lime, lemon and the medicinal citron), bananas and rice. But the primary money-making activity of the Spanish in the island Caribbean after 1510, and throughout the remainder of the sixteenth century, lay not in crop production but in animal rearing, particularly involving cattle (for hides), horses and pigs, although sheep and goats were also present. Virtually all of these were raised on an open-range basis, the animals being left to fend for themselves for much of the year on a rich diet of local roots, herbs fruits and berries, obtained at times from abandoned *conucos*, before being rounded up for sale. Most did very well in the wild, breeding vigorously to produce large numbers. Thus 30 000 hogs were noted in Cuba in 1514, only three years after the introduction of these creatures. Española was especially noted for its cattle, horses and hogs, as also was Jamaica, with large numbers of cattle and horses too in Puerto Rico. Pigs were left on almost every island with which the Spanish came into contact, a traditional practice.[27] It is to be noted that all these creatures were the first large herbivores to inhabit the island Caribbean (the previous largest being iguanas), and their presence was to modify considerably the environment in the sixteenth and subsequent century.

Environmental modification arising out of these activities became pronounced from the second decade of the sixteenth century, especially following the demise of the Indian population. This was especially the case in those areas formerly covered by seasonal rainforest, which appear to have had the highest Indian population density and the greatest number of *conucos*. There, as elsewhere, *conucos* quickly reverted to wild scrub, and then secondary forest, as Indians increasingly were no longer available to tend them. After abandonment, facultative rapidly-spreading shrubs can overwhelm a *conuco* within a year or two, and this process was further accelerated by the fact that in many of them introduced European grazing animals tended to eat the nutritious seeds of native grasses, herbs and shrubs, encouraging both the seeds' viability, and their rapid dispersal. Species which gained a competitive advantage in this way, and which were often the first shrub colonizers on abandoned *conucos*, included native acacias, the guava, and also the native sage (*Lantana camara*), one of the world's worst weeds.[28] These were then shortly replaced in the succession by taller shrubs, such as shrub cottons (*Gossypium* species) and several of the introduced citrus. Eventually these were also replaced by a range of palms and rapidly-growing trees such as the trumpet tree (*Cecropia peltata*), tree ferns (*Cyathea*) and eventually trees of the mature seasonal forest.[29]

This process of forest recolonization on previously cultivated land appears to have been widespread, though little is yet known of it in detail. However, on many islands (Barbados is one of them), it is recorded that one century subsequent to the removal of Indians, extremely dense forest covered all land down to the seashore on the arrival of English and French colonists: the full transformation back to seasonal, or full rainforest had by then taken place. Other environmental changes were also afoot. As a result of overgrazing by introduced cattle and other herbivores, some of the more palatable native island grasses (e.g. an Espanolan thatch grass) were quickly rendered extinct. Although extinction among animal groups went largely unnoticed, some of the forest ground animals, and ground-nesting birds must also have succumbed to introduced European rats and cats early on. In Española, though not elsewhere, the predations of feral dogs had a similar effect. Culling and predation of native animals, such as the hutia and iguana, by the Spanish were, on the other hand, always light. In agricultural areas a few of the more common Old World weeds began to take over from native species (the purslane is one example), as they were introduced at first from mainland Spain and the Canary Islands, and then subsequently, as the slave trade from Africa was put into effect from the 1510s onwards, from the Gulf of Guinea and the Cape Verde islands.[30]

In addition to their grazing requirements, which at times helped to favour the growth and dispersal of introduced weeds at the expense of native grass species, and so in some small way alter the balance of native versus introduced species in heavily grazed areas, European domesticates also modified the environment in a more general way though their trampling activities. Trampling along animal pathways in time compacts the soil, reduces the soil infiltration capacity of rainfall, encourages surface runoff, and the channelling of water downslope along these pathways. Bearing in mind that tropical soil structures tend not to be well bonded, these processes could, and often quickly did, lead to gully erosion on mountain land. In Española there is documentary evidence to suggest that many of the major *barrancas* and *arroyos* which are now so characteristic of its mountain land-scapes, and which have given rise to massive soil loss in Haiti, are directly linked in origin to the establishment of such trampling effects. Indeed, there is no reason to suppose that they would have been a feature of the land-scape in pre-Hispanic times under the conditions of *conuco* agriculture, which was erosion-resistant and on land which, prior to the arrival of European domesticates, supported no animals which could have had a major compacting effect. However, the formation of such gullies in the early six-teenth century would appear to have been small in scale; they are unlikely to have expanded to their present proportions until much later, possibly during the eighteenth and nineteenth centuries, when they were extended consider-ably following the clearance of land for sugar cane cultivation.

Unlike elsewhere in Hispanic America, most of the decline in Indian populations in the island Caribbean seems to have eventuated before the introduction of Old World disease organisms, to which aboriginal groups had little or no antibodies for resistance. That at least is the traditional view. Certainly, by the time that smallpox entered, through Santo Domingo in 1518, and then spread rapidly to San Juan, Puerto Rico and subsequently elsewhere, few Indians were left in either island, and those that were quickly succumbed to the new disease. Probably by 1522 no full-blooded Indians remained in either island. Their death rates at this time are also likely to have been enhanced by the onset of yellow fever and malaria, introduced no doubt from West Africa following the commencement of the slave trade, at roughly the same time. But it is still not clear whether other Old World organisms might have reached the island Caribbean earlier than these dates, and thus facilitated in part the rapidity of Indian population decline which hitherto has been largely ascribed to Spanish mistreatment. However, Kiple[31] has made out a good case for the presence of influenza (to which the Indians also had no resistance, and which to them was also a killer disease) in Española as early as 1496. There is also the question as to whether enteric dysentery, contracted aboard ships en route to Española, and which killed many settlers, might not additionally have been passed to Indian populations, perhaps at an even earlier date. If these suggestions are proved, then many of the arguments for Indian population decline will need to be re-evaluated.

Few New World diseases appear to have affected the new colonists to any great extent, though syphilis was one. Endemic to the Indians, it was of minor consequence to them, but became extraordinarily virulent and lethal within the bodies of Europeans, especially in the first years of settlement.

Taken as a whole, the direct and indirect environmental changes induced by Hispanic colonization were in the short term relatively small, though they were significant in that they pointed the way towards the much larger scale of environmental degradation which was to follow. They also, in time, brought home to Europeans the vulnerability of the natural environment of the island Caribbean to economic pressures. This vulnerability was to be expressed in full later, following the introduction of plantations for commercial crops into the region, by the British and French in particular, after 1645, and which has remained in many areas through to the present day.

NOTES

1   J.M. Cruxent and I. Rouse, 'Early man in the West Indies', *Scientific American*, Vol. 221 (1969), pp. 42–52

2   David A. Hodell, Jason M. Curtis, Glenn A. Jones, Antonia Higuera-Grundy, Mark Brenner, Michael W. Binford and Kathleen T. Dorsey, 'Reconstruction of Caribbean climatic changes over the past 10,500 years', *Nature*, Vol. 352 (London, 1991), pp. 790–3.

3   Cruxent and Rouse, 'Early man in the West Indies', pp. 42–52.

4   Betty J. Meggers and C. Evans, 'Lowland South America and the Antilles', in J.D. Jennings (ed.), *Ancient Native Americans* (San Francisco, 1978), pp. 543–92.

5   Carl Sauer, '*The Early Spanish Main*' (Berkeley, 1966), pp. 184–5.

6   Sauer, *The Early Spanish Main*, p. 48.

7   David Watts, *The West Indies: patterns of development, culture and environmental change since 1492* (Cambridge, 1987), p. 69.

8   Watts, *The West Indies*, p. 55.
9   Sauer, *The Early Spanish Main*, p. 61.
10 The Lucayas was the Spanish name for the Bahamas group, used until the seventeenth century.
11 Sauer, *The Early Spanish Main*, p. 37.
12 W.C. Sturtevant, 'Taino agriculture', *Antropologica, Supplement*, Vol. 3 (1961), pp. 69–82.
13 Peter Hulme and Neil L. Whitehead (eds), *Wild Majesty: encounters with Caribs from Columbus to the present day* (Oxford, 1992), p. 17.
14 Robert H. Fuson, *The Log of Christopher Columbus* (Camden, Maine), p. 89.
15 John S. Beard, 'The classification of tropical American vegetation types', *Ecology*, Vol. 36 (1955), pp. 89–100.
16 Sauer, *The Early Spanish Main*, p. 183.
17 Bartolomé de Las Casas, *Historia de las Indias* (Madrid, 1520–61).
18 William M. Denevan (ed.) *The native population of the Americas in 1492* (Madison, Wisconsin, 1992).
19 Sturtevant, 'Taino agriculture', pp. 69–82
20 Denevan, *The native population of the Americas in 1492*, p. 22.
21 Peter L. Drewitt, Mary H. Harris and E. Wing *Prehistoric Barbados* (Denbigh, 1991), p. 106.
22 P. Bowman-Boyd, 'Patterns of Spanish emigration to the Indies until 1600', *Hispanic American Historical Review*, Vol. 56 (1976), pp. 580–605.
23 Watts, *The West Indies*, p. 116.
24 Sauer, *The Early Spanish Main*, p. 61.
25 Las Casas, *Historia de las Indias*.
26 Hugh Thomas, *Conquest: Montezume, Cortes, and the fall of old Mexico* (New York, 1993), pp. 609–14.
27 Alfred W. Crosby, *The Columbian exchange: biological and cultural consequences of 1492* (Westport, Connecticut, 1972), p. 88.
28 Robert M. May, 'The world's worst weeds', *Nature*, London, Vol. 290 (1981), pp. 85–6.
29 David Watts, *Man's influence on the vegetation of Barbados, 1627 to 1800* (Hull, 1966), p. 21.
30 Sauer, *The Early Spanish Main*, pp. 210–12.
31 Kenneth Kiple, *The Caribbean slave: a biological history* (Cambridge and New York, 1984), p. 16.

2

THE INITIAL LINKAGE WITH AMERICA: A GENERAL FRAMEWORK

Ruggiero Romano

The first expeditions from the Spanish mainland

Although in 1490 Spain's overseas possessions (the Canaries, enclaves in Africa) covered no more than 4000 sq. km, between 1493 and 1500 they spread to encompass 50 000 sq. km, and from 1502 to 1515 there was a further increase to 250 000 sq. km. Eventually, by about 1530, they totalled one and a half million square kilometres.

Despite the approximate nature of these figures (and the fact that they are largely unchecked), they are nevertheless revealing from several different viewpoints. Firstly, and most obviously, they are a clear indication of Spain's precipitate haste in its territorial expansion, but the most significant fact to emerge is undoubtedly the following. Expeditions to conquer new territories set sail from the Spanish mainland. Those conquests, however, were inevitably restricted by the limitations imposed by the technical, financial and human difficulties of transport. The occupation of the first 50 000 sq. km was, in itself, something of an exploit and established a sort of frontier. More ambitious expeditions, setting out from the old continent, would have been impossible. And so it was from the islands that the 'American' conquest of America was launched.

It all began in the Antilles. The name itself is an old one, dating back to 1367, when it appeared on a map by Pizigano, illustrating the location of the island of Corvo in the Azores. Later, in 1435, Becario's chart referred to a certain 'Antilla' to the west of the Azores. Most significantly, it appeared in the famous charts drawn by Paulo dal Pozzo Toscanelli, a copy of which Columbus is reputed to have owned.

It would be tempting to interpret this as an earlier discovery, but it is more likely that we are dealing with an imaginary island, as the name itself suggests, and '*ante-ilha*' ('island lying beyond') was based on the pure conjecture that an unknown island lay beyond the last known island. In 1492 this fiction became a reality. The old theory was recalled and the name 'Antilles' was given to the group of islands 'lying beyond'.

Although the islands are outlying, at the same time the possibility of travelling from one to another makes them rather like a bridge. The early years of colonization were years of just such a progression from island to island, not only in terms of equipment but also with regard to building and the layout of the various settlements, from La Navidad to Isabela, and from Isabela to Santo Domingo (the town was founded in August 1494). The latter was used, especially between 1503 and 1508, as a base for expeditions to Higüey, the island of Saona, Puerto Rico, Cuba and others.

It was from 1506 onwards that the move towards the permanent settlement of the continent got under way, with the founding of Acla (1516) and Panamá (1519).

Later voyages set out, again from the Antilles and from the American continent itself, to conquer the Mayan and Mexican territories. It must be stressed, however, that such initiatives were possible only when Santo Domingo and Cuba, i.e. the Antilles, could provide shipbuilding facilities and guarantee maritime supremacy. Only then could voyages be undertaken to discover other lands, and only then could 'the American Mediterranean' become a reality.[1]

The foregoing is a brief summary of the historical background to the conquest of this vast continent which will be described in greater detail in the other chapters of this volume. However, events of such significance which, in print, seem to follow a logical sequence, cannot be reduced to a mere succession, even if their more complex interconnections are brought out. There are other factors worthy of consideration.

Let us turn our attention to a problem which, although insoluble, should be mentioned, if only as a reminder. Frequent reference is made to the 'discovery' of America. This description overlooks the fact that, when the first steps were taken on American soil and the first natives encountered, it was for the latter, too, the 'discovery' of another world, since there stood before them individuals not naked as they were, but fully dressed (what was the significance of this 'discovery' of clothes?). Everything was different – weapons, language, gestures, attitudes. Much more could be said on this subject, but nothing definite will ever be known about the 'discovery' of white people and their culture by the indigenous population of America.

Let us return, therefore, to our European explorers. It was in the Antilles, in fact, that the word 'discovery' took on its full meaning, since *everything* seemed new. Take, for example, Amerigo Vespucci who, as early as 1503, referred constantly to a *Mundus Novus*. After the Antilles came many more new discoveries, but by then the impact of the initial, total novelty had worn off, and later many of the things encountered by the *conquistadores* were already 'familiar' (which explains why, in New Spain and Peru, the Spaniards gave so many flowers, plants and fruits the names learned from their earlier days in the Antilles. More important than the names of flowers, fruits and plants is the example of the word '*cacique*', which, throughout America, came to replace the local word for 'chief').

The inhabitants of the New World in their natural surroundings

Before discovering the nature of the New World, the *conquistadores* encountered its inhabitants. Christopher Columbus observed: 'They are all of good stature, their hair not frizzy, but flowing and thick...'.[2] Ten years later, Vespucci wrote: 'Their bodies are well-formed and in proportion, they are fair-skinned, their hair long and black and the men have little or no beard'.[3]

It is interesting to note the insistence on their long, straight hair, a characteristic which distinguished these people from negroes and made them seem more similar to whites. Similarities, not differences, were emphasized. With regard to their skin colour, Columbus initially described them as fair-skinned (a version he subsequently changed), whereas Vespucci was more specific, describing the colour of their skin as 'tawny, like a lion's'. However, he hastened to add that this was an impression heightened by their nudity and that 'if they were to wear clothes, they would be as fair-skinned as we are.'[4]

The urge to identify common features rather than differences was only a first reaction. It would not be long before opinions changed, and differences emerged only to be instantly condemned: tattoos, cranial deformities, filed teeth, the perforation of nostrils and lips – all of these were incomprehensible and therefore 'barbaric'. The split was thus complete between civilized beings on one side and savages on the other. Moreover, the gulf became total and unbridgeable, with the advent of anthropological arguments (certain etymological theories suggest that the very word 'cannibalism' is derived from the Caribs – Canibs – Cannibals). Cannibalism (which, together with incest, represented the maximum deviation from accepted social mores) was considered beyond the pale, and the savagery of the American native was thus irrevocably confirmed.

Their long hair and their pale, not to say white, skin on the one hand, and their tattoos, sacrifices and cannibalism on the other, constituted an *ensemble* of contradictions, in which the overriding impression was one of ferocity and brutality. These contradictions did not disappear since, strangely enough, these primitive beings also inspired the idea of a social order which recalled the Golden Age. Peter Martyr said so explicitly when, on the subject of the Antilles, he wrote, 'They belong to the Golden Age'.[5] And he was not alone in so thinking, since P. Bembo (possibly a pseudonym), Acosta and Vespucci made similar observations. It should be noted that this reference to a Golden Age as a contemporary reality is of great significance, since, according to Christian doctrine, the Golden Age existed only in the Garden of Eden prior to Adam and Eve's original sin. Hence, 'it was unacceptable that a Golden Age should exist on earth in the mid-sixteenth century'.[6] Nevertheless, the idea prevailed for quite some time, if not strictly as a vision of the Golden Age, then at least as the acknowledgement of the existence of an earthly paradise, thereby sowing the seeds of the later myth of the noble savage.

At this point, a brief methodological observation should be made: we have noted the constant vacillations and contradictions in the various attitudes adopted towards these 'new' people – their gentleness/savagery, similarity/differences, cannibalism/innocence. These contrasting attitudes gave rise to a series of clichés, stereotypes which were to spill over into European culture (discussed later in this chapter) and which only luminaries, such as Montaigne, had the wisdom and the desire to challenge. In this instance, the crux of the matter is that, in the context of the local (internal) history of the Caribbean (and of America in general), the contradictions disappeared, leaving only the negative stereotypes. Thus, the indigenous populations, as seen by its conquerors, was not perceived as noble, but only as savage.

Having considered the inhabitants, let us now examine the natural surroundings. Here, too, the impact was tremendous. The earliest accounts clearly reveal the reactions of the explorers from the Old World to the flora and fauna of the New World. Vespucci, once again, gives an excellent description: 'This land is most pleasant, covered with countless immensely tall, green trees, which never shed their leaves and all of which exude most sweet, aromatic odours and produce an abundance of fruits, many of which are delicious to eat and nourishing. In the fields grow a variety of herbs, flowers and root vegetables, so sweet and good that I am sometimes amazed at the fragrance of the herbs and flowers and the taste of the fruit and vegetables, so much so that I seem to be nearly in an Earthly paradise. In the midst of such fruits, I could imagine myself almost there'.[7] As G. Ugolini observed,[8] 'first impressions are determined by smell and taste, but, in this case, all the senses were assailed, even the sense of hearing'. To quote Amerigo Vespucci again: 'And the other birds in the trees sang so sweetly and melodiously that we were often overcome by the beauty of their song. The trees are so magnificent and graceful that we seemed to be in an Earthly Paradise'.[9] It is most probable, even certain, that Vespucci's comments were influenced by descriptions of paradise to be found in the Bible and in Dante's *Divine Comedy*.[10] Most importantly, these landscapes alone were capable of inspiring in Vespucci thoughts of an earthly paradise; any reference to other literary sources could only be the consequence of actual experience, and his descriptions should not be seen as a mere literary exercise. Accordingly, his writings should be appreciated not only on account of their quasi-poetic tone but also as a true description of his amazement, wonder and enchantment on first encountering the natural beauty of these American landscapes which seemed so primeval that he was inevitably reminded of the Garden of Eden.

Admittedly, there were also disadvantages, as the Spaniards discovered on 30 June 1502, when a hurricane (another word from the Antilles which has passed into many other languages and is still in use today) destroyed 20 ships.[11] This was a new and terrible aspect of the natural phenomena of America; not only were the trees immensely tall, but the winds were exceedingly violent.

In their first contacts with the natural world in the Caribbean, the *conquistadores* could only describe what they saw by resorting to analogy. For instance, a pineapple was described as a kind of artichoke or fir cone, native canoes were called *zopoli* (flat-bottomed boats from the Venetian lagoon), maize was known as sorghum, and even the name Venezuela means little Venice.[12]

The 'laboratory' of history

The Caribbean was a great 'laboratory' of history (and so it still seems today to the observant historian), in which a profusion of contrasting attitudes coexisted – friendly contacts, hostile encounters, understanding and misunderstanding. There was the thirst for knowledge and, at the same time, the rejection of it, the refusal to understand countered by endeavours to understand. Any attempt to examine these exhaustively would get bogged down in a welter of images, all of them interesting, but not necessarily useful for purposes of historical reconstruction. Accordingly, rather than plunging into a comprehensive survey, punctuated by occasional quotations, I intend to concentrate on three lines of investigation which I think are of particular significance.

The language
The cardinal importance of language is underlined by the fact that, on this first voyage, Christopher Columbus took with him a linguist who spoke Arabic and Hebrew. The idea may seem extraordinary to modern readers, but it clearly demonstrates the importance Columbus attached to linguistic communication (Columbus thought he was travelling merely to Japan and China).

The Requerimiento

The problems posed by the need to communicate emerged most conspicuously in the use of the *Requerimiento*. What was it exactly? It was a kind of declaration, drawn up in Spain, which had to be read out to the native population. It required that they accept Spanish sovereignty and the 'true' Christian faith. If they refused they were threatened with war, slavery and extermination.[13] The first known *Requerimiento* to be used in America dates back to 1513, but there had been earlier examples of similar documents used during the conquest of the Canaries.

The opening words are unequivocal.

> In the name of the most high, most powerful, most Catholic Defender of the Church, always victorious, never vanquished, Don Hernando, the mighty King of all the Spains, of the two Cecilias, of Jerusalem, of the islands and mainland of the Ocean, etc., Conquerer of the savage peoples, and, in the name of the most high and powerful queen, Doña Juana, his dearly loved daughter, our sovereign lords, I, Pedrarías Davila, his loyal servant, emissary and captain, make known to you, as best I can, that the one and eternal Lord God created heaven and earth, and a man and a woman, from whom we and you and all mankind are descended, and all those who come after us; but for all the generations who succeedded them for more than 5,000 years since the creation of the world, it was necessary that some of them be in one part of the world and others in another part, and they were divided among many different kingdoms and provinces, since it was impossible for them all to live and survive in one alone.[14]

Thus a declaration was made, 'as best I can', reciting a sort of universal history purporting to emanate from God and the King of Spain. The important point, however, is the realization that this declaration was issued to the best of the speaker's ability and not always very clearly.

The declaration went on to explain who Saint Peter was and his successor, the Pope, and the authority invested in him. It was the Pope who, in God's name, 'granted' the islands and the mainland to the King of Spain. Either they accepted this situation, this *donación*, and the consequences thereof, or else a bloody war would ensue.

Naturally the whole declaration was read out in Spanish and addressed to indigenous populations with whom the *conquistadores* had come into contact only hours beforehand, and with whom linguistic communication was clearly nil. No matter – they *had* to understand:

Therefore, as best I can, I beseech you and demand of you that you understand correctly what I have said to you, that you take the necessary time to understand and consider all these things, that you recognize the universal supremacy of the Church, and the Supreme Pontiff, called the Pope, in his name and in the name of the King and the Queen, our sovereign lords in their position as rulers of these islands and the mainland, by virtue of this concession, and that you accept what these Holy Fathers declare and preach.[15]

They were required, therefore, to understand a declaration which was incomprehensible to them, a fact of which the Spaniards were fully aware, so much so that, on certain occasions, they even went as far as reading it out of their hearing:

They gave notice from a distance of the requirement that they promise allegiance to the Catholic King; the declaration was made by Ayora in the presence of an official so that he might verify the said requirement, which was delivered in the Spanish language, of which the *cacique* and Indians knew and understood nothing, and, moreover, it was done at such a distance that, even if they had known the language, they could not have heard it.[16]

For a better understanding of these aspects of the *Requerimiento*, we should bear in mind that this institution was part of the kind of anxiety that animated the Spaniards (and the Europeans in general): legitimacy. One could kill, massacre, and destroy, but the fundamental problem is to know if it is a 'just' war, a 'legitimous' conquest. What does this 'legitimacy', this 'justice' imply? A sovereign can occupy the realm of another sovereign if the latter's ownership is not 'legitimous'. Thus, to give the most obvious example, Charles V was really anxious to know if Montezuma and Atahualpa were 'legitimous' sovereigns. He was assured that they were not, because they had occupied their 'realms' by chasing out the ancient legitimous sovereigns... . All this may, perhaps, help to understand how the conquest of America was effected while many of the European medieval ideas remained operative. Although this situation may seem ridiculous, it nevertheless gives

a clear indication of the attitude of the *conquistadores* towards the native population, and vice versa. In the first place, of the two individuals or groups concerned, one delivered a statement, to which the other listened; one laid down the law, delivering an incomprehensible message, while those listening found themselves in a position of anxious expectation through their lack of comprehension, and were thus at a disadvantage.[17]

There were undoubtedly instances (in Darien, for example) where, if it was possible to communicate with the native population, even through an interpreter, their reaction was one of open disdain:

> And they replied: that when I said that there was only one God and that he ruled Heaven and Earth and that he was Lord of all, they accepted this; but when I talked about the Pope and said that he was the Lord of all the universe as God's representative and that he had made a gift of all this land to the King of Castile, they replied that the Pope must have been drunk when he did so, because he had made a gift of what was not his, and that the King must be mad if he had asked for and accepted such a gift, since he had demanded what belonged to others.[18]

After the Antilles and the Mainland, the *Requerimiento* continued to play an important role in the conquest of New Spain and Peru, albeit with some modifications. Cortés – who was politically very astute – avoided the brutal tactics employed by Juan de Ayora on the Mainland, but there were still plentiful examples of brutality (Pizarro's execution of Atahualpa, for example). In any case, what should be remembered is that it was in the Caribbean laboratory that this particular invention was developed and refined.

With regard to the development of the language and unrelated to the problems of communication already mentioned, it is important to note that it was in the Caribbean that what could justifiably be called 'colonial Spanish' evolved, with the creation of *linguae francae* amongst the sea-faring communities of the Antilles.[19]

Sexuality

The Spaniards who arrived in the Caribbean had behind them a long tradition of a religion founded, in part, on monogamy. When they first discovered the New World, it seemed like paradise for several reasons, not least of which was the practice of polygamy which was prevalent among the indigenous population and which they readily adopted.

Their initial reaction was naturally one of licentiousness, but there were other factors which should not be overlooked. Here is yet another example of a failure of understanding, particularly with regard to the nudity of the population, which was described, for example in Hispaniola, by Peter Martyr, in almost classical terms,[20] whereas Fernández de Oviedo[21] saw it as nothing short of the sign of irredeemable sin. But setting aside the opinions expressed by writers, famous or otherwise, libertine or authoritarian, let us consider instead what the nudity of the population could have meant to the 'average' *conquistador*. It was perceived as an invitation. This was, of course, a misinterpreation, but history, on a grand and on a trivial scale, is full of just such misconceptions.

It was not just a question of an initial misunderstanding. The *conquistadores* found further evidence of the 'barbarity' of the natives in the fact that they 'offered' them their women. Naturally it was not an offer in the ordinary sense of the word, since the gift of these young women was intended to strengthen bonds of kinship as the basis for peaceful coexistence with the new arrivals.

However, not all the women were 'given' or 'offered'. Many more were taken by force or abducted. Invariably, however,

> a new man emerged, more violent and more cruel, more in control of his actions, with fewer restrictions and likewise fewer transgressions – or many more, but permitted by a conscience which had begun to forget the essential commandments. The New World, in its initial phase, was so immense, so tolerant, that in most regions of America, despite the presence of a number of clergy and monks, who were also affected by the New World, and despite sermons and the first royal decrees, this man, who was part of the conquest, rapidly turned into a polygamous, vigorous, and fertile specimen of the male sex.[22]

The considerations of A.M. Salas are certainly very much justified, but they have, of course, to be fitted into a framework which allows for a better evaluation. In other words, the violence and brutalities towards women during the conquest are not different from those in the course of the wars which took place in Europe in the same period (and in all periods). The difference (that makes the *conquistadores* new or rather 'different') arises from the American context. Everything will be new (different) in America, the sexual relations, but also the clergymen, the traders and the landowners.

Here again it is not just a matter of sexual appetite. These events marked the beginning of the still widespread phenomenon of interbreeding, implying not only the birth of mestizo offspring from such liaisons, but also the process of mutual acculturation between Spanish *conquistadores* and native women, since although in some cases the relationship lasted only a day or even an hour, there were many cases in which it lasted longer and still others where the woman or women accompanied the *conquistador* on his subsequent voyages of discovery.

These intimate liaisons clearly 'implied the violation of many practices, customs, taboos and inhibitions of which the carefree lover was totally unaware. Indian women had to abandon their traditional customs and strict, unwritten laws and adopt others that were very different, imposed by their new masters.'[23] The same was true of the *conquistador*. These liaisons encouraged a rapid process of acculturation, inculturation and transculturation, affecting amatory techniques, but also food and its appreciation, clothing and ornamentation. In addition, they provided a useful opportunity for learning each other's language.[24]

Any temptation to romanticize these liaisons should be restricted, since they were frequently marred by violence and, in some cases, by terrible brutality. What should be remembered is that, despite the violence and brutality, these relationships forged a link between two worlds hitherto unknown to each other.

The three different factors that we have considered – language, the *Requerimiento*, and sexuality – posed one fundamental problem: that of interpreters.

Interpreters

We stated earlier that Cortés was a gifted diplomat. That much is incontrovertible. But it must be added that he was more fortunate than others in being able to express his subtlety through interpreters. Although examples abound, let us consider only the most outstanding episode. In 1511 a Spanish vessel was wrecked off the Jamaican coast. Taking to a lifeboat, some of the men succeeded in reaching the shores of Yucatán. Taken prisoner, some were killed as sacrificial offerings, and others became slaves. Of the latter, two survived, and much detailed information about them is available.[25] They were Gonzalo Guerrero and Jerónimo de Aguilar. The former became totally integrated into the local community, eventually rising to the rank of a military commander who even fought against the Spanish invaders.[26] When Cortés met him in Gozumel, Guerrero refused to follow him, preferring to stay with those who were now his 'own' people.

Aguilar's attitude was quite different; he had survived thanks to 'a submissive slave-like demeanour which had saved his life', and immediately offered his services to Cortés as an interpreter of the Mayan language.[27]

This was just the beginning. In Tabasco, Cortés was presented with the gift of 20 young girls, among whom was a certain Doña Marina, who later became known as La Malinche. It so happened that she knew both Mayan and Nahuatl and thus, with Aguilar who spoke Spanish and Mayan, they formed a useful linguistic combination. It was only after some considerable time that Cortés (speaking in Spanish) was able to communicate directly with La Malinche (Spanish-Nahuatl). So far the only problem that has been dealt with is that of translating from Spanish *into* American Indian languages, a phenomenon which undoubtedly ran into many difficulties in the early stages of the conquest. But it should be remembered that subsequently there arose the problem of communication between victor and vanquished which would finally be solved by the adoption, albeit partial, of bilingualism by the subject population. The Spanish reinforced their supremacy by retaining their monolingualism.[28]

The relationship between *conquistadores* and subject peoples

The emphasis on the 'cultural' aspects of the earliest contacts between the European adventurers and the Caribbean world is easily explained; *their* contact with *this* new world marks the turning-point in the establishment of the Spanish 'empire' in America.[29] For a full appreciation of the internal structure of such an empire, it is important to consider the true nature of the relationship between the *conquistadores* and their subject peoples. A relationship of this kind is never straightforward; in other words, there is a big difference between the function of the Spanish governor of the Duchy of Milan and that of New Spain. There are countless reasons for this, the most important of which is the fact that, in different parts of the world, the conquering nation's 'cultural' conception (cultural in the wider, anthropological sense) of its subject peoples varies radically. These variations are determined by religious and linguistic criteria as well as by differences in skin colour (not racist in the contemporary meaning of the word) – in short, by cultural parameters. It was certainly true that the attitude adopted towards the American Indian as part of a group of subject peoples was one of total superiority. The evidence is overwhelming, but the most striking example may be found in *Buscom*, where the innkeeper describes as 'Indian' a person (a Spaniard!) who is unable to express himself clearly. In the plays of Lope de Vega, as a rule the 'barbarian' is inevitably the Indian.[30] This is the crux of the matter. As mentioned earlier, certain observations in the writings of Columbus and Vespucci foreshadow the myth of the noble savage. However, the word 'savage' was not widely used until the eighteenth century (although it did appear sporadically in the seventeenth century, particularly in England), whereas it was not long before the American continent and its peoples were described as barbarian.

This idea originated primarily in the Caribbean, starting in the islands and spreading to the mainland. It was here that the notion of the American Indian as an inferior being began, thus laying the foundation for the overall structure (political, social and economic) of the whole Spanish 'empire' in

America. If these simple facts are ignored, there is a danger of overlooking the mainspring of American history. It goes without saying that it should not be thought that this contempt was reserved exclusively for the aboriginal Americans, for testimonies can be found of similar behaviour *vis-à-vis* African peoples. The attitude towards Asians (in particular the Chinese) and even towards Arabs was more shaded, partly because the latter were the traditional enemy and nearest of all.

Personally, I find it hard to believe that capitalism existed in Europe as early as the Middle Ages or the sixteenth century.[31] Nor do I believe in the existence of a form of pre-capitalism or commercial capitalism, both of which strike me as fairly ill-defined categories and more likely to confuse the issue than to clarify it. However, in this context, my own personal views are irrelevant and, for the sake of the argument, I am prepared to acknowledge that capitalism was prevalent in Europe towards the end of the fifteenth century. It thus becomes possible to accept the thesis that the American conquest was motivated by capitalistic expansion in Europe. Moreover, the capitalistic nature of the ventures in America undertaken by Spanish (and European generally) trading companies is evident. And here we approach the heart of the matter; what was the situation on the other side of the Atlantic? Did capitalism (commercial or otherwise) exist there, too, on strictly American terms, peculiar to the history of the American continent?

Let us begin at the beginning. It is a well-documented fact that approximately two-thirds of Columbus's first voyage was financed by the Crown and one-third by private investors; let us therefore qualify the latter as 'capitalistic'. But let us also consider the system under which the large-scale conquest of America (and more particularly of the Caribbean) took place.

For this, we have at our disposal the excellent book by the late Mario Gongora,[32] the main conclusion of which, with regard to the conquest of the American mainland, was that the key factor was the *compaña* (not to be confused with *compañia*, a much more complex legal instrument combining the concepts of 'capital' and 'work'), which was basically 'the whole group of those taking part in the conquest, the band of *conquistadores* in its entirety'.[33] Interestingly enough, the *compaña* existed as early as the thirteenth century in the form of the *Fuero de Cabalgadas* (law of cavalry raids), highlighting two important facts: firstly, that it was a feature of the early Middle Ages (possibly feudal) and, secondly, that there was indeed a link between *compaña* and *cabalgadas*. The latter were 'rapid, spontaneous forays made from a certain town or fortress or with an army detachment'.[34] The important point here is that in America the essential purpose of these 'lightning' raids was to capture slaves and 'recover' gold and pearls, the inverted commas in the latter case implying that these activities can scarcely be described as commercial. Consider this incident, dated 1529, which took place between

Caribana, Sinu and the islands of Baru and San Bernardo...: 'Later that day the Indians came to the coast to recover their wives and children and they recovered the children and then they began to shoot arrows at us'.[35] Were these commercial ventures? They seem more like strictly military operations. It may be claimed that these were isolated incidents, occurring sporadically. But this claim is invalidated if it is true, as it certainly was, that between 1514 and 1520 'the gold, pearls and slaves carried off by the *conquistadores* were much worth than the profit gained from individual transactions [...] or gold from the mines'.[36] In other words, the gains from plunder and pillage were greater than those generated by any form of production (which in any case could hardly be described as 'capitalistic', since it was based on coercion, ranging from actual slavery to the *encomienda* system of bonded labour).

Although these activities were admittedly characteristic of the early stages of the conquest and circumstances did gradually change, it can also be said that, during the conquest of Mexico, there were no longer any such 'forays' since, with Cortés, there was a transition from a 'slave-based conquest' to the 'development of a seigneurial-colonial structure'.[37] It nevertheless remained true that 'from 1509 onwards and for several decades, the north-eastern regions of the South American continent were subject to constant military incursions from bases in the coastal towns. These towns were typical assembly points for the *conquistadores* who had not yet settled to manage estates and farms'.[38] Let us now turn our attention to the other extreme, the 'seigneurial-colonial structure'. There seem to have been two main systems, the *encomienda* (rights over the native population) and the *mercedes de tierra* (land ownership). Contrary to widely held belief, the *encomienda* was not an 'Indian' system but was Spanish in origin. It was a mediaeval, feudal institution, even if there was already some evidence of it in Roman times. It was transplanted to America, albeit in a form adapted to local conditions. (The American version of the *encomienda*, for instance, required the *encomendero* to guarantee religious education, an obligation which did not exist in the Spanish system.)

Briefly then, the *encomienda* was a feudal, some would say seigneurial institution. But without entering into this old controversy, we have to admit the fact that it was not capitalist.[39] Moreover, the fact that it was exploited by persons who had succeeded, by other means, in appropriating land, accentuated still further the feudal (seigneurial) aspects of the system.

It was in the Caribbean 'laboratory' that the dual system of *encomienda* and *mercedes de tierra* was refined. After an initial period of unadulterated slavery, disguised under the name of *repartimiento*, there followed the *encomienda*, or the rights acquired by a Spaniard over a group of Indians from whom tribute could be levied, most often in the form of personal services. The transition from *repartimiento* to *encomienda* solved the problem of the status of the aborigines, at least on the surface; to hand them over under the system of *repartimiento* meant not to recognize that they were vassals of the King. It was certainly not by chance that, on learning, in 1499, that Columbus had distributed 300 Indians, Isabella exclaimed: 'On whose authority does the Admiral dispose of my vassals?[40] The *encomienda* solved this problem at least formally, since under this system, again at least formally, the Indian *encomendado* or bondservant remained a vassal of the Crown. However, between the *de facto* and the *de jure* situation, it was the former which prevailed and, in actual fact, the Indian bondservant became alienated and reduced to the vassal of his *encomendero*.

Since the dire impact of this situation has already been well documented, there is no need for further elaboration. What should be noted is that, at the same time as the *encomienda*, the practice of land grants became more widespread, and it was the combination of these two policies which formed the basis for the economic structure of America.[41] It was a model that evolved (and changed) over time, but nevertheless retained its traditional character and contributed to the establishment and subsequent perpetuation of the cornerstone of the socioeconomic pattern which was to prevail in the Caribbean and throughout Hispanic America, namely a system of people without land and land without people. Only a system based on an apparent contradiction allowed for land acquisition and, at the same time, coercive and cost-free (or virtually cost-free) methods of assembling a work force. Admittedly, the whole economy could not be reduced to land, and it should be remembered that the above observations also apply to mineral resources; nor should it be forgotten that the *encomienda* system also operated to produce 'industrial' goods: bonded Indians also worked in the textile mills.

Trade and commerce

No study of this sort would be complete without reference to trade and commerce, of which there were several categories – transatlantic, inter-regional and local, confined to one particular region.[42] The transatlantic trading activity of the time has always seemed to me to be on a very small scale, not only in comparison with the modern concept of international trade, but also in relation to the world as it was then. The volume of precious metals exported to Spain was undoubtedly extremely high, but two factors must be taken into account. Most importantly, during the period described by Pierre Chaunu as the first 'gold cycle', between 1493 and 1520, with a yield of 80 per cent from Santo Domingo, 10 per cent from the other islands and the remaining 10 per cent from the Castilla del Oro, total production did not exceed 35 tons.[43] More significant than these details were the means by which the gold was obtained: by liquidating the island populations. Can such extermination be described as a 'capitalist method of production'? It must be said that the system of forced labour which prevailed in the Caribbean and in Spanish America in general was also to be found in the context of international trade. Several years ago, an Italian study of the accounts of the transatlantic commercial ventures undertaken by a Florentine company showed how amazingly low were the costs of transport between Veracruz and Mexico. Yet the distance covered was considerable and the route a harsh one. There was an attempt to explain the phenomenon by referring to the 'low cost of living in Mexico', but more likely was the fact that the goods were transported on the backs of Indian bonded labourers, resulting in low transport costs (and high profits).[44]

With regard to inter-regional trade, even at an early stage, the Caribbean was an area which proved interesting in many respects; a vast number of ships transported goods from one place to another within the confines of the 'American Mediterranean' – cocoa from Venezuela to Mexico, livestock between Cuba and Santo Domingo, and grain from Mexico to Cuba, establishing at an early date a busy network of trading links which continued throughout the entire period of Spanish domination.[45] Another form of locally-based commerce sprang up around towns and mining areas, but this particular trading system was never widely developed in the Caribbean, particularly since very few major cities and even fewer mining complexes were founded. The point is that, once any grandiose claims to international trade are discounted, it is clear that life in the Caribbean during the period in question was basically austere and offered few opportunities for development, nor even for some growth.

Spanish colonial strategy

Any attempt to give an account of the Spanish conquest of America should emphasize how it was confronted, locally, with two different situations – that of structured societies on the one hand and, on the other, that of societies which were fragmented. Whereas the former (in Peru, Mexico, etc.) offered little resistance, and could be 'assimilated', with their own traditional hierarchy intact, into the new state structure imposed by the Spanish, the latter, having never known any form of rigid state control, refused to comply. Their resistance resulted in the extermination of the aboriginal population or, at least, its drastic reduction, to a much greater extent than occurred anywhere on the American mainland between the early sixteenth and mid-seventeenth centuries. The elimination or drastic reduction of the population meant difficulties in procuring labour and led to the necessity of importing African slaves at great expense. It is certainly no coincidence that it is in the Caribbean that the African influence, from skin colour to cooking and Africanisms in the language, is still today more widespread than in other areas of Spanish America, with the exception of Yucatán. The population of Yucátan, which had a sociopolitical structure, accepted the colonial system without much opposition. But which colonial system did it accept? It would appear to be more that of New Spain than the old Spanish model. Yucatán can be defined as a sort of sub-colony of Mexico, just as Chile was a sub-colony of Peru. In any case, the basic ethnic structure has remained unchanged to this day, a virtually unique oasis in the Caribbean area.

However, a simple observation demonstrates that this demographic factor was of great significance in many parts of the Caribbean; of the entire American continent, it was only in the Caribbean that Spain relinquished territories: Curaçao, Jamaica and many other 'abandoned' islands fell into foreign hands during the first half of the seventeenth century. Others, even though they remained under Spanish rule, were more or less abandoned, as in the case of Hispaniola, the northern part of which was almost totally abandoned in the late sixteenth century, while the life of the island was confined to the town and port of Santo Domingo.

It was not long before large gaps opened up within the Caribbean. It is a well-known fact that nature abhors a vacuum. It was therefore no coincidence that pirates and buccaneers had no difficulty in establishing themselves in the Caribbean islands and along the coasts. Nor was it by chance that, by the end of the sixteenth century, the whole area had become like a vast strainer into which poured pirates of every nationality.[46] But above all, sufficient proof of the attraction exerted by the empty space in the Caribbean is furnished by the frequency and daring of the raids by pirates (particularly the English).

This leads to another subject. Even today, an impression of the 'physical' reality of the former Spanish 'empire' in America is conveyed by the many fortresses and fortified buildings which stretch from Cartagena to Havana and to Santo Domingo. The fact is that between Cuba, Veracruz, Cartagena and Portobelo, the whole Spanish 'empire' was at stake. It was here that the momentous contest took place to determine the control of the trade routes between Spain and America and, more importantly, to prevent (whether through losses or defeats) too many English, Dutch, French and Danes from hurrying in to fill the gaps.

From these observations it is clear that, once the gold years were over (by about 1540) and the period of pearl exports from Cubagua and Margarita was at an end, (about 1580), the Caribbean was of little economic importance in the Spanish colonial system. What could be exported from the area? Sugar was a major item (but Brazil soon offered serious competition).

What else was there? Nothing that really amounted to very much – ginger, cochineal, indigo, cane, lignum vitae.

Moreover, even granting that a more or less commercial form of 'capitalism' existed in the fifteenth and sixteenth centuries, it is hard to understand how the Welsers (who were certainly true champions of such 'capitalism' or, at least, key figures in the alleged 'commercial and/or financial capitalism') failed so spectacularly in Venezuela. Their American adventure lasted from 1528 to 1541.[47] The export of Indian slaves 'was the mainstay of German commerce in Venezuela'.[48] Caracas (1567) and La Guayra (1568) were founded after the Germans had left. To quote again from the writings of Pierre Chaunu: 'During the period of German influence, no form of permanent settlement occurred. Thus, the coast of central Venezuela became one of the sources of slave labour within the Caribbean. The Welser concession probably delayed the effective colonization of mid-Venezuela by several decades during the 13 years that it lasted, and even longer as a result of the mass elimination of the potential work force that it entailed'.[49]

Strangely enough, the failure was total in countries where the colonizers were champions of 'capitalism'. Were the Welsers to blame? If we were to allow that they really were 'capitalists', it would be necessary to add that their particular form of capitalism was not sufficient to boost the Venezuelan economy. In reality, the Welsers were merchant bankers, used to a certain form of economy (definitely not capitalist, but at least non-colonial). Their early American experience taught them that they had no choice but to follow local 'custom', which in America was already clearly defined: it amounted to plunder. And the Welsers were quick to conform.

Nevertheless, the Caribbean remained central to Spain's colonial strategy; the mineral wealth of the whole continent converged here, if only in transit. Its local economy was seriously limited, but its strategic importance, globally, was highly significant. Admittedly, strategic value implied economic importance, but it must be remembered that the source of the latter lay outside the area of the Caribbean.

I have already used the term 'laboratory' to refer to the Caribbean. In my view, it conveys the history of the area most effectively – in the first instance, as a place where the procedures of conquest were devised, to be put into practice later on the American mainland, though with some variations. It was here that the system of exploitation originated (agrarian and mineral), based above all, if not exclusively, on forms of forced labour; and it was here, too, that the model for the unequal exchange between the home country and its colonies first existed.

There is another reason why the Caribbean can be described as a laboratory. As already mentioned, the gradual weakening of the economy was offset by the gradual strengthening of its strategic role. But that role was not sufficiently extensive to preserve Spanish domination (threatened though it was), since it left too many 'gaps' on which the French, English, Dutch and Danes converged. Thus the Caribbean saw the emergence of a host of different models of exploitation and principles of domination, which would perhaps repay more thorough scrutiny and careful comparison by historians.

NOTES

1 G. Harvey Gardiner, *Naval Power in the Conquest of Mexico* (Austin, 1956).
2 Cited in B. de Las Casas, *Historia de las Indias* (Mexico-Buenos Aires, 1951), 1, p. 205.
3. A. Vespucci, *Lettere di viaggio* (Verona, 1984), p. 22.
4 *Ibid.*, p. 40.
5 P. Martyr d'Angheira, *Extrait des îles trouvées* (Paris, 1533), p. 23.
6 G. Atkinson, *Les nouveaux horizons de la Renaissance française* (Paris, 1935), p. 139.
7 A. Vespucci, *Lettere*, p. 22.
8 G. Ugolini, 'Paesaggio e società delle Indie Occidentali nelle "Lettere di viaggio" di Amerigo Vespucci', *Archivio Storico italiano*, CXLIV (1986), p. 201.
9 A. Vespucci, *Lettere*, p. 4.
10 P. Bush, 'Nature in the New World: its impact on European observers and settlers in the colonial period', in T.A. Riese (ed.), *Vistas of Continent. Concepts of Nature in America* (Heidelberg, 1979).
11 Cf. A. Gerbi, *La nature delle Indie Nove* (Milan-Naples, 1975).
12 G. Folena, 'Le prime immagini dell'America nel vocabolario italiano', *Bollettino dell'Atlante linguistico mediterraneo*, 13–15 (1971–3), pp. 676–7.
13 With reference to the *Requerimiento*, cf. S. Benso's splendid *La conquista di un testo – Il requirimiento*, Rome, 1989. Also recommended, the article by B. Biemann, 'Das requirimiento in der Spanischen Conquista', *Neue Zeitschrift für Missionwissenschaft*, IV (1950), pp. 94–114.
14 In S. Benso, *La Conquista*, p. 49.
15 *Ibid.*, pp. 56–7.
16 *Ibid.*, pp. 77–8.
17 *Ibid.*, p. 79.
18 F. Martinez de Enciso, *Suma de Geografia (1519)* (Madrid, 1948), pp. 220–1.
19 Cf. P. Henríquez Ureña, *Para la historia de los indigenismos (Papa y batata. El enigma del aje, Boniato, Caribe, Palabras Antillanas)* (Buenos Aires, 1938), and G. Friederici, *Amerikanistisches Wörterbuch und Hilfswörterbuch für den Amerika-nisten* (Hamburg, 1960).
20 P. Martyr d'Angheira, *Décadas del Nuevo Mundo* (Buenos Aires, 1944), p. 54.
21 G. Fernández de Oviedo, *Historia general y natural de las Indias, Islas y Tierra Firma del Mar Oceano (1535)* (Ascunción, 1945), p. 241.
22 A.M. Salas, *Crónica florida del mestizaje de las Indias* (Buenos Aires, 1960), p. 21.
23 *Ibid.*, p. 17.
24 Cf. A. Dupront, 'De l'acculturation', *Rapports du XIIe Congrès International des Sciences Historiques* (Vienna, 19 August–5 September 1965), I, (Vienna, 1965), pp. 7–36. The more detailed publication: A. Dupront, *L'Acculturazione, Storia e*

scienze sociali (Turin, 1966), (with an interesting introduction by G. Viventi) is even more valuable.

25   Cf., for example, Bernal Díaz del Castillo, *Historia verdadera de la conquista de la Nueva España* (Mexico, 1960), **I**, pp. 102–11; Lopez de Gomara, *Hispania victrix* (1877), p. 230; B. de Las Casas, *Historia de las Indias* (Mexico,1951), III, pp. 230 ff.

26   A.M. Salas, *Crónica florida*, p. 78.

27   *Ibid.*, p. 77.

28   L. Terracini, *I codici del silenzio* (Turin, 1988), pp. 13–23 and pp. 197–229.

29   A reference to M. Ganci and R. Romano's 'Governare il mondo – L'impero spagnolo dal XV al XIX secolo', proceedings of the congress held in Palermo (4–10 May 1988).

30   M.A. Morínigo, *América en el teatro de Lope de Vega* (Buenos Aires, 1946), pp. 142–3.

31   Cf. R. Romano (and A. Tenenti), *Die Grundlage der modernen Welt* (Frankfurt am Main, 1967) (Spanish translation *Los Fundamentos del mundo moderno*, Mexico City, 1970).

32   M. Gongora, *Los grupos de conquistadores en Tierra Firme (1509–1530)* (Santiago de Chile, 1962).

33   *Ibid.*, p. 39.

34   *Ibid.*, p. 10.

35   *Ibid.*, p. 27.

36   *Ibid.*, p. 24.

37   *Ibid.*, p. 38.

38   *Ibid.*, p. 38.

39   R. Ramano, 'American Feudalism', *Hispanic American Historical Review*, 64 (1) (1984), pp. 121–34.

40   L. Hanke, *La lucha por justicia en la conquista de America* (Buenos Aires, 1949), p. 29.

41   R. Ramano, 'Entre encomienda castellana y encomienda indiana: une vez más el problema del feudalismo americano (siglos XVI–XVII)', *Anuario IEHS de la Universidad Nacional del Céntro de la provincia de Buenos Aires*, 3 (1988). It should be noted that in addition to the *mercedes de tierra* there were also land seizures proper.

42   R. Ramano, 'Algunas consideraciones sobre los problemas del comercio en Hispanoamérica durante la época colonial', *Boletín del Instituto de Historia Argentina y Americana, Dr. E. Ravignani*, III S, No. 1 (1989), pp. 23–49.

43   P. Chaunu, *Conquête et exploitation des nouveaux mondes* (Paris, 1969), p. 301.

44   F. Melis, 'Il commercio transatlantico di une compagnia fiorentina stabilita a siviglia a pochi anni dalle imprese di Cortés e Pizarro', *Estudios del V Grongeso de Historia de la Corona de Aragón*, III (Zaragoza, 1954).

45   Cf. the classic study by E. Arcila Farias, *Comercio entre Venezuela y Mexico en los siglos XVII y XVIII* (Mexico City, 1950).

46   G. de Roboles, *América a fines del siglo XVII – Noticias de los lugares de contrabando* (Valladolid, 1980).

47   G. Arciniegas, *Los Alemanes en la conquista de América* (Buenos Aires, 1941), and J. Friede, *Los Welser en la conquista de Venezuela* (Caracas-Madrid, 1961).

48   P. Chaunu, *Séville et l'Atlantique (1504, 1650)*, VIII (Paris, 1959), p. 596.

49.   *Ibid.*, p. 627.

3

The establishment of primary centres and primary plantations

Frank Moya Pons

The need for gold

The discovery of America can be interpreted as the result of the efforts made by the Western European states to overcome the economic stagnation of the late Middle Ages, which had been worsened by the dynastic wars of the fourteenth and fifteenth centuries. These wars left the emerging monarchical states heavily in debt and with limited economic means to enjoy their newly-won political gains. The gold mines which had been exploited since Roman times were almost totally depleted, money was scarce due to the lack of gold and silver, markets expanded slowly, and productivity in agriculture and manufacturing was very low.

One factor behind Europe's economic problems in the fifteenth century was the rise of prices of Oriental luxury goods and spices upon which Europeans had become dependent. While such goods as silk, precious stones and perfumes were prerequisites for the nobility, the spices, which included cloves, pepper, cinnamon, nutmeg and ginger, were essential for the preservation of meat as the livestock were slaughtered in early winter for lack of pasturage and fodder. The trade with the East had always been a drain upon Europe's gold supplies, since Europe had very little of value other than gold to offer in exchange for those imports.

Even the Italians, who had controlled the Oriental luxury trade and had been the bankers of Europe for several centuries, were experiencing difficulties in the fifteenth century. The Turks had captured Constantinople in 1453 and had imposed heavy taxes along the trade routes which passed through Constantinople and the Bosphorus Strait, thus limiting the control previously exerted by the Venetians and the Genoese. Thus, trade with the East was restricted in such a way as to make prices rise. Florence, the home of the principal banking houses of Europe, suffered from internal political problems and from the default on some major loans made to various European states.

Since the Venetians, the Genoese and the Florentines held a virtual monopoly of trade and finance in the Eastern Mediterranean, the Atlantic offered the only other possibility of a sea route to the Orient. The Portuguese made a serious effort to explore the Atlantic throughout much of the century, but their expeditions did not venture far enough, and the most they could do was to establish several trading settlements, called *factorías*, on the coast of West Africa where they found some gold and pepper. Eventually, the Portuguese discovered the Cape of Good Hope, in 1486, and reached India by sailing east of Africa in 1498.

A sailor named Christopher Columbus, who had worked for the Portuguese along the African coast for several years, became obsessed with the idea of sailing west across the Atlantic to reach Asia. After travelling to various European courts, where his ideas were treated with interest but also with scepticism, Columbus returned for a third time in 1492 to the Court of Spain. On this occasion, the Spaniards were in a state of exhilaration with the conquest of Granada, and Columbus managed to persuade the Spanish Queen of the immense possibilities of his plan. He motivated her with the vision of monopolizing a more direct trading route to the sources of gold and spices in Asia.

The Catholic monarchs reached an agreement with Columbus which arranged for a business partnership in which Columbus was to receive one-eighth of the net profits in return for investing one-eighth of the needed capital. After all the preparations were made, Columbus set sail from Palos on 3 August, 1492, and reached the Bahamas on 12 October, after nearly two months at sea. Believing that he had reached the coast of Asia, Columbus pushed on and landed on the large island of Haiti, which he christened Española on 5 December, 1492. There he made contacts with the natives and found them wearing some roughly-made gold trinkets which he quickly exchanged for European artifacts. On 4 January, 1493, he began his return voyage to Spain, where he arrived on 15 March, 1493. The news of the discovery of new lands containing gold created so much excitement that one of his letters announcing the event was published in seventeen editions and widely circulated throughout Europe during the remaining years of the fifteenth century.

Despite the general shortage of money in Spain, the Crown made immediate arrangements to establish a *factoría* in the island Columbus named Española. Columbus had learned about the *factorías* when he sailed with the Portuguese in Africa several years earlier. Now he and the Crown would have absolute ownership. They would divide the profits, while labour would be provided by 1200 soldiers and workers employed under a rigid wage system. Columbus hoped to obtain from the conquered Indians not only the gold awaited by the monarchs in Spain but also food for his men.

The natives were forced to cultivate large cassava plantations, or *conucos*, to feed the Spaniards since there was a shortage of wheat flour coming from Castile.

The frequent military raids unleashed by Columbus and his men to recruit native workers, as well as the forced labour, terrorized the Indians. Many fled to the mountains to escape the violence of the Spaniards. At the same time, Columbus alienated his own men by imposing upon them very harsh working conditions. As a result, a rebellion soon broke out and the *factoría* collapsed just after Columbus had returned to Spain, leaving his brother Bartholomew in charge of the government of the settlement. The *factoría* was completely depopulated. The rebels went to live in other regions of the island, while Bartholomew Columbus moved the settlement to a new place, later called Santo Domingo. This new town was closer to the recently discovered gold mines at Haina River, in the south of Española.

Columbus's inability to rule the *factoría* forced the Spanish Crown to reconsider its colonization scheme in the New World. The monarchs removed Columbus from the colonial administration in 1500, and designed a new scheme for the settlement and colonization of the New World. The instructions given to Nicolás de Ovando, appointed governor of Española in September 1501, were very precise concerning the defence of royal interests and the regulation of the social life of the island.

Forced Indian labour and *encomiendas*

Meanwhile, a problem with the Indians was developing. For years, the Indians had been put to work in the mines as slaves and were treated as an inexhaustible resource. Small groups of Spaniards had become owners of thousands of Indians controlled through fearful or complacent *caciques* despite the fact that the Queen had declared that the Indians were free vassals and should be treated as such. In 1503 Ovando made the Crown realize that if the Indians were not forced to work in the mines, the Spaniards would leave the island, and thus the whole enterprise would be lost. Pressed by a need for gold to pay expenses in Europe, the Crown legalized the system of distributing the Indians among the Spaniards to work in the mines and on the farms, with the only condition that the recipients of Indians teach them the Catholic faith. This consent was given on 20 December, 1503, and legalized the system of *encomiendas* in Española.

Once they entered the mines, hunger and disease killed the Indians by the thousands. Those who managed to survive eight to twelve months in the mines became so desperate that they committed mass suicide by drinking cassava juice or by strangling themselves with their own hands. Mothers killed their own children and pregnant women aborted so as to prevent children from living in slavery. The result was that by 1508, when a census was made, there were only 60 000 Indians left on the island, of the original population of 400 000. Two other countings registered 40 000 in 1510 and 33 523 in 1511. A new census taken in December 1514 registered 26 334.

The decrease in the native population created a consciousness of an approaching labour crisis. The solution adopted was the importation of Indians from Jamaica, Cuba, the Bahamas, and the Lesser Antilles where it was said that the natives would never be Christianized because they were too distant from the Spaniards. Although some 40 000 were imported between 1508 and 1513, the decrease in the number of Indians continued. As a result of these expeditions the aboriginal population of the Bahamas was completely wiped out, and that of Cuba was decimated. In Puerto Rico, settled by the Spaniards in 1508, the decline was as fast as that of Española. An Indian census taken in 1530 registered only 1148 Indians. Jamaica, without gold, attracted a few Spaniards when it was settled in 1509 by some colonists from Española who abandoned the island and moved to Cuba in 1512. Yet another group arrived in 1515 to develop cattle ranches. Cuba was also settled in 1511, but since gold proved to be elusive for more than ten years, the Spaniards dedicated themselves to cattle ranching. In Cuba there were only 2781 Indians left in 1522, all concentrated in the hands of only 19 *encomenderos* who lived practically by themselves in five 'towns'.

Thus, during the first decade of the sixteenth century, Española was the only centre where gold was produced in the Antilles. By 1510 the Spaniards had been able to extract 4.9 million grams of gold from Española. With the inclusion of Puerto Rico and Cuba, the Spaniards extracted another 9.1 million grams between 1511 and 1520. During this decade, Española and Puerto Rico produced almost the same amount, with Cuba producing substantially less. But by 1514 there were already clear signs that this bounty would not last. The Indian population was dwindling very fast, the mines were becoming exhausted, and many colonists were leaving the islands after failing to make a fortune as *encomenderos*. Emigration from Española, which was already quite intense by 1512, greatly accelerated at the end of 1515, leaving behind only 715 households in all the towns and cities of Española.

Realizing that gold production could stop at any moment, the colonial authorities began in 1516 a frantic search for new sources of wealth to substitute for gold and the Indians. They made great efforts to reorientate the island's economy towards agriculture. They proposed to the Crown the importation of European labourers, and they experimented with European seeds to determine what crops would be feasible in the unfamiliar tropical environment. Eventually, only two of the proposed schemes would stand out for the advantages they offered in the European market: the cultivation of sugar cane and the planting of *Cassia fistula* trees whose fruit was widely used in Europe as a purgative.

Meanwhile, a major smallpox epidemic broke out and killed more than two-thirds of the remaining 11000 Indians of Española between December 1518 and January 1519, thus reducing the native population to less than 3000. Without labour to work in the almost depleted mines, only 2000 gold pesos (86000 grams) could be extracted in 1519. Facing the collapse of the mining economy, the colonial authorities dedicated themselves to furnishing loans to those who wished to remain on the island and invest in the construction of sugar mills.

From mines to ranches and plantations

The depletion of the gold mines and the extinction of the indigenous population brought about a radical transformation in the Caribbean islands. Cattle raising and sugar production replaced gold mining as the main economic activities. These new enterprises were also dominated by the bureaucratic élite while the poorer Spaniards emigrated, convinced of the impossibility of surviving on the islands without having previously accumulated wealth. Emigration was further intensified after news arrived telling of new lands in Mexico heavily populated by Indians. In Española two towns disappeared even before 1520, while the inhabitants of two others had merged to ensure their survival. So intense was emigration that by 1528 five more towns had been abandoned. The remaining towns barely held a combined population of 1000 Spaniards.

Those who remained on the islands invested their fortunes in sugar production or livestock raising. These activities offered good possibilities of profit in the European market. Sugar was still a luxury item and its prices had increased in Europe after 1510, remaining high throughout the century. European livestock did not yield sufficient hides to cope with demand. Hence these products enjoyed high prices in Europe during the entire sixteenth century. Cow hides had numerous industrial, military, domestic, and even cultural uses. The armies needed hides to make harnesses, crossbow strings, armour and footwear, as well as leather bottles for wine and water and other necessary containers. Industry required hides in large quantities to make the ropes and pulleys used in workshops. The population in general needed hides for shoes, hats, coats, pants, straps, and numerous other domestic articles, including the lining of furniture, doors, books, and even beds in the better homes.

The development of livestock raising came as a spontaneous response from the colonists to the depopulation of the islands and to European demand. Those who were not directly involved in sugar production became ranchers or hunters of the hundreds of thousands of livestock which roamed wild in the islands' plains in large herds. The livestock business constituted an important source of income for the inhabitants of Santo Domingo, San Juan and Santiago de Cuba. In these cities resided a small and influential group who possessed tens of thousands of heads of livestock which were sacrificed for their hides alone with the meat being discarded, since there were not enough people to consume it. Speaking of Santo Domingo in the 1540s, chronicler Gonzalo Fernández de Oviedo, said that 'there are men and families of this city with seven and eight and ten thousand heads of cattle and some with eighteen, twenty thousand heads or more, and even twenty-five and thirty-two (thousand) ...'[1] Among this group were the Bishop of Puerto Rico and Venezuela, Rodrigo de Bastidas, who had some 25 000 heads of cattle, and a rich widow named Maria de Arana, who owned 42 000 cattle on her ranches between 1544 and 1546. These ranches were often located near the *ingenios* where transportation facilities were available.

The first sugar plantations

Experiments with sugar production began as early as 1506, when a resident of Concepción de La Vega, by the name of Aguilón, began making sugar for local consumption with the help of some crude instruments. The sugar cane planted by Aguilón descended from the seeds brought by Columbus from the Canary Islands in 1493. Aguilón's business did well and in 1514 the mayor of Concepción, Miguel de Ballester, also constructed a small mill to make sugar to sell in the city. This early production did little more than demonstrate the feasibility of the sugar industry on Española since the output of this primitive mill only supplied the local market and the sugar consumed in the Caribbean still had to be imported from Spain or the Canary Islands.

Shortly after 1516 a colonist, named Gonzalo de Vellosa, constructed a mill on the southern coast of Española to take advantage of the port of Santo Domingo. Vellosa's success demonstrated that mills should be constructed near this city where there were transportation facilities available. Thus, most of the new *ingenios* were built on the banks of the rivers close to Santo Domingo, making the southern region the centre of sugar production in the colony. The sugar industry began in earnest between 1518 and 1520 when the colonial authorities furnished loans to construct the new mills and received permission from the Crown to import African slaves to work in the plantations. The first shipment of sugar left the island in 1521. In the following year some 2000 *arrobas*[2] were exported at a price of two ducats per unit, thus giving high returns. By 1527 there were 19 *ingenios* and six *trapiches* operating at full capacity on Española. The average production of each mill was about 125 tons of sugar per year. All but two were located in the south and exported their sugar through the port of Santo Domingo. The remaining two mills were located in the north near Puerto Plata.

Unlike livestock raising, the sugar industry was a major undertaking which required both technical skills and heavy investment. The sugar estates, commonly called *ingenios*, included not only the plantation area but also the mill and the boiling house where the cane juice was processed into sugar. There were two types of mills: *ingenios*, which moved with water power, and *trapiches*, which used animal power, usually horses or oxen. The land of the plantation was divided into four sections: a large part was dedicated to the cultivation of cane, since one acre of land was required to produce a ton of sugar; another part was used for the cultivation of cassava and other crops necessary for feeding the workers; a third part was for the cutting and collection of wood to feed the furnaces for the cauldrons; and the fourth section was land used to feed the oxen, horses and mules. The plantations contained large herds of livestock whose meat was used to feed the labourers and whose hides provided a secondary export product.

Santo Domingo had more importance for the sugar industry than just its port. In 1520 this city had the only residents wealthy enough to invest in the construction of mills. It was also the seat of the government and finance of the colony, as well as the political centre of the Caribbean. Here, investors could obtain loans with relative ease, but credits were only granted to those individuals who for several years had belonged to the bureaucratic élite and the top of the *encomendero* class. In this manner, the sugar industry served as the economic basis to support the continuity of power among the greatest *encomenderos*, who quickly transferred their fortunes from the mines to the mills.

The Spanish Crown promoted the development of the sugar industry and fostered the interests of the sugar producers as much as possible without jeopardizing royal interests. The *señores de ingenios* thus were exempt from import taxes on all machinery and copper necessary for the construction of their mills as well as from the payment of church tithes. In 1529 the Crown passed a law which established that no *ingenio* could be seized or executed juridically for the debts contracted by its owners. Other privileges accorded by the King to the *ingenio* owners included the right of patronage over the church clerics and chapels on their plantations, and the right of primogeniture. This privilege sought to assure that the plantations passed from father to son, so that the death of the owner would not bring the industry to a standstill through disputes over succession.

The development of the sugar industry brought about sweeping changes in the social and political structure of the island. The *ingenios* became the most important centres of population, containing not only large numbers of slaves but also Spanish overseers and foreign technicians called *maestros de azúcar* who were responsible for managing the mills. These 'sugar masters' generally came from the Canary Islands, Sicily or Portugal where there was a long tradition of sugar production. They were contracted for very high wages since they determined the quality of the final product. In 1535 there were 200 Portuguese working on the plantations, with a lesser number of Sicilians and Canary Islanders. The self-sufficiency and relative isolation of the plantations brought as a consequence a noticeable decentralization of political power, since the *ingenio* owners gradually became the foci of authority in the regions where their estates were located. This process, together with the absence of a stable government in the Antilles from 1523 to 1528, consolidated the political power of the *señores de ingenios*.

The wealth generated by the sugar and livestock industries gave Santo Domingo a particularly lively and cosmopolitan flavour. During the sugar boom, Santo Domingo contained several wealthy merchants connected to the great commercial houses of Seville, Germany, Genoa, and Portugal. For several decades in the middle of the sixteenth century, men could be seen in the streets dressed in expensive silks, taffetas, embroideries and brocades brought from Europe, while in the seignorial plantation houses highly-priced imported foods and drinks were consumed daily. Santo Domingo also lodged hundreds of unmarried European men who worked on the *ingenios* and visited the city to spend their earnings in the bordellos legally installed in 1526.

Indeed, this city, which held 3000 inhabitants in 1527, was the only real urban area of the Caribbean which managed to survive the wave of emigration toward Mexico and Peru between 1520 and 1540. To her port came foreign technicians to work on the *ingenios* as well as thousands of African slaves periodically auctioned by Genoese, German and Portuguese traders to whom the Spanish Crown successively conceded import licenses. Since the planting, cultivation and cutting of sugar cane required a large quantity of workers, African slaves were imported to replace the ever decreasing Indians in the early plantations. As early as 1520 King Charles granted one of his courtiers a licence to import up to 4000 African slaves to Española where they were to be sold to those building *ingenios*. This individual decided not to go directly into the business and sold his rights for 25 000 ducats to the Casa Centuriona, a Genoese company which had already been shipping slaves to Española since 1518. Thus, the first *ingenios* to go into operation were manned by a few hundred of the remaining Indians and several hundred of the recently-arrived African slaves. Although the first licence granted by King Charles implied a monopoly for eight years, the Crown paid little attention to this aspect and almost immediately favoured other courtiers and members of Española's oligarchy by conceding each of them the right to import anywhere from a dozen to 400 Africans.

Gradually, the plantations became predominantly populated by African slaves. As the Spanish population continually decreased through emigration, the slave population kept increasing, both by importation and by natural increase. In 1526 the Crown had decreed that each group of slaves imported to Española should contain one-third of females. Given the cost of each slave, which fluctuated between 90 and 150 pesos, the owners looked after their welfare so as not to lose their investment. In 1546 there were already some 12000 slaves as opposed to a white population of less than 5000. By 1568 the number of slaves had increased to around 20000, and there was such an availability of slaves that some plantation owners connived with the authorities to export their surplus workforce to Central America and *Tierra Firme*, thereby earning a net profit of 30 to 40 pesos per head.

Slave rebellions

The demographic difference between the white and black population had a decisive effect on the life of the colony. With such a small Spanish population it was difficult to maintain a strict control over the workers, and the slaves continually escaped from the plantations. The problem of runaways and uprisings had been faced as early as 1502 when a few black slaves introduced as servants escaped and were never captured. In 1515, when plans to import black slaves for the proposed sugar plantations were being discussed, the colonial officials agreed that the slaves should be brought directly from Africa and not from those already living in some Spanish cities. They argued that these blacks knew Spanish very well and could communicate with each other to contrive plots and rise up against their masters. These already-Westernized blacks were called *ladinos* to differentiate them from the *bozales* who were taken directly from Africa. Despite these precautions, the *bozales* imported by the Genoese in 1518 proved to be dangerous since they belonged to the Joloff, a Senegalese tribe famous for its pride and obstinacy and its rejection of mistreatment. In December 1522, the first slave rebellion broke out on the sugar plantations.

This rebellion was promptly repressed, but the repression of this revolt did not prevent a mounting wave of individual runaways, known as Maroons. Official reports calculated the number of black fugitives between 2000 to 3000 in 1542. Girolamo Benzoni, an Italian traveller who spent several months on the island in the same year, believed that the number of runaway slaves reached 7000. Once free, these Maroons sought to regroup themselves with others who spoke the same language and belonged to their own tribe or to related tribes. These groups lived in organized communities complete with their own social and economic structure, and even with a fiscal system which permitted them to maintain their leaders. Socially, they were organized according to the cultural patterns of the African regions from which they came and tried to reconstruct in the new Maroon communities their native familial and religious organization. They earned their livelihood from the raids which they conducted against the small Spanish population of the interior of the island or against the *ingenios* and cattle ranches they encountered in their path.

Fear among the Spanish population grew since the Spaniards were convinced that, due to the numerical superiority of the blacks, the day was not far off when all the island would be under their control. In 1543 fear was so prevalent among the white population that the Spaniards did not dare to leave their farms unless in parties of 15 to 20 armed men since the Maroons went about with lances and other weapons, and riding horses stolen from the Spaniards.

In the following three years squadrons of armed men were sent to the mountains, where they fought and killed the Maroons in a bloody war in which many of the main black leaders lost their lives. Captured slaves were hanged, shot with arrows, burned or punished by having their feet cut off. So effective was this campaign that many eventually asked for pardon and offered their services in capturing their former companions in exchange for their lives. The Spaniards accepted the offer and with this valuable aid did great harm to the rest of the runaways. In June 1546 the Spanish governor could at last write to the Crown that the problem of the runaway black was better than it had been for twenty years in this part.

The runaway slaves were a constant source of fear and concern for the Spanish colonists, but they did not decisively affect the sugar industry in Puerto Rico and Santo Domingo. During this period the merchants and planters continued exporting sugar to Spain, either directly to Seville or by way of Portobelo in Panama. Between 1536 and 1565 some 803 ships entered and departed from the port of Santo Domingo and other ports, bringing merchandise and manufactured goods and returning to Spain with their ships stores loaded with sugar, hides, and other products of the island.

In those thriving years few bothered with activities other than sugar production, cattle raising, and the exploitation of *Campeche* wood and *Cassia fistula* trees. These were the activities which provided the income to import those goods that made life comfortable and tolerable in the islands, where the construction of imposing stone buildings was financed by the money earned in the sugar business. As the sugar industry flourished, the city of Santo Domingo became a thriving port and the centre for investors in

TABLE 3.1   Sugar production in Española and Puerto Rico, 1568–1607

Year	Española (arrobas)	Puerto Rico (arrobas)	Total arrobas	Tons
1568	6 960	22 200	29 160	364
1569	57 250	11 370	68 620	732
1570	62 070	8 010	70 080	876
1571	51 570	8 520	60 090	751
1581	44 130	–	44 130	552
1583	31 110	2 370	33 480	418
1584	42 150	5 580	47 730	596
1585	180	–	180	2
1587	10 350	–	10 350	129
1589	–	1 170	1 170	14
1593	–	5 640	5 640	70
1594	–	9 105	9 105	113
1603	13 451	–	13 451	168
1604	6 961	–	6 961	87
1605	8 438	–	8 438	105
1606	10 000	–	10 000	125
1607	4 220	–	4 220	52

Source: Pierre et Huguette Chaunu, *Seville et l'Atlantique*, (Tables Statistiques), Vol. VI, pp. 1004–9 (Paris: Armand Colin, 1955–8), and J. Marino Incháustegui, *Reales Cédulas y Correspondencia de Gobernadores de Santo Domingo*, Vol. III, pp. 861–3 (Madrid: Gráficas Reunidas, 1958).

the sugar industry. In 1548 there were 35 sugar *ingenios* in Española and 11 in Puerto Rico, all controlled by the bureaucratic élite and some Spanish merchants associated with the big mercantile houses of Seville. The relevance of the *señores de ingenios* could still be seen twenty years later, in 1568, when nine of the 12 council men of Santo Domingo were plantation owners.

The decline of sugar production

What happened to the sugar industry in the Antilles in the last quarter of the sixteenth century? Why was it that the planters of Española and Puerto Rico got out of the market after having accumulated decades of experience in their mills and plantations? The answers to these questions do not lie solely in the Antilles but in the evolution of the world sugar market and in the rise of other products that came into competition with sugar cane.

Although some local factors can be pointed out as having led to the destruction of the sugar industry in Española and Puerto Rico, the most decisive ones rest on the international market. Not even the smallpox epidemic that ravaged the slave population in 1586 and subsequent years, killing more than half of the blacks, can explain the decline of sugar production in the Antilles. For despite the enormous loss of life, nearly 10 000 slaves remained alive, and only 10 per cent of them were used in the production of sugar.

Ginger production, on the other hand, did contribute to the decline of the sugar industry in the Spanish Antilles at the end of the sixteenth century. Ginger is a plant of Asian origin, introduced into Mexico in 1547, which spread out into the Antilles some years later. Its root was much used as a remedy for stomach aches and as a spice. It took nearly two decades to convert ginger into a large-scale commercial crop, but by 1574 some *vecinos*[3] of Santo Domingo were already harvesting up to 6000 *arrobas* worth. Starting in 1576, ginger began to appear in the export statistics of Española, and in those of Puerto Rico in 1583. The *vecinos* of La Habana also experimented with ginger cultivation for a time, but production in Cuba remained almost negligible, apparently due to the lack of manpower and to the colonists' preference for cattle raising.

In Española and Puerto Rico there was an excess of slave labour that could be turned to ginger production. There is abundant evidence of sugar mill owners from both islands who used a portion of their slaves in the cultivation of this plant to such an extent that many canefields were converted into ginger plantations at the end of the century. Observing the decline of sugar exports each year, the Spanish Crown attributed it to ginger and prohibited its cultivation in 1598, threatening the sugar mill owners with taking away from them privileges they had enjoyed for decades. In 1601 the *señores de ingenios* of Puerto Rico replied that they would prefer to lose their privileges than give up the cultivation of ginger, and it seems that their colleagues in Española reacted similarly. According to a population census of Española taken in 1606, only 800 out of the 9648 slaves on the island worked in the sugar mills. Of the rest, 6742 worked mainly on ginger farms, alternating with the planting of maize, yucca, plantains, and other foodstuffs. Only 88 slaves were mentioned as domestic servants.

This obstinate preference for ginger cultivation among the *señores de ingenios* can be explained by the difference in price with sugar, and by the lower production costs of ginger. Looking at the available export statistics for both products between 1581 and 1615 (Table 3.2), it can be observed that while the average price for a pound of sugar remained relatively stable at 25 *maravedíes* during the last two decades of the sixteenth century, the average price of a pound of ginger kept rising from 45 *maravedíes* a pound until it reach a record high of 80 *maravedíes* in 1615. Besides, sugar was much more difficult to produce than ginger. In addition to planting the cane, it had to be harvested then transported from the plantation to the mill, where it had to be ground. Its juice had to be boiled until it became molasses, before it was finally crystallized into sugar. Sugar manufacturing was an extremely complicated process which consumed an extraordinary amount of capital, entrepreneurship and energy.

Ginger, on the other hand, is a small root that retains its properties for a long time after being unearthed, and does not need to be specially processed for export. Furthermore, ginger was a product that could be easily transported and hidden in the ships, making it very popular as a medium of exchange in the contraband trade in the Antilles. Therefore it is not surprising that ginger, along with tobacco later on, became the colonists' preferred crop. The 1606 census of Española reported that nearly the entire population was engaged in ginger production. As a result, production increased substantially at the turn of the century. By 1607 Española was exporting 17 000 quintales of ginger, in contrast to the 2000 quintales exported 10 years before (Table 3.2).

Ginger alone cannot sufficiently explain the sugar crisis in the Antilles at the end of the sixteenth century. Two more factors have to be taken into account. One is the increasing difficulties imposed by piracy to navigation in the Caribbean, as well as the isolation of Española and Puerto Rico from the main trading routes. The other is overwhelming competition from Brazilian production in the European market. As to the first cause, the explanation is very simple. As the religious wars dominated European life throughout the sixteenth century, the war waging nations sent their corsairs to the Caribbean

TABLE 3.2   Ginger exports and prices, 1581–1615 (in *quintales* and *maravedíes*)[4]

Year	Española	Puerto Rico	Cuba	New Spain	Price
1581	3 334		390		45.5
1583	8 624	33	42		44.8
1584	9 598	214			43.0
1586	3 750				
1587	22 000	6		406	41.3
1589	2 560	403			40.9
1593	947	2 089	12		40.1
1594	2 175	3 168			51.0
1596	3 418				51.7
1597	2 086				60.0
1607	17 261				60.0
1615				86	80.0

Source: Pierre et Huguette Chaunu, *Seville et l'Atlantique*, (Tables Statistiques), Vol. VI, pp. 1030–1 (Paris: Armand Colin, 1955–8).

to harm the Spanish trade with the Indies. To protect its trade between Seville and the New World, the Spanish Crown ordered in 1543 that its ships should make their trips together in well-guarded fleets. These fleets were to leave twice a year from Seville and return through the ports of Veracruz in Mexico and Nombre de Dios on the Isthmus of Panama. This system of fleets did not function regularly until 1566 when the use of galleons was inaugurated.

The system of fleets notably altered the rhythm and flow of navigation in the Caribbean and eventually completed the isolation into which Santo Domingo, Puerto Rico and Jamaica had been falling as other colonies, especially Mexico and Peru, were gaining in importance. Now the ships to Santo Domingo could only sail from Spain together with the fleet. However, upon arriving in the Caribbean, they would have to go alone without protection through pirate-infested waters as the fleet continued on to other ports. Thus, navigation to Española, Puerto Rico and Jamaica became more expensive. Freight rates rose in proportion to the worsening international situation, and maritime insurance was much cheaper for Mexico than for Santo Domingo. Havana became the most important port in the Caribbean while Santo Domingo was sidelined. Havana was on the Gulf route and its port was much more convenient for the fleets to stop at to take on provisions of food and water for the return voyage.

Lacking regular transportation for their products, the colonists of Puerto Rico and Española resorted to smuggling, but since sugar was a highly-supervised and regulated business, contraband could not help the *señores de ingenios* to ship their product regularly, making it a less profitable activity than others, such as ginger cultivation, cattle ranching, or *Cassia fistula* farming. By the middle of the century investment in new mills had stopped, and in the following fifty years, investment in modernization or maintenance dwindled.

The other major factor behind the decline of sugar production in the Antilles was competition from Brazilian sugar. Sugar production in Brazil started in 1532 under royal protection, and soon enjoyed the financial backing of German and Dutch investors connected with the principal trading houses of Lisbon. Initially, Brazilian production grew slowly. In 1575 there were only 55 sugar mills in operation. Part of the reason why this initial phase was so slow has to do with the long-standing controversy on the use of Indian slaves in the plantations. This controversy was finally resolved in 1570 when the Crown decreed that Indians should be paid salaries, but it forced the Brazilian planters to look for African slaves as an alternative source of labour.

The use of African slaves in the sugar plantations had already been authorized since 1559, but given the availability of Indian labour, the

75

importation of blacks was not significant until after 1570. Then, the rise in demand for sugar in Europe in the following years encouraged the Brazilian planters to build 70 new mills between 1570 and 1583, and 72 additional ones between 1584 and 1610. As it had happened in the Antilles before, the importation of African slaves rose accordingly, fluctuating between 10 000 and 15 000 per year at the turn of the century.

With such a large number of mills and slaves, Brazilian sugar production increased substantially and reached more than 25 000 tons per year by 1610, dwarfing the 500 tons produced by the Antilles and even the 2500 tons produced by Madeira in the mid-sixteenth century. Thanks to the Dutch mercantile connections, the Portuguese were able to compete successfully with the Venetians and the Genoese, and eventually drove them out of the market which the Italians had dominated since the fifteenth century. In 1598 Amberes (Antwerp) alone imported more than 40 000 tons of sugar from Portugal. Most of this sugar was produced in Brazil and the Portuguese Atlantic islands. Sugar from the Antilles, reaching Seville, could barely make an impact in the Spanish market, and was insignificant in the Mediterranean still dominated by the Italians.

Tobacco

As for tobacco, its legal production did not start until very late. Tobacco was adopted early by the black slaves of the first sugar plantations in the Antilles and by the *cimarrónes* who went around with the Indians in the mid-sixteenth century, but not by the Spanish colonists because the Spanish authorities discouraged its use for many years.

The popularity of tobacco smoking and chewing among sailors, who used it to combat phlegm and colds and to protect themselves from the humidity, quickly incorporated tobacco on to the list of products exchanged for merchandise in the contraband trade in the Antilles, and thus tobacco entered into the European pharmacopoeia. The Spanish Crown authorized apothecaries to utilize tobacco in their medicines and to sell it legally despite the fact that tobacco cultivation had been prohibited in Panama, in November 1586, in an attempt to prevent contraband.

The penetration of French, English and Dutch corsairs in the Caribbean helped spread tobacco throughout the taverns of European ports where sailors and drinkers alternated wine and liquor with the inhalation of snuff. By 1600 this product was one of the most prized among the Dutch smugglers who patrolled the Antillean coasts. Tobacco leaves were even used as a sort of primitive paper money among smugglers. Those colonists who were too poor to enter into sugar production soon discovered tobacco as an important means of earning a living. It took relatively little effort to produce since family labour was sufficient for the harvest.

Precisely because tobacco, together with cow hides, was the preferred means of exchange with the smugglers, the Spanish Crown prohibited its cultivation for ten years in Puerto Rico, Española, Cuba, Margarita, Cumana, Venezuela and Nueva Andalucia in August of 1606. In that year Venezuela was the most important tobacco production centre and the main supplier of the leaves to the Dutch. The zone of Barinas in the Venezuelan flatlands, produced some 35000 lb of the best tobacco. Although in Española there were 95 *vecinos* who produced tobacco in 1606, its leaf was not as highly desired by the Dutch as that of Barinas.

Most of the tobacco produced in Española was used by the *ingenio* owners to entertain their slaves at the sugar plantations. The surplus was exported to Spain where it was sold as medicine. In Cuba and Puerto Rico tobacco was still not cultivated for export in 1607. Despite prohibition, tobacco smuggling continued and the Caribbean colonists continued harvesting it clandestinely. Taking into account that the main beneficiaries of the contraband trade were foreigners, and that the Crown was not collecting taxes on this trade, in 1614 the Spanish government ordered that all that was not consumed within Venezuela and the Antilles had to be exported under official supervision to Seville.

The political truce in Europe favoured this effort to control the tobacco market. The ultimate goal of the Crown was to become the intermediary for Caribbean and Venezuelan tobacco that entered England, of which the annual volume was estimated to be more than 50000 lb in 1616. For this purpose, the Spanish Crown dictated a series of measures creating a state monopoly on tobacco in 1620. During the first quarter of the seventeenth century the consumption of tobacco expanded considerably in Europe. The Dutch and the English spread the use of pipes, as well as the habit of smoking, which soon became more popular than the inhalation of snuff.

The success of Virginia, based on the cultivation of tobacco since 1613, soon attracted thousands of immigrants who also settled in other North American territories. However, in 1625 the English Crown also imposed a monopoly on tobacco. With this new legislation, the English Crown prohibited the cultivation of tobacco in England as well as the importation of foreign tobaccos, thereby authorizing the production of tobacco only in the colonies on the condition that the product would be sold exclusively in England. The story of tobacco cultivation in England's North American colonies, as well as in the Lesser Antilles in the seventeenth century, falls out of the scope of this chapter, but both developments are connected to the culture of tobacco in the Spanish Main, as should become evident in the subsequent volumes of the UNESCO *General History of the Caribbean*.

Conclusion

As can be seen, the Spanish colonists in the Antilles spent most of the sixteenth century searching for an export staple which could substitute for gold once the mines became depleted and the Indian population disappeared. During the early years of colonization, many Spaniards thrived through live-stock rearing for the expeditions bound to *Tierra Firme* and Darien. Those expeditions needed horses, ham, bacon, cassava, cattle, and other livestock for the new settlements. So many colonists eked a living out of their ranches, pork pens, or yucca farms. In the first twenty years of the sixteenth century there were in Santo Domingo and Puerto Rico extensive yucca plantations, worked by Indians, which supplied the early *conquistadores* with cassava bread. The Mona Island, between Española and Puerto Rico, as well as the Saona Island, were converted into important production centres of cassava bread which attracted the *carabelas* (caravels) and *navios* (ships) of the early expeditions. But as the Indian population disappeared, and as the focus of the conquest moved to Mexico and Peru, those settlements were abandoned and the colonists had to content themselves with producing cattle, sugar, *Cassia fistula*, and eventually ginger and tobacco for export.

NOTES

1   Fernández de Oviedo, Gonzalo, 'Historia General y Natural de las Indias', Biblioteca de Autores Españoles, 5 vols, (Madrid, 1959).
2   An *arroba* is about 25 lb or 11.5 kg.
3   *Vecinos*, residents or heads of household.
4   A *maravedí* (nm) is an old Spanish coin; a *quintal* is one hundred weight or 46 kg.

Spanish expansion in America, 1492 to c. 1580

Horst Pietschmann

Introduction

The historical assessment of the Spanish – and to a lesser extent Portuguese – colonization of America has undergone a radical change in the present century. Until the Second World War, or thereabouts, it was regarded, in a self-assured Europe and in the countries of the American continent which were themselves heavily oriented towards Europe, as a largely positive process conducted by farsighted and bold seafarers and *conquistadores*. The fact that brutalities had been committed against the indigenous population was conceded with varying degrees of ambiguity; but it was still felt that the process had ultimately brought about Europeanization of the continent. Only the comparatively small group of ethnologists who specialized in America called persistent attention to the destruction of flourishing native cultures and lamented the resulting loss to the cultural heritage of mankind. Under the influence of the decolonization movement of the post-war years, worldwide emphasis on human rights and the reflection now being fostered by many countries of Latin America on their pre-Hispanic Indian past in the wake of a new nationalism, together with the waning fascination of the European model, a rapid reappraisal of the process of Iberian expansion in America set in. The emphasis was now placed on the cruelties perpetrated by the conquerors, the incredible suffering of the ancient inhabitants of the continent with the loss of population numbers and of their cultural identity, followed by repression and exploitation by the new colonial masters. This trend was favoured by a move in historical science away from the great historical problems and the acts of prominent figures to research into structural relationships and developments. The *conquistadores*, who had originally been fêted for their heroic deeds, were now placed in the dock of history, while the defeated peoples were elevated to the status of true historical heroes as helpless and innocent victims. At the same time, it was felt that justice must now be done to their suffering descendants by giving them a bigger share of the blessings of Western civilization.

Faced with these two biased interpretations, historical research which draws heavily on the relevant sources has, in recent decades, put forward many references based on extensive individual study to show that the historical truth lies somewhere between the two views which have characterized the broader historical consciousness at different times. Each in its own way, these two lines of interpretation remain on the whole Eurocentric. Self-evident in the older view, this fact does not immediately spring to mind in what is currently the dominant interpretation. The biased presentation of the original inhabitants of America as innocent victims has its true roots in the myth of the *bon sauvage* dating from the European enlightenment, i.e. the good savage who, unspoiled by European civilization, lives in harmony with his environment. Precisely because of his unspoiled nature he was bound to be destroyed by the brutal onslaught of this civilization which he had no means of resisting. That myth is perpetuated in the more recent historical view which sets out largely from the assumption that the original inhabitants of America were, and still are, incapable of actively influencing history. They were also thought to be unable to impart any significant features of their cultural heritage to the rising colonial societies and later to the independent states, over whose historical development they could not exert any sustainable influence.

In actual fact, the seizure of lands by the Iberians led to the creation of new societies whose main feature was a more or less pronounced – of course to widely varying degrees – mestizo character in ethnic and/or cultural, socioeconomic and even political and religious terms. That view is now increasingly gaining ground, as was apparent in the attitude of the Mexican government – i.e. the state which most consciously accepts its mestizo character – to the jubilee marking the 500th anniversary in 1992 of the voyage of Columbus. The Presidential decree which set up a national commission to prepare for this year of celebration, drew specific attention to the fact that these ceremonies were to be planned under the guiding theme of 'an encounter between cultures', reference being necessarily made to the reciprocal influence of the two cultures, i.e. to the process of mixing of the peoples which began at that time.[1]

The early European colonization and Indian culture

The accuracy of that view is reflected in the course of the European colonization and its early history. Depending on the cultural level of the original inhabitants of the different regions of Central and South America, these processes took place in totally different ways, at different epochs, and over varying lapses of time. The differences in the nature of the conquest and colonization of what is now Argentina and Mexico can only be explained by the different population density and cultural level of the original inhabitants, as the conquering Castilians generally proceeded with the same scheme of organization, inspired by the same motives and with a largely homogeneous cultural makeup. After all, an overwhelming majority of them came from Andalusia and Extremadura. Simplifying greatly, the original Indian inhabitants of the continent can be classified into three different groups in terms of their cultural development: 1) The high cultures of Mexico, Central America and the Andean area with their dense population, highly structured and hierarchical order of society, an economy based on the division of labour with an almost exclusively agrarian and craft structure, and a rigid political and religious organization; 2) the sedentary tribes of the Caribbean and the tropical and sub-tropical parts of America with incipient arable farming, hunting and fishing, a far less pronounced social structure and a rudimentary political and religious organization with the people living essentially in small (tribal) groups; and 3) the nomadic or semi-sedentary tribal groups in the temperate latitudes of South America or in northern Mexico and the south-western part of what is now the USA, who were mostly hunters and gatherers with little social differentiation and crude forms of political and religious organization.

In the areas populated by the people belonging to the first group, the European conquest went ahead quickly after military conflicts which frequently, in view of the extremely small number of *conquistadores* in relation to the native population density, took the form of Indian civil wars, as the Spaniards soon found allies who rose up against their Indian lords. Here, a process of biological and cultural interchange occurred from the outset. To some extent the Spaniards respected the social, economic and political structures of the Indians.

From the peoples of the second group the Europeans encountered either temporary resistance or none at all. However, to the extent that they set about integrating the natives into the Spanish or Portuguese (the Portuguese mainly came across original inhabitants belonging to this group) social and economic system, their organizational structures generally collapsed. The natives either resisted in a last vain revolt and were decimated or wiped out by war and new diseases, as was largely the case in the Caribbean, or else they soon intermingled biologically with the Europeans, as was the case in Paraguay. In the first instance, their cultural influence on the European settlers was less and the decimated or destroyed Indian population was gradually replaced by black African slaves. In the second case, a process of cultural mixing again occurred. As in many regions belonging to the first group, it sometimes even extended to use of the native language by the Europeans.

In the regions populated by peoples belonging to the third group, the Europeans met with bitter resistance from the outset. These peoples did not accept domination. They escaped Spanish pressure, if necessary by withdrawing to adjoining territories. They preserved their specific character, at best taking over from the Europeans tools and forms of behaviour which helped them to assert their own strength: domestic cattle, especially horses, and weapons. In a few regions, such as the La Plata estuary, these peoples were wiped out towards the end of the sixteenth century but in most cases they preserved their independence until well into the nineteenth century when they mixed to some extent with the Europeans (the South American Gauchos for instance are the result of these processes of mixing). Some have even managed to survive until today in a state of relative independence. In all these territories, European colonization made extremely slow progress, if any, and a frontier phenomenon, lasting for centuries, occurred, as in nineteenth-century USA.

This brief outline shows that different Indian forms of culture had widely varying influences on the rising colonial societies, and were able to leave a lasting mark on them. It is repeatedly claimed that the natives occupied the lowest social rank in the new societies. However, this applies only to the mass of the indigenous population who remained in their village communities and not to the Indian élite. Nor should we overlook the fact that in Europe the mass of the rural population occupied the lowest position in the social hierarchy until the nineteenth century, often living under conditions which were still typified by the feudal order of the late middle ages and the early modern era. The massive migration from Europe in the nineteenth century shows that comparisons would need to be drawn between the living conditions of the lower social groups on both sides of the Atlantic at different periods. Such studies would be essential to enable the fate of the native population of America under European colonial domination to be assessed in a more informed manner. However, there can be no doubt about their active role in history.

The term 'active role in history' must not be understood here from the perspective of history written in terms of great political leaders and national deeds, but rather from the angle of an historiography which is interested in long periods of time and slowly-changing structures. From that angle, the European seizure of land in America signified the integration into the global context of a continent which had hitherto lived in almost total biological isolation. The microbes, plants, animals and techniques brought over by the Europeans signified a dramatic change for the continent, affecting its people and the indigenous fauna and flora alike. Hitherto unknown sicknesses spread among the natives much faster than the Europeans themselves. They were passed on by the native people, already in contact with the Europeans, to other population groups. European cattle sometimes multiplied explosively and brought specific parasites with them, as did European domestic plants. This ecological revolution, which has been the subject of recent research, resulted after the conquest, with the political, religious and social changes brought about by the conquerors, in a population decline which lasted for about one and a half centuries and gathered pace dramatically, especially in the sphere of the densely-populated Indian high cultures. Even before the Spanish conquest, these cultures had made the greatest possible use of the ecosystem. The weak dietary base of the high cultures soon collapsed altogether under the impact of the conquest. That process further accelerated the demographic and cultural disaster facing the original population.

At the same time, however, the conquerors began to borrow Indian techniques, domestic plants, etc. A process of cultural transformation set in and soon spread to Europe in the early modern era where it also ushered in far-reaching changes. The great economic and political changes which American precious metal brought about in Europe and to some extent also in Asia – via the Philippines or Europe – are already widely known. Less well-known are the transformations to which the adoption of American cultivated plants and products led in Europe, for example, medicinal plants, dyestuffs, cocoa, maize, and the influence on European thought, art and culture. A wide-ranging and detailed study of these processes from the angle of cultural history is still lacking. In the German-speaking countries, situated as they are in Central Europe, these far-reaching changes on both sides of the Atlantic which resulted from the European colonization have so far attracted insufficient attention. The fact that this is the case in historical science clearly emerges from the major historical manuals.

The prehistory of Atlantic expansion

How did this expansion come about? Why did the Iberian kingdoms set out on this process of transatlantic expansion at the transition from the middle ages to the modern era and how did it take place? In our quest for the underlying criteria and reasons for this expansion we must look back far into the European middle ages and, in particular, at the medieval developments which took place in the Mediterranean region. The relevant processes must be mentioned here, at least in very general and concise terms. To begin with, they were not directly bound up with this expansion but included such factors as: population growth in the middle ages, the rise of an urban bourgeoisie, the expansion of the monetary economy and the development of banking associated with the growth of trade with remote countries, new forms of trade organization, progress in shipbuilding and navigation, ecclesiastical and religious trends such as the crusades, the endeavour of the papacy to gain world power and the creation of the mendicant orders with their dedication to missions to the peoples, or the survival of the Aristotelian tradition with its impact on the medieval worldview and the resulting commitment to empirical thinking and the creation of new sciences. Nor must we forget the survival of ancient myths, legends and the faith in all kinds of exotica. The colonization of the East should also be taken as a point of comparison.

In the narrower sense, the prehistory of Atlantic expansion includes the consolidation of the trading empires of Italian city-states in the Mediterranean regions and their colonial experience in the Black Sea and Eastern Mediterranean, the progress of the medieval Iberian *Reconquista*, and the recovery of the Iberian Peninsula from the dominance of the Moors which reached the Straits of Gibraltar in the mid-thirteenth century. This permitted Christian navigation from the Mediterranean out in to the Atlantic so that regular shipping and trade contacts were soon established between the Mediterranean and Western Europe or the North Sea region. The Iberian kingdoms of Castile and Portugal quickly rose to the status of European maritime powers. They also became important centres for long-distance European trade where Italian and French merchants met with their counterparts from Flanders and the Hanseatic League. Here too, seagoing ships began to be built. They were able to sail on the Atlantic with its high waves and long swell. The transition from the prevailing coastal shipping to high-sea navigation then became possible. The extent to which these developments stimulated the imagination of the seafaring cities is apparent from the fact that, in 1291, a Genoan expedition tried to sail southwards along the African coast but failed to return from this venture. In the first third of the fourteenth century, the Genoans rediscovered the Canary Islands which had already been known in ancient times. At much the same period Marco Polo's report on his voyage to China caused a sensation in Europe. The desire to reach Asia by the sea route was now rekindled. In parallel, the conviction that the earth was round took root. In 1344 the Infant Luis de la Cerda of Castile was rewarded by the Pope with the Canary Islands and given the task of spreading the message of Christianity among the indigenous population. This led to the announcement of claims of possession by the Castilian Crown and also by Portugal. Subsequently, the two powers were rivals for Atlantic shipping rights and domination, associated with their joint wish to carry the *Reconquista* and the Christian mission from the peninsula to North Africa. But the Catalans and Mallorcans, who were subjects of the Crown of Aragon, also took part in these early ventures in the Atlantic at the beginning of the fourteenth century. With their highly-developed cartographic skills, they helped to disseminate the acquired knowledge until, at the end of the same century, Norman G. de Béthencourt, acting with the permission of Castile, made the first systematic attempt to colonize the Canary Islands and convert the indigenous population.

In the fifteenth century this initiative came increasingly from Portugal. After the conquest of Ceuta in North Africa in the year 1415, Portuguese seafarers, acting at the behest of the Crown, Prince Henry the Navigator and his brothers, voyaged along the African coast and out into the Atlantic. In early 1530 they discovered the unpopulated Atlantic island group of Madeira and the Azores which Prince Henry went on to settle. The Portuguese advances along the African coast soon led to territories inhabited by black Africans, i.e. to the discovery of non-Islamic, heathen (in the true sense of the term) peoples. In the early fifteenth century the Roman Curia prohibited their enslavement on condition that they tolerated the Christian mission. Here the Portuguese developed commercial colonization by taking possession of the territories for the Portuguese Crown without seeking to subjugate or control the indigenous population. They were satisfied with the establishment of trading bases along the coast, small fortified strong points, generally in agreement with the coastal population from which they sought to acquire precious slaves, gold and spices, by barter trade. It was in the Portuguese seafaring environment that Columbus later gathered the experience that permitted his venture to discover the western sea route to Asia. The latest research assumes that Columbus was already aware of the existence of a country beyond the known island groups. The two most prominent Columbus researchers who subscribe to that view, Juan Manzano Manzano and Juan Pérez de Tudela, hold differing opinions as to the source of this information. Perhaps that circumstance answers the question as to why Columbus stuck so tenaciously to his plan to reach Asia by the western sea route, although the most experienced cosmographs of Portugal and Castile gave him convincing evidence that his calculations of distances were far too short.

In the fifteenth century Castile was engaged in protracted internal conflict, so that the Crown could do little more than defend its title of ownership to the Canary Islands. For the rest, Andalusian maritime navigation was allowed a free hand. This did not change until Ferdinand of Aragon and his wife, Isabella, enforced their hereditary claims to the Castilian Crown in the early 1470s. Immediately afterwards, in 1478, the two rulers definitely incorporated the Canary Islands into the Kingdom of Castile. However, in the Peace Treaty of Alcàçovas with Portugal in 1479 they had to accept a delimitation of their interests in the Atlantic which seemed less favourable to them. Portugal secured exclusive shipping rights south of an imaginary line running east-west from Cape Bojador, so that the Castilian Kings were only left with the possibility of expansion to the north of that line in a westerly direction.

This dividing line meant that the Canary Islands were the limit for navigation by Castilian vessels sailing to the south. Then domestic policy matters, and soon afterwards the war against Granada, the last Moorish kingdom on the soil of the peninsula, laid full claim to the attention of the Kings. That is why Columbus' project met with little interest here when he came to Castile in 1485 to escape from his creditors in Portugal and offer his project to the Castilian Crown after it had been rejected by the King of Portugal. Acting on the advice of a group of experts, the Kings also decided not to finance Columbus' project. But, for reasons that are not entirely clear, they changed their minds immediately after the conquest of the city of Granada and a decision was then taken to implement the plan even though Columbus provoked a risk of failure until the last minute by making exaggerated claims. With an eye to the Treaty of Alcàçovas which only permitted westerly expansion by Castile, the Crown accepted the proposals of the Italian adventurer because if, contrary to all expectation, he were to prove successful, a great opportunity would arise to outmanoeuvre Portugal. If not, on the worst assumption, three ships would be lost. That risk seemed perfectly acceptable to the rulers who had been uncommonly strengthened by their victory over Granada.

The legal form of the venture was defined in 1492 in the capitulation of Santa Fe – the fortified field camp of the Kings in front of Granada – between the Catholic Kings and Columbus. In this document, Columbus bound himself to take any islands and mainlands discovered in the western ocean into the possession of the Kings. In return, he was given the title and offices of Admiral of the Ocean, Viceroy and Governor of the territories to be taken into possession as inheritable estate, together with a number of economic privileges and income from the anticipated trade with those territories. The contracting parties reserved a clearly-defined trading and shipping monopoly with those territories and stipulated that only full-time employees of the monopoly could be allowed to travel to, and reside in, those countries. Despite the order given to Columbus to take possession of the territories discovered by him, the venture was conceived entirely on the lines of the trade colonization developed by the Portuguese; economic advantages were the main reason for the expedition. A decisive contributory factor to success lay in the participation of the Andalusian seafaring family of Pinzon from the little port town of Palos, as it enabled experienced seamen to be recruited under the supreme command of a foreigner. After just three months navigation past the Canary Islands and onward in a westerly direction, on 12 October 1492, the three ships sighted Guanahani which is one of the Bahamas Islands and forms part of the American land mass, before going on to discover Puerto Rico and Haiti. Leaving behind a small force which was soon destroyed by the natives in Fort Navidad built in Haiti, Columbus sailed back to Europe via the Azores after the loss of his flagship. His two ships were separated by a storm and Columbus sailed into the port of Lisbon so that the King of Portugal was the first to learn of the success of his venture. He at once suspected an infringement of the Treaty of Alcàçovas which he had caused to be ratified by the Pope. Vigorous diplomatic activity was therefore the immediate consequence of Columbus' discovery. The Catholic Kings turned to Pope Alexander VI who came of a noble line from Valencia. On the strength of their missionary intentions, they persuaded the Pope to issue a series of papal bulls transferring possession of the newly-discovered territories and any further territories in that part of the world to them. That is how the Crown of Castile was able to bring about a revision of the Treaty of Alcàçovas in 1494 in the shape of the Treaty of Tordesillas. An imaginary line running from north to south 370 nautical miles west of the Cape Verde Islands was now defined as the dividing line between the territories of mutual interest. All territories discovered to the west of that line were to fall to Castile, while Portugal reserved the lands found in the southerly direction of the east of that line. It must not be forgotten that, a few years previously, Bartolomeu Dias, acting in the service of the Portuguese Crown, had sailed round the southernmost tip of Africa and, just a few years later, in 1498 Vasco da Gama reached India. As a consequence of the definition of this dividing line, the eastern tip of the South American continent fell to Portugal. The origin of the modern state of Brazil therefore lies in the Treaty of Tordesillas.

A further consequence of this political interlude was the fact that, on his second voyage, Columbus took with him a group of missionaries drawn from various religious orders in order to set about the conversion of the natives. However, that endeavour was to remain fruitless because of disputes between the missionaries themselves and between the colonists. Despite new discoveries, Columbus' venture soon faced crisis when commercial income failed to materialize. Some of the indentured employees of the trading monopoly began to rise up in mutiny against Columbus and his supporters and demanded permission for settlement colonization. They also wanted to make greater use of the indigenous population as a workforce. Columbus was strongly opposed to this as he wanted to maintain his good relations with the original inhabitants of Española/Haiti and because such a step was not in his own interest. After 1498 or thereabouts the Crown for its part began to relax the monopoly and allow other navigators to set out on voyages of discovery. Columbus' attempts to offset the economic deficit by trapping indigenous slaves and shipping them to Spain failed because of a decision of the Crown which, following the practice already adopted on the Canary Islands and acting on papal instructions, prohibited the shipment of natives who had not yet become Christians to Europe against their will. The deteriorating circumstances in the first settlements on Haiti under Columbus' command and court intrigues directed against him, fomented in particular by Bishop Rodriguez de Fonseca who had been entrusted with the organization of the fleets of discovery (he was said to be more skilful in seafaring and trade matters than in saying mass) finally led the Crown to send an examining judge to Haiti. The judge relieved Columbus of his offices and sent him back to Spain. Despite rapid rehabilitation, Columbus had now definitely lost his influence over the further development of America. His deposition not only spelled the end of the monopoly concluded with the Crown but also the transition to a new concept of settlement: *de facto* occupation of the new territories, settlement of them by colonists travelling out for their own account but with royal approval, the creation of an order emulating the conditions prevailing in Castile and – as a direct consequence – the full incorporation of the indigenous population into this new order. In short, it marked the transition to settlement colonization.

Settlement colonization

For the first time since antiquity, the concept of the creation of European plantations overseas emerged. At all events, the colonization of the Caribbean islands which was now set in motion represented a new feature of late medieval-early modern history. Despite the absence of systematic comparisons with other forms of ancient, medieval and modern colonization, it can nevertheless be asserted that in this form of settlement colonization economic interests did not dominate in the early days, given the policy of the Crown. On the contrary, general considerations of power politics and civilization went on to leave their mark on subsequent development. The Crown wanted first of all to put an end to the highly-unprofitable monopoly with Columbus without, however, endangering the progress of colonization. It therefore endeavoured to roll the costs on to the private sector, while at the same time securing control over development by making voyages to America and other expeditions conditional on its approval. At the same time the conversion of the natives and their incorporation into a society based on Spanish lines were to be promoted. The last will and testament of Isabel the Catholic from the year 1504 makes that intention particularly clear. The efforts of the Crown to obtain patronage over the future ecclesiastical organization and to establish bishop's dioceses reflected the same intention, while the foundation of a state trading house in Seville, the Casa de Contratacion, clearly indicated the fact that not just shipping, trade and passenger transport with America were to be controlled, but customs revenues and levies from the overseas ventures were also to be secured for the Crown. The disputes over the succession following the death of Isabella in 1504 interrupted these efforts until the return of Ferdinand as the Regent of Castile in the year 1507/8.

Ferdinand's return soon gave fresh impetus to the American venture. In 1508 the Pope granted the Crown unlimited patronage over the church in America. In return the Crown undertook to finance the church organization until the newly-created ecclesiastical establishments became capable of financing themselves on the European model through church tithes, i.e. the payment of one-tenth of annual agricultural income. Columbus' son, Diego Colón, was reinstated in his father's rights, but only for the territories discovered by the latter and taken into his possession. Missionaries from the mendicant orders were sent out and Diego Colón led the conquest of the island of Cuba. In 1511 Ferdinand, following the Castilian model, set up a royal court of appeal, the *Audiencia*, in Santo Domingo.

Another decisive impetus was to follow from a totally different quarter in the year 1511. The Dominican, Montesinos, launched a massive attack on the Spanish colonists in his Advent sermon in Santo Domingo. He accused them of merciless exploitation and repression of the natives and criticized the fact that their behaviour could not be reconciled with the moral principles of Christianity. He threatened them with excommunication and finally raised the central question: by what right did they claim to dispose of the natives? This raised the question of Spanish legal titles which touched directly on the Crown. After all, it was the Crown which had authorized the colonists to travel to America. King Ferdinand first reacted outspokenly against the Dominicans, but soon went on to grasp the serious nature of the problem. In 1512 he convened a 'junta' made up of theologians and lawyers to debate this topic. At the same time, the departure of a big expedition to the Panama Isthmus was delayed until the conclusion of the deliberations. That was the beginning of the great debate over the Spanish legal title which was to exercise the minds of Spanish spiritual experts constantly in the sixteenth century and was destined to have a far-reaching influence on politics, legal developments and the attitude of the church towards the heathens.

Montesinos' sermon had another consequence. It made the colonist, Bartolomé de Las Casas, aware of the dubious nature of his actions, and caused him to join the Dominican order. That was the start of the career of a resolute defender of the rights of natives who was to have a decisive influence on the debate through his actions and writings in his long life. From now on a broad distinction can be made, in respect of motivation, political interest and concrete action, between three main factors in the process of Spanish expansion. Each such factor was to have a different impact while the interplay between them set the tone of Spanish expansion and colonization: the Crown and its central apparatus of government, the *conquistadores* and colonists, and the church, represented primarily by the three mendicant orders, the Augustinians, Franciscans and Dominicans. The relationship with the two latter orders was the most significant in every respect.

The *conquistadores*

Let us now turn our attention to the *conquistadores*. In the early days of expansion, when Columbus held a monopoly and the concept of commercial colonization was being pursued, the Spaniards who travelled to America were for the most part recruited from the Andalusian port cities which had the closest links with trade and navigation. However, the end of the war against Granada left a large number of persons with a military and warlike mindset at a loose end. In the central and southern part of the province the last years of the war had seen the onset of a kind of war economy geared both directly and indirectly to siege warfare against the fortresses of Moorish Granada. Towards the end of the campaign 50 to 60 000 men were recruited each year in Castile, largely by the urban militias. They were used either to supply the fighting troops or as combatants themselves. The war brought many people from the lower ranks of the nobility and poor rural population hope for economic betterment through regular wages or the prospect of booty. Following the end of the war against Granada there was, therefore, a substantial human potential which saw a chance of social betterment in the new adventures or military campaigns. Since the mid-1490s many people had set their hopes on the war in Naples, which the Catholic Kings were seeking to wrest from the French on grounds of old hereditary claims. However, as Columbus' first voyages brought America to public prominence, many of these people, who were willing to seek better living conditions and hence social advancement through warlike ventures, voyages of discovery, etc., now turned their attention to the New World. Their goal was not so much emigration and settlement in newly-discovered lands as the hope of material gain. They wanted to grow rich and return to their homeland to lead a respected life, preferably with the privileges of the nobility. Accession to the nobility through the devious route of money was relatively easy in Castile in those days. The country was rather thinly populated. Its rural population was living under straightened circumstances, while the cities were experiencing a period of economic boom and offered a visible incentive for a more agreeable way of life. As a result of the *Reconquista* wars which had lasted for centuries, the urban and rural populations, especially in the centre and south of the country, were accustomed to a constant obligation of military service in the militia system as the need to ward off the assaults of the Moors frequently arose. The male population was therefore familiar with the alternation between civilian life and war service.

When the Crown adopted the policy of settlement colonization with which it furthered the course of expansion, while seeking to leave the financial risks to private initiative, sufficiently large numbers of people were available who wanted to take part in such ventures in the hope of personal enrichment. They were also well equipped for campaigns but, for the most part, had no interest whatever in permanent settlement overseas, let alone in setting to work there with their own hands. However, there was also an entrepreneurial class which had learnt in the *Reconquista* wars to turn war to economic advantage in order to secure long-term income and social status. Many of the leaders of the voyages of discovery and conquest came from that group. They were certainly willing to settle permanently in the newly-acquired lands, provided that they could acquire lordships, offices and privileges which could be handed down by inheritance. Out of this complex situation there very soon developed, on Columbus' own model, the institutional system which was to underpin the entire Spanish expansion in America. Entrepreneurs of this kind sought from the King the right to take possession of a particular territory, generally inadequately defined because of the vague knowledge of geography, for the Crown of Castile. In return, he demanded supreme military command over the expedition, together with the main civilian and military offices in the conquered region and various economic privileges for himself and his descendants. In legally-binding documents, known as Capitulations, the Crown granted the entrepreneur an order to pursue the conquest and vested in him the desired offices and privileges as inheritable possessions. In addition, it fixed general rules which the person concerned was supposed to apply in his various official duties after the conquest and during the colonization of the country. In turn, the entrepreneur gave an undertaking to fit out the expedition at his own expense.

On receipt of this document the person enjoying the privilege had to organize the venture. That was increasingly done from the soil of existing Spanish territories in America. Ships and equipment were almost always financed by capital providers who for the most part did not intend to be present on the voyages themselves. Crew members were recruited by advertising for volunteers who were required to pay for their own kit and often had to take out loans for that purpose. These volunteers undertook to show military obedience to their leader until the end of the campaign, but not beyond the victory which was taken for granted. In consideration of their services, they were promised a percentage share of the earnings of the venture. The share was based on traditional military principles. A cavalryman received more than a cannoneer or crossbow archer, while they in turn were paid more than foot soldiers armed with the usual kinds of pikes and swords. The motivation of the participants was already high, but the debts incurred by many of the expedition participants, in particular by its leaders and officers, were a further incentive to succeed as they faced economic ruin and legal proceedings by their creditors in the event of failure. Many of the participants in these campaigns had quite literally little or nothing more than their own lives to lose. Commentators generally overlook the fact that the loss of human life among the *conquistadores* was extremely high, as a result of illness, hardship or battles. This in turn tended to strengthen rather than weaken the resolve of the survivors. These circumstances are important to assess what actually happened; not to call attention to some kind of heroism, but rather to explain why such well-organized kingdoms of the ancient Americas so quickly fell pray to the onslaught of troops who were very few in number. The indigenous peoples were unaware of the motives which drove the *conquistadores* on. That is why they underestimated their force because of their small numbers. Often their ability to resist was also impaired by their own traditional myths and omens. Under these circum-stances it is easy to understand that, regardless of their own feeling of civilizing-Christian superiority or awareness of their missionary role, these *conquistador* troops had concerns other than the conversion of natives to Christianity or compliance with the rules for the protection of Indians uppermost in their minds. On occasion, and to varying degrees depending on their psychological and political make-up, the leaders did try to take account of these higher considerations. After all, invoking of the faith by the spiritual representatives who always took part in such ventures created legit-imation, and conversion, even if only formal, nevertheless represented acknowledgement of the claims of the *conquistadores* to domination. Considerate treatment of the natives also encouraged them to submit and cooperate. During the military phase of the conquest the best possible treat-ment was therefore meted out to the indigenous population and the procla-mation of the faith was harnessed in the service of the war aims. Cruelty and massacres were a poor second-best way of achieving the *conquista-dores'* aims if the population showed stubborn resistance or broke their promises of subservience.

The critical stage of these ventures was generally reached at the moment of victory when the leaders were confronted with the need to estab-lish a permanent organization for their domination, while the other partici-pants were entitled to return home with their booty. New incentives were now required to keep the participants in such campaigns hard at work and to complete the transition to sustainable rule and colonization. Ultimately, this aim was achieved by three institutional mechanisms: the founding of cities, the acknowledgement of the rights of the middle Indian leadership strata, the *caciques* or *curacas*, who were often granted the status of a Spanish hidalgo, i.e. a relatively low noble rank, and, lastly, the payment of tributes in kind or in labour by individual groups of Indians, so prolonging

pre-hispanic customs (*repartimiento/encomienda*). By making the participants in successful expeditions, and the neo-colonists who followed them,
citizens of the newly-founded cities with a simultaneous entitlement to
varying tributes in kind and in labour, it proved possible to persuade them to
stay in the country and remain willing to take up military service. At the
same time they were encouraged to settle permanently in the country.
Although these allocations of Indians were not associated with any juris-
dictional authority, the *conquistadores* saw this as something like landlord's
rights on the Castilian model, i.e. a social status symbol and at the same time
an instrument of enrichment at the cost of Indian productivity and labour,
which would assure them of a magnificent life in the long term and preferably one which could be handed down by inheritance indefinitely.
Considering the fact that the leaders were hereditary owners of the civilian
and military offices over the conquered region, there was an evident danger
of feudalization of the newly-acquired territories and the Crown was exposed
to the risk of losing its influence over their internal development.

The colonists and the missionaries

A rapid influx of missionary clergy from the mendicant orders built up the
new ecclesiastical hierarchy in the absence of any other clergy, and ran the
missions to the natives. They soon came to regard the aspirations of the conquerors and colonists *vis-à-vis* the Indians as a serious obstacle to the propa-
gation of the faith. In that regard, it will be noted that the Catholic Kings had
already favoured a church reform in Spain in the late fifteenth century, anti-
cipating in many respects Tridentine reforms. In particular, the mendicant
orders had been reformed so that they now observed the original rules of
their orders and most of the missionary clergy who went to America were
drawn from the circles of proponents of monastic reform. They were, therefore, often endowed with a strong sense of missionary zeal, and some even
expected that an ideal Christianity of a Utopian kind could be achieved in
America, free from the negative profit and pleasure-seeking aspects which
prevailed in Europe. With that fundamental attitude, these people must obviously have been critical of the position adopted by the colonists, especially
as they soon came to realize that the right of the colonists to dispose of the
native population made the task of conversion more difficult, if not impossible. The Dominicans in particular soon became bitter opponents of the
colonists; they fought against their privileges, especially the institution of
the *encomienda*, and advocated the widest possible separation between the
Indians and the rising colonial society. They opposed the behaviour of the
colonists locally and also at the court by exerting pressure on the conscience

of the King through the discussion of legal title in an attempt to bring about statutory reforms. This strategy was to prove highly successful.

The Crown already reacted to Montesinos' 1511 sermon with two major legal innovations. In the Laws of Burgos dating from 1512, it laid down stringent regulations governing the coexistence of Spaniards and Indians. It declared the indigenous people living under Spanish rule to be free vassals of the Crown. However, they were expected to live in the closest possible community with the Europeans to enhance the spread of Christianity and Europeanization. With that end in view, they were to live in villages near to European settlements and be governed by a priest and a lay official who would encourage them to adopt a Christian way of life, regular work and orderly life in society. The hours and forms of work were regulated in detail, as was religious life. In addition, all the leaders of campaigns of conquest were instructed to cause the *Requerimiento* to be proclaimed by interpreters to the Indians before opening hostilities. This text explained to the natives that the Pope had transferred these territories to the Kings to enable them to disseminate the Christian faith here. That message was followed by a brief explanation of the content of the faith and a reference to the role of the Pope as Christ's representative on earth and an appeal to conversion and recognition of the King in return for the assurance of benevolent treatment. Only if the Indians rejected this offer was warfare to be opened. This document, and its significance (if any) has been the subject of great controversy. But commentators have tended to overlook the fact that it was basically a version of the ritualized European declaration of war, with the resulting legal consequences.

In addition, a more far-reaching identity of interests soon arose between the missionary clergy and the Crown. In the age of incipient monarchical absolutism, the Crown could not remain indifferent to the risk of feudalization of the overseas territories. What is more, it had accepted responsibility to the new vassals and – having regard also to the low population density of Spain – was inevitably interested in the rapid integration of the natives into a Christian state structure based on the European model. On the other hand, it had to treat the *conquistadores* and their justified claim to reward for their military feats with a degree of caution so as not to endanger the cause of further expansion. It therefore tried gradually to curtail the powers of the colonists and to satisfy their demand for reward through all kinds of financial and social favours. In the long term it was helped by the circumstance that, following a successful conquest, disputes always tended to break out among the leading *conquistadores* and also between the leaders and their followers. These disputes generally centred on the distribution of the spoils of war, favours in the award of *encomiendas* or measures which disadvantaged other groups. The kingdom made use of this circumstance to appoint investigating judges with far-reaching powers who generally relieved the leaders of their offices or drastically restricted their authority. In parallel, a state-controlled administrative system was set up with civil servants appointed for limited terms of office and starting from the highest level. First the creation of a central authority in the motherland, the Council of the Indias, was followed by the introduction of royal appeal courts overseas and the creation of the vice-royalties of Mexico and Lima. Finally, provincial administrations were set up and the councils of the cities founded by the Spaniards placed under the control of state officials. With the help of this administrative system, it was possible in the long run to limit the rights of the colonists over the Indians and to reduce the *encomiendas* largely to a source of automatic income. This whole process was accompanied by an increasingly effective policy to protect the Indians. It culminated in the physical separation of the two communities and divided the overseas territories into two *republicas*: the Indian communities which were also administered under Spanish local law and guaranteed the Indians a degree of local self-administration with freedom to choose their local authorities under the supervision of a Spanish civil servant and allowed the integration into Spanish colonial law of all previous Indian traditions that did not oppose Christian moral traditions; on the other hand were the Spanish municipalities which were placed under state control. However, this development took place very slowly and was accompanied by many disputes, some involving military action. The colonists for their part always found ways and means by bypassing the state legislation and defending their own interests, especially as the newly-established civil service made common cause with the colonists in many ways, so as to acquire the same wealth. Laymen did not travel overseas in the service of higher ideals but in the expectation of personal gain. On the other hand, the Crown did not pursue a colonial policy in the modern sense in relation to the new possessions, i.e. with emphasis on achieving the highest possible financial return, as late as the 1980s. The newly-conquered territories, although colonies in the modern sense, were still treated constitutionally as Kingdoms of the Crown of Castile with formally equal rights. Each of their inhabitants, Indians, black Africans and Europeans alike, was able to appeal directly to the King to safeguard his rights. At least in the sixteenth century the policy of the Crown struck a balance between missionary and civilizing interests on the one hand and economic and political goals on the other.

The Caribbean influence in the development of the colonial system

What part was played by the Caribbean in this general context that we have just outlined? What importance attached to the Caribbean at which periods in the Hispano-American colonial system that expanded rapidly in the sixteenth century, while at the same time undergoing political, economic and social changes? A first point to note here is that, from the perspective of royal policy, much the same processes took place in the different regions, albeit at different times: 1) the seizure of land, mostly by bands of *conquistadores* organized on private lines; 2) the phase of colonial rule which, to begin with, developed more or less autonomously at the instigation of the *conquistadores*; 3) the process of disempowerment, first of the leaders of the *conquistador* groups by the appointment of governing bodies designated by the Crown (governors and captains-general and/or viceroys and supreme courts organized on collegiate lines, *Audiencias*), followed by the replacement of the second level of *conquistador* government by the introduction of a state-run provincial and district administration with the simultaneous limitation of the authority of the *conquistadores* to decide on the working and productive activities of the native population, i.e. through regulation of the *repartimiento/encomienda* systems; 4) as a result, the *conquistador* society with its parasitic tendency was obliged to embark upon entrepreneurial economic activity in the areas of agriculture, mining, commerce and trade. Depending on the availability of labour, the pace of this process of a new economic 'valorization' of the individual regions varied, with the concomitant formation of the different types of colonial society referred to earlier.

Before looking at developments in the Caribbean in their chronological sequence and varying patterns against the background of this general model, it will be noted that this part of the world was particularly affected by the further course of Spanish expansion in the Americas. This was because the conquest and colonization of the American continent had stronger feedback effects on the Caribbean island world than can be observed, in the same sustained manner, in any other region of the Spanish colonial empire on the American continent. Nowhere else were internal and external processes so strongly superimposed in the sixteenth century as in the Caribbean, making it practically impossible to determine which of the two had a more decisive impact on internal development.

Let us look first at internal developments. The seizure of the land and the subsequent phases occurred at different points in history, depending on whether the region is regarded as a whole or the West Indian islands – at least the largest of them – considered individually. If we also count the region of the Isthmus of Panama, the Atlantic coast of what is now Colombia, Venezuela and Florida as part of the Caribbean, the first phase, namely that of the Spanish seizure of land, lasted until about the mid-sixteenth century. Significantly, Spain made scarcely any serious endeavours to take effective possession of areas such as Guyana, the Mississippi delta or the smaller West Indian islands and to populate them. Venezuela, Florida and Yucatán were also conquered and colonized at a relatively late stage. Until the waning sixteenth century, the rest of the Caribbean was a kind of Spanish Mediterranean, controlled and progressively opened up from the effectively populated and colonized big West Indian islands. For a long time its ecclesiastical, cultural and economic life was controlled, at least loosely, from Santo Domingo with its Court of Appeal, the *Audiencia*, and its diocese, soon to be elevated to the status of an archbishopric, university and harbour. After the creation of the vice-royalty of New Spain, centring on Mexico in the year 1536, large parts of the region came initially under the political, and then increasingly also under the economic, influence (after the discovery of the big silver deposits in around the year 1550) of the new vice-royalty. With the conquest of Peru in 1532/33 and above all following the establishment of another vice-royalty in Lima after 1542, the Isthmus region soon fell within the sphere of influence of Peru and the role of the big West Indian islands was transformed from the function of a central colonial region into that of an intervening region between the home country and the fast-developing new colonial metropoles. In parallel with this process, the Caribbean gold deposits were depleted and the original Indian population decimated, so that the economic base of this old colonial core region soon disappeared and large parts of the Spanish colonial population migrated to the new centres on the American continent.[1]

The European corsairs, who made increasingly frequent incursions into this region in the second half of the sixteenth century, expedited the process of decline. They not only seriously disturbed the Spanish colonial economy and colonial trade, but also obliged Spain to take costly measures to fortify the major cities which, despite high subsidy payments from Lima and Mexico, still had to be financed in part from the declining resources of the region itself. In addition, this threat compelled Spain to take military action to safeguard its own shipping and commerce with America in the Atlantic sea routes between the Iberian Peninsula and the Canary Islands and within the Caribbean itself. After the 1540s, this led progressively to the introduction of a rigid fleet system under which two commercial fleets sailed each year from the Guadalquivir estuary via the Canary Islands and the small West Indian islands before reaching Santo Domingo. One fleet then sailed to Nombre de Dios and later Portobelo on the Panama Isthmus and on to Cartagena de Indias, while the second navigated through the Gulf of Mexico to Veracruz. Finally, a few individual ships sailed down the coast of Honduras to supply Central America.

In the final third of the century, Havana became the central home port in place of Santo Domingo where the ships gathered again for the return journey via the Bahamas. Up to then, the port cities of Puerto Rico, Haiti and Cuba had been in direct contact with one another and also with Spain. But, in the second half of the sixteenth century there was just one central port, first Santo Domingo and later Havana, which remained in direct contact with Europe and the new colonial metropolises. The supply of European goods to the other parts of the region suffered greatly from this system, especially as the region's gold deposits had been worked out since the 1540s and financial resources were tight. Considering that Spanish-American commerce primarily involved items of daily consumption, means of production (cattle, tools, metal goods, etc.) and even basic foodstuffs, which were delivered to America until the 1560s – after which high-quality luxury goods for the new colonial élites came to predominate – it is clear that the Caribbean was bound to quickly lose its importance in the Hispano-American empire as resources were no longer sufficient for the restructuring of its economy. The significance of the region was quickly reduced to its strategic role and it became a burden on the new colonial metropolises of Peru and Mexico. These countries, in the interests of their maritime routes to Europe, paid financial subsidies to the Spanish settlements in the region – even supplying them in some cases with goods for daily consumption. The former central region of the rising Spanish colonial empire thus became a forecourt of the Spanish colonial metropolises of the American continent in which it was ultimately easy for other European colonial powers to gain a foothold since Spain now attached priority to the development and protection of the more densely-populated and economically richer continental areas. In the Caribbean, Spain was obliged to confine itself to the protection of its shipping routes at a time when even its European empire was increasingly threatened by France and the Protestant powers in the age of Philip II.[2]

This development was brought about in large measure by the demographic development of the region. We have already called attention to the dramatic decline of the indigenous population, which has been considered in more detail elsewhere in this volume. In addition, the level of civilization of the indigenous inhabitants of the Caribbean was much less receptive to the economic techniques and social forms of the Spanish immigrants than the indigenous population of the high cultures of Meso-America and the Andean zone. A majority of the Spanish immigrants came from Andalusia and Extremadura where large parts of the population were still tied in to a traditional system of seizing booty. It will be recalled that the conquest of the last Moorish kingdom on Spanish soil was the outcome of just such an *entrada*. The mechanisms of these incursions were, of course, reflected in the Spanish seizure of lands in America. It is true that more modern intensive, market-oriented agriculture with a high degree of commercialization did also exist in Western Andalusia, but the farmers concerned were mostly members of the higher nobility, debarred by the Crown from participation in the expansion to the Americas. The part of the Andalusian population involved in modern capital-intensive trade with far-flung countries was concentrated in the small triangle of Cadiz, Seville and Huelva. Essentially, it provided the entrepreneurs and crews for the voyages of maritime discovery with commercial objectives which were highly mobile, and focused on the most economically-promising regions in the framework of Spanish expansion in America. The more economically dynamic group of immigrants originating from the commercially active central and northern parts of Castile represented a minority of the new Spanish arrivals. The Basques, Galicians and Navarrese did not follow until the end of the sixteenth century when the economy of Castile lapsed into crisis because of the price revolution and the people emigrated in larger numbers. Between 1520 and 1539 the numbers of Spanish migrants to the big West Indian islands declined. P. Boyd-Bowman calculated 1372 immigrants to Santo Domingo, representing 11 per cent of the total migratory movement, 195 to Cuba equivalent to 1.6 per cent and 108 to Puerto Rico or 0.9 per cent of the total. These figures declined still further between 1540 and 1559: Santo Domingo 389 (4.4 per cent), Cuba 32 (0.3 per cent) and Puerto Rico 51 (0.5 per cent).[3] However unreliable these sources may be on this issue, these percentages do probably give a dependable reflection of the general trend.

Following the Treaty of Tordesillas with Portugal, Spain had no direct access to black Africa so that it had few opportunities to make good the losses of the indigenous population by importing black African slaves. The progress of Spanish expansion, the decline of the indigenous West Indian population, the depletion of the precious metal reserves, the rapidly falling numbers of Spanish migrants and the difficulty of obtaining supplies of African slaves resulted in a self-reinforcing downward spiral of development for the region as a whole. This began in 1520–1 on Haiti as the gold deposits were worked out. The conquest of Mexico was just beginning. Together with that of Peru, it led to the departure of the immigrants. When the Cuban precious metal deposits were worked out in the 1540s, the migratory movement gathered pace. The cycles by which the chronological history of the Caribbean economy is generally characterized (a procedure that seems methodologically dubious from our modern perspective as it is an oversimplification of the complex human and social development of this region) document this decline: the cycle of gold, the cycle of sugar and, less frequently cited although no less relevant, a cycle of domination of extensive cattle farming and subsistence farming.

Let us turn now in more detail to the phases of development on the big West Indian islands and in particular to the political developments. Recent research clearly shows that an historical reappraisal is made necessary by a series of factors: the many political conflicts between Columbus and some of the settlers; the dismissal of Columbus himself and developments after

Columbus's deposition until the arrival of the new governor, Ovando, followed by the reinstatement of the Columbus dynasty with the appointment of Columbus's own son, Diego Colón, to the post of governor and his conflict with King Ferdinand; the Advent sermon of the Dominican father Montesinos leading to the enactment of the Laws of Burgos and the concept of the *Requerimiento*, together with the dispatch of an examining judge after 1516 and the formation of a commission of Hieronymite monks; last but not least, the convening of an assembly of municipal representatives on Hispaniola/Haiti.[4] We have the impression that these problems ultimately entailed a conflict between three different models of colonization or society which were defended by different interest groups. As is well known, Columbus himself subscribed to a concept of trade colonization of the type developed by the Italian city-states in the Eastern Mediterranean and successfully practised by the Portuguese in the Atlantic since the days of Henry the Navigator. This model of colonization, which sought commercial profit and was organized as a monopolistic venture between the partners, i.e. the Catholic Kings and Columbus, worked with paid colonists and failed because of the high costs and the inability of the indigenous population to make available sufficient gold or other goods for trading to cover the expenditure incurred. That situation led to a rebellion of some of the colonists who wanted to exert direct pressure on the natives because of their experience of the *Reconquista* in order to achieve their ends.

When the examining judge, Bobadilla, arrested Columbus and sent him back to Castile, many of the paid settlers also returned to Spain. The next two years and the conduct of the remaining 300 or so Spaniards generally receive little attention from historiographers, but they are essential to an understanding of subsequent developments – especially if we bear in mind what Bartolomé de Las Casas had to say about this short phase.[5] Many of the Spaniards spread out over the islands and went on to live among the natives, adapting in many respects to their customs and habits. As a grotesque derivation of the seigneurial customs of their homeland, they caused themselves to be treated as 'lords' by the natives. They set up a Spanish-inspired noble 'court' staffed by Indians, had themselves carried around in hammocks wearing rags or half-naked and held orgies with the natives. They married the daughters of the Indian *caciques* and neglected their religious obligations or even profaned the Christian religion. As these Spaniards also adopted the language of their new environment, from the standpoint of the Crown there was not just the threat of a process of hybridization but also that of complete assimilation of the Europeans by the natives. The expedition by which the new governor, *comendador* Ovando, a member of a Castilian knightly order, was sent to Haiti in 1502 and the instructions given to him, clearly show that the Crown had, in the light of this experience, reached the conviction that the model of repopulation of the territories conquered from the Moors must be followed on the island. In putting together the Ovando expedition of around 1500 men, the Crown was also at pains to send members of the higher social strata of Castile noblemen and priests to Haiti. At the same time, orders were given to found cities in which the Spanish colonists were required to live. Instructions were also given to concentrate the indigenous population in villages near the Spanish cities where they could pursue their farming activities and provide labour for the colonists on a regulated scale. The aim was to achieve an agrarian colonization based on the experience of the *Reconquista* with the express stipulation that the Castilians, who were required by reason of their status in Europe to earn their own living through work, must do so also in America. At the same time, an attempt was made to secure by legal provisions the elevated status of the Indian *caciques*. In the light of subsequent events, it must be concluded that these dispositions were attributable to the influence of Queen Isabella, as King Ferdinand later pursued a different policy when he became Regent. The guidelines given to Ovando for his activity in Haiti therefore clearly show the intention to create a mirror image of the Spanish society on Hispaniola, while the measures ordered for the foundation of cities etc. were designed to create social discipline of the colonists and integrate the indigenous population into the *Reconquista* society on Spanish lines.[6] The fact that, for the last time in the history of Spanish expansion, an *Encomendero* of a Spanish knightly order was appointed to an elevated political position lends credence to this interpretation. In parallel, the Crown made representations to the Pope to achieve recognition of its patronage over the newly-founded ecclesiastical organization in America. In the first instance it only obtained control over the anticipated income of the churches in return for pre-financing of the development costs and a right to propose appointments of the bishops to the new dioceses. This too, confirms the fact that Castile now wanted to pursue in America the concept of a settlement colonization based on the model of the *Reconquista* tradition. Isabella's death in 1504, the enforced withdrawal of King Ferdinand from Castile and the outbreak of a gold rush on Hispaniola prevented the implementation of this policy.[7]

Following the death of Philip of Burgundy, who had ruled Castile because of the inability of his wife, Queen Johanna, to govern in the year 1506, King Ferdinand took over the regency again. He appointed Diego Colón, who had in the meantime married into the high Andalusian nobility, governor of Santo Domingo. He developed the city in the seigneurial style of Andulasian towns[8] and, on the instructions of the Crown, enacted a *repartimiento* of the indigenous Indian population which was intended to regulate the work to be provided by them.[9] The indigenous population of the island was already in a state of rapid decline due to the impact of imported epidemics, compulsory labour in the gold washing plants and the extensive collapse of traditional Indian agriculture with the resulting food shortages. The enslavement of the island population was admittedly prohibited, but this did not mean very much as the collapse of the traditional order and forced labour through the *repartimiento* system (the theoretically regulated and paid provision of work for limited periods) had so debilitated the population that the European sicknesses caused particularly large numbers of victims among a population that had already been weakened. Slavery of the Caribs, who were accused of cannibalism, was still permitted on the small West Indian islands. The shortage of labour on Haiti had already resulted in slavery practically throughout the region, based on the cursory assertion that these people were 'mere cannibals'. These slaves were brought to Haiti to work.

In the enforcement of the *repartimiento*, Diego Colón now made an interesting distinction and became embroiled in violent controversies with King Ferdinand. He allocated the indigenous population of Hispaniola exclusively to agricultural work in the vicinity of the settlements and ordered slaves taken on the other islands and along the continental coast in the Caribbean to be used in the gold washing plants. The new governor was visibly attempting to enforce the concept of colonization ordered by Queen Isabella in 1502, which consisted of agrarian settlement with the involvement of the indigenous population. This system was by then only being practised to a limited degree because of the gold rush. Under the influence of Portuguese successes in Asia, King Ferdinand had in the meantime, however, made sustained endeavours to find a western passage through the Caribbean island world to Asia. He needed gold or capital to finance the necessary ventures. As an Aragonese who had travelled to his kingdom of Naples following his enforced departure from Castile (Naples had increasingly became the centre of his influence since the days of his uncle, King Alfonso the Magnanimous), he was in any case more closely bound up with the modern Mediterranean developments, especially in Italy, than his wife Isabella who was far closer to the Castilian tradition of the *Reconquista*. In the meantime, Venice had also failed in its endeavour to prevent the Portuguese advance into the Indian Ocean with the help of the Egyptian Mamelukes. Ferdinand may therefore have hoped to be able to mobilize Italian commercial capital for the continuation of the conquest with the Portuguese on the western sea route to Asia so as to achieve still more privileged access to the wealth of Asia. Be that as it may, Ferdinand strongly disapproved of Diego Colón's policies and gave orders that the exploitation of gold deposits must on no account be neglected. He was clearly interested primarily in the economic benefits of the island, as he was far more inclined to favour the Italian commercial capitalism as a socioeconomic model for the future than Isabella had done when she laid out her instructions for colonization of the island in the year 1502.

The situation began to become increasingly acute on the island. In 1509 Dominican monks arrived as missionaries. They were clearly influenced by the 'observant' current within the order which had already caused religious and social unrest in Italy, for example with Savonarola in Florence, and soon they would intervene in the political discussions. Diego Colón, who already had put forward the legal proceedings against the Crown regarding the extent of his father's rights under the capitulation of 1492, became the object of strong criticism. He decided to create a *fait accompli* and accordingly prepared to conquer Cuba and Puerto Rico, but since King Ferdinand had made generous donations to many of his courtiers from the island income, political schemes and personal interests complicated the situation and increased the pressure on Diego Colón and his supporters.

In the year 1511 decisive steps were taken on three different fronts. Diego Colón began the conquest of Cuba and Puerto Rico, while King Ferdinand set up an *Audiencia* in Santo Domingo, i.e. a court of appeal whose members were also to have governmental functions in order to consolidate authority. Finally, the Dominican father, Montesinos, gave his famous Advent sermon in which he described the conduct of the colonists against the indigenous inhabitants as unjust and unjustifiable in law and threatened them with excommunication – an essentially religious measure which did, however, have far-reaching civilian consequences. In the light of the previous history and spiritual background of the Dominican monks, it may be suspected that Montesinos' criticism was not directed against all the colonialists, but essentially against the proponents of King Ferdinand and ultimately against King Ferdinand himself and his 'Italian model' of commercial exploitation of the island. However, this aspect would require further study. The uproar caused by the sermon was such that the Dominicans took the independent decision to send Montesinos back to the Court. Ferdinand was sufficiently irritated to order Montesinos to appear at Court where he managed to persuade the King and his advisers to take action.

As noted in Chapter 2, the Crown reacted to Montesinos' 1511 sermon with two major legal innovations. In the Laws of Burgos dating from 1512, it laid down stringent regulations governing the co-existence of Spaniards and Indians. It declared the indigenous people living under Spanish rule to be free vassals of the Crown. However, they were expected to live in the closest possible community with the Europeans to enhance the spread of Christianity and Europeanization. With that end in view, they were to live in villages near the European settlements and be governed by a priest and a lay official who would encourage them to adopt a Christian way of life, regular work and orderly life in society. The hours and forms of work were regulated in detail, as was religious life. In addition, all the leaders of campaigns of conquest were instructed to cause the *Requerimiento* to be proclaimed by interpreters to the Indians before opening hostilities. This text explained to the natives that the Pope had transferred these territories to the Kings to enable them to disseminate the Christian faith here. That message was followed by a brief explanation of the content of the faith and a reference to the role of the Pope as Christ's representative on earth and an appeal to conversion and recognition of the king in return for the assurance of benevolent treatment. Only if the Indians rejected this offer was warfare to be opened. This document, and its significance, has been the subject of great controversy. But commentators have tended to overlook the fact that it was basically a version of the ritualized European declaration of war, with the resulting legal consequences.

The Laws of Burgos not only signified a return to the policy set in motion by Queen Isabella in 1502, but also their elevation into a kind of basic law governing the further policy of colonization in America. On the other hand, they still left sufficient latitude for politics. It was now clear that the treatment of the American indigenous population and the institutions of the *repartimiento* or the *encomienda,* as it was later known in the region, in which a more highly-developed native population enabled tributes to be demanded in the shape of Indian products to sustain the *conquistador* society, would be the central points of contention over Spanish colonization policy. The fact that the Laws of Burgos were a concession to some of the colonists on Hispaniola is reflected in the development on the Isthmus of Panama in those years. Here Vasco Nuñez de Balboa had not only discovered the Pacific Ocean, so arousing new hopes on the part of the King of finding a western sea route to Asia, but also pursued a policy similar to that of Diego Colón towards the native population which aimed to achieve a more harmonious co-existence between the Spaniards and the Indians.

As a result of the crisis sparked off by Montesinos' sermon, an expedition was sent out to the Isthmus under the command of Pedrarias Dávila. However, the Crown held this expedition back until the crisis was settled and only allowed it to set out when the Laws of Burgos had been defined in 1512 and enacted – together with the text of the *Requerimiento* citing the papal bull of 1493 and the missionary intent referred to therein as justification for the Spanish advance into America. All this gave satisfaction at least to the Spaniards directly concerned. On the strength of the two texts, Pedrarias was now to take over governmental authority on the Isthmus. Not only did he put an end to the Indian policy of Balboa, he even ordered Balboa himself to be sentenced to death and executed, and began an unrepentant exploitation of the native population. He also applied the new texts, in particular the *Requerimiento,* in a particularly cynical manner which was later sharply criticized by Las Casas; it was almost as though he wanted to prove that the previous political line of King Ferdinand still remained valid.

Diego Colón, who had conquered Cuba and Puerto Rico with his followers, was relieved of his office in 1515 by King Ferdinand. Bartolomé de Las Casas, who must have been on Hispaniola since 1502, where he was later consecrated a lay priest, took part in the conquest of Cuba and became the proprietor of an *encomienda*. However in 1514 he gave up that *encomienda* after a Dominican had refused him absolution in the confessional as he was making Indians work for him. He then began his energetic campaign for the rights of the American Indians.

The economic crisis in Haiti also broke out in 1514, after clear signs of the exhaustion of the gold reserves had become public knowledge, and the constant decline of the native population made the labour shortage increasingly acute. Already at this time the view was taken that the economic future of the island could only be ensured by the widespread development of sugar cane cultivation and the introduction of black African slaves. That opinion was ultimately reminiscent of the Italian-Portuguese model of colonization of the Atlantic islands uninhabited before the Portuguese found them.

A detailed study of the political controversies cannot be discussed here, but developments reached a climax after the death of King Ferdinand in 1515 under the regency of Cardinal Jimenez de Cisneros. The latter began to make a thorough study of the prevailing circumstances, not least on the basis of the ideas of Montesinos and Las Casas who had travelled to the Court. He dismissed persons from the close circle of King Ferdinand, who had previously administered American affairs, and sent an examining judge to Santo Domingo who was to review the conduct of the *Audiencia* and the other authorities. Last but not least, he appointed a committee of three monks of the Hieronymite order to clarify the question as to whether Indians could live independently on the island while nevertheless becoming Christians. In the context of this revision of colonial policy, in 1518, at much the same time as the new King Charles – later to become Emperor Charles V – had reached Spain and the Assembly of the Cortes was convened in Valladolid, an assembly of the representatives of the different cities was also summoned on Santo Domingo. At this assembly two parties are to be identified. They are described in older literature as the supporters of Diego Colón and the followers of King Ferdinand and his policy.[10] In fact, however, the political demands put forward by them show that they were the partisans of two different models of colonization if their political demands are classified according to the two models: i.e. the Spanish Andalusian *Reconquista* model and the Italian commercial model. The former called for a review of the allocation of Indians: Indian labour was only to be assigned to settlers living on the island. Smaller numbers of Indians were to be allocated and not sent to the mines or, if there was no other solution, only in the lowest possible numbers. The Indians were to be allowed to eat meat on fast days if there was no other food available and the parish buildings in the Indian villages were to be occupied. This political group also called for the free immigration of all Spaniards and foreigners to be permitted, with the exception of the Genoese, Jews, Moors and sentenced delinquents. In addition, all the bishops were to reside in their diocese and the church tithes used to build cathedrals and churches. The capital city of the island was to be transferred to Concepción de la Vega in the interior and Diego Colón allowed to appoint a life governor of the whole island. A voting right was also sought in the Castilian Cortes. This grouping further demanded a strengthening of the authority of the municipal administrations, the abolition of lifetime membership of the town councils and the introduction instead of an election system for all urban offices, together with tax abatements and an extension of the highway network.

The other party placed much greater emphasis on commercial privileges, freedom of trade and shipping, the promotion of sugar cane cultivation by importing the necessary seed stock and means of production and the importation of slaves, etc. In addition, it called for the retention of the existing system of government by a governor to be reappointed regularly by the King and by the *Audiencia*. This group also wanted to promote settlements, but insisted more strongly on the acquisition of Indian slaves from neighbouring islands and the exploitation of natural resources. These two groups did not, in the final analysis, simply represent different models of colonization for America, but different economic and social models of the kind which had already become controversial in Castile and intervened in the revolt of the *Comunidades* in Castile when King Charles left for Germany in 1520/21 to accept elevation to the dignity of Emperor. Many of the demands of the first group were reflected in a much more radical form in the claims of the Castilian rebellion. Regrettably, historical research has as yet hardly dealt with the question of the extent to which the conflicts in America were related to the conflicts in Spain itself in those years.[11]

When King Charles took up his reign over Spain in 1518, his advisers from Flanders included two central figures with different attitudes to these questions. The first, his chancellor Jean le Sauvage, had been greatly influenced by the humanistic thinking of Erasmus of Rotterdam and was close to the line of Cardinal Cisneros, another strongly humanist if not Erasmic personality in Spain. Then there was his own educator and adviser, Chièvres, who was far more interested in economic objectives. When the Hieronymite monks from Santo Domingo finally proposed that the *repartimiento* policy was necessary in relation to the indigenous population and that only the expansion of sugar cane cultivation and the importation of black African slaves could create a sound economic basis for the island, it was Chièvres who received from King Charles the first *asiento* or permit to import African slaves to Haiti. It would seem that King Ferdinand's political line was also adopted by his successor.

However, the Court gave no clear answer to the open questions. King Charles left Spain hastily, leaving the country in a state of open rebellion: the revolt of the *Comunidades* spread quickly in Castile while the 'Germanias' rose up in Valencia. This movement, like the revolt in Castile, was led by the modern urban middle classes involved in the craft trades and the new intellectual professions together with parts of the begging orders of monks of the 'observant' line. The classes that were interested in foreign trade, and the high nobility, tended to side with the Crown, as did large parts of the traditional rural population which supported the rural nobility. In parallel, the expedition of Hernán Cortés, which was to conquer Mexico by 1521, was being put together in 1519 in Cuba under Governor Velázquez appointed by Diego Colón. This venture, like some of its predecessors, was intended firstly as a barter expedition which set out to pursue strictly commercial goals on the Mexican coast. The skill of its leader led, through the foundation of the city of Veracruz, the appointment of a town council and the designation by the latter of Cortés himself to the post of Governor and Captain General, to an act of open rebellion against Velázquez and the conquest of the first Indian high culture on the American continent. Here Cortés soon recognized that under these conditions the attainment of a model of colonization in the Spanish *Reconquista* tradition subscribed to by Queen Isabella and Diego Colón would be far easier than in the West Indies. The political measures taken by Cortés after the capital of the Aztec kingdom had fallen, clearly reflected his interest to implement this seigneurial model in practice. Francisco Pizarro, who sought extensive advice from Cortés in Spain, tried the same endeavour a little later in Peru. It was to take until well into the reign of Philip II for the Crown to win the definitive political battle against this seigneurial model of colonization.

However, for the Caribbean area, this trend meant that the conflicts fought out there were brought to a surprising conclusion. The proponents of Queen Isabella's concept of settlement colonization on the Spanish model found an opportunity to achieve this on the continent under far more favourable conditions, so that many of its advocates – and not just them – moved to the continent. As a result, the plantation economy was the only remaining commercial option for the West Indian islands. That option had already been taken up by King Ferdinand. Both Haiti and Cuba now ceased to play a significant role in the controversy over the Spanish policy of colonization and economic change languished because of lack of capital and working forces. The debate was now between Mexico and Peru on the one hand and the Court on the other. All the other territories became ancillary venues, although it took them a long time to come to terms with that minor role.

In parallel with these developments, from 1519–22, Fernâo de Magalhaes or Magellan embarked upon the voyage around the world which had been started on the order of the Castilian King who was still pursuing the search for the western sea-route to Asia and the access to the spice trade. Thus, from this perspective too the geographical and geopolitical circumstances became clearer. The Caribbean was now definitely relegated to the geographical status of a forecourt of the American continent – especially after attempts had been made from New Spain/Mexico since 1527 to reach the spice islands by the Pacific route. Ultimately, in 1529, under the Treaty of Zaragoza, Portugal and Spain drew a similar dividing line between their mutual spheres of influence in the East as they had in the Atlantic by virtue of the Treaty of Tordesillas of 1494. Consequently, the Philippines fell to Castile but the spice islands, i.e. the Indonesian island archipelago, fell to Portugal. Charles V, having meanwhile married a Portuguese princess, resigned himself to a long-running rivalry with Portugal, although preferring an alliance with Portugal probably because of the increasing conflicts with France and the reformation-movement spreading all over Europe.

As the precursors of developments to come, foreign corsairs made their first appearance in the Caribbean in 1522. In this context, it is symptomatic that the Crown transferred the privilege of colonization of Venezuela in 1528 to the Augsburg trading house of the Welsers. Although this may have been the outcome of commitments given by Charles V to this venture, the privilege was nevertheless an indication that the Court clearly had different priorities in America than to concern itself directly with the colonization of a region which had up to then proved profitable, albeit for a short period.

The remaining phases of political development can be readily summarized. In 1536 the legal proceedings between the Crown and the heirs of Columbus ended in a compromise: the heirs waived all their claims and in return were elevated to the Dukedom of Veragua and the Marquisate of Jamaica with rule over the corresponding region of the Isthmus of Panama and the islands. In this way, Cuba and Puerto Rico reverted directly to the Crown. In the same year Charles V established the vice-royalty of New Spain in Mexico to which the Caribbean was subjected, with the exception of the Isthmus region. In 1538 the University of Santo Domingo was established at the request of the city. In 1546 Santo Domingo was elevated to the status of an archbishopric to which the dioceses of distant areas such as Honduras, Florida and Venezuela were subordinated. In other words, the main Caribbean territories not only constituted a uniform jurisdiction under the *Audiencia* of Santo Domingo, but also a single ecclesiastical province and at least the embryo of an intellectual centre with the University of Santo Domingo. In 1555 the French freebooter, Jacques de Sores, plundered Havana, one of the major cities of the region, for the first time and in 1563 the English sea falcons began their raids in the Caribbean. As a result, the Spanish Crown definitively set up the fleet system, to which we referred previously, in 1564. In 1567 the city of Caracas was founded, heralding the slow consolidation of the Spanish position on the north coast of South America, after Pedro Menéndez de Avilés had put down the French Huguenot revolt in Florida and founded Fort San Augustin two years before. Both these measures helped to secure the flanks of the Spanish Caribbean and this process continued in 1574 with the foundation of Maracaibo. In parallel, fortress construction measures began on a grand scale in the main Spanish harbour towns of the Caribbean. The policy of settlement was now progressively replaced by protective military measures, so clearly showing that Spain, in view of its growing European and Mediterranean involvement, was confining its ambitions to the defence of its principal strategic positions in the Caribbean. At the same time, this reflected the recognition by the Crown of the decline of the region and, to a certain extent, acceptance of the fact that the decline was inevitable.[12]

Finally the question arises as to whether the development defined in broad outline in the sixteenth century in the Spanish Caribbean was no more than a protracted conjunctural cycle, or whether it in fact reflected longer term structural and/or mental attitudes in a historically conceived approach to the issues. There is good reason to suppose that the controversy over the future of the islands and the desired model of society which was interrupted in 1518 and never restarted because of subsequent developments, may in many respects have had sustained consequences. On the continent itself, this debate resulted in the inception of a true cultural identity which became clearly perceptible in the seventeenth century and soon culminated in the assertion of an American identity against the Spanish homeland. On the other hand, the Spanish Caribbean islands were increasingly tending to look outwards as they became isolated; Haiti even lost some of its Spanish character. The numerically small élites now looked entirely towards remote Europe and co-operated with practically anyone who came from there to engage in commerce or seek escape from adverse weather conditions in the Caribbean.

At the beginning of the nineteenth century this extrovert attitude and dedication to Europe was detected by such an acute observer as Alexander von Humboldt who commented in detail on it in his 'Political essay on the island of Cuba'. It is therefore hardly surprising that, in the nineteenth century, people in the Spanish-speaking areas of the West Indies tended to discuss whether they should become part of the USA or stay with Spain rather than envisaging their own independence. In Puerto Rico this problem remains unsolved to this day. The phenomenon of Fidel Castro in Cuba must surely also be seen against this background.

NOTES

1   On the above synthesis, see my studies: Horst Pietschmann, *El Estado y su evolución al principio de la colonización española de América*, (México, 1989), in which the earlier historiography is mentioned and discussed in detail; cf. also *idem*, 'La Conquista de América: un bosquejo histórico', in Karl Kohut with Jürgen Bär, Ernesto Garzón Valdés, Sabine Horl Groenewald and Horst Pietschmann (eds) *De conquistadores y conquistados. Realidad, justificación, representación*, (Frankfurt/M., 1992), pp. 11–28; *idem*, 'La resistencia española al imperio: Las Indias en los años iniciales del reinado de Carlos V', in Universidad Complutense de Madrid (ed.) *Estudios de Historia del Derecho Europeo. Homenaje al Prof. G. Martinez Diez*, 2 Vols, (Madrid, 1994), Vol. 2, pp. 13–30; *idem*, 'La evangelización y la política de poblamiento y urbanización en HispanoAmérica', in Pontificia Commissio pro América Latina (ed.) *Historia de la evangelización de América. Trayectoria, identidad y esperanza de un Continente*, Simposio Internacional, Ciudad del Vaticano, 11–14 de mayo de 1992, actas, (Vatican City, 1992), pp. 489–510; *idem*, Walther L. Bernecker, Raymond Th. Buve, John R. Fisher, Horst Pietschmann and Hans Werner Tobler (eds) *Mittel-, Südamerika und die Karibik bis 1760-Handbuch der Geschichte Lateinamerikas*, Vol. I, (Stuttgart, 1994).

2   Cf. Antonio García-Baquero González, *La Carrera de Indias: Suma de la contratación y océano de negocios*, (Sevilla, 1992); Pierre Chaunu, *L'Expansion européenne du XIIIème au XVème siècle*, Nouvelle Clio, 26, (Paris, 1969); *idem*, Pierre Chaunu, *Conquête et exploitation des Nouveaux Mondes*, Nouvelle Clio, 26bis, (Paris, 1969); José Luis Martínez, *El mundo privado de los emigrantes a Indias*, (México, 1992); Pablo E. Pérez-Mallaina, *Los hombres del océano. Vida cotidiana de los tripulantes de las flotas de Indias. Siglo XVI*, (Sevilla, 1992); Carmen Bernand and Serge Gruzinski, *Histoire du Nouveau Monde. Vol. I: De la découverte à la conquête, une expérience européenne, 1492–1550*, (Paris, 1991); Jacques Heers, *La ruée vers l'Amérique. Le mirage et les fièvres*, (Bruxelles, 1992); David A. Brading, *The First America. The Spanish Monarchy, Creole Patriots, and the Liberal State, 1492–1867*, (Cambridge, New York, 1991); Renate Pieper, *Die Vermittlung einer neuen Welt. Amerika im Nachrichtennetz des habsburgischen Imperiums (1493–1598)*, (Mainz, 1997) (in print); Pieter Emmer and Femme Gaastra (eds) *The Organization of Interoceanic Trade in European Expansion, 1450–1800*; A.J.R. Russel Wood, *An Expanding World. The European Impact on world History, 1450–1800, Vol. 13*, (Aldershot, 1996); Susan Socolow (ed.) *The Atlantic Staple Trade: Commerce and Politics*; A.J.R. Russel Wood (ed.) *An expanding World. The European Impact on world History, 1450–1800, Vol. 9*, (Aldershot, 1996).

3   Cf. Peter Boyd-Bowman, *Patterns of Spanish Emigration to the New World (1493–1580), Special Studies*, Council on International Studies, State University of New York (Buffalo, 1973); *idem, Indice Geobiográfico de más de 56 Mil Pobladores de la América Hispánica*, 5 Vols. (Mexico, 1985); Magnus Mörner, *Evolución demográfica de Hispano-América durante el periodo colonial*, Institute

of Latin American Studies, Stockholm, Research Paper Series, No. 14, (Stockholm, 1979); Ida Altman and James Horn (eds) *To make America: European emigration in the early modern period*, (Berkeley, 1991); Sherburne F. Cook and Woodrow Borah, *Essays in population history: México and the Caribbean*, 3 Vols., (Berkeley 1971–9); Bernard Grunberg, *L'Univers des conquistadores. Les hommes et leur conquête dans le Mexique du XVIème siècle*, (Paris, 1993); Enrique Otte, *Cartas privadas de migrantes a Indias, 1540–1616*, (Sevilla, 1988); Götz Simmer, *Die deutsche Auswanderung nach Mittel- und Südamerika im 16. und frühen 17. Jahrhundert. Kleine Beiträge zur europäischen Überseegeschichte*, Heft 23, (Bamberg, 1993).

4   Cf. José Maria Pérez Collado, *Las Indias en el pensamiento político de Fernando el Católico*, (Borja, 1992); Luis Arranz Marques, *Don Diego Colón, Almirante, Virrey y Gobernador de las Indias*, Tomo 1, (Madrid, 1982); *idem, Repartimientos y Encomiendas en la Isla Española (El Repartimiento de Alburquerque de 1514)*, (Madrid, 1991); Frank Moya Pons, *Después de Colón. Trabajo, sociedad y política en la economía del oro*, (Madrid, 1986); Manuel Giménez Fernández, *Bartolomé de Las Casas*, 2 Vols., (Sevilla, 1958–60); *idem*, 'Las Cortés de la Española de 1518', in *Anales de la Universidad Hispalense*, Vol. XV, No. 2 (1954), pp. 47ff; Antonio Muro Orejón, with Florentino Perez-Embid, José Antonio Calderón Quijano, Francisco Morales Padrón and Tomás Marin Martínez (eds) *Pleitos Colombinos, Vols. 1–4 and 8* (Sevilla, 1964–89) (no further volumes published yet); Consuelo Varela, *Colón y los florentinos* (Madrid, 1988); Manuel Ballesteros Gaibrois and Roberto Ferrand Pérez, *Luis de Santángel y su entorno. Cuadernos Colombinos*, 20, (Valladolid, 1996); Luis Weckmann, *La herencia medieval de México*, 2 Vol. (Mexico, 1984); Ovidio García Regeiro, *Oro y población (La producción aurífera cubana: 1518–1542)*, (Madrid, 1994); Demetrio Ramos, *Hernan Cortés. Mentalidad y propósitos*, (Madrid, 1992); Claudio Esteva Fabrega, *La Corona española y el Indio americano*, 2 Vol., (Madrid, 1989); Georges Baudot, *La Corona y la fundación de los Reinos Americanos* (Madrid, 1992); Johannes Meier, *Die Anfänge der Kirche auf den Karibischen Inseln. Neue Zeitschrift für Missionswissenschaft*, Suplementa, Vol. XXXVIII, (Immensee, Schweiz, 1991); Paulino Castañeda Delgado, *La teocracia pontifical en las controversias sobre el Nuevo Mundo*, 2 ed., (México, 1996); José García Oro, *El Cardenal Cisneros. Vida y empresas*, 2 Vols. (Madrid, 1992); Pedro Borges, *Misión y civilización*, (Madrid, 1986); Joseph Pérez, *Isabelle et Ferdinand. Rois catholiques d'Espagne*, (Paris, 1988); Federico Chabod, *Carlos V y su imperio*, (México, 1992); on Las Casas, cf. Paulino Castañeda Delgado (ed.) *Fray Bartolomé de Las Casas. Obras Completas*, 14 Vols., (Madrid, 1989) ff.; also Isacio Pérez Fernández, O.P. *Inventario documentado de los escritos de Fray Bartolomé de Las Casas*, (Bayamon, Puerto Rico, 1981); *idem, Cronología documentada de los viajes, estancias y actuaciones de Fray Bartolomé de Las Casas*, (Bayamon, Puerto Rico, 1984). These two works, each comprising around 1000 pages are fundamental, because of the many chronological and source-related problems which the long activity of Las Casas poses for the historian, not only for an understanding of his personal character and action, but also to the entire early history of the Caribbean region.

5   Cf. Bartolomé de Las Casas, *Historia de las Indias, libro II, capítulo I. Edición de Agustín Millares Carlo y estudio preliminar de Lewis Hanke*, 2 Vols (Mexico-Buenos Aires, 1951), Vol. 2, pp. 202ff. On the relation between Italy and the

events in Spain and America in those days, see also the important work by Charles Verlinden, *Précédents médiévaux de la colonie en Amérique*, (México, 1954); *idem, Les origines de la civilisation atlantique. De la renaissance à l'âge des lumières*, (Neufchâtel-Paris, 1962); Nelson H. Minnich, *The Fifth Lateran Council (1512–17). Studies on its Membership, Diplomacy and Proposals for Reform*, (Aldershot, 1993); John W. O'Malley, *Rome and the Renaissance Studies in Culture and Religion*, (London, 1981).

6   Cf. also legislation in Richard Konetzke (ed.) *Colección de documentos para la historia de la formación social de Hispanoamérica 1493–1810*, 3 Vols., (Madrid, 1953–63), Vol. 1, pp. 9ff.

7   On political developments in Spain and America between 1504 and 1507/8, cf. Manuel Giménez Fernández, *Bartolomé de Las Casas*, cit. Note No. 4, in particular Vol. 1.

8   Cf. also Erwin Walter Palm, *Los monumentos arquitectónicos de la Española*, (Santo Domingo, 1984).

9   See Luis Arranz Marques, *Repartimientos*, cit. Note 4. On the problem of cannibalism, see a recent publication by Annerose Menninger, *Die macht der Augenzeugen. Neue Welt und Kannibalen-Mythos, 1492–1600*, (Stuttgart, 1995).

10   On the events of 1511 ff, cf. Manuel Giménez Fernández, *Bartolomé de Las Casas*, cit. Note 4; also Ernesto Schäfer, *El Consejo Real y Supremo de las Indias. Su historia, organización y labor administrativa hasta la terminación de la Casa de Austria*, 2 Vols., (Sevilla, 1935–47); Alberto de la Hera, *Iglesia y Corona en la América Española*, (Madrid, 1992); Josep-Ignasi Saranyana (Director), Carmen José Alej-Grau, Luis Martínez-Ferrer, Ana de Zaballa and Maria Luisa Antonaya, *Historia de la Teología LatinoAméricana. Primera parte: siglos XVI y XVII*, (Pamplona, 1996); Manuel Giménez Fernández, *El plan Cisneros-Las Casas para la reforma de Indias*, (Sevilla, 1953); Elisa Luque Alcaide and Josep-Ignasi Saranyana, *La Iglesia Católica y América*, (Madrid, 1992); Francisco Morales Padrón, *Teoría y leyes de la Conquista*, (Madrid, 1979); Annie Lemistre, 'Les origines du "Requerimiento"', in *Mélanges de la Casa de Velazquez*, Vol. VI, (Madrid, 1970), pp. 161–209; Silvio Zavala, *Las instituciones jurídicas en la conquista de América*. 2nd edition, revised (Mexico, 1971); Demetrio Ramos, *Audacia, negocios y política en los viajes españoles de descubrimiento y rescate*, (Valladolid, 1981).

11   Marcel Bataillon, *Erasmo y España. Estudios sobre la historia espiritual del siglo XVI*, (Mexico-Madrid-Buenos Aires, 1950); Joseph Pérez, *La révolution des 'comunidades' de Castille (1520–1521)*, (Bordeaux, 1970); Manuel Giménez Fernández, *Hernán Cortés y su revolución comunera en la Nueva España*, (Sevilla, 1948); J.H. Elliott, 'Cortés, Velázquez and Charles V', in Anthony Pagden (ed.) *Hernán Cortés, Letters from México*, (New Haven-London, 1986); Guillermo Lohmann Villena, *Las ideas jurídico-políticas en la rebelión de Gonzalo Pizarro. La tramoya doctrinal del levantamiento contra las leyes nuevas en el Perú*, (Valladolid, 1977); J.A. Fernández-Santamaria, *The State, War and Peace. Spanish Political Thought in the Renaissance, 1516–1559*, (Cambridge, London, 1977); Anthony Pagden, *Spanish Imperialism and the Political Imagination. Studies in European and Spanish-America Social and Political Theory 1513–1830*, (New Haven-London, 1990); *idem, The Uncertainties of Empire. Essays in Iberian and Ibero-American Intellectual History*, (Aldershot, 1994).

12   On the more general developments in Spanish-America at a later period, see
Manuel Lucena Salmoral, ed., *El descrubrimiento y la fundación de los reinos
ultramarinos hasta fines del siglo XVI. Historia General de España y América,
tomo VII*, (Madrid, 1982); José Andrés Gallego, ed., *La crisis de la Hegemonia
española. siglo XVII. Historia General de España y América, tomo VIII*, (Madrid,
1986); Demetrio Ramos Pérez, Guillermo Lohmann Villena, (eds) *América en el
siglo XVII. Los problemas generales. Historia general de España y América, tomo
IX*, 1 (Madrid, 1985).

5

French, English and Dutch in the Lesser Antilles: from privateering to planting, c. 1550–c. 1650

Anne Pérotin-Dumon

War for trade in the island Caribbean, the 'Gate of Peru'

After they discovered America, the Spaniards claimed to possess the archipelago that lies between the north and south masses of mainland America. Their slave trading raids in the first decades of the sixteenth century had led them to reconnoitre fairly extensively the insular Caribbean originally occupied by Indians, as well as its margins of Central America, Florida, Guiana (between the Orinoco and Amazon rivers) and Venezuela and Colombia (or *Tierra Firme*) in South America. However, the islands themselves had remained unevenly occupied by the European invaders, who did not speak of one entity called 'Caribbean islands' but rather perceived these as belonging to several distinct entities:

1 The four Greater Antilles were part of the Spanish possession in America, *las Indias occidentales.*
2 Looking toward the North American coast of Florida, the Lucayos Islands, later to be called Bahamas, had been neglected by the Spaniards after the depletion of their Indian native population.
3 Closer to the continent than the Bahamas, and off the coast of Venezuela, were Curaçao, Aruba and Bonaire. These islands were more an appendix of South America than a part of the Caribbean archipelago.
4 A fourth entity was the Lesser Antilles, a chain of forty habitable islands (and many more deserted islets) which face the Atlantic, from east of Puerto Rico south to Trinidad.

Outbound Spanish ships took advantage of the trade winds blowing westwards at the latitude of the Lesser Antilles to cross the Atlantic. As a result, these islands were the first the Spanish encountered *en route* to the Indies. Since Columbus, the best entrance into American waters was the passage between Guadeloupe and Dominica. However, the Lesser Antilles were not settled by the Spaniards, who only used them regularly to water and provision their ships *en route* to the Indies. For the Spaniards they were a hostile world of wilderness, the domain of Carib Indians. Before the arrival of the Spanish, the Caribs of the Lesser Antilles appear to have been already on hostile terms with their neighbours of the Greater Antilles, with whom they regularly engaged in warfare. Spanish perception lumped the islands they did not occupy, east of the Greater Antilles, the *Islas del Mar del Norte*, with other margins of Spanish America. This included Florida and the Eastern part of *Tierra Firme*, inhabited by similar Indian tribes as the Lesser Antilles, where a Spanish presence was thin or nil and where reconnaissance and communications were limited to the coastline.

In the course of half a century of Spanish occupation the Greater Antilles had experienced a dramatic change. Santo Domingo had been established as the centre of the enterprise of the Indies and had known a boom linked to a gold rush (1500–10). But for the Spanish, interest in the Caribbean was soon displaced by Mexico, which they conquered in 1519–21. The energies and resources of the Spanish invaders shifted from the Antilles to the west, to mainland America, stretching from Mexico to Peru. In Hispaniola and Cuba the Indian population, which had been distributed among the conquerors, declined precipitously, causing the latter's ruin and exodus. Ghost towns were left behind and large tracts of empty land were abandoned to wild cattle pasture. The Greater Antilles entered an acute economic depression. The production of sugar, indigo and ginger declined considerably, and mineral resources were negligible compared to those of Mexico and Peru. The Spanish Antilles became merely the gate to the heart of the Indies, the silver-producing mainland of America.

In the early decades of the sixteenth century, ships from north-west Europe began sailing into the Atlantic Ocean to West Africa and to America, in the wake of the earlier Portuguese and Spaniards. Promoters of maritime ventures obtained royal licences to 'search for certain islands and countries where it is said there are greater quantities of gold'. They formed corporate syndicates of merchants who invested jointly in these trading ventures. The merchants expected a return proportionate to their share in the joint investment. Already joint-stock companies of non-Iberian merchants, which later would finance settlements, were then making their way into the Caribbean behind the ships that reached regions left empty or loosely controlled by Iberians.

To non-Iberians, the Spanish Indies were largely unknown: the English referred to *Tierra Firme* as the 'Spanish Main', the French called the Antilles the 'islands located at the entrance of Peru'. More accessible (because of the north-east trade winds) were the coasts of Brazil, which the French visited frequently, led by Portuguese pilots. Portuguese merchants and ships also enjoyed an active role in the early enterprises in Spanish America. They were the first non-Spanish presence in the Caribbean and used the Lesser Antilles as way stations between Brazil and Portugal from the early decades of the sixteenth century on. In the late 1520s, the first mentions of the French and English appear in Spanish sources. From then on, and following the Portuguese, French incursions were alleged to be most active into the Caribbean, Isthmus of Panama and *Tierra Firme* areas. In the 1560s the English presence grew, and so, by the 1590s did the Dutch.

It is as contraband traders that Europeans began cutting into the Spanish domain of the Isthmus of Panama and the Greater Antilles: they bartered their hardware, foodstuffs, clothes and shoes against ginger, indigo, and later cacao and sugar from Spanish colonists. European cloth (particularly from Rouen, Normandy, a main textile and leather centre) and hides from Hispaniola seem to have been the most substantial items for the exchange trade. Bartering took place with Indians on the margins of the Spanish empire. To obtain valuable raw products – tortoiseshells, pearls, dyes (dyewood) – the French traded weapons, alcohol, hardware tools and trinkets. In the second half of the sixteenth century an enduring pattern of barter and petty trade was established between northern Europeans and Spaniards, of which the French seem to have had the largest share. It largely reproduced the trade practised in Brazil in the first part of the century. This trade had to be clandestine, since the Spanish Crown refused to grant trading licences to aliens beyond the Canary Islands.

The northern Europeans hoped, however, that once having crossed the Atlantic, they could obtain licences of tacit agreements from local authorities to trade with Spanish American colonists or their local intermediaries. If an agreement could not be worked out locally, smugglers might have to resort to violence to force the exchange of valuable commodities against European stuffs. Along with French contraband, such *rescates* or illicit exchange obtained through violence were reported by Spanish authorities from the 1540s on. A shipowner who undertook a venture overseas, having bribed a Portuguese pilot to sail along Caribbean and American coasts, had to be ready both to trade and to raid. If obstacles thwarted clandestine trade, it could be simpler for non-Iberians to take a cargo from another ship as a prize, or to go on a raid ashore – to sack a town of the Isthmus where merchandise awaited transshipment, to loot an estate on the coast, or to ransom Spanish colonists for cash. This pattern of mixed contraband trading with

116

raiding was long to remain a characteristic of the Caribbean. It derived from understanding overseas trade as a predatory activity – a way to make quick profits by preying on the valuable commodities of the outer world or a search for precious products to bring back rather than an enterprise to establish markets.

The association between trade and violence was further encouraged by the more general spread of warfare, as northern Europeans challenged Spain's primacy in Europe. By stepping into the Spanish domain, northern Europeans challenged the Habsburg pretention of remaining mistress of the seas, in Europe as well as in America. In the absence of standing navies, war on the seas was essentially a private and commercial affair. French and English sovereigns granted commissions to privateers to attack Spanish trade. Privateering was encouraged as an official form of warfare in America; it legitimized the use of violence by smugglers in Spanish America. Under such commissions, which were often of dubious value, true private enterprises of piracy flourished, the English and the French being almost continually at war with Spain from the 1520s until the beginning of the next century.

After 1550 large cargoes of American silver were shipped back regularly to Spain, along with other commodities. This enormously increased the value of potential Spanish prizes. Northern Europeans who were involved in active smuggling in the Caribbean area began combining this with privateering attacks on the Spanish-American homeward trade (also intercepting Spanish ships around the Atlantic islands and Spanish coasts). Such operations were officially encouraged. In 1559 the King of France instructed his ambassador in Lisbon of his intention to 'make enterprise on silver that our neighbours expected from Peru'.[1] Smuggling raids and *rescates* in the Greater Antilles were now a preliminary stage to pirate raids on the Isthmus of Panama and *Tierra Firme*. Compared to what the French Jacques de Sores and Jambe de Bois could get in the 1540s and 1550s (hides, a bit of sugar and ginger, even slaves, all bulky cargoes of little value), plunder in the 1570s and 80s in the Isthmus by the English pirates Hawkins and Drake were much more profitable. But to seize rich cargoes from the Isthmus remained exceptional; often they had to fall back onto petty contraband in the Spanish Antilles. They had to be alternatively ready for one form of raid or another. Even though the islands attracted foreigners simply as smuggling coves, as bases of pirate forays for the riches of the Spanish-American continent, there is no doubt that both types of operations made northern Europeans quite familiar with the Caribbean in the second half of the sixteenth century.

Religious motivations added to political rivalries: this element of sixteenth-century European culture and warfare also made its way into the Caribbean as non-Iberians came to challenge Spain. Most of northern Europe embraced Protestantism in the second part of the sixteenth century. Since

Spain was, throughout, the uncompromising champion of Catholicism, she was consequently the enemy of northern heretics or *luteranos*. The possibility for the Low Countries freely to profess Calvinism caused their revolt in 1566. After 1580 the seven northern United Provinces continued to wage war against Spain until achieving *de facto* their independence (officially recognized in 1648). The Dutch consciously expanded their war of independence into a commercial war overseas. The rising identity of England as a Protestant country was another reason to encourage its sea rovers to harass the Spanish in the Caribbean. French Protestants – Huguenots – also saw the American venture as an outlet. After having been strongly affected by the rise of Reformation, France ultimately remained officially Catholic. While anti-Protestant persecution in the kingdom continued, the state observed a certain tolerance towards Huguenot gentlemen who sought overseas ventures.

For Spain, the struggle against northern intrusion presented a double challenge: she had to protect the homebound passage of her silver export against their attacks, and she had to root them out from their contraband bases in the Greater Antilles. This was an exorbitantly expensive policy for a country at war with the rest of Europe, including some of her subjects. Drastic choices had to be made. Spain chose to concentrate her resources on protecting her main Atlantic sea-lanes for the benefit of the King and Seville merchants: warships escorted merchant ships and followed fixed routes and schedules. As one would expect, the protection of the outbound route through the Caribbean was a main aspect of this policy. On the outer perimeter, key ports such as Cartagena and Veracruz, from which the *Tierra Firme* and Mexican fleets respectively sailed out, were fortified. In the Greater Antilles, Havana became the stronghold where the fleets rendezvoused before undertaking their homebound voyage through the channel between Cuba and Florida, while at the eastern tip of the Spanish Caribbean, the fortress of San Juan in Puerto Rico protected its entry. Spain thwarted French, English and Dutch attempts to set foot in Guiana, Trinidad and Florida, where they intended to threaten outbound fleets and secure a springboard for further conquest. With San Juan, the fortifications of Florida now formed the eastern outposts that buttressed Spain's mainland possessions.

For the Spaniards to control the whole Caribbean region with such vast and undersettled territories was impossible. Outside the strongholds mentioned above, the rest of the Spanish Caribbean was left pretty much to itself. What had been the centre of Spanish power in the insular Caribbean, Santo Domingo, was deserted, in favour of the north-west corner of Cuba. Havana was now the hub for strategic control of the Atlantic shipping routes, the new centre of the Spanish Antilles. Elsewhere, the main policy to counter further intrusions of northern Europeans was forcefully to relocate coastal settlements into the hinterlands. Those forced resettlements, or *devastaciones* as Spanish colonists denounced them, aimed at cutting foreigners' attempts to create free-trade enclaves, particularly as they had existed in the east of Cuba and north of Hispaniola (or, for that matter, on the Venezuela and Guiana coasts of South America).

This policy ruined the northern Europeans' hopes that the islands would be the gates to the riches of the Indies. Indeed, pirates' captures of the Spanish fleets remained, from a statistical standpoint, exceptional. But the marginalization and desertion of the Spanish Antilles made it easier for corsairs to continue harassing inter-regional trade in the Spanish Caribbean. By 1600 the economic decline of the region was such that this petty plunder and contraband by northern Europeans had probably become less profitable in the Greater Antilles than on the Brazilian coast. But as pirates tried relentlessly to capture the silver fleet, their presence as smugglers was continuous and widespread: 'Coming and going, we always have a corsair in sight. If this continues either the island will be depopulated or they will compel us to do business with them rather than with Spain,' complained an official from Santo Domingo, the capital of Hispaniola in 1595.[2]

Transferred from Europe, a situation of international conflicts around trade turned the Caribbean into one of the world's hotbeds of piracy for a long time. The result was to alter dramatically the Spanish Caribbean in its configuration and centre of gravity, while northern Europeans, *en route* to privateering and contraband in the Greater Antilles and the Isthmus increasingly stopped in the Lesser Antilles. The next section of this chapter will analyse how the privateers' diffuse, clandestine and predatory presence in the Lesser Antilles led to 'planting' expeditions sponsored by European merchants and their respective states. Further sections will show how commercial settlements, originally intended to extract or produce commodities, came to be the beginnings of new societies in the Lesser Antilles.

Tobacco and the shift from privateers' way stations to planting

From the 1540s on, the Spaniards reported that northern Europeans were infiltrating the Lesser Antilles. This is confirmed by numerous French sources indicating the presence of French smugglers and corsairs on these islands. We know of French corsairs based in Dominica in 1549. It was on the same island, in 1564, that Hawkins stopped to water *en route* to the Spanish Caribbean, on a voyage from Sierra Leone with a cargo of 300 slaves. In 1609 a French crew was using the island of St Christopher (now St Kitts) as their base of operations. Northern Europeans did not seem to have fixed plans for colonization. Instead, from those temporary bases, they intended to exert pressure on Spaniards until they could force them to yield on the main issue, trade.

The process seems to have begun with random stops. Some men were sent ashore to hunt (pigs introduced by Spaniards and Portuguese had proliferated), fish, and cut wood, to get fresh water and produce, to gather salt (the Caribbean region offers abundant saltpans) and to cure fish or meat for the rest of their trip. When ships stopped at islands which were occupied by Caribs – such as St Christopher, Nevis, Montserrat, Guadeloupe and St Vincent – the Indians seem to have accepted temporary stays by the Europeans well. This attitude seems to have been motivated partly by a sense of common hostility towards the colonizing Spaniards. This was, in time, a rationale exploited by Europeans in negotiating with Indians. As happened against the Spaniards at the end of the fifteenth century, Indian reactions would change when the northern Europeans ceased only to pass and stay briefly and began to occupy lands and grow crops.

In 1619–20 French corsairs, returning from a failed venture that had led them throughout the Atlantic and the Pacific, stayed several months with Caribs in Martinique. Their sick and starving crew members were rescued and adopted by the Indians. The evocative account of their stay reveals that it had been a current practice for several decades. Mutineers, fugitives or maimed sailors left behind by their captains immersed themselves in the native culture. John Hilton recalled shipwrecked Frenchmen, who 'got ashore, did live among the Indians, went naked and did go to war with them'.[3] We have accounts of sailors who, when their ship returned to pick them up, decided to stay on the island upon seeing their exhausted and skinny companions on board.

In less desperate circumstances entire crews often organized temporary stays in the Lesser Antilles in between expeditions to the Spanish Caribbean. In an area long used to this process, ships were emptied, and the goods carried ashore and stored in sheds hastily built to receive them. Using ship sails, tents were pitched on the beach to house men. Forges for smiths and armouries were set up for a sort of weapon manufacture and to produce iron bolts and nails needed for ship repair. Other men cut and sawed timber; from part of it they produced charcoal for the forges. Another important task was to trim and caulk vessels, using whale oil, since pitch and tar were not available. In their self-sufficiency the tasks and tools made life ashore an extension of that on board, establishing what would be a pattern of early life in the Caribbean for non-Iberians.

Some sailors extended their stay ashore to make a living by catering to the needs of other passing ships for fresh meat, fruits and wood. They drew from an abundance of wild pigs and cows (introduced over the century by

Spanish sailors who had used the islands as watering places). From Spanish Caribbean hunters, called *masteurs* by the French, northern Europeans learned hunting techniques with dogs, and from Indians the curing technique of grilling meat above a fire of green woods (or *boucan* in French). A style of life was set for more than a century, which the last buccaneers made famous in the 1670s.

Around 1600 we begin to know more precisely where northern Europeans were establishing their footholds in the Lesser Antilles, generally in the vicinity of navigational passages. A first area was the upper Leeward islands to the east of Puerto Rico: the islands of Nevis and St Martin were conveniently located for pirate expeditions. Spanish officials reported in 1621 that 'the islands of Nevis and Virgin Gorda ... are the enemy's safe places and anchorages, where most years they winter, preparing and careening their ships and fortifying their spirits.'[4] In the same area French ships also anchored at St Croix between pirate campaigns. There, during several weeks, sometimes months in the bad season, they repaired and careened their ships. The southern islands, such as Trinidad, St Lucia, Tobago and St Vincent, were another zone where northern Europeans often stayed. St Vincent appears to have been a watering place and operational base for Dutch, French and English operations *en route* to Brazil and Guiana.

Thus, the Europeans' infiltration in the Lesser Antilles was linked to a similar one on the nearby South American coast. It was strengthened by a host of new extractive activities by which Europeans seem gradually to have supplemented either the volatile returns of piracy in the Caribbean or their trading ventures along the coasts of *Tierra Firme* and Brazil. Searching for their resources led to a thorough exploration of all islets, in both north and south of the archipelago. Among a very rich Dutch literature on navigation and trade, two classics stand out: *Toortse der zee-vaart* (1623) (The Torch of Navigation) by the sailor Dierick Ruyters, and *Nieuwe Wereldt ofte beschrijv-inghe van West Indien* (1625) (The New World or Description of the West Indies), by Johannes De Laet, a director of the West India Company. Both books reveal an extensive knowledge from several decades of exploration, particularly in the Lesser Antilles, of those many small islands which 'from the eastern coast of the island of Puerto Rico down to mainland South America ... form an arched barrier across the sea.'[5]

One new activity was loading ships with various types of rare woods and salt that crews found in the Lesser Antilles when stopping to water, pro-vision or careen on the way back from trading ventures in Brazil. Also, instead of simply gathering salt for their own consumption, Europeans began exporting it as return freight. In the late 1500s the Dutch were particularly busy exploiting large saltpans at Punta de Araya, a peninsula near Cumaná, in the eastern part of Venezuela. Salt was a commodity much needed for curing herring, which represented the largest share of Dutch trading activity in the North Sea. Saltpans in Araya were an alternative source of supply for the Dutch, now that the Spaniards had banned them from their traditional Portuguese sources of salt supply. Salt-gathering, like the fur trade in North America, meant systematically extracting raw products.

The Dutch, French and English also regularly visited the islands of Margarita and Cubagua to buy pearls collected by Indians, although pearl fisheries were already on the decline. The coast of *Tierra Firme* offered a more substantial resource, tobacco, which northern Europeans bought from Spanish colonists or Indians, establishing factories to trade it in contraband in Cumaná, La Guaira and Trinidad. In 1606 Spaniards prohibited colonists from growing tobacco, in an attempt to curtail the intrusion of other Europeans. Northern Europeans then looked for sites to plant tobacco themselves in eastern regions of *Tierra Firme*, which were even more isolated and therefore more poorly-controlled by Spain: the Wild Coast between the Orinoco and the Amazon deltas, and the island of Trinidad.

The project of 'setting forth a ship and men for ye design of tobaccoes', on the margins of Spanish America–Guiana (between the deltas of the Orinoco and Amazon rivers), Virginia, Bermuda – caught the imagination of West European merchants as a possible investment. Between the 1590s and 1610s, 'to settle a plantation to make tobacco', to invest in sending settlers and ships, became a new type of project for joint-stock companies or merchants who had hitherto speculated on privateering or contraband-trading ventures. To produce commodities, *'faire de la marchandise'*, as the French put it, caused temporary way stations to become more permanent settlements, for the new enterprise required regular visits of ships from Europe to bring immigrant settlers and to load tobacco (and salt) in America. Tobacco was the one commodity everybody was betting on. An entrepreneur in the Guiana tobacco trade predicted in 1612–13: 'It is planted, gathered, seasoned and made fit for the merchant in short time, and with easy labour .... I dare presume to say, and hope to prove within a few months ... that ... this commodity tobacco ... will bring as great a benefit and profit to the undertakers, as ever the Spaniards gained by the best and richest silver mines in all their Indies.'[6] As far as Guiana was concerned the dream remained unrealized; expeditions repeatedly organized by northern Europeans between the Orinoco and Amazon rivers throughout the next decades all ended up, sooner or later, in failure.

The first projects to plant tobacco in the Lesser Antilles appear to be immediate spin-offs of those that failed on the Wild Coast, as Guiana was then called. In 1605 an expedition of settlers that had tried in vain to reach Guiana landed in Santa Lucia and decided to stay. Then in 1609, a joint-stock Anglo-Dutch company fitted out three ships and sent over 200 men directly to Grenada. Both settlements were destroyed and the settlers massacred by the natives. Those, wrote one member of the expedition, 'were often disturbed by Indians, nor indeed were they persons fit for the settling of plantations, being the greater part the people of London no way inured to hardship and not so capable of encountering the difficulty that attend new plantations in the West-Indies.'[7] The reasons stated for the failure – a lack of experience in planning the expedition, and the Carib resistance to Europeans who were more than passing crews – should have been a lesson. Instead they became a leitmotiv in the subsequent decades.

Further to the north other small parties of sailors had started growing tobacco. Their enterprise caught the eye of privateers in difficulty. In 1622 a member of Captain Roger North's expedition to Guiana in 1620, Thomas Warner, landed at St Christopher. He found there a community of European islanders who were growing tobacco. 'He, well viewing the island, thought it would be a very convenient place for the planting of tobaccoes, which ever was a rich commodity.'[8] Two trips to London secured the English entrepreneur the financial backing of merchants and a royal patent as King's lieutenant: 'having lately discovered toward the continent of America St Christopher, Nevis, Barbados and Montserrat inhabited of savage people and not in the possession of any Christian prince or state, and having begun a plantation and a trade there ....' Warner was granted 'licence to traffick to and from the said islands, to transport men, and do all such things as tend to settle a colony and advance trade there, to govern and rule all persons there.' In 1624 and 1625 the first shiploads of settlers, equipment and provisions arrived from London.

In the early 1620s a factor was sailing throughout the Caribbean and along the Guiana coast on behalf of French merchants of Rouen. Back in Normandy he seems to have reported on a company of Frenchmen based at St Christopher, who lived on good terms with the Indians and grew cotton and tobacco like them. It was suggested that with very little capital involved, the operation of the Frenchmen at St Christopher could become a lucrative venture for the Rouen merchants. Thus, the latter sent Belin d'Esnambuc, a gentleman-adventurer from Normandy, who had traded in Brazil and the Caribbean, to St Christopher. In St Christopher, d'Esnambuc joined up with another gentleman-privateer, du Roissey, whose last operations had been unsuccessful. The combined initiatives of these gentlemen, together with the merchants' capital, led to the formation of a company which received a charter from Richelieu, the minister of Louis XIII. The official project as stated in the charter of the *Compagnie de Saint-Christophe* was 'to leave in the islands of St Christopher, Barbados and others located at the entrance of Peru a number and quantity of men that they deem necessary to work there, trade, grow tobacco and all other sorts of merchandizes, to barter and trade money and merchandize that it will be possible to gather and extract from the said islands and neighbouring places.' From France, settlers, provisions and tools were sent in 1627 to grow tobacco, cotton, anatto dye from French *rocou*, and spices.

During the next two decades non-Iberian settlements spread into the Lesser Antilles. Following an old pattern in the history of colonization, some settlements were spin-offs from the first ones – whether because there were too many people for the land available, or from a few restless characters whose energies and ambitions led them elsewhere (as with Spaniards in the Greater Antilles), or through the need to replace the loss of previous settlements. Other settlements were planned and launched from Europe by merchants trying to match initiatives from veterans of the first settlements.

From tiny St Christopher (65 sq. m.) were settled nearby Nevis, followed in 1632 by Antigua (108 sq. m.), which had the best lands, and Montserrat (32 sq. m.). Too barren for any significant yield were the tiny islands of Anguilla, Barbuda and Tortola, although they too were occupied by the English. In 1627 the English settled in Barbados. Its planting began as an afterthought from operations on mainland America. On a return trip from Bahia, in north-east Brazil in 1622, Captain Henry Powell and his ship spotted the island and 'stayed some time to inform themselves of the place.'[9] Sir William Courteen, for whom Powell was working, had previously invested in Dutch ventures on *Tierra Firme*. He agreed to participate in the Barbados venture, obtaining a patent in 1627. Soon numerous settlers arrived at Barbados. A trip to Powell's former Dutch associates in Guiana procured tobacco seeds and a labour force. On the return trip, Powell took a prize which supplied the first cargo of African slaves. A bigger island (166 sq. m.) extending to the south-east of the archipelago, Barbados was inhabited neither by Spaniards nor by Indians. It had a better acreage of cultivable lands and a better climate than the other Leeward Islands, which may explain why the island soon became the main English settlement in the Caribbean.

St Christopher also operated as a springboard for the French, who began looking for larger islands. An older settler in St Christopher, L'Olive, knew of Guadeloupe (619 sq. m.) and Martinique (380 sq. m.), which were occupied by Caribs and used by Spaniards as watering places for their fleets. L'Olive made a trip to Paris and gathered together investors from his native port of Dieppe for the settlement of Guadeloupe. In 1635 the expedition from Dieppe headed by Liénart de L'Olive landed in Guadeloupe, with 550 men and four missionaries. In the preceding days, L'Olive had attempted briefly to land in Martinique. This island was finally settled the same year by d'Esnambuc, bringing 80 soldiers and 40 settlers from St Christopher. Within the next few years new settlements were launched from those two islands. Settlers from Martinique landed on St Lucia and Grenada, but new settlements on the Grenadines remained extremely precarious for about a century. Those who went from Guadeloupe toward the islands Saintes, Désirade and Marie-Galante appear to have set up more stable communities.

Those episodes are well-documented because their enduring character gave them an official status in the historiography of the origins of European colonization in the Lesser Antilles. They were part of a much broader trend, if not always equally well-documented. Richard Ligon has aptly summarized the repeated process: 'This discovery being made, and advice given to their friends in England, other ships were sent with men, provisions and working tools.'[10] Private investors from different countries launched tobacco planting, sometimes concurrently on the same islands, after small communities of sailors growing tobacco had drawn the attention of a promoter who was able to raise capital and send settlers from Europe. Such seems to have been the case with French, English and Dutch settlers reported at Nevis and St Martin, with the Dutch and English at St Croix in the 1620s, and in the following decade with the Dutch and English in Tobago, and with French and English in Grenada. Because of their private nature and smaller scale, as well as their more volatile character, the beginnings of such settlements are less traceable by historians.

Without the active naval presence of Dutch privateers throughout the Caribbean, it is doubtful whether French and English settlements in the Lesser Antilles would have survived. After two decades of the Dutch offensive against Spanish commerce, a truce was concluded in 1609, allowing the former to reconquer some of their European markets. However, in 1621 the Dutch resumed their offensive against Spain. It soon meant their unprecedented naval presence in Caribbean waters in the form of regular campaigns by privateers' fleets. Dutch annual fleets sometimes combined operations towards other regions of America, particularly towards Brazil, using St Vincent or Tobago as way stations. Dutch fleets also called at St Martin, Bonaire and Curaçao.

The Dutch armed presence needed more permanent bases. Their ability to set a foothold in the Caribbean was dictated by military considerations: 'the destruction of our hereditary enemy could not be accomplished by the trifling trade with the Indies or the tardy cultivation of uninhabited regions.'[11] Thus St Martin, which had not been occupied officially by any European nation, was targeted. In 1632 a fort was built there and a hundred men were garrisoned. A second objective for the Dutch settling in the Lesser Antilles was salt-gathering. The repeated attacks by the Spanish on the Dutch saltworks at Araya for two decades had forced them to give up altogether on this source of salt supply and look for alternative ones. The Dutch had exploited saltponds at Tortuga, along the northern coast of Hispaniola, but Spanish attacks on Tortuga also forced them to abandon this place.

Large sea-salt deposits had been discovered at St Martin by passing fleets (among them was the fleet of Pieter Schouten in 1627) even before a fort was built by the Dutch on St Martin. The West India Company and some traders it had licensed, brought back the first loads of salt. Soon hundreds of ships licensed by the West India Company were going regularly to the island, thus establishing maritime connections with Europe. De Laet accurately described the island's situation: 'No one lives on this island, there is no fresh water, but there is a huge saltpan.'[12] Fresh water had to be supplied from St Christopher. The English reported in the 1630s that the Dutch fleet came 'laden with salt from St Martin to water at St Christophers, because there is no water but brackish, a strange place to fortify in wanting of this commodity.'[13] Out of those regular visits, a brisk trade was established which justified the choice of St Martin as a base. Soon St Martin was a bustling entrepôt. Sir Henry Colt observed in 1631: '48 saile of hollanders, all unrigged, their sails ashorre, their ships not ballasted for they mean to ballast with salt.'[14] Lost to the Spaniards in 1633 (as we will see later), St Martin was reconquered in 1644 by the Dutch who considered 'this island … remarquably situated … to load the tobacco ship with salt, if (one fails) to have a full cargo, or at least for ballast.'[15]

Another active branch of Dutch trade was tobacco. After the loss of the Wild Coast establishments, they settled on St Eustatius, which was still officially unclaimed at the time. In 1635, backed by Flushing merchants, 50 colonists led by the promoter Pieter van Corselles, a veteran of an unsuccessful expedition to Tobago, founded the settlement of New Zealand. In 1640, from St Eustatius, the neighbouring island of Saba was colonized to grow cotton, indigo and tobacco. From that time on, St Martin, Saba and St Eustatius were to form the Dutch Leeward islands.

The loss of St Martin in 1633 deprived the Dutch of a naval base as well as of their main salt supply. Amsterdam merchants pushed the West India Company to acquire another Caribbean base that could strengthen the Dutch position in Brazil (the conquest of which had begun in 1624), from where the movements of Spanish fleets could be watched and naval offensives mounted. Previous reconnaissances indicated that Curaçao (and nearby Aruba and Bonaire) in the Windward islands was well suited; it also had salt, wood and cattle. However, the islands had to be taken from the Spaniards, something that no one had ever attempted. The fact that the Dutch were successful gives a measure of both their combativity and their confidence in the Caribbean. The expedition was carefully planned and well-financed by the state. It was made up of 255 soldiers, an equal number of sailors, nine months of provisions, and materials to build a fort. The conquest was executed in 1634 under the command of Pierre le Grand. Johannes van Walbeeck, a veteran of Brazilian endeavours and an official of the West India

Company, was designated to be the new governor. After four weeks, the entire island was in the hands of the Dutch. The Spaniards put up little resistance, assuming the Dutch attack amounted to nothing more than a contraband raid. In the south of Curaçao, two good harbours offered a base. A fort was erected, and a garrison set. The abundance of cattle made up for resources in salt that proved disappointing. From Curaçao, Aruba and Bonaire were conquered; they also supplied salt, wood and cattle. Curaçao, Aruba and Bonaire together formed the Dutch Windward islands, the most important Dutch Antilles.

Patents, tobacco and servants

Non-Iberian colonies in the Antilles were started up in the wake of a host of commercial operations (described above), in a similar way to those taking place in Brazil and along the *Tierra Firme* and the Wild Coast. The Dutch and the French were actively gathering and exporting hides, various sorts of woods, and salt. As noted above, another type of venture, needing more capital, was to send settlers with provisions, equipment and ammunitions, to expand a series of small and semi-clandestine tobacco plantations which had been started by sailors living among Indians, in order to export the crops to Europe. At the beginning of the seventeenth century, these activities became more active in the Lesser Antilles.

When shown samples of crops, by captains back in the home port, merchants who had financed contraband and privateering expeditions saw a potential for promising new ventures. By the 1620s they were willing to venture capital in the planting of settlements to produce marketable agricultural commodities in the Lesser Antilles. In the usual corporate fashion, they made joint-stock investments and sent expeditions to the Antilles, as well as Guiana and Virginia. To reinforce the initial small sailors' communities in Indian territory, ships carried several hundred settlers who had been contracted to plant colonies and work in the Lesser Antilles. The corsair captain would become the leader of a settlers' community. The new settlements depended on stockholders who had jointly raised money for those ventures. Merchants were the real movers behind the settlements in the Lesser Antilles, but unlike previous merchant guilds, their companies were open to any new investor beyond the initial shareholders. They authorized and licensed other traders to operate within their privilege. As a result, merchants' investments in Caribbean settlements extended increasingly beyond the small number of initial company members.

The new situation developing in the Lesser Antilles was also recognizable in Virginia, Guiana and the Bahamas islands. It had a political dimension in that new settlements implied territorial expansion and the creation of communities overseas. This required the establishment of some political power which had to derive from a legitimate authority in order to be effective. As soon as a European settlement involved expeditions and capital from Europe, states had in one way or another a say in the undertaking. They had begun to consider overseas colonization as a way to enhance national power for the economic benefits that it could yield to its subjects. By fostering commercial settlements in America, non-Iberian states threatened the Spanish Indies and challenged Spain's economic power, which was so heavily dependent on its American riches.

Merchants' ventures received royal approval, with the rights, privileges and duties falling to each side being set out in a charter. From the state, a merchant company obtained privileges of exclusive trade with the intended settlements and a delegation of political authority for several decades. In exchange, the company often had to supply a specified number of settlers and ships for maritime connections. Commercial companies which were chartered by English and French monarchs exhibited an interplay of state control and merchants' initiatives; they combined in varying proportions state subsidies and private capital. In 1626, as the war with Spain was about to start, the French statesman Richelieu chartered the first French commercial company interested in Caribbean settlements, the *Compagnie des Seigneurs de Saint-Christophe*. Richelieu appointed his financiers, faithful courtiers and advisers as members, and personally subsidized the venture by underwriting a substantial proportion of stock. In England, the Tudor monarchy also officially encouraged such ventures, but it was less committed to them financially.

Richelieu's model was the Dutch West India Company, chartered in 1621. This company combined the two goals of damaging Spain and enriching national subjects. The country was still engaged in the war of independence which was primarily maritime and commercial. As a result, within the broad mandate of its charter, the 'octroy' or military and political objectives, clearly prevailed over purely commercial ones, and the company was well subsidized by the States-General. Its interest in promoting colonization primarily derived from its military mandate. But military objectives and privateering alone did not seem to be enough to attract potential shareholders. Only when the Dutch company was allowed to include salt-gathering (the main extractive activity of the Dutch in the Antilles) among its commercial privileges was it able to attract a sufficient number of shareholders to finance its projects in Brazil, Guiana and the North American coast, as well as the Antilles. As other merchant companies started settlements, the Dutch company outfitted ships, contracted settlers, supplied equipment and provisions, built forts and garrisoned them.

If a settlement managed to survive a couple of years and to yield merchandise sent homeward, a patent was granted by the King to the merchants

128

who had been its promoters, and a commission of governor to the ex-corsair (who would often retain in his new functions the title of captain). The captain of a settlement might need several trips back and forth between the islands, Paris or London, his home port and the Court, to secure the settlement financially as well as politically, to get enough investors and obtain for them the 'privilege and power to settle and people' by virtue of a proprietorship patent. 'Persons of considerable wealth and socially prominent' who were influential at the Court and occupied key political functions were indispensable; they backed the enterprise financially and were its advocates in political circles. After Captain Thomas Warner had landed at St Christopher in 1623, he had about two years of hardship struggling to get things started on the island with the support of ships from the Merrifield merchant firm. He then returned home, recruited more settlers and obtained a patent of lieutenant for St Christopher (as well as Nevis, Barbados and Montserrat) to exercise in the name of the company powers and privileges granted by the King.

The text of Warner's commission encapsulates the purpose of the settlement, the way public functions were delegated to private corporations and exercised by the individuals appointed by them as well as the role of all partners involved.

> 'Whereas Thomas Warner', reads his commission, 'having lately discovered towards the continent of America four islands ... inhabited by savage people and not in the possession of any Christian prince or state, and having begun a plantation or a trade there. Has been an humble suitor to His Majesty to take the said islands into his royal protection and to grant licence to the said Ralph Merrifield his partes and agents to trafique to and from the said islands ... to transport men and (to) do all such things as tend to settle a colony and advance trade there. And also to grant the said Thomas Warner ... the custody of the said islands and rule all persons there ... and by force to repress all such as shall seek in hostile manner to invade the said islands.'[16]

The commission given in 1635 by the *Compagnie des Iles d'Amérique* (a new, enlarged version of the previous *Compagnie de Saint-Christophe*) in the name of the King of France to Captain Liénart de L'Olive for the settlement of Guadeloupe similarly read:

> having chosen the island of Guadeloupe, where you have begun to settle and clear the grounds, and where you have built forts with the decisions to stay there, keep the island for the King's and company's service, and establishing a colony of Frenchmen.[17]

The first patents of proprietors were granted to syndicates of merchants who had financed settlements, for example, the Courteen Company, the Dutch West India Company and the *Compagnie des Iles d'Amérique.* Gradually, French and English trading companies were superseded as patentees by members of the gentry. This may have been linked to the fact that most merchant companies, being in deficit, stopped fulfilling their mandate and licensed individual merchants to exercise their trade privileges. Even the powerful Dutch company proved at times unable to raise enough capital. It then relied on individual merchants instead, delegating them as a political authority known as 'patroon'. In 1628 merchants from Flushing, who had financed the settlement of Tobago, also received political power over the settlement (which eventually failed). The patroon system was also the regime on St Eustatius.

In England, individual entrepreneurs competed early on with merchants to obtain proprietor patents. Some were gentlemen adventurers who became interested in settlements after careers as corsairs; planting appealed to them in that it combined conquest and feudal power. Other wealthy members of the gentry secured a proprietorship patent for themselves at the invitation of merchants who sought an influential aristocratic patron. The rivalry between the Earls of Carlisle and Pembroke (with merchants behind the latter) is well known. It played an important part in the British West Indies political factions and disturbances of the early debates. The Earl of Carlisle in 1627 received the lord proprietorship of all Caribbean islands. Angered by this grant to Carlisle, the Courteen Company and his merchant associates pushed forward the Earl of Pembroke. The conflict was settled in 1629 when Carlisle's patent was limited to the jurisdiction over Barbados, while the rest of the (less wealthy) West Indies was granted to Pembroke.

Proprietors – individual or corporate – were generally absentees. At the head of a settlement, an agent or governor was appointed by the state or with its approval. The governors of Curaçao and St Martin were appointed and paid by the Dutch company. The governor of St Eustatius, however, was appointed in the same way as those of the French islands. French and English governors were recruited among a gentry who carried a tradition of seeking booty and conquests through arms, but lacked the capital to secure a proprietor patent for themselves. French governors were relatively independent of the French Company which in 1649 sold to each of them its proprietorship rights. Houel in Guadeloupe, Du Parquet in Martinique, and Poincy in St Christopher became the owners of the island they governed. In the Dutch Republic, the maritime towns of Holland and Zeeland dominated mercantile and colonial activities. The governors of Dutch settlements were Company officials, burghers, ship captains or soldiers. In the course of their career as colonial officials, Jan Claeszoon van Campen, Johannes van Walbeeck and

Pieter Stuyvesant moved between Brazil, Curaçao, St Martin and North America, thus, they were more immune to local pressure from colonists than in the English and French islands. Whether holding his powers from an individual or a corporate proprietor or ruling the island as proprietor, or whether operating independently or in close dependency on proprietors, an energetic local leadership was essential for early political institutions to function.

The general pattern, for English and French as well as Dutch settlements, was that the company hired settlers who became its employees for a given length of time. To repay the cost of their passage, immigrants were to work for the company and receive a percentage of the crops for each year of their contract. Whether stipulated in the contract or not, the expectation of receiving a land-lot after completion of their term was a powerful incentive to sign up. Their passage paid, equipped and provisioned, and under the leadership of a ship captain or that of a gentleman soldier, who was it from these European societies who left for the islands? The first expeditions were organized without a clear idea of the types of skills, tasks and tools needed to start planting. People of all ranks were recruited in the homeland of the captain of the expedition – or around the port where the ships outfitted by the companies departed, such as London, Bristol, Plymouth in England, Dieppe, Rouen, La Rochelle, Nantes, Honfleur in France, and the maritime towns whose chambers controlled the Dutch company. Family kinship or regional clienteles seem to have played an important role in the recruitment of settlers.

From the beginning, English and French settlers placed a greater emphasis on agriculture than on the privateering and extractive activities characteristic of most Dutch settlements. Land was available for several decades to start a plantation, but the labour needed to work it was in chronically short supply. The existence of this problem – experienced earlier in the Spanish Antilles and, contemporaneously in other regions in North America – meant that the main investments and entrepreneurial efforts were directed towards recruiting a labour force. After a few shiploads, most companies were unable to continue recruiting and send people so they licensed individual settlers and merchants to do so instead. The role played by merchants in recruiting settlers is particularly well documented with respect to the French islands, through thousands of notarial contracts between merchants and immigrants that have been preserved. Once the initial settlers that companies had recruited became landholders, they invested their first profits in turn in recruiting servants, either going themselves to Europe or using the services of relatives and partners.

Merchants and artisans advanced colonists' passages for two or three servants; they were repaid by a share in the return, when the products sent from the Antilles were sold in Europe. Hundreds of contracts set conditions similar to these. For example, in 1636 an innkeeper entered a partnership with a burgher of Honfleur (a port in Normandy). Together they paid passages for the innkeeper's brother along with four other men who were leaving to go and grow tobacco in the islands. The two partners would divide equally among themselves the return made out of the crop sale.[18] Indeed, contracting servants became the way for new merchants to invest in planting overseas.

In the letters sent back by settlers to their homeland that have been preserved, requests for more servants was a leitmotiv. For example, in 1627: 'Send me some 2 or 3 men, that they be bound to serve me in the West Indies, so 3 or 5 years, which you do think good to bind for, and get them as reasonable as you can.'[19] In the early 1630s, Sir Henry Colt, who had brought on his ship some twenty servants from England, wrote to relatives and friends with whom he had various business arrangements: 'I need more men', and again: 'I could use fourty more', and shortly after: 'I want at least fourty men more. I have a great plantation and I will keep afoot … I have great need of them.'[20] Along with the ones hired by companies, servants were now hired by settlers to whom they owed their services for several (in general three to seven) years. The name initially given to servants in French – *alloué* – referred to the medieval practice of placing oneself in a position of personal servitude for a specific length of time (later, the word *engagé* replaced *alloué*). Contracts of servitude called 'indentures' (by reference to the physical aspect of the document) were drawn up between settlers and servants. These resembled other types of individual contracts made at the time to learn or perform various types of activities and duties, as in apprenticeship, division of shares or privateer's booty and payment of land-dues.

These contracts of servitude enabled servants to emigrate, and masters to own the latter's labour for a given time. During the time of the contract, the master supplied (besides the passage) clothes, food and lodgings. At the end of their services, servants were entitled to receive a wage in crop (tobacco). Servants could be sold during the time of their term, along with a plantation that changed hands, although contracts signed up before the departure had bound servants nominally to a given settler. As plantations and a class of the first landholders got established, the nature of the tasks required became better understood. The recruitment of labour increased and became more impersonal. Within about two decades, the contracts of indentured labourers became standardized. In European ports, merchants hired gangs of 10 to 40 young males at a time. Upon arriving on the island, ship captains who had taken indentured servants aboard sold them to any settler who could afford them. Speculating on cargoes of servants for the Antilles (as well as Canada, Guiana or Virginia) became a form of commercial venture in which merchants from Bristol and La Rochelle became specialists.

English and French sources point towards a common sex-age-ethnic profile of indentured labourers; the overwhelming majority were young males in their late teens and early twenties. Some came as apprentices to serve merchants or artisans. Their indentured service corresponding to an early stage of their lives, they were able to acquire professional training. But most of them came as poor and unskilled labourers who had no further prospect in life. The proportion of women – less than 10 per cent – remained virtually unchanged during the three decades in which the indentured system was the dominant form of recruiting a white immigrant labour force from Europe. The most striking point that stands out consistently – whether from testimonies of former indentureds themselves, merchants back from the islands, or officials, missionaries and ministers posted there – is the exploitation of this immigrant labour force. When servants came from a stock distinct from that of their masters – as the Irish were from the English – exploitation and ill-treatment overtly had a racist component.

It was widely commented at the time that merchants speculated on the eagerness of people to seek the happiness and riches they did not have in their initial condition. 'They are remarkably good at achieving their prosperity by speculating on others' misery'[21] wrote Paul Boyer, Sieur de Petit-Ouy, observing in the early 1640s the recruitment for an expedition to Guiana that turned out to be disastrous. Mass recruitment organized by companies themselves were particularly sordid. Wonderful promises were made and obstacles carefully concealed by company recruiters when immigrants signed up to leave for the islands. About the way settlers were recruited in 1655 for a settlement similar to those in the Antilles, a Jesuit, Father Pierre Pelleprat, observed:

> The majority of those who do this trafficking take advantage of the innocence of some persons whom they have made believe that everything is easy in the islands, that the land is abundant in everything, that they will have to work little and will earn a lot. They abuse not only the poor, but also induce some children of good family, telling them that in America one only lives on the fanciest meats, that houses are sugar-roofed (because they are usually covered with straw of sugar-canes) .... They put them into their ships under a variety of pretexts, and when they are there, they hold them by force and ship them against their will to the islands, where they sell them often to masters who feed them very badly, demand excessive work from them that is beyond their strength, and treat them with such inhumanity that several die within a short time.[22]

Esquemeling, the well-known buccaneer, began his adventurous career as an indentured servant. He left a vivid account of the harsh treatment inflicted on him and his companions; they were displayed for sale in front of the planters, forced to attend their houses and plant provision after their

working hours in the fields, and put in a pit as a punishment. The indentured servants' lot was frequently defined as a form of slavery limited in time.
Father Du Tertre wrote that *engagés* 'were treated worse than slaves; they
could only be forced into work by hitting them with sticks and halberds.'[23]
The Englishman Richard Ligon came to Barbados a grown man, after having
suffered hardship in his life. About indentureds beaten by overseers, Ligon
wrote: 'I have seen an overseer beat a servant with a cane on the head till
the blood had followed, for a fault that is not worth speaking of ... Truly I
have seen such cruelty there done to servants, as I did not think one
Christian could have done to another.'[24] Along with white servants, there had
been from the beginning of European settlements a few Caribs and African
slaves, almost all enslaved for life. On Dutch settlements, particularly on their
log-cutting and salt gathering sites, were working gangs of Indians (captured
in neighbouring islands as well as on the Wild Coast) and of African slaves
(brought initially to Spanish colonies in the Greater Antilles).

Henry Colt, a gentleman from Essex, left Weymouth in Dorset in 1631.
He recalled the moment of the departure, 'Now are we all met, our joy not to
be expressed ... but aboard we are ... Neither do we lose time, for we
presently weigh anchor, hoist up our sails, putting ourselves to sea.'[25]
Similarly a Frenchman who left for Guiana in 1642 wrote that 'all of us
expressed the greatest joy. Our hope to acquire a share of those inexhaustible riches that people say are to be found in the Indies made us
incredibly impatient to leave.'[26] For the *engagés*, the loathsome, stinking food
served aboard soon produced a different impression. One of them,
Guillaume Coppier, went to work in St Christopher in 1630. Coppier
complained of brackish water, 'its colour like the double dark beer from
Amsterdam.'[27]

As soon as the ship touched land, pressing tasks had to be performed
to ensure the survival of the newcomers. After pitching tents made with ship
sails and having the first supper of fresh produce, served on a chest, the first
tasks attended to were defence and food. A fort of *palisadoes*, with tree
trunks planted vertically, was built. The first peas and squashes were sown
which would feed people after a few weeks. Only then could the first crops
of tobacco or cotton be sown. For this, newcomers had to clear the grounds.
Esquemeling recalled the slash-and-burn operations with precision. 'The first
endeavour was to root up the shrubs and little trees; afterwards to cut down
the great ones; these they gathered into heaps, with their branches, and then
set them on fire, excepting the roots, which, last of all, they were constrained
to grub and dig up after the best manner they could.'[28]

The primeval landscape, where woods were so thick and trees so tall,
was daunting, 'Newcomers ... are almost at a stand and do sigh to see how
many trees they have to fell and how their hands are blistered.'[29] This was

the painful moment when people realized that they did not have the right tools: a whole day could be lost in making an axe-handle that had been forgotten. Soon, amidst the evergreen tropical paradise, some rows of potatoes and beans emerged between the boughs. As a result of clearing, the areas surrounding the settlers took on a devastated aspect which sometimes lasted for years: 'like the ruins of a village recently burned ... all things carrying the face of a desolate and disorderly show to the beholder.'[30] It was much easier to spot a place where there had been an Indian garden. Even better, when one could afford it, was purchasing a ready-made plantation. Soon some made a living out of selling lands they had opened up to others, felling trees, building shacks, clearing fields and planting provisions for newcomers.

The objective when setting up a plantation was to produce marketable commodities for regular shipment to Europe. Just about everything that Indians and Spaniards were already producing in the Caribbean and *Tierra Firme* was tried, not only tobacco and cotton, but also ginger and dyewoods like green-blue indigo and the red annatto dye plant, and of course sugar. But the results were, by and large, of poor quality. It was during the decades when settlements got started in the Lesser Antilles that tobacco was becoming an item of mass consumption (with Dutch manufactures of clay pipes). Tobacco thus became the commodity most commonly grown. It did not require much know-how or capital, and above all, tobacco could be sown, harvested and processed for export in the course of a single voyage. Four years after the settlement of St Christopher had begun, we read of Captain Warner sending home a cargo of 20 000 lb. of tobacco to Ralph Merrifield and his associates – and then the following month another cargo of 10 000 lb. In the years 1637–40 St Kitts and Barbados shipped one-fifth of the total amount of tobacco produced by Virginia planters.

As more settlers came during the decades of tobacco growing, the large original allotments of arable land seem gradually to have been divided up into smaller units, advancing inland. The larger estates belonged to the proprietor – the lord or syndicate of merchants – or to merchants to whom they had been leased out. Some lots were held in common by the company but were operated individually by settlers; others, held and operated by individual merchants, were apportioned to their shares in the company. There were also 'private plantations', financed by groups of subscribers who might or might not have been among the initial stockholders. On the remote, hilly parts, former indentured servants opened up smaller lots, which they had been granted by the governor, or that they simply occupied. With time, it became difficult for initial patentees to receive rents on the lands initially leased out and to raise taxes on crops.

Most companies did not survive long. It became difficult for them to raise further capital for the young settlements, so they dissolved into separate joint-stock ventures. Thus, each year a different set of subscribers financed a corporate cargo sent to the settlement. More and more merchants from Europe received individual licences from the company to invest in overseas planting. They placed on their share of land a tenant 'as half', or they entered into partnership with a settler already established on an island, often a relative or a friend. As mentioned, the most important aspect of the arrangement between partners consisted in the supply of labour and equipment sent in the expectation of a return on crops produced. Thomas Modyford, a future governor of Jamaica, bought in 1647 an already established plantation of 500 acres and planted sugar. He described how his brother-in-law, a merchant, sent him from London 'all the supplies ... at the best hand, and I returning him the sugars, and we both thrived on it.'[31] French notary archives contain numerous instances of partnerships between colonists from the Antilles and merchants from European ports, like the following one. In 1657 Joseph Cazenove, a merchant established overseas, embarked on the *Poirier*, captained by Nicolas Vignon of Amsterdam, to return to his 'magazin' in Martinique. Two Nantes merchants entrusted him with a cargo of aquavit to dispose of there. Cazenove was to send back the value of the sale in cash and commodities. After those commodities were sold in Nantes, he was to get half of the returns.[32]

On Dutch islands that functioned as trade factories the problems of a labour force were no less acute than on plantations. Private shipowners licensed by the Dutch company, or the company's personnel, organized campaigns of woodcutting and salt-gathering to load ships as soon as they arrived. Extractive activities and loading ships required a large but seasonal labour force. Gangs of black slaves who gradually replaced enslaved Indians were sent for a few weeks to Aruba to cut dyewoods and capture cattle, and to the saltpans of Bonaire and Curaçao. Servants were hired by the company as artisans to do construction works, to maintain tools, ships and weapons. The chronic scarcity of such artisans was a recurrent complaint of the governor of Curaçao. He needed a baker, having authorized the one he had to return to Holland 'because he has been engaged for some years to a widow there whom he fears otherwise might chance to marry another during his long absence.'[33]

The Dutch official also needed a blacksmith. He had unfortunately hired a Frenchman from a privateer who pretended he was a blacksmith 'but cannot repair the soldiers' weapons much less an axe or knife.'[34] Servants of the company as well as freeholders (ex-servants) were encouraged to grow some cotton and tobacco, and above all provisions to feed a large population of clerks and soldiers as well as labourers involved in extractive activities. Soldiers of the forts were reluctant to work at any of those tasks, as a letter of Governor Stuyvesant, from 1657, made clear: 'Your honours shall also find it difficult to believe that the soldiers who are sent out to catch fish as we ordinarily do, as well as with the fishnet, consider it to be an extraordinary degradation if they have to trouble themselves with it ... and they dare boldly to suggest that if they observe their ordinary professional duties concerning military services, they are not obliged to do more.'[35]

Then there was the trade with other Europeans. The Dutch sold the latter their outbound freight of European goods (wine, cloth, even ships) as well as African slaves, and bought tobacco and cotton to complete their freight return of salt and wood. Soon, these Dutch ships provided maritime connections with Europe to all settlements in the Antilles, while English and French merchant companies failed to do so. English and French settlers described how they owed their survival to providential Dutch ships that happened to pass the island. At St Christopher, Father Du Tertre wrote:

> The French had barely landed (and were still struggling to survive) when they received an unexpected assistance by the arrival of a ship from Zealand, loaded with victuals, linen and all sort of goods needed in the islands. As the captain found that the tobacco was excellent and well processed, he trafficked with the colonists of his goods; he even gave them credit for some of it, encouraged them to work, comforted them of their misfortunes and asked them to prepare a good quantity of tobacco, giving them his word he would come back within six months, bringing them victuals and all the things they needed.[36]

Having been helped by foreigners the Frenchmen took heart again, returned to clear the woods, to plant provisions, grow lots of tobacco (*petun*) and build huts (*cases*).

Thus, from rescuers, the Dutch became trading partners. Indeed, to trade with Spain's enemies was part of the Dutch company strategy. 'From the commencement of our administration we preferred to proceed in a warlike manner against the common enemy .... We found that even the new nations who are independent of the King of Spain could be brought to St Eustatius; there were also Dutch warehouses and merchants established in Guadeloupe, Martinique, Barbados.'[37]

Dutchmen were particularly appreciated, firstly, because they were willing to operate as mere factors or even carriers (*engagés* as well as return cargoes frequently used Dutch ships). They also supplied ships among goods they offered. The second reason was their price, reliability and range of merchandise offered: 'In the entrepôts of their (Dutch) several islands, among which was Curaçao, 'Du Tertre wrote,

> one finds everything that planters are in need of. (Dutch) merchants are careful to have such a wide variety of goods that the planter needs not

to go from one place to the other to find what he wants ... The Dutch have always supplied the islands abundantly. This is the main reason why our planters have stopped trading with French ports and put all their business in Dutch hands ... (they) had a large number of good and beautiful ships and they accepted half of what the French carriers asked for freight fare.[38] ... trade with us in no other way than by declaring ourselves in their favour.'

Deeds from the English Leeward planters show that the Dutch commercial strategy was successful. Among many, one contract of 1642 shows two mariners from Holland, Albert Jocheme and Cornelius Heertjies, agreeing with Christian Brodehaven of Barbados to send him goods valued at 400 pounds every year 'or so much more as occasion shall present', in such merchandises as he shall give advice in his letters. Jocheme and Heertjies were to buy the merchandise at ready-money prices and to ensure its delivery at his storehouse. Brodehaven would in return send cotton on such ships as his Holland partners direct, to repay in full the 400 pounds with 40 per cent insurance.[39] French settlers' correspondence with Dutch merchants that was seized by the British Admiralty shows that all were debtors to the Dutch.

French and English governors organized a virtual trade monopoly with Dutch traders for a few decades. Dutch boats and *shallops* from St Eustatius visited the other islands. They also established their warehouses and merchants in Guadeloupe, Martinique and Barbados. They were reliable, offered a wide range of merchandise at prices cheaper than the English and the French, and bought crops at the highest prices. By 1660 both the French and English reached the same conclusion: most of the colonists 'were Dutch at heart', because, as the author of the *History of the Caribee Islands* (1666) observed: 'The Hollanders are the great encouragers of the plantations ... give great credit to the most sober inhabitants ... they managed the whole trade of the Western colonies, and furnished the islands with negroes, copper, steels ... This,' he concluded 'I take to be the true and original cause of the riches of the colony.'[40]

A young, small and incipient society

This section presents a general picture of the early white European settlements and their relationships with Indian Caribs and African slaves. A preliminary issue is that of the size, and more broadly, of the population in the Lesser Antilles in the first half of the seventeenth century. How many Caribs were there in the Lesser Antilles when non-Iberians began settling, and what, as a result of this intrusion, was their population decline? This question may never receive a satisfactory answer. Until the second half of the seventeenth century, when the first official censuses were taken, we have only general, vague and contradictory data about the young settlements.

On white immigration a variety of sources exist, but none of them offers substantial longitudinal data. French notary records (from French ports) provide lists of settlers shipped by French merchant companies in the 1620s and 1630s, as well as numerous individual contracts of immigrants. English sources appear to be more reliable but no less sketchy; indentureds' registers (for instance for the port of Bristol, 1654–86) or lists of taxpayers for Barbados, 1635–9. The first substantial shipments of African slaves (several hundred) which arrived in Barbados or in Guadeloupe in the 1640s are recorded, but we do not have any statistical figures for the first decades of systematic deportation from Africa. We are left with demographic orders of magnitude rather than figures.

During the first years the companies that financed settlements usually sent several shipments of settlers. Doing so was required of them by the charters granted by the French monarchy. The *Compagnie des Iles d'Amérique*, founded in 1635, was scheduled to send 2500 persons within eight years. The previous company did send 1200 persons in five shipments to St Christopher between 1627 and 1629. But mortality, already high during the ocean passage, continued to strike the settlements in the first years following the arrival, sweeping away between a third and a half of the new-comers. From the 1200 Frenchmen who had departed for St Christopher, there were only 350 left there in 1629. Malaria, dysentery, etc., coupled with famine, plagued the infant colonies. Repeatedly, contemporaries observed an eerie combination of utmost misery, rampant death and entrepreneurial achievement.

Ligon, who visited Barbados in 1647, noted that: 'Notwithstanding all this appearance of trade, the inhabitants of the islands, and the shipping too, were so grievously visited with the plague (or as killing a disease) that before a month was expired the living were hardly able to bury the dead ... It was doubtful whether this disease, or famine, threatened most, there being a general scarcity of victuals throughout the whole island.'[41] The figures available for French and English immigrants suggest that departures ranged, according to ports, from a few hundred to a few thousand yearly. Actual numbers were likely to have been higher. The destination given for immigrants was often vague, for example, 'to St Christopher and other islands in America'. Dutch settlements, consisting of garrisoned forts surrounded by a few gardens or extractive sites, received even fewer settlers.

Until about 1640 population growth depended mainly on white immigration. These settlements, conceived as commercial ventures, were peopled by males without the intention to settle and take root, had chronically too few in number and were continuously stalked by premature death. As a result, it took about a decade for an English or French settlement to reach a few thousand. Promoters and merchant-colonists made frequent trips to Europe to raise funds, to sell their merchandise and to bring back servants. A portion of the latter (though this is difficult to assess) returned to the mother country after completing the term of their contracts. To this turnover were added movements (equally hard to assess) between settlements caused by the volatile economic conditions that accompanied initial development. All this makes it difficult to state precisely a settlement's population at a given time. Ligon (who erroneously estimated the population of Barbados in 1643 at 50000 inhabitants) remarked, 'It was somewhat difficult to give you an exact account of the number of persons upon the island ...'.[42]

At any rate, we are talking of very small societies. A fresh look at both English and French data available (some of the latter neglected by literature in English) suggest a demographic trend which cannot be too far from reflecting the overall situation, for the figures for the Dutch are also likely to have remained very low. Three different stages in the demographic trend, i.e. the 1640s, 1650s and 1670s, point to three successive formative factors: the Carib wars which slowed down the growth of settlements, then the introduction of large numbers of African slaves which decisively boosted them, just as the attraction of new enterprises in the Greater Antilles siphoned off a large number of landless males who could not afford to start sugar plantations. The fact that Barbados was spared Indian wars and that slaves were introduced in substantial numbers earlier than anywhere else in the Lesser Antilles made its situation exceptional. The white settler population of Barbados grew rapidly in the late 1630s (sevenfold in four years) and that of the slaves in the late 1640s. This explains observations by contemporaries that the island was congested.

In the early 1640s reasonable estimates would put the French population just under, and the English just over, 10000 each. At this time, the French were still centred on St Christopher – Carib resistance undoubtedly thwarting the progress of French settlements on Guadeloupe and Martinique – while four out of five of the English were already on Barbados. A set of figures for 1655–60 appears to put the French around 25000, while the English were by then twice that number. In both cases the Upper Leeward islands were not part of this growth, which was centred on Barbados, Guadeloupe and Martinique. The make-up of these populations had considerably changed as compared to the previous decades. African slaves were now a quarter of the population on the French islands and almost half on the English. The massive introduction of slaves was the cause of a quantitative leap in population between the 1640s and 1660s. The last set of data for the 1670s confirms that the slaves were the main factor of demographic growth, the white population having stagnated (as many left the Lesser Antilles for the Greater). The difference in population between the English and French islands remained in a proportion of more than two to one: Barbados retained the considerable advance it had gained in the previous decades, due to an earlier and continuing predominance in its slave population.

The white settlers' socioeconomic profile is distinctively Caribbean. They were overwhelmingly young males; females initially made up less than 10 per cent and only approached 25 per cent by the middle of the century. Since white male servants comprised 90 per cent of the population, their features as a group tended to characterize the settler population as a whole. They averaged 20 years of age; 70 per cent were between 15 and 24 years old. Almost a quarter were between 10 and 15. In an age when the majority of the population was put to work early in life, these young adolescents had come as part of the labour force, too. What Richard Dunn summarizes for the case of the British West Indies applied to other white immigrants: 'Few people over the age of 40 came over, scarcely any married couples and almost no children below working age.'[43]

Research on comparable male immigrant populations in other times and regions helps us to identify a pattern in which poverty, youth, and remaining single reinforced one another. In the Lesser Antilles of the 1630s–50s, too, young people were more likely to be unmarried and poor (some climbing the social ladder with age); poor people often could not afford to get married at all. More recently gender studies have identified patterns of behaviour, including mobility, restlessness, and regionalism, that characterize *garçons*, or bachelors, from 15 to 25, when working as servants away from a home with which they still strongly identified. In the Lesser Antilles of the mid-seventeenth century, young males, bachelor, poor and transient, made up a large part of the population. As a result and for several decades, these insular, very small societies were arrested in distinctive categories. Immigrants who returned to their homeland after spending some time in the Antilles in business or as indentureds, were likely to be replaced by others from the same region (predominantly the west and south-west of both England and France). Had they taken root in the islands, it is likely that they would have blended earlier into the Caribbean creole society.

Religious or political conflicts imported from Europe also stirred the islands. They were often translated into regionalist factions that tore apart small Caribbean communities: Protestants against Catholics, royalist Anglicans against independent Puritans, Normans against Parisians and Picards, English against Irish. One such European event was the French Fronde in the 1640s. Even more, the English Civil War (1642–6), setting Cavaliers against Roundheads, had a strong impact, particularly on Barbados, as this island received an influx of Cavaliers who had fled from England. These young men suffered alienation and boredom, and were prone to drinking. This fact was often noted by early narrators: 'Who is he who can live long in quiet in these parts? For all men are here made subject to the power of their infernal spirit and fight they must, although it be with their friends.'[44] Heavy drinking led to quarrelsome behaviour, young men angrily rioted against absentee proprietors, as in 1643, when the Barbadian assembly stopped paying proprietary rents to the Earl of Carlisle, or when French colonists in 1649 rose up against incompetent management of the *Compagnie des Iles d'Amérique*.

On each island political authority tended to be exercised by strong individuals: Houel on Guadeloupe, Du Parquet on Martinique, and Poincy on St Christopher. Some of them turned into petty tyrants: Henry Hawley in Barbados in the 1630s and 1640s or the Sieur du Bu in French Grenada in the 1650s. The latter, a man of modest origins, dubbed himself 'King of Grenada' and declared that the power of the King of France did not extend beyond the country's natural boundaries. In the 1650s, as the settlement was trying to survive repeated Carib attacks, du Bu submitted male settlers to a variety of arbitrary practices and measures and he sexually abused female settlers of any age. The death of a proprietor, which raised questions of inheritance, frequently led to expulsions and murders. Levasseur, governor of Tortuga island, was murdered by his two designated successors. A bitter feud erupted between clans in the Du Parquet family in Martinique and in the Houel family in Guadeloupe. As remarked upon, Dutch governors enjoyed more independence from the local élites and were less exposed to local opposition from colonists.

The famous line of Hobbes, 'nasty, brutish, solitary, poor, and short' has been aptly quoted by the English historian V.T. Harlow, to describe life in the early decades of the seventeenth century. Famine and death were omnipresent, causing frequent fights between settlements over resources like salt and cattle, slowing down necessary work for defence or agriculture. Hunger, with the disturbances and lack of loyalty it bred, is a leitmotiv. In 1636, two years after the Dutch had conquered Curaçao, Spanish spies reported that 'Dutch soldiers were so hungry that they wished the Spaniards would come back so that they could surrender to them.'[45] In October 1643 the storehouse of the Company had at the most three weeks supplies of fish, beans and vinegar; meat had become extremely scarce, extensive hunting having depleted the cattle. Pieter Stuyvesant, the well-known director of the Company, and his staff drew resolution after resolution restricting daily rations. They finally resorted to sending a small ship with half the garrison to neighbouring settlements in search of meat and other food.

The problem was still acute in the following decade. In 1655 the vice-director of the Company at Fort Amsterdam wrote that not much cotton and tobacco would be planted because everyone was preoccupied with provi-

Papayer franc 187.

Je Clerc. f.

1 A Carib man and woman, from J.B. Du Tertre, *Histoire Generale des Antilles,* Paris, 1667

2 Amerindians using tobacco, from Girolamo Benzoni, *La historia del mondo nuevo,* Venice,
1565

3 Havana, a famous port in North America, on the island of Cuba, by Peter Shank

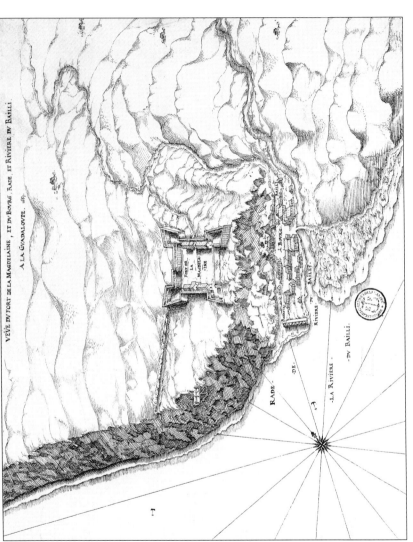

4 Fort and Bourg of Magdelaine, Guadeloupe, from J.B. Du Terre, *Histoire Generale des Antilles*, Paris, 1667

*Jeune Negre dans un Canot fait du Tronc d'un seul arbre,
qu'il conduit et gouuerne auec une pagaye.*

5 A young negro paddling a canoe made out of a single tree trunk, from Theodor de Bry,
   Americae, Frankfurt, 1590-1643

Mulastre qui fume, et qui est vestu de la maniere que les mulastres esclaues sont vestus dans les Isles Françoises de l'amerique,

6 A female mulatto slave, dressed in the local fashion, smoking a pipe, from Theodor de Bry, *Americae,* Frankfurt, 1590-1643

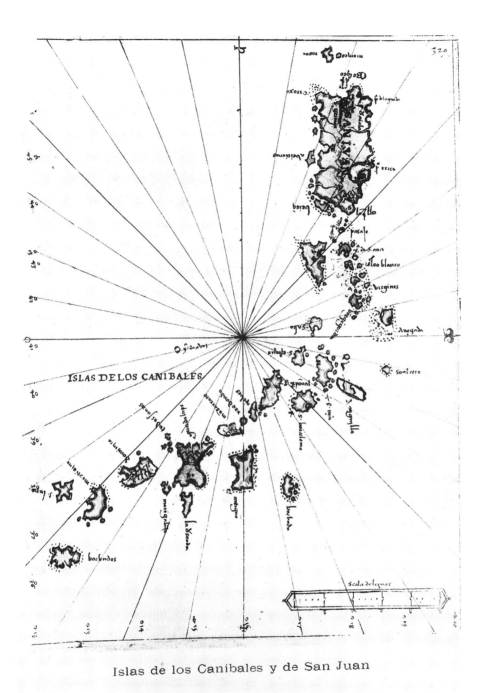

Islas de los Canibales y de San Juan

7 Islas de los Canibales y de San Juan (Islands of the Cannibals and San Juan) c. 1621

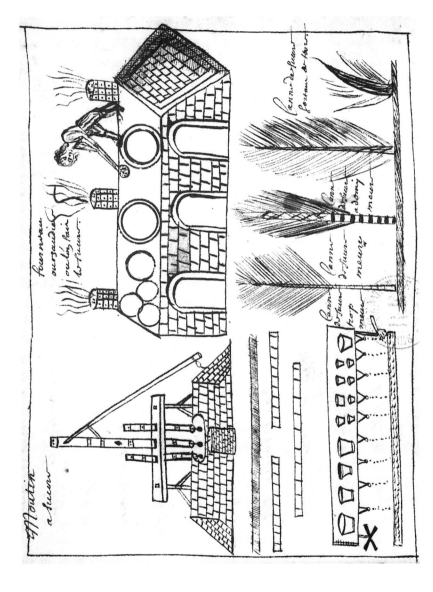

8 Sugar canes and the method of producing sugar

sions. 'I was not able to produce one pount of bread per week for the company's servants, so that they had to go into the country to dig up certain roots [likely to be cassava] and bake cakes from them in place of bread in order to fill up their hungry stomachs.'[46] Father Breton remembered shortly after his arrival a funeral in which a dead man, carried by a slave in his arms, was then buried in palm leaves in lieu of a shroud. The scarcity of goods that resulted in frequent famines led to exorbitant prices. Guillaume Coppier, who came as an indentured servant to St Christopher in the 1640s, remarked that prices could multiply a hundred times between Europe and the islands.[47]

Apart from Barbados, which neither against the Spaniards nor against the Indians ever experienced war, virtually all settlements feared attacks and destruction. They were a regular part of life. Father Labat noted as a general point that: 'the beginnings of every settlement [are] dangerous unless settlers take provisions.'[48] The passage of Spanish outbound fleets between non-Iberian settlements caused regular panics. Energetic Spanish commanders of the fleet strove to clear up the passages for their ship on their way toward the Greater Antilles. In 1629 Don Fadrique de Toledo destroyed the French and English settlements at St Christopher and Nevis; in 1633 he expelled the Dutch and French settlers from St Martin. At great cost, a Spanish fort and garrison were kept in St Martin from 1635 to 1646, before being reoccupied by the Dutch. On the southern passage for their fleets, a Dutch settlement which was just starting at Tobago was destroyed in 1636. For non-Iberians sailing on frail skippers and *pinnaces*, to find themselves on the passage of a powerful Spanish fleet was always frightening. Until well into the 1640s, the Dutch were the only ones to send naval forces from Europe to challenge the Spaniards. The French and English could only continue to harass the Spaniards by small plundering raids and smuggling operations. When they established smuggling coves around the Greater Antilles, as in Providence or Tortuga, they were regularly expelled by the Spaniards.

The danger posed by Carib attacks was different and a far more continuous experience. The Caribs had tolerated crews who went ashore for wood and water, and small bands of sailors ready to barter and mingle among them. When they saw large numbers of settlers arriving in search of land, the Caribs 'Displeasure [grew] in their hearts, at seeing the French settling on their own lands and making themselves the masters of their country.'[49] The hostility displayed by the Indians towards settlers repeated what Spaniards had experienced a century earlier in the Greater Antilles; it was also occurring in North America at the same time as in the Lesser Antilles. As settlements progressed, they raised increasing concern among Indians. When the governor of Martinique decided to launch a settlement on Grenada in 1649, the person he sent to elicit the best site was instructed to tell the 'wild men' that the French were just looking for fisheries, and to ease the atmosphere by plenty of liquor. After the expedition from Martinique had landed and men were busy building a fort, Carib chiefs, according to a missionary with the expedition, came to ask: 'We don't go to your lands. Why then do you come to ours? We do not want your land. Why do you take ours? We are satisfied with ours. Why are you not with what you have?'[50]

When Europeans occupied a site on an island, sooner or later they faced a confrontation with the Indians. The process began with the English and French at St Christopher in 1629. The Indians who had not been massacred generally retreated onto the leeward coast of the island (only they could sail on those rough seas), leaving to the newcomers their valuable 'gardens' on lands that were already cleared. The map of Martinique drawn by Mariette in 1645 shows the partition that had been taking place in the first decade of official settlement between the French to the windward and the Indians to the leeward. It was a matter of time before Indians were driven out of an island altogether by the Europeans' thrust for more lands. 'As our weapons frighten the wild men, our settlers [*habitants*] grow more and more numerous. No longer are they satisfied with the lots that these barbarians had left them; they are opening up new lands, clearing the forest (felling trees) at the same time that they are planting provisions and tobacco.'[51]

Thus, an uneasy pattern of relationships was initiated where bartering alternated with ambushes, and trickery was practised by both sides. 'Neither siege nor pitched battle, but a lot of surprise-attacks and a lot of ambushes; it's their way to wage war.'[52] Settlers built forts, and organized sentinels and militia, primarily to protect themselves against Indians. In times of crisis, everyone retreated into the fort; plantations had to be abandoned. Being exposed to frequent Indian attacks, Antigua for years looked more like a garrison than an agricultural settlement.[53] Stray settlers who went hunting or were clearing new grounds were easy targets for the Indian ambushes. English settlers at St Christopher had gone fishing for turtles when they 'were suddenly attacked with 7 or 8 naked Indians painted red and feathers in their heads.'[54] As elsewhere, endemic guerrilla warfare was nerve-wracking and caused panics: 'Red leaves in the woods looked to them [the French] as if they were wild men who were chasing after them ... and every floating log they took it to be a pirogue loaded with their enemies.'[55]

Relationships were particularly strained when settlers came directly from Europe. Totally unequipped, they relied on Indian provisions for their survival. In exchange for their hospitality and generosity, acknowledged over and over in the sources, Indians expected not only glass trinkets, such as mirrors and beads, that had been part of bartering since Columbus' first voyage, but also coloured cloth and feathered hats that they had integrated into their body adornments. Increasingly, alcohol, weapons, and tools such as sickles and axes also formed part of the exchange, for they had become vital to the Caribs. However, the Caribs had problems of supply to maintain their side of the exchange. Their resources in pigs, lizards and tortoises, and other products of their hunting and fishing, were soon strained by settler demand and then exhausted.

Father Bresson, a French missionary, described the repressive and murderous dynamic that a conflict over provisions set in motion when bartering arrangements collapsed. In 1651 he witnessed a retaliatory expedition that set fire to Carib *carbets* (settlements) in Grenada.

> When they had not come [to barter provisions], there were always people to complain that one should go and kill them, and take their provisions. Then three piroques showed up in one week with a lot of merchandise considering the season. Some clever elements then complained that they had only come to spy, and that they should be got rid of, and twice did their best to massacre those poor people who had come in good faith.

Restless and irresponsible elements pushed for raids to seize lands and provisions from the Indians. Their designs were initially resisted by others among the settlers. The governors could not but be concerned about the disastrous consequences a state of war could have for infant settlements. But once such a dynamic was set in motion, it was not easily stopped. 'Rushing to take to the sea and being so eager to catch the savages by surprise made people forget to eat and drink, or, at least, it did not give them time to do so,' recalled Father Bresson. In the 1640s Guadeloupe faced some of the most murderous 'Indian wars'.

Between 1620 and 1635 the threat posed by European intrusion extended southward. The Carib could not retreat into vast rainforest areas, as in the Amazon basin. They resisted steadily on one island after another in the southern Lesser Antilles. Expelled from Guadeloupe, they made Dominica and St Vincent their strongholds. They organized joint attacks and repeatedly dislodged Europeans from Tobago, St Lucia and Grenada. Mock treaties were concluded with the help of much alcohol. But they were only truces in a conflict that was brutal and merciless on both sides. A last treaty was concluded in 1660 between the governor of Martinique and the Indian chief of Dominica, leaving only this latter island to the Caribs. If this one seems to have been respected, it is because at this point Carib resistance had been exhausted. The individual bravery and intelligent strategy of the Caribs throughout those wars have been vividly narrated by French Dominican missionaries. They evoke qualities found in many subsequent colonial wars in the world.

Father Raymond Breton stands out as the most articulate critic of the northern intrusion into a long-standing state of war between Caribs and Arawaks. A good disciple of Las Casas, Breton believed that 'it was not legitimate to wage war unfairly on a free nation, to rob her of her properties and lands.' The missionary arrived at Guadeloupe with the first French settlers from Dieppe in 1635. Much to the displeasure of other colonists who thought he should attend to their religious needs, the Dominican considered his first duty to be the evangelization of Indians, according to the mandate of the Company. He made several stays in Dominica, documenting Carib culture and language in the 1640s. 'Had the Indians been left alone', Breton wrote, 'they could have been converted to Catholicism by missionaries who had learned their language.'[56]

Let us now consider the internal challenges faced by settler communities of young males. With the risks 'to raise commodities' being death and famine, settlers were, out of necessity, riveted to immediate demands and material constraints on life. Their communities have often been depicted as materialistic, deprived of any spiritual or moral values, and lacking artistic creativity or intellectual interest. A fresh look at the issue, however, leads to a slightly different conclusion. On the one hand people came with a minimum baggage of convictions and knowledge, among which religious convictions were central. When they were literate, Protestants brought along their Bible and Calvin's *Institutions*. French missionaries travelled with quite a supply of handbooks for homilies and confessions. Between them theological differences often led to vehement discussions. At an inn in Basse-Terre, Guadeloupe, in the 1640s, a Calvinist ship captain and a Catholic local merchant got into such heated debate that the governor deemed it necessary to go to the inn himself and interrupt the dispute.

On the other hand, an intensive and creative process took place within these settler communities in a broad cultural sphere, crowned by musical expression but reaching down to the humblest artifacts and processes. Jack Greene speaks of this process as 'cultural reformulation'. The process resembled the earlier cultural synthesis among Spaniards and Arawaks in the Greater Antilles. In the Lesser Antilles it began with the communities of sailors living with Caribs. It then drew both from European influences regularly injected by new European settlers and from a local Caribbean culture. As the latter rapidly thinned out, a growing group of newcomers, the African slaves, contributed to the cultural reformulation.

Observing that very few Barbadians enjoyed playing musical instruments, Ligon concluded: 'I found others whose souls were so fixed upon, and so riveted to the earth, and the prosperity that arises from it, as their souls were lifted no higher, and those men think and have been heard to say, that three whip-sawes, going all at once in a frame or pit is the best and sweetest musick that can enter their ears.'[57] But Ligon's negative remark followed his description of one of the most remarkable instances of cultural reformulation between Europeans and Africans. Ligon had shown a string instrument to a slave, explaining how strings of different length could produce different tunes. The next day, the English settler found the slave, while on duty on a provision ground, fabricating accurately, out of his memory, the musical instrument.

This process of cultural reformulation engendering a creole material civilization was most active among proletarian labourers. Here three ethnic groups collided. Almost from the very beginning settler communities in the Lesser Antilles regarded some slaves as on a par with white servants. Slaves were sometimes Indian (from the islands as well as from a broad area extending from *Tierra Firma* to Carolina), but increasingly most were African. Whites predominated numerically until the 1640s or 50s, depending on the islands. The difference between slaves and servants were clearly stated: the former were enslaved for life, the latter only for the period of their contract. This meant different food, clothing and lodgings. When cattle died by disease, Ligon observed, 'servants ate the body and negroes the skin, head and entrails';[58] servants drank a potato-alcohol while negroes had plain water. Some of these differences, however, may have been blurred by the fact that early slaves, Indian and African, were often reserved for domestic tasks while white servants worked in the fields. The significance of slave-servant distinctions was further lessened by social context. Indians particularly, and Africans at the beginning, were minorities, working in close proximity with whites, who were the more numerous among labourers.

Class differences that allowed masters to exploit servants were perceived by everyone. 'Most eminent persons' were frequently contrasted with 'humblest indentured servants' – just as their mutual prejudices were expressed toward alien cultures. But colour and class had not yet collapsed around one rigid divide. Hardships and rebellious behaviour were often similar for both servants and slaves. Alike they were press-ganged, kidnapped, displayed to be purchased, and sold along with an estate. 'Poor negroes and Christian servants', as Ligon noted,[59] 'both ran away and rose up to escape or protest cruel conditions'. In 1635, in St Christopher, French servants rebelled against their masters. 'They were plainly talking of servants becoming masters and masters the servants.' On one occasion when the Spaniards attacked St Christopher, servants threw away arms, crying 'Liberty, joyful liberty!' and swam to the Spanish ships. Colt commented 'But these servants of the planters rather desire the Spaniards might come, that by it they might be freed, than any willingness they show to defend their masters.'[60] As early as 1639, a group of 60 Africans in St Christopher was reported to have become Maroons. From the mountains where they had sought refuge, the Maroons were sending arrows down among the settlers.[61] It is fascinating to observe those cultural transfers operating outside European settlements. Indian slaves running away; African runaways joining Caribs, fighting naked with arrows, their bodies dyed with red annatto; Carib Indians owning African slaves that they sometimes kidnapped from white settlers; Caribs and Arawaks raiding on each other's islands to capture enemies.

In this early period the process of social division along colour and class lines was still incipient, as indicated by the number of attributes applied indifferently or successively to both servants and slaves. Spaniards called white servants *esclavos*, while a missionary began a remark, 'When one has a servant, white or black ...'[62] An ordinance of 1664 by Governor Tracy, in the French islands, 'forbids any plantation owner (*maître de case*) regardless of his religious confession, to prevent servants and negroes from going to mass on Sundays and holidays.' One still had to specify to which group some provisions applied, which later would be exclusively, therefore implicitly, associated with one given group. In 1636 Governor Hawley from Barbados ruled 'that negroes and Indians that came here to be sold should serve for life, unless a contract was before made to the contrary.'

The élite of these settlements lacked a clear economic orientation, another sign of a young society. Those who went there had only vague ideas about commerce. Soldiers by career, the model they had in mind was Cortés, who found land and riches through conquest. Merchants and gentleman-promoters invested their joint-stock capital in both privateering and planting ventures. When Sir Henry Colt arrived at St Christopher in 1631, he started tobacco planting. While the crop was getting ready, Colt went with his ship to load salt at nearby St Martin. When his ship was severely damaged by a storm, he decided to go to the Spanish Main and trade with the Indians. Yet, while making such plans, the gentleman from Essex was writing to relatives that they should send him more men to 'keep afoot' the 'great plantations' he had set up.[63]

Routinely the trading privileges granted by a charter included commodities produced, traded or taken in prizes, all seen as elements of trading ventures. The fact that settlements in the Lesser Antilles were launched when the war against Spain resumed, gave privateering a sustained importance in merchants' and promoters' plans. The first settlers' ship sent by the French to St Christopher and Guadeloupe, as well as those the English sent to St Christopher and Barbados, all took prizes en route to the Antilles. To obtain the settlement of the prizes by the Admiralty might delay the beginning of a settlement, but prizes were seen as a welcome means of survival in the first months of a settlement.

Settlements could be used as bases for piracy and contraband. St Martin and Curaçao were settled by the Dutch primarily as naval bases located between Europe and Brazil and nearby Spanish possessions. Promoters developed enterprises alternatively in privateering or planting. In England, the Earl of Warwick had the most successful enterprise in the 1610s. After the end of the war between England and Spain in the 1630s, Warwick invested in planting the colony of Providence off the Mosquito Coast. The proximity to Spanish colonies offered him 'opportunities of gaining by prizes'.[64] Warwick also tried to set foot on the island of Tortuga; he bought the proprietorship rights over Barbados. Neither Providence nor Tortuga settlements were successful. Spanish reprisals against both islands ended the days of the Company. Warwick returned to privateering. His own fleet constituted a large part of the Royal Navy, the command of which he received in 1642.

The expedition of Captain William Jackson that threatened Jamaica in 1642 was sent by Warwick. As Dutch filibustering campaigns were foundering, the English and French entered a new era of privateering toward the Greater Antilles and the Isthmus that would last until the beginning of the eighteenth century. Semi-private navies sent from Europe recruited additional forces among communities that were beginning to be established in the islands surrounding the Spanish Greater Antilles: Tortuga, the Cayman Islands, Providence and San Andrés in the Bahamas. As their former bases were being turned into plantations, freebooters who had been part of the Caribbean since the sixteenth century, did not disappear. Rather, they carried their male, maritime and migrant culture from the Lesser Antilles to the Greater Antilles, where it continued to receive a steady stream of landless young males expelled from the Lesser Antilles by the progress of sugar plantations after the middle of the century. As Esquemeling made clear in the *Buccaneers of America*, settlers might choose piracy after attempting other economic alternatives. 'The first plantation was tobacco', wrote Esquemeling of Tortuga's economy. 'They attempted likewise to make sugar but by reason of the great expenses necessary to defray the charges, they could not bring it to any effect... So that the greatest part of the inhabitants ... betook themselves to the exercise of hunting and the remaining part to that of piracy.'[65]

The buccaneers knew their heyday in Tortuga, Providence and other coves from the late 1620s to the 1670s–80s. Their success rested on an economic foundation encompassing privateering, smuggling, tobacco and hide-producing (along with hunting tortoises and collecting salt or wood). The contraband with Spanish colonists in which the pirates engaged, as well as their ties with the hide market in Europe, contributed in no small way to the formation of non-Iberian empires in America. Their fame, however, came from their military activities. With an efficiency not always proven, they regularly cooperated with freebooters and navy campaigns in the Caribbean.

The Lesser Antilles in the Caribbean region, 1640–60: changes and legacy

Between 1640 and 1660 a wide variety of changes took place in the Lesser Antilles which gradually affected most of the islands. In various ways those changes seemed to solve problems, overcome limitations, and complete processes initiated in the early years. The labour force of the early decades, primarily based on white indentured immigration, supplemented by some Indians and African slaves, had been chronically scarce. The problem, from the colonists' point of view, was solved by a massive introduction of African slaves. Both male and female, these Africans replaced European white males as the largest social group. As a result, Caribbean populations became half African and slave, and the process of miscegenation was activated.

Tobacco ceased to be the major commercial crop, when ten boom years ended with soil exhaustion and overproduction. Its place was taken by a much more lucrative commodity, sugar. In fact, sugar had been cultivated since 1520 in Santo Domingo and the Greater Antilles. It had become insignificant by the time the non-Iberians began settling in the Lesser Antilles. They soon tried to produce sugar, following the example of Brazil. The crop was given a decisive boost, first when the Barbadian planters received technical assistance from Dutch merchants versed in sugar production in Pernambuco, and then in the 1650s, after the Dutch lost Brazil (1654), from the arrival of Dutch and Jewish colonists and merchants who sought asylum with their slaves in the French islands. Unlike tobacco, sugar would enjoy a steadily growing demand in Europe. The islands with an earlier development based on tobacco lost importance. St Christopher in particular, for decades the centre of French and English colonization in the Lesser Antilles, entered a decline. 'If you go to Christophers, you shall see the ruins of a flourishing place', remarked a visitor in 1645.[66]

Other changes stemmed from the assertion of political and economic control over the islands by the French and English monarchies. Commercial companies and lord proprietors had managed control with varying degrees of royal supervision and a great many local disturbances. In the 1640s political troubles came to a head in the French and English islands. The next two decades saw the beginning of officials appointed by the state, while the privileges and powers of commercial companies were limited to commercial matters. In 1664 the French *Compagnie des Indes Occidentales*, brainchild of minister Colbert, was granted trading privileges for 40 years, but the governor-general of the French islands was appointed by the King. Within ten years, even trade was directly controlled by the King of France. At the same time, political dissidence was curbed and religious tolerance put to an end, be it of English Royalists or of French Huguenots.

The way the rights of state authority were successfully imposed on Barbados illustrates the fact that economic necessities played their part. After members of the local assembly revolted against the Earl of Carlisle in the 1640s, Barbados became largely autonomous. During the Cromwell era the island was dominated by Cavaliers. With the Restoration, however, Barbadian planters had to surrender much of their independence, which meant they had to accept the protectionist policy established by the Navigation Acts of 1651 and 1660 and deal only with the English market and merchants, as the price of sugar was only half what it had been in 1640. Likewise France established a national trade monopoly which excluded foreign merchants and ships – mostly the Dutch.

The rise of national trade monopolies in the French and English islands did serious harm to the Dutch. Dutch Caribbean entrepôts, merchants, and ships had to operate entirely on an interloper basis in importing African slaves and European goods, and exporting sugar. But before they lost a substantial part of the English and French trade, they were already busy organizing an entrepôt in Curaçao primarily to smuggle slaves into nearby *Tierra Firme*. The official correspondence from New Netherlands related the efforts of this colony to equip its harbour with docks, warehouse and repair facilities, to initiate a small trade of hides for slaves with Spanish colonists that would lead to 'a trade of importance'. 'May the Lord God give His blessing that the Spaniards may be encouraged by this small beginning to come here to trade,' wrote Matthias Beck, the vice-governor from Fort Amsterdam in 1657.[67] The new charter received in 1647 by the West India Company clearly reflected this emphasis on contraband. It responded to a new international context: the peace which was to be concluded with Spain made privateering irrelevant.

The end of Dutch primacy in the Lesser Antilles was contemporary with the defeat of the Caribs who retreated to two islands, Dominica and St Vincent (from which they would finally be deported at the end of the eighteenth century). Father Labat's epilogue on the Caribs seems to convey the view of the time:

> Our Caribs were always a warrior people, proud and unsubmissive, who preferred death rather than servitude. Europeans were not able to civilize Caribs enough so that they could all dwell together in the same places [...] Instead [Europeans] were forced to destroy and hunt [the Caribs]; they had to corner them where they are today, in two islands alone, that are Dominica and St Vincent, in order [for the Europeans] to live somehow safely in the other islands.[68]

The elimination of the Caribs was one point on which colonists and metropolitan states were in agreement. In 1661 Louis XIV's instructions to his governor-general for the French islands was 'To wage war with them [the Caribs] until we exterminate or expel them.'[69]

As the Carib threat was removed, so was that posed by Spain, which faced an economic and political crisis after 1640. The Treaty of Westphalia recognized the independence of the Netherlands and its overseas possessions. The Spaniards gave up trying to keep the non-Iberians off the route of their outbound fleet through the Lesser Antilles. Instead they were subjected to an offensive by the non-Iberians in the Greater Antilles. From Tortuga, in the 1640s, the French gained a foothold in the north-west of Hispaniola (the colony of Saint-Domingue was to be recognized in 1698). In 1655 the English conquered the Spanish colony of Jamaica. This was the sole result of Cromwell's 'Great Design', which had aimed at seizing larger pieces of the Spanish domain in America, while replacing the Dutch as Spain's successful rivals in the Caribbean. England and France both then turned against the Dutch Republic: each waged three wars against the Dutch between 1652 and 1713. Starting in 1672, the Anglo-Dutch war initiated a new era of generalized warfare which pitted European countries against one another.

A new balance of power was established and the centre of gravity shifted within the Caribbean region. The Spaniards and the Dutch were now on the defensive while the English and French became successfully aggressive. While the Lesser Antilles remained the main centres of Caribbean colonization officially until the end of the century, this western frontier attracted more and more of their white immigrants from the 1650s on. A move westward had been initiated which, in the next century, would shift the Caribbean centre of gravity for all the metropolises toward the Greater Antilles.

These changes signalled that around the middle of the seventeenth century the phase of the early settlements was coming to a close. The founding of new societies had started as trading ventures in which merchants and settlers, each in different ways, expected to profit by getting rewards unattainable in Europe. Hardships, factions and famine, fear of the Indians, conflicts with them over land which ended in the Indians' elimination – all had been part of the price for undertaking this venture. The fear of being abandoned had also been pervasive. The impression gained is that in developing plantations the first settlers, daunted and incapacitated by inexperience, were sometimes not so much responding to the promoters' blandishments as driven by the fear of being totally abandoned by traders, who would allow them to starve if they had nothing to offer in exchange. Avoiding starvation often depended on the food a ship could bring, and inducing a ship to stop depended on their ability to produce something worthy of being traded.

Chronicling the first year of Guadeloupe's settlers, Father Breton writes: 'The ships were passing by, afar, for they could not have found her anything to trade.'[70] And Richard Ligon, about the first generation of Barbadians: 'Their supplies from England coming so slow and so uncertainly, they were often driven to great extremities; and the tobacco that grew there, so earthly and worthless, as it could give them little or no return from England or else-where; so that for a while they lingered on in a lamentable condition.' It was only when colonists were able to grow indigo, cotton and wood 'to traffick with, [that] some ships were invited (in hope of gain by that trade) to come and visit them, bringing for exchange such commodities as they wanted, working tools, iron, steel, clothes, shirts and drawers, hose and shoes, hats and more hands.'[71]

New institutions, activities and policies had been transferred onto the islands without clear ideas or direction. Following Iberian precedents, the French and English monarchies grafted feudal institutions onto commercial enterprises. Rights over islands were granted which provided economic rewards in the form of tributes, land-rents, and trade-duties, and could be parcelled out to followers. Soon, however, the initial feudal pattern of power and profit was undermined by market forces which began integrating the metropolitan and the islands' economies and by state authority which reclaimed justice, taxation and defence prerogatives. Even without this temporary coexistence of competing economic and political principles, there would have been political disturbances as a result of the broader sorting-out process experienced by societies in the making. These conflicts had an almost biological quality, as different groups or factions competed for control of resources, before efficient mechanisms of regulation, control and arbitrage were created. None of this, it should be said, was peculiar to these societies; it was the lot of other equally recent non-Iberian settlements in America, as it had been earlier that of Spanish and Portuguese settlements. But it is useful to remember that difficulties, confusions, tragedies, and a halting, sporadic tempo were intrinsic characteristics of the beginnings of the Lesser Antilles.

At the same time, features appeared in those early decades that would constitute enduring patterns for the Caribbean as a whole. The significance of this early era should not be reduced, as is unfortunately common, to being a mere prelude to the later classic age of slave and sugar plantations. The first long-term result of the settlement by non-Iberians in the Caribbean was to give a territorial existence to islands that during the sixteenth century had merely served as watering places and provisioning stations among the Caribs, *en route* to the Spanish Antilles. The Greater and Lesser Antilles now together formed the insular part of America, a new entity, constructed by the Europeans.

By 1660 the insular Caribbean was clearly differentiated between Spanish and non-Spanish spheres, as were more broadly the old Iberian America and the more recent non-Iberian one. Barbados was, by 1650, the most populated and wealthiest colony in British America, and the French Lesser Antilles had six times more white settlers than French Canada (where there were 2000 in 1660). Yet both English and French Caribbean colonies were young, rough and frail as compared to Havana or Cartagena. At the same time, however, what had emerged in the Lesser Antilles was an imbricated pattern of European nationalities and languages which was to be duplicated in the Greater Antilles. 'If they had been free to choose, they would not have formed enclaves as they have, in such a way that the English are in Nevis, Montserrat, Antigua, between St Christopher and Guadeloupe, and the Dutch, who own St Eustatius, between St Christopher and St Croix, just as the French who as the masters of Martinique and Guadeloupe between Barbados and Antigua, so badly they bother (*s'empêchent*) one another, and put serious obstacles to trade between them, particularly during war,' wrote the governor-general of the French islands in 1670. By then, the political and linguistic map of the Caribbean had been set for a century. It would remain roughly the same until 1760 (St Christopher officially becoming English in 1702).

A second legacy had to do with ecological modifications. Once Europeans cleared and established plantations, the primeval forest, which earlier Indian slash-and-burn and extensive garden agriculture had touched more lightly, receded quickly, leaving the most inaccessible hills as refuges for runaways. In 1620, passing French freebooters noticed that Barbados had abundant wild pigs. Ten years later, Sir Henry Colt recorded that they had been 'well nigh eliminated ... They usually killed 1500 a week, a waste too great to be continued... But this plentiful world of theirs is now past... They needed not have made such a hasty destruction of them.'[72] In the following decade, Father Du Tertre observed how many Caribbean animal species, fish and mammals, had disappeared from the French islands: 'The abundance of these things had either diminished or been entirely destroyed.'[73] Supplies in wood and cattle were being exhausted, as settlers kept arriving. In Curaçao in 1656 the vice-governor explained his difficulty in provisioning the garrison with local fish and cattle and the need to receive foodstuffs from Europe. When the Spaniards were the masters of the island, Matthias Beck said, they could still sustain themselves with what existed there. But then there were few families and no garrison to maintain.[74]

Agricultural settlements occupied the leeward coasts, the lots gradually extending inland in terraces parallel to the seashore. It was in the Lesser Antilles that an intensive agricultural landscape (rather different from that of Spanish early plantations in the Greater Antilles) was created that was to spread to a large part of the colonial Caribbean over the next two centuries.

Vegetable gardens and cattle pastures surrounded the lots planted with commercial crops. Human settlements were dispersed, rather isolated from one another; piers and boats linked them to the main harbour, that is, to the outside world. In the Dutch as well as the French and English islands, this harbour was protected by a fort, surrounded by the wealthiest estates. Around the site of the harbour an incipient *bourg* was emerging: a church, a few inns, shops and warehouses along the harbour edge. Soon the reinforcement of administrative and trade controls and the growth of population would create the first urban concentrations around this single fortified point.

A third important legacy of those beginnings was to provide the basis for centuries of a colonial economy based on trade. As with the Iberians earlier, trading connections across the Atlantic had begun to integrate the economy between Europe and colonial America, through the import of European goods and export of agricultural commodities. Trade routes were being established, which favoured some islands and left out others. When the French tried in the 1650s to establish a colony in Grenada, one of the difficulties allegedly preventing its development was: 'This island is quite off the route of the ships.'[75] In contrast with the poor quality of the commodities exported from the islands, commercial techniques appeared already quite sophisticated. They involved cash to grow cash crops, to pay money-rents, and to hire wage labour. The pattern established early on with the tobacco trade was amplified during the next century of French and English trans-Atlantic trade. From the seventeenth century on, trading connections between the Lesser Antilles and Europe were more frequent than those to the Spanish Caribbean. This created a dependency on outside resources which had important cultural consequences in the patterns of consumption. Whether it was clothing, foodstuffs, or construction materials, the better materials came from Europe for the wealthiest.

Ships also carried immigrants from Europe and from Africa. Until well into the eighteenth century the lethal climate of the tropics, coupled with the exploitative nature of the work on plantations, slowed the natural growth of the population considerably, which depended mainly on immigration for renewal. From the very beginning, it had been an immigration mainly geared toward supplying a labour force. Such large-scale unskilled immigration never ensures a good treatment for the immigrants, even though they were in demand. The conditions of servitude to which indentured white servants were submitted served as a pattern for African slavery. As David Galenson wrote: 'Wherever slavery ultimately developed, indentured servitude had earlier been in use.'[76] And Eric Williams: 'White servitude was the system upon which negro slavery was constructed.'[77] The Lesser Antilles were among the regions in which an earlier reliance on servant labour paved the way to slave labour.

As the slave population grew in the Lesser Antilles, poor whites became a numerical minority, skilled and used as overseers on plantations. They retained frontier activities as fishermen, cowboys, salt-producers, loggers and hunters. (With the urban growth of the next century, they would also form a class of urban artisans.) Poor whites lived on the margins of plantations, in areas not yet cleared and poorly connected; some moved to the Greater Antilles, where their communities survived well into the eighteenth century. Poor whites were also left in charge of local maritime connections, cabotage and contraband. In wartime, they shifted to privateering. Until the beginning of the nineteenth century, Caribbean white freebooters retained a distinctive lifestyle. All their property was contained in a trunk: their arms, miscellaneous personal belongings, and legal and financial documents that established their rights to shares and promises from merchants.

As their heyday passed, freebooters acquired a legendary stature. They also provided mythical origins to Caribbean non-Iberian communities that was called forth in the defence of political rights. In the French islands popular riots invoked the privileges of freebooters against the establishment of royal control over trade in the 1660s-80s. In the eighteenth century the myth of free and egalitarian communities, not subjected to royal authority, living on a boundless sea and not tied up to any land or family, in a society with neither big sugar planters nor slaves, was also employed to buttress political claims. In Saint-Domingue in 1788 radical political thinking held that a compact had been made between the King of France and freebooters: they had freely recognized the King's authority, and in exchange he defended them and their properties. 'Saint-Domingue was neither conquered nor subjected ... Brave [gallant] Frenchmen, independent ... whose only dwelling was the sea ... expelled the Spaniards ... this conquest was their sole property. They kept it during ten years in their quality of freebooters. Having sovereign rights of possession, they were absolutely free to give it to the one among European kings they deemed most worthy.'[78]

NOTES

1   Andrews, K.R., *The Spanish Caribbean. Trade and Plunder, 1530–1630* (1978), p. 85.
2   *Ibid.*, pp. 119–120.
3   Hilton, J., 'Relation of the First Settlements of St Christopher and Nevis' in Harlow, V.T. *et al.*, (eds) (1925) *Colonising Expeditions to the West Indies and Guiana, 1623–1667*, p. 3.
4   *Ibid.*, p. 237.
5   De Laet, I., *De Nieuwe Wereldt ofte bechrijvinghe van West-Indien* (1625), Bk. I, Ch. XVII, p. 106.
6   *Ibid.*, p. 231.

7   *Ibid.*, pp. 241–2.

8   Hilton, 'Relation of the first Settlement of St Christopher and Nevis', p. 1.

9   Ligon, R., *A True and Exact History of the Island of Barbados* (1654) p. 23.

10 *Ibid.*, p. 24

11 Goslinga, C.C., *The Dutch in the Caribbean and on the Wild Coast, 1580–1680* (1971) p. 505.

12 *Ibid.*, p. 129.

13 Harlow, 'The Voyage of Sir Henry Colt', p. 94.

14 *Ibid.*, p. 81.

15 Gehring, C.T. and Schiltkamp, J.A., *Curaçao Papers, 1640–1665*, p. 33.

16 Harlow, *Colonising Expeditions*, XVI–XVII.

17 Petitjean Roget, J., *La Société d'habitation à la Martinique: Un demi-siècle de formation, 1635–1685*, 2 Vols, (1985).

18 May, L-P., *Histoire économique de la Martinique, 1635–1763* (1930) p. 31.

19 Innes, F.C., 'The Pre-Sugar Era of European Settlement in Barbados', in *Journal of Caribbean History*, I (1970), p. 7.

20 Harlow, 'The Voyage of Sir Henry Colt', p. 101.

21 Chatillon, M. and Debien, G., 'La propaganda imprimée pour les Antilles et la Guyane au 17e siècle, recrutement ou racolage 2', in *Notes d'Histoire Coloniale*, 217, p. 65.

22 'Relation des missions des Pères de la Compagnie de Jésus', in Chatillon and Debien, 'Propaganda imprimée pour les Antilles', p. 94.

23 Du Tertre, J.B., *Histoire générale des Antilles*, I, (1667–1671) p. 84.

24 Ligon, *True and Exact History*, p. 44.

25 Harlow, 'The Voyage of Sir Henry Colt', p. 54.

26 Chatillon and Debien, 'Propaganda imprimée pour les Antilles', p. 65.

27 Coppier, G., *Histoire et voyage des Indes Occidentales*, (1645), pp. 3–4.

28 Esquemeling, J., *Buccaneers of America* (1684–5) pp. 42–3.

29 Pares, R., *Merchants and Planters*, (1970), p. 18.

30 Harlow, 'The Voyage of Sir Henry Colt', pp. 66–7.

31 Dunn, R.S., *Sugar and Slaves (1972), p. 81.*

32 Debien, G., 'Colons, marchands et engagés,' p. 8.

33 *Curaçao Papers*, p. 83.

34 *Ibid.*, p. 85.

35 *Ibid.*, p. 99.

36 Du Tertre, *Histoire générale*, I, p. 23.

37 Pares cites a deed among many kept at PRO 75, p. 30.

38 Devèze, M., *Antilles, Guyanes*, vol. 2, (1977), p. 196.

39 Pares, *Merchants and Planters*, 75, p. 30.

40 J. Davies, in Harlow, V.T., *A History of Barbados 1625–1685* (1926), p. 42.

41 Ligon, *True and Exact History*, p. 21.

42 *Ibid.*, p. 43.

43 Dunn, 'Experiments Holy and Unholy 1630–1631', p. 275.

44 Harlow, 'The Voyage of Sir Henry Colt.'

45 Felice Cardot, *Curazao hispánico*, pp. 229–31.

46 *Curaçao Papers*, pp. 80–7.

47 Coppier, *Histoire des Indes Occidentales*, p. 53.

48 Labat, J.B., *Nouveau voyage aux isles de l'Amérique* (1722), p. 168.

49 Du Tertre, *Histoire générale*, I, pp. 117–19.

50   Roget, J.P. (ed.) *Histoire de l'Isle de la Grenada en Amérique, 1649–1659* (1975), p. 55.
51   Du Tertre, *Histoire générale*, I, p. 107.
52   Labat, *Nouveau voyage*, pp. 242–3.
53   Pares, *Merchants and Planters*, p. 62.
54   Harlow, 'Voyage of Sir Henry Colt', pp. 76–7 and 96.
55   Du Tertre, *Histoire générale*, I, p. 93.
56   Breton, R., *Relations de l'Île de la Guadeloupe (1647) p. 158.*
57   Ligon, *True and Exact History*, p. 107.
58   *Ibid.*, pp. 37–8.
59   *Ibid.*, p. 107.
60   Harlow, 'Voyage of Sir Henry Colt', p. 87.
61   Du Tertre, *Histoire générale*, I, pp. 157–9.
62   Labat, *Nouveau Voyage*, p. 56.
63   Harlow, 'Voyage of Sir Henry Colt', p. 101.
64   Craven W.F., 'Earl of Warwick' (1930), p. 469.
65   Esquemeling, *Buccaneers of America*, p. 41.
66   Dunn, *Sugar and Slaves* (1972), p. 121.
67   *Curaçao Papers*, p. 106.
68   Labat, *Nouveau voyage*, IV, p. 242.
69   Quoted in Ly, A. 'La formation de l'économie sucrière', (1957), p. 9.
70   Breton, *Relation de l'Iles de la Guadeloupe*, p. 92.
71   Ligon, *True and Exact History*, p. 24.
72   Harlow, 'Voyage of Sir Henry Colt', p. 92.
73   Du Tertre, *Histoire générale*, IV.
74   *Curaçao Papers*, pp. 97–8.
75   Roget, *Histoire de l'Isle de la Grenada*, p. 21.
76   Galenson, D.W., *White servitude in Colonial America* (1981) p. 120.
77   Quoted in Galenson, *White Servitude.*
78   Frostin, C., *Les révoltes blanches à Saint-Domingue aux XVIIe et XVIIIe siècles* (1975) pp. 44–5.

6

FORCED AFRICAN SETTLEMENT. THE BASIS OF FORCED SETTLEMENT: AFRICA AND ITS TRADING CONDITIONS

Enriqueta Vilá Vilar with *Wim Klooster*

Although the forced emigration of Africans to the Americas may be considered an accident or an unusual scheme which had to be introduced for the development of new societies, it is certain that the slave trade arising out of this emigration was in no way haphazard. It had in fact been practised for centuries, but now it started to grow in a spectacular way. A few years after the first Spanish settlements in the West Indies were founded, the slave trade expanded in proportion to the amount of land being incorporated under the Crown of Castile and to the resulting decimation of the indigenous population.

In effect, European trade with Africa was well established in the Mediterranean world. It increased considerably with the growth of Islam and the commercial expansion associated with it. The Arabs, as large distributors of products of the Eastern and Western worlds, were in constant contact with the great traders of the Italian city-states, and were able to set up a trading network dealing mainly in expensive oriental fabrics, gold, marble and slaves between southern Europe, Egypt and the Maghreb. Centuries later, the nation-states of Portugal and Spain, long-standing enemies of the Arabs, would exploit these established routes in order to perpetuate hostilities against the Muslims in their own lands.

Portuguese contact with the African continent in the early fifteenth century served to confirm officially what the sailors of the west coast of the Iberian peninsula and the intrepid Italian traders had known for many years – that is, that there was land across the Sahara that was rich in gold and marble, and not too well controlled by their rivals. Drawing from the experience of the Atlantic sailors, the Portuguese came into contact with sub-Saharan Africa in the 1440s. In 1441 an expedition returned from the Guinea coast with the first black slaves, and in 1444–5 the Portuguese reached the

Cape Verde Islands and the mouth of the Senegal River, where they set up their base for rapid penetration into these territories. Various states in West and South-west Africa facilitated a profitable and constant trade, which would be an important feature in their development.

By the mid-fifteenth century Lisbon became an important port from which slaves were sent to other European centres, particularly the Atlantic islands of Madeira and the Azores, where black slaves once used as mere house servants were tested on sugar plantations with promising results. This served as the basis for the later success achieved in the Caribbean, as the spread of slave labour exceeded the limits of the Mediterranean and impacted on the Atlantic.[1]

The African background

When European merchants first called on the West African coast, slavery had for long been a common feature of African societies. The institution existed throughout the continent, as a consequence of the legal impossibility to reproduce wealth by buying land. In Africa, land was relatively scarce and private land property non-existent. People who wanted to invest their wealth had to turn to purchasing slaves. Slaves were to be found among soldiers, servants, high-ranking officials, as well as humble producers, since not only private persons employed slaves, but rulers also relied on their services. Some of these slaves might end up in European hands by means of trade that took place on the coast or at inland markets.[2]

For students of Afro-American history, the origin of slaves imported into America is extremely interesting. From the outset, the anthropological, physical, cultural and linguistic diversity of the Africans who landed at Caribbean ports in growing numbers became evident. In the early seventeenth century, the Jesuit Alonso de Sandoval was able to discern over 300 ethnic groups, evidence of which can be found in documents, since slave traders kept records of the area from which the slaves came, in order to determine their physiological or psychological characteristics. Soon, in the murky and complex world of the slave trade, it became possible to discern docility or rebelliousness and skill or lack of it among the different nations arriving in the Caribbean, just as it was to distinguish their language and tribal 'marks' or scars. In 1532, for instance, the Spanish King prohibited the export to America of Jolof slaves from Upper Guinea, because of their alleged pride, disobedience and rebelliousness.[3] It also became possible to identify, generally speaking, which regions of Africa had the greatest ethnic and cultural influence in the Caribbean and to understand the shift of the

160

centre of the slave trade towards the coast of south-western Africa during the sixteenth and seventeenth centuries.

Along with the slaves, traits of various African cultures were transferred to the Caribbean. Already by the 1540s, as an Italian traveller reported, the African nations of Hispaniola had their own kings or governors. The various African groups living in the town of Cartagena de Indias appointed their officials annually and celebrated their traditional feasts under cover of Christian holidays. Ethnic articulation would take place in the *cofradías*, the religious brotherhoods that cared for the churches and organized festivals for the patron saints.[4] Black slaves also reconstructed elements of their African cultures in their runaway communities. These were mostly short-lived, but some survived for more than a century without outside contact.

At the risk of being simplistic, we can identify three large areas along the continent which competed with one another in selling slaves to the Americas: 1) Upper Guinea, the area from Senegal to present-day Liberia, 2) Lower Guinea, the area between Ivory Coast (now Côte d'Ivoire) and Cameroon, and 3) the Angolan coast.

We can situate in these areas the different 'nations' which constituted the majority of the captives in Africa. No one nation emerged victorious over the others, at least until 1650, when the Portuguese lost control of the slave trade. From then on, the European slave trade became a well-organized business, and the ethnic origins of slaves in the different Caribbean islands were in large measure influenced by the European power to which they belonged. For instance, the strong Arara influence in the French West Indies had its origin in the French colony of Dahomey.[5] This meant that the people belonging to this old culture ended up in the French West Indies.

Towards the end of the sixteenth century ships arrived in the Caribbean from many distant regions of Africa. In these regions the slavers needed time, skill and patience to obtain a 'cargo' provided by the African merchants, kings and warlords. There is a notable difference between the hurried expeditions into the interior occasioned by the arrival of a slave ship, and the organization of powerful traders from the coast with agents in the interior with an organized army of skilled blacks in their service who acted as middlemen and bartered for slaves.[6] European traders offered a wide range of goods in return for the slaves: European and Asian cloth, iron, copper, weapons, cowry shells (which were used as currency), trinkets and beads. None of these goods were unknown to central Africa, which could boast an impressive metal and textile production, but African trade with Europe was largely moved by prestige and fancy.[7]

161

The trade in black slaves constituted the basis of a veritable economic revolution, not only by facilitating the start of a form of mercantile capitalism, but also by constituting the cornerstone of a new form of labour which revolutionized production. Slavery transported to America assumed special characteristics which were very different in nature and scope from slavery in Europe, with its Graeco-Roman tradition. Slavery in the Americas was also a more complex phenomenon than the terms 'slave society' or 'plantation economy' would suggest. According to Sidney Mintz, it was an intrinsic component of European capitalism, and he supports this statement by a quotation from Marx who stressed that the work of the African in America was the driving force behind trade and changed the economy by producing raw materials for the industry.[8] If the slave trade was one of the cornerstones of early capitalism, it can be easily understood why it was supported by those nations where a strong bourgeoisie had developed during the sixteenth century, namely England, Holland and France. These countries ended Spain's monopoly in areas where Spain lacked the political and military power to maintain its domination.

A dynamic market: the slaves as merchandise

If we admit that the early form of capitalism, based, *inter alia* on trade with far-off lands, emerged in the early sixteenth century, it is clear that the slave trade contributed significantly to the development of many of the great commercial metropoles. It was one of the most lucrative enterprises of early European colonization in America. What appeared in the beginning to be no more than a series of royal concessions granted on a somewhat questionable basis to courtiers, high-ranking officials, nobles and *conquistadores*, the granting of a quota of licences for bringing in Africans became, in reality, a sale and resale enterprise which finally fell into the expert hands of the Italians, as well as those of the Corsicans and the Portuguese who were the real traders, as they were the ones who specialized in the procurement of slaves. The Italian bankers, on the other hand, were the ones who controlled the finances.[9]

Most of the slave trade was therefore not conducted by Spanish subjects. Apart from lacking influence on the African coast, Spain had no dynamic merchant middle class that could support this risky and costly trade. Although slavery still remained quite deeply rooted in the Iberian Peninsula in the fifteenth and sixteenth centuries, it was maintained by the use of a high percentage of people from outside sub-Saharan Africa. The slaves that were bought and sold on the Seville market in the mid-fifteenth century were mainly Moors, Muslim converts (*moriscos*), Canarians and some Jews.[10]

It appears that the slave trade had a definite impact on the development of the various societies in the Caribbean, given that it was the most widely-used method of immigration. It is therefore necessary to devote some time to the administrative development of the slave trade, its legal framework and the events and circumstances that caused it to veer away from its initial path. Towards the end of the period of colonization and implantation under study (1492–1650), the slave trade, as we have mentioned, was in the hands of the Italians and Portuguese, and under the administrative control of the Spanish Crown. In 1640, however, the Portuguese rebelled and Spain lost administrative control. Northern Europeans then came on the scene and challenged Portugal's primacy in the Atlantic slave trade.

Dutch merchants had been trading on the West African coast since the late sixteenth century. However, it was only in the 1630s that Dutch interest was aroused in obtaining slaves to fulfill the labour needs of their newly conquered territories in Brazil. The occupation of a number of Portuguese forts, both in West Africa and Angola, must be seen in this light. It was not until peace was concluded with Spain in 1648 that the Caribbean became a major destination of the Dutch slave trade. With the exception of an expedition which, in 1606, delivered 470 slaves to the Spanish colonists in Trinidad, there is no evidence of wartime slave voyages by Dutchmen from Africa to the West Indies. In this period, the Dutch role in the Caribbean slave trade was largely confined to privateers who intercepted Portuguese ships and sold their merchandise in the Antilles. In addition, small groups of slaves were transported from Dutch Brazil to the Lesser Antilles.[11]

After losing their Brazilian captaincies, the Dutch set up an important slaving centre in Curaçao. Curaçao was one of many Caribbean islands Spain lost in the 1620s and 1630s, when France, England and the United Provinces established themselves in the region. Neither of these countries relied on African labour from the outset. Unlike Spain, they initially made use of contract labourers from Europe, but eventually the English and French plantation economies could not survive without slave labour. To meet the crying need, two conditions had to be fulfilled: active engagement of England and France in the slave trade and a substantial increase of African supplies. Indeed, the spectacular growth of the Caribbean slave trade in the years after 1650 could only take place because of the rise of African slave exports, especially from Angola and the region stretching from the Gold Coast to Cameroon.[12]

In the slave trade to the Spanish Caribbean there were three distinct phases until 1640, judging from the administrative and legal principles: 1) acclimatization and evaluation (1492–1513), 2) licences (1513–1595), and 3) monopolistic settlements (1595–1640).

According to the extensive literature on the subject, there is no doubt that from the very beginning of colonization, blacks were taken to America.[13] Santo Domingo was the country in which blacks were first acclimatized to conditions prevailing in the Caribbean, and from where the first of them were probably taken to Puerto Rico and Cuba with the earliest settlers. It appears that the first quota of slaves arriving for a specific job were imported by Governor Nicolás de Ovando, who in 1503 brought in scores of Africans bound for the gold mines. In the early years the African slave trade was partly organized by private persons without the permission of the Crown. In 1513 the Spanish administration decided to take advantage of a trade that they could not stop, and a tax was imposed on the import of blacks. This was set at two ducats per imported slave, and eventually rose to sixteen ducats. From then on, licences were introduced, and this facilitated the keeping of records for emigration.

The sale of slave-trading licences was increasingly considered by the Crown as a possible source of income, and the desire to earn revenue from it led to changes in the legal framework governing the trade. During the sixteenth century, up until 1595, slave licences were used as an incentive to reward deserving subjects. While the *Casa de Contratación* (House of Trade) sold small concessions, the King was busy granting larger ones to his friends and bankers. Besides, they fell into the hands of financiers, as the acquisition of the annuities of national debt obligations was often accompanied by a slave licence.[14]

This practice began with the courtier Laurent de Gubenot and the Welser bankers, who in 1518 and 1528 were granted permits to import 4000 slaves into the Caribbean. These permits set two important precedents for the control of the trade – the fixing of quotas for a specific period, as well as the destination to which the slaves were to be transported. Perhaps the most remarkable licence of the period was the one for the import of 23 000 black slaves at the price of eight ducats each, granted by Philip II to the banker Hernando de Ochoa in 1553. This disproportionately large and little studied licence also stipulated the selling price for these slaves in Caribbean ports.[15] Estimates of the number of licences granted in the sixteenth century vary between 130 000 and 150 000. Existing research on the distribution of these licences only allows for conjectures based on available information, because there is considerable confusion over the demand, the number of licences granted and the number of slaves which were actually imported.

Santo Domingo was definitely the major destination in the early years, so much so that it was the scene of the first uprising of black slaves in 1522.[16] In Puerto Rico, where immigration had been restricted in the first two decades, there was a total of 2292 coloured inhabitants around 1530.[17] The first large cargo going directly to Cuba from Africa might have arrived in 1526, when 145 blacks were imported from the Cape Verde islands. Until then they had come from Hispaniola, but in the 1540s there must have been about 1000 slaves on the island. In Venezuela some 80 black slaves arrived in the mid-sixteenth century to work in the Buría mines near Barquisimeto, and a large number of them worked in the Tocuyo mines and in the pearl diving areas.[18] Florida received few slaves, except for those who were brought in illegally at the end of the century, and some who went on the expedition of Menéndez de Avilés in 1565, which laid the foundation for permanent settlement in this colony.[19] Similarly, it is difficult to determine the numbers that landed in Jamaica or along the mainland between Trinidad and Veracruz. In order to do this, we would need a systematic study, which is not available. If indeed there were large concessions, the beneficiaries rarely achieved their objectives. The slaves arrived in small numbers on fleet vessels, and in large numbers on the slave ships coming directly from the African continent. It was only during the period of monopoly concessions to the Portuguese that the growing demand for slaves in the Americas was met by a regular supply, both legally and illegally.

The 45 years of the Portuguese monopoly (1595–1640) are significant for a number of reasons. Firstly, the control exercised by the *Casa de Contratación* gives a fair indication of the total number of ships sailing from Africa to America, and what is more difficult, of the number of blacks transported without licences. Secondly, in order to gain control, in 1602 only two ports were authorized to receive African cargoes – Cartagena, which distributed slaves throughout the southern continent and the Caribbean islands; and Veracruz, which received those bound for the vice-royalty of Mexico and Florida. Thirdly, Portuguese expertise in the trade and their agents in every port and region of Atlantic Africa, created a network which sustained the trade for a long time. These agents were usually Jews and, occasionally, retired civil servants. In spite of this control, or as a result of it, the Caribbean was no longer exclusively a Spanish domain. During the 45-year period, the Antilles, Margarita, Caracas, Santa María and other places which were no longer included on the direct slave route, had recourse to illegal means to obtain slaves.[20] This not only enabled other powers to mobilize themselves in order to do away with this monopoly which was a source of serious conflict between the Dutch and the Portuguese, but also led to certain fraudulent practices by civil servants in ports closed to direct traffic. In fact, the existing monopoly automatically gave rise to organized smuggling of slaves. These illegal imports were a way of evading taxes, as slave ships would exceed the quota of slaves that they were authorized to transport, and as unauthorized ships came in from Africa in violation of the monopoly system. The latter practice was more common in the Río de la Plata region than in the Caribbean.

The widespread belief that the slave trade was used as a cover for European contraband in other products is true only from 1640 onwards when the Dutch and the English gained control of the slave trade. Up until then neither of these nations needed to smuggle their products to the less closely guarded ports – something which happened in the Caribbean from the mid-sixteenth century onwards. It was only when these countries dominated the slave trade that they adapted its trading routes, and Jamaica and Curaçao became distributors not only of slaves, but of every type of commodity that would yield a profit.

At any rate, many irregularities occurred during the period of the Portuguese monopoly. The neighbouring ports of Santo Domingo, Puerto Rico and Portobelo, which were always in need of slaves, had to find their own means of obtaining them. Despite the ban, the civil servants of the Crown authorized the sale of some or all of the cargo of any slave ship that arrived in their ports.[21] Fernández Delvas, a supplier from 1615 to 1622, noted that one of the reasons that the galleons carried so little silver from the sale of slaves was that the profits from these sales remained in Jamaica, Yucatán, Río de la Hacha, Santo Domingo or Puerto Rico, where the slaves had been sold illegally. According to new information it appears that Santo Domingo was of great importance for illegally receiving and distributing slaves.[22] The same was probably true of Jamaica. Official figures from the import of slaves to these ports are therefore of little or no importance. The only figures of note are those taken from the records of the suppliers themselves, or from officials of the Crown. The most reliable and systematic are unquestionably those for the ports of Cartagena and Veracruz, the only slave ports authorized to receive slaves at the time. Based on this information, we can get a general picture of the way in which the first African slaves were distributed.

Using demographic calculations, and making allowances for smuggling, we can venture to give some figures for this period. Some 135 000 slaves may have been coming to Cartagena between 1595 and 1640; 70 000 slaves landed at Veracruz, and around 20 000 at other Caribbean ports. These figures refer to the *bozales*, the slaves brought in directly from Africa.[23]

Forced African settlement and the new societies

There is, undoubtedly, a notable difference between the societies which were established before the second half of the sixteenth century, and those which were just emerging during the following century. Some, such as the Spanish colonies of the Greater Antilles and permanent establishments on the South American coast and the Gulf of Mexico, were the product of a quasi-Renaissance, aristocratic philosophy. Others were less stable and were soon caught up in the changes being wrought in the Spanish system by pirates and corsairs. This was particularly evident in Tortuga island, to the north of Santo Domingo, in parts of Honduras and in Trinidad. Still others arose out of another, more advanced type of colonization, organized by Europeans with a clearly mercantile philosophy who settled in previously unsettled places, or in those which had been abandoned by Spaniards attracted to the wealth of the continent – the Lesser Antilles and the Guyanas. From the arrival of the earliest colonists to the last, there is a period of almost 150 years during which ideology, social and economic structures, and therefore the concept of colonialism, were able to change. This span of time was also sufficient for a transformation of the geopolitical scene in the Caribbean.

In addition to the time factor, space, and therefore resources, have to be taken into account to characterize the new societies. The first areas to be settled were of course those where it was easy to earn money through the gold deposits above or below the surface, and the deep banks of oysters. Santo Domingo, Puerto Rico, the mainland and islands of Margarita, and the Pearl Coast were chosen for the early settlements. The colonists required workers for the gold mines and expert divers to plunge the depths of the crystal-clear Caribbean waters. Almost as urgently as they needed men for the exploitation of gold deposits, they needed field hands, or livestock herders to ensure their survival, construction workers, allies to help them defend them against less docile groups, and house servants. These require- ments were too numerous for the small-scale, primitive Amerindian society that could not cope with the type of work that its members were expected to perform, and who, above all, had no biological defences against European diseases. Therefore it became necessary to seek alternative sources of labour. The first alternative considered was that of the African, and the idea of slave imports from Africa first emerged probably as a casual suggestion which then gained credence as the Africans proved to be physi- cally more resistant. On the other hand, the impact of some diseases on the native Caribbeans was probably exaggerated by those people who made out a case for the import of African slaves.[24]

Still, there is no doubt as to the considerable losses suffered by the indigenous West Indian population. Historians seldom agree as to the number of natives who occupied the islands when the Spaniards arrived. For Santo Domingo, for instance, the figures vary between 100 000 and 8 000 000 and although it is very difficult to decide on either figure, it is certain that in 1508 there were 60 000, while in 1554 only 30 000 remained, and in 1570 their numbers had dwindled to 500.[25] Because of their former isolation, they became a likely target for diseases such as smallpox, and later measles, and within a few years a considerable number of natives were wiped out. In colder, more salubrious climates, where the Amerindians were better pre-pared and more skilled, they were able to recover during the latter half of the sixteenth century. But in the unhealthy tropical atmosphere of the Caribbean where food was scarce, the mortality rate rose spectacularly as the inhabitants fell victim to dysentery, diarrhoea, new infections and parasites which were brought by the Africans and which found an ideal place to mul-tiply at an alarming rate. The Amerindians, under biological attack from the European and African fronts, found it impossible to recover. Only the more isolated populations of the mainland, or the larger, more developed groups such as those in Guatemala and Yucatán, where there was much less African immigration, were able to survive.

Less is known about the Indians' encounter with African diseases, probably because the whites, who were the first to witness the decimation of the Indian population, also fell victim to these diseases. But malaria and yellow fever, the two major endogenous African diseases, also caused significant losses much earlier than had been supposed.[26] The Africans, on the other hand, were more resistant. Their constant contact with other people, particularly Muslims, and their acclimatization to unsanitary tropical conditions rendered them immune to yellow fever and malaria.

The impact of African slavery in the Caribbean was felt most where the indigenous peoples were very vulnerable, and was less pronounced, yet more complex and diverse, where these peoples were more developed. From the earliest years of Spanish colonization in the Caribbean, blacks were used to meet a variety of needs – panning for gold, pearl diving, farm and ranch work, general transport, mule-driving, iron-working, public works, fortifications, and domestic service. This range of occupations, the number of slaves so employed, and the number of deaths per year, are given in an interesting document which dates from the mid-seventeenth century, from which we quote the parts relevant to the Caribbean.

– Panamá had 17 000 slaves who are used to drive mules from Portobelo, as crew on frigates, boats and pearl brigs, for work in shipyards, and as live-stock herders. Five hundred *piezas* are lost each year.[27]
– Cartagena and its dependencies have 12 000 blacks who work at many of the occupations mentioned above. Losses are in the amount of 350.
– Along the mainland, in the areas of Santa Marta, La Grita, Caracas, Cumaná, La Margarita, La Guayana, there are 12 000 blacks working

in pearl diving and tobacco, cocoa, and fruit plantations. Losses total 350.
- The Windward islands of Cuba (Havana), Santo Domingo and Jamaica have 16 000 blacks working in the sugar mills, leather-making, lumber and shipbuilding. Losses total 600 in each area.
- The province under the jurisdiction of Guatemala in Honduras have 10 000 blacks, and losses amount to 350.[28]

In some of the Caribbean societies development was long in coming; in others, the diversity began a few years after the arrival of the Europeans and the Africans. Through ethnic, cultural and religious syncretism many of the newly-implanted societies acquired a personality of their own. A decisive part of this development was the Africans' continuous resistance against their slave status.

The runaways, or Maroons, show that the slave was in no way a passive, resigned individual, as has been suggested by some authors. Eric Williams described the slave as having the potential to be a present-day revolutionary from the time he was taken on board.[29] With the aid of the hazardous terrain, peasant villages, help from outside forces, and the pillaging of the caravans which travelled regularly into the interior, the slaves were able to escape to the mountains or the jungle. They banded together to form pockets of resistance, which took many forms, starting from the early years of colonization in America.[30]

The threat of Maroon uprisings was particularly strong in the region of the Isthmus of Panama, but it was kept in check in areas around Cartagena, Havana and Santo Domingo. The runaways were a constant threat to the Spanish settlers; they interacted with the pirates and occasionally with the Indian populations which had not been enslaved. In many places where Maroons crossbred with the remaining members of indigenous communities, the resulting racial mixtures were given special names. For instance, in some small Caribbean islands, like Saint Vincent, they were called 'Black Caribs'. In the early days of this contact, when the slave ships were not regular, they had a tangible impact on the cultures of these societies. Seeds, animals and some utensils from Africa were introduced among the Indians, together with certain types of tubers and chickens. The blacks in turn learned how to make flour, cassava bread and fermented drinks, and how to cultivate land using wooden tools.

Crossbreeding with the natives occurred in those remote areas where it was impossible to enforce the stringent legislation aimed at protecting the Indians. The whites, on the other hand, mixed readily with the blacks, and there soon emerged mulattos of various shades. Because most of them were illegitimate, and often the 'master's children', their prospects for freedom were quite good. There was a shortage of white women, and female slaves were imported in large numbers, since it was stipulated that they should constitute one-third of the slave quota. This encouraged concubinage and the practice of illegal marriages. Thus began the ethnic intermixing in which anyone with African blood, no matter how little, was in a less favourable position in the radical conflicts which soon erupted. Consequently, it became just as important to 'become whiter' in order to improve one's social status as it was to attain or to buy one's freedom.

The increasing number of blacks who had attained freedom during the sixteenth century by means of personal purchase or testamentary provisions made by their masters, gave rise to a skilled labour market, since the majority of them had acquired a skill of some kind. A certain number of these skilled workmen were able to climb the social ladder, so much so that in Panamá during the early seventeenth century, they had managed to displace the whites in some minor clerical positions (in 1607, 11.5 per cent of all clerics were freed slaves). The freed population generally formed part of the urban society. They were considered subjects of the Crown, and had to pay an annual tax, which was one *peso* in the sixteenth century.[31] However, their so-called status as subjects did not improve their social or economic position. Many of them joined the ranks of the Indians, and problems of vagrancy and looting were a direct result of the social and economic crisis. In an attempt to control this, the Spanish authorities introduced a number of repressive measures. Only in the early seventeenth century was there an attempt at integration, with the formation of 'black' and 'free mulatto companies', and more often 'mixed companies' which played an important part in the defence of the Spanish Empire.

The ideology of slavery

Although slave societies were not new to mankind, there is no doubt that it was in the New World that they developed fully. The situation in the Americas necessitated a legal framework which did not exist in other types of colonialism. The legislation had three major concerns regarding slaves and former slaves. It intended:

1) to avoid close interaction between them and the slaves,
2) to prevent the existence of Maroon communities and combat them, once they were formed,
3) to channel unproductive slave labour into productive economic activities.

In other words, there was an attempt to improve economic output by means of strict social control, and by maintaining an hierarchical view of society.[32] Compared to slavery elsewhere, a certain degree of protectiveness exercised by the clergy, and the control measures necessary to avoid mixing with the Indians, paints a gentler picture of the form of slavery practised in the Spanish colonies. This has been the subject of great debate in the literature, rendering impartiality difficult.[33] But slavery can in no way be considered gentle, and in the final analysis, the severity of working conditions would be determined by the social and economic factors described above, rather than by the existing degree of benevolence towards the slaves. Though from the outset members of the clergy argued on behalf of the slaves and denounced the bad treatment they received, very few of them actually called for its abolition. Slavery was seen as the sole means to sustain the development of colonies which needed manpower in every economic sector. The slave was always seen as a tool similar to any beast of burden, and was bought and sold like a piece of merchandise. This situation was justified on the grounds of racial inferiority of the African, the poor living conditions in his native land and that baptism was the means of his salvation.

Life on a sugar plantation was basically the same in Havana as it was in Jamaica, Guadeloupe or Brazil. Similarly, the perception in Europe of slavery in the Americas was largely the same. There, the sole concern of colonizing nations was to obtain the greatest possible output by encouraging the slave trade and thus by making Africa and the Africans a vital element in the development of American societies. In the case of the Caribbean, which received large numbers of immigrants, the Afro-American symbiosis is a quintessential part of these societies.

Appendix

AFRICAN SLAVES TAKEN TO CARIBBEAN PORTS (1595–1601)

Years	No. of ships	No. of licences	Official no. of slaves brought in
Port of Cartagena			
1595	8	710	1 435
1596	11	2 066	2 536
1597	20	3 850	3 542
1598	19	3 345	3 555
1599	24	3 881	4 749
1600	22	3 177	4 231
1601	19	2 386	3 323
Total	123	19 415	23 371
Port of Veracruz			
1596	1	240	210
1597	1	150	149
1598	5	775	723
1599	7	1 010	1 101
1600	5	654	777
1601	8	–	1 604
Total	27	2 829	4 564

Other ports[*]

Ports	Years	No. of ships	Official no. of slaves brought in
Havana	1596–1600	4	778
Margarita	1598–1599	3	529
Sto. Domingo	1596–1598	3	256
Puerto Rico	1597–1598	5	292
Cumaná and Río Hacha	1596	2	238
Caracas	1599	1	237
Total		18	2 330

[*] Figures on licences are not supplied in original text.

AFRICAN SLAVES ARRIVING IN CARTAGENA AND VERACRUZ IN THE FIRST
HALF OF THE SEVENTEENTH CENTURY

Year	Official no. of slaves brought in	Year	Official no. of slaves brought in
Veracruz			
1604	144	1623	–
1605	1 399	1624	421
1606	165	1625	420
1607	269	1626	290
1608	1 866	1627	152
1609	755	1628	–
1610	1 728	1629	–
1611	1 608	1630	–
1612	659	1631	368
1613	1 036	1632	–
1614	133	1633	237
1615	172	1634	690
1616	281	1635	301
1617	910	1636	193
1618	709	1637	–
1619	1 814	1638	692
1620	1 713	1639	755
1621	3 362	1640	180
1622	1 183	no date	482
Total			25 987
Cartagena			
1622	1 418	1633	–
1623	1 588	1634	–
1624	1 566	1635	–
1625	1 204	1636	1 010
1626	1 199	1637	636
1627	985	1638	693
1628	911	1639	494
1629	746	1640	243
1630	905	1641	250
1631	1 287	no date	542
1632	709		
Total			16 306

AFRICAN SLAVES ARRIVING IN OTHER CARIBBEAN PORTS IN THE FIRST
HALF OF THE SEVENTEENTH CENTURY

Year	Official no. of slaves brought in	Year	Official no. of slaves brought in
Havana			
1609	14	1625	22
1610	3	1636	347
1611	2	1637	3
1612	6	1638	11
1613	160	1641	310
1623	102		
Total			980
Santo Domingo			
1601	144	1611	150
1605	129	1612	2
1606	812	1613	199
1607	277	1617	5
1608	11	1631	16
1609	43		
Total			1 788
Puerto Rico			
1607	34	1618	85
1608	55	1621	152
1609	53	1623	3
1611	256	1625	185
1612	123	1627	12
1615	112	1628	8
1617	36		
Total			1 114
Venezuela			
1597	388	1619	1
1608	2	1623	2
1612	207	1625	118
1615	37	1626	100
1617	141	1627	100
Total			1 096

Year	Official no. of slaves brought in	Year	Official no. of slaves brought in
Santa María			
1609	84	1620	6
1610	1	1625	3
1613	156	1636	80
1614	1	1638	60
1617	3	1640	129
1619	246		
Total			769

NOTES

1　For further information on this interesting acclimatization process, see Charles D. Verlinden, 'Esclavitud medieval en Europa y esclavitud colonial en América', *Revista de la Universidad de Córdoba* (1958), pp. 175–91.

2　John Thornton, *Africa and Africans in the making of the Atlantic world, 1400–1680* (Cambridge, 1992), pp. 87, 76, 91, 105–8; D. Laya, 'The Hausa states' in B.A. Ogot (ed.), *UNESCO General History of Africa*, V (Los Angeles and London, 1992), pp. 483–4; Beatrix Heintze, 'Traite de "pièces" en Angola: ce qui n'est pas dit dans nos sources' in Serge Daget (ed.), *De la traite à l'esclavage. Actes du Colloque international sur la traite des Noirs, Nantes 1985*, 2 vols. (Paris, 1988), I, pp. 162–4.

3　Luis M. Díaz Soler, *Historia de la esclavitud negra en Puerto Rico* (Rio Piedras, 1965), pp. 203–4.

4　María del Carmen Borrego Plá, *Cartagena de Indias en el siglo XVI* (Seville, 1983), p. 429; Thornton, *Africa and Africans*, pp. 202–3; Carlos Esteban Deive, *La esclavitud del negro en Santo Domingo (1492–1844)* (Santo Domingo, 1980), p. 379.

5　The African origin of blacks in America has been the subject of studies by anthropologists such as Fernando Ortiz, Artur Ramos or Gonzalo Aguirre Beltrán. More recently, historians such as Miguel Acosta Saignes for Venezuela, Alfredo Castillero Calvo for Panamá, and Frederick Bowser for Peru, have been paying attention to the geographical origins of the slaves as supplied by the documents, which give us some insight into the degree of influence exerted by the various nations or castes. For general information on this topic see the following titles: Alonso de Sandoval, S.J., *De instauranda aethiopium salute* (Seville, 1626); Philip D. Curtin, *The Atlantic slave trade. A census* (Madison, 1969); Gonzalo Aguirre Beltrán, 'Tribal origins of slaves in Mexico', *The Journal of Negro History*, XXXI/3, (1946); Franco Fernández Esquivel, 'Procedencia de los esclavos negros analizada a través del complejo de distribución desarrollado desde Cartagena', *Revista de Historia*, II/3, (Costa Rica, 1986).

6   A slave trader stated in 1677 that there were areas bordering Angola with over 300 of these blacks in his service, who were employed on long journeys of 150 to 200 leagues (one league = approximately three miles) into the interior. These trips sometimes lasted one or two years. Archivo General de Indias (AGI) Consulados 1605.

7   Thornton, *Africa and the Africans*, pp. 44–53.

8   Sydney Mintz, 'Africa en América Latina: una reflexión desprevenida' in Manuel Moreno Fraginals (ed.) *Africa en América Latina* (Paris, 1977).

9   Rodrigo Baso and Juan Antonio Corso, two of the most influential traders of Italian origin in Seville in the sixteenth century, were also important slave traders. See Eufemio Lorenzo Sanz, *Comercio de España con América en la época de Felipe II* (Valladolid, 1979). For information on Juan Antonio Corso, see Enriqueta Vilá Vilar, 'Los Corzos: un clan en la colonización de América', *Anuario de Estudios Americanos*, XLIII (1985), pp. 1–42, and *Los Corzo y los Mañara: tipos y arquetipos del mercader con América* (Seville, 1991). Italian involvement in the slave trade dates back many centuries earlier, and the loans which the Catholic monarchs received from Italian bankers to pay for a part of Columbus' first voyage derived from the slave trade. But the presence of the Portuguese on the African coast, and their discoveries in the Atlantic, brought the slave trade under their control. Consequently, they became so firmly entrenched that from 1595 to 1640 they were granted a royal monopoly of the slave trade. See Enriqueta Vilá Vilar, *Hispanoamérica y el comercio de esclavos. Los asientos portugueses* (Seville, 1977).

10   Vicenta Cortés Alonso, *La esclavitud en el Reino de Valencia durante el reinado de los Reyes Católicos. 1479–1515* (Valencia, 1964); Alfonso Franco, *La esclavitud en Sevilla y su tierra a fines de la Edad Media* (Seville, 1979); Manuel Lobo Cabrera, *La esclavitud en Canarias orientales en el siglo XVI (negros, moros y moriscos)* (Las Palmas, 1982); Charles Verlinden, *L'esclavage dans l'Europe médiéval* (Bruges, 1955), Vol. I.

11   Ernst van den Boogaart and Pieter C. Emmer, 'The Dutch participation in the Atlantic slave trade, 1596–1650' in Henry A. Gemery and Jan S. Hogendorn (eds), *The uncommon market. Essays in the economic history of the Atlantic slave trade.* (New York, San Francisco and London, 1979), pp. 354–7, 371–5; W.S. Unger, 'Bijdragen tot de geschiedenis van de Nederlandse slavenhandel', *Economisch-Historisch Jaarboek*, 26 (1952–4), p. 136.

12   Thornton, *Africa and the Africans*, pp. 117–19.

13   There is an extensive literature on the slave trade, but most of the works are based on two classics: George Scelle, *La traite négrière aux Indes Castille*, 2 vols. (Paris, 1906), and José Antonio Saco, *Historia de la esclavitud de la raza africana en el Nuevo Mundo* (Havana, 1938). Both authors deal with the legal aspects of the trade. Philip D. Curtin attempts to quantify the Atlantic slave trade in his *Atlantic slave trade*, although many of his figures have been revised in later publications. See Magnus Mörner, 'Investigaciones recientes sobre la esclavitud negra y la abolición en América Latina', *Revista de Historia*, II/3, (Costa Rica, 1976), pp. 9–41.

      Also of importance to the study of the slave trade is the compilation of documents by Elizabeth Donan, *Documents illustrative of the history of the slave trade to America*, 4 vols. (Washington, 1930); Luis Bonilla, *Historia de la esclavitud* (Madrid, 1961); James Pope Hennessey, *La traite des noirs à travers l'Atlantique*,

1441–1807 (Paris, 1969); Hubert Deschamps, *Histoire de la traite de noirs de l'Antiquité à nos jours* (Paris, 1971); Louis Lacroix, *Les derniers négriers* (Paris, 1972); and Lesley B. Rout Jr., *The African experience in Spanish America, 1502 to the present day* (Cambridge, 1976). Besides, UNESCO has published on this subject *La traite négrière du XVe au XIXe siècle* (Paris, 1979). Two publications attempt to quantify the number of slave licences granted in the sixteenth century: Lorenzo Sanz, *Comercio*, and Lutgardo García Fuentes, 'Licencias para la introducción de esclavos en Indias y los envíos desde Sevilla en el siglo XVI', *Jahrbuch für Geschichte von Staat, Wirtschaft und Gesellschaft Lateinamerikas*, 19, (1982), pp. 1–46.

The period of the Portuguese *asientos* was studied by Vilá Vilar, *Hispanoamérica*, and with regard to the period 1663–73, when the Genoese Grillo and Lomelin held the *asiento* there is a work of Marisa Vega Franco, *El tráfico de esclavos con América* (Seville, 1984). For information on the two years immediately following, see Enriqueta Vilá Vilar, 'El Consulado de Sevilla asentista de esclavos: una nueva tentativa para el mantenimiento del monopolio comercial', in *Actas de las Primeras Jornadas de Andalucía y América* (Huelva, 1981).

14   Richard Konetzke, *Süd- und Mittelamerika I. Die Indianerkulturen Altamerikas und die spanisch-portugiesische Kolonialherrschaft* (Frankfurt am Main, 1965), p. 78.

15   Saco makes mention of this in his work *Historia de la esclavitud*, II, p. 39, as does Scelle in *La traite*, I, p. 205. F. Cereceda considers the moral aspects of this practice in 'Un asiento de esclavos para América en el año 1553 y parecer de varios teólogos sobre su ilicitud', *Missionalia Hispánica*, II/9 (1946), pp. 580–7.

16   Carlos Larrazábal, *Los negros y la esclavitud en Santo Domingo* (Santo Domingo, 1967).

17   Luis María Díaz Soler, *Historia de la esclavitud negra en Puerto Rico (1493–1890)* (Madrid, 1953), p. 50.

18   Eduardo Arcila Farías, *Economía colonial de Venezuela* (Mexico-City, 1946); Miguel Acosta Saignes, *Vida de los esclavos negros en Venezuela* (Caracas, 1962), p. 144.

19   John Tepaske, 'The fugitive, intercolonial rivalry and Spanish slave policy, 1687–1764' in Samuel Proctor (ed.) *Eighteenth-century Florida and its Borderlands* (Gainesville, 1975).

20   For further details on this topic see Enriqueta Vilá Vilar, 'La esclavitud en el Caribe, la Florida y Luisiana; algunos datos generales para su estudio' in *La Influencia de España en el Caribe, la Florida y Luisiana (1500–1800)* (Madrid, 1983).

21   Many examples of this can be found in Vilá Vilar, *Hispanoamérica*, Chapter VI.

22   To provide new information on this type of smuggling, we have used the port of Santo Domingo over a three-year period as an example. In 1623 the following were noted: a ship coming from Angola to Brazil, belonging to Pedro Gómez Pereira, sold 44 slaves at this port. Diego Suárez Cardo, with a licence for 70 slaves, had taken from an unknown location in Africa 372 slaves, of which he declared 158 at this stop in San Juan. He sold 38 in Santo Domingo, and took the rest to Veracruz. Francisco Viera de Lima, with an undisclosed register, sold 343 in Santo Domingo and transported several others to Havana. He declared a total of 258. Xil Franco, who had a register of 80, took 217 out of

Angola, of which he sold 38 on the island. Diego Fonseca, who had a register of 150, left Angola with 295. Upon inspection, 199 were declared, but in reality 500 were taken, and of these 146 were sold, and the rest were transported in two frigates to Caracas and New Spain. In 1624 Andrés Núñez, with a register of 100, took 341 out of Angola, while only 151 were declared upon inspection. Francisco Núñez, with a register of 120, took on 276 in Angola. Upon inspection, 148 were declared, but in Santo Domingo alone 155 were sold, and the rest were taken to Havana and Puerto Rico. Luis Méndez, with a register of 150, took 522 out of Angola. He had received a licence to sell 30 slaves in Santo Domingo, and sold 170. In 1625 Duarte Díez, who had no register, declared 28. He was charged duty on 36, but in Santo Domingo alone he had sold 93 from a cargo of 339 from Angola. Leonardo Váez, with a register of 80, took 173 from Angola, and declared 75 upon inspection. Simón Riberos, with a register of 150, transported 400 from Angola to Santo Domingo, and declared only 99. Miguel Rodríguez, who had no register, took on 408 in Angola, declared 182, but 400 were sold in Santo Domingo and then distributed to other ports. Nicolás Lemus, who had no register, declared 68, but there was proof that 200 were landed in Santo Domingo, and taken to other ports. Information taken from AGI Escribanía de Cámara 21A, piece no. 1. Case against Fernández Lamiago and Antonio de Ordás for fraud. Fewer slaves were recorded in Puerto Rico at the time. It appears that 46 were sold in 1620, 118 in 1621–2, 55 in 1623, 92 in 1624–5 and only 28 in 1626. AGI, *ibid.*, piece 3.

23 Vilá Vilar, *Hispanoamérica*, pp. 204–11. The term *negros bozales* was used to designate those who came to America directly from Africa, without having had any contact with whites, apart from the slave traffickers. They had no knowledge of the language or of the Catholic religion. On the other hand, those who had been latinized in some way were called *ladinos*.

24 Francis J. Brooks, 'Revising the conquest of Mexico: smallpox, sources, and populations', *The Journal of Interdisciplinary History*, XXIV/1 (1993), pp. 18–19.

25 See Mellafe, *Breve historia*, p. 22. As in other regions of America, the methods used by Cook and Borah record the highest figures, which seem to be disproportionate. Seabourne F. Cook and Woodrow Borah, *Essays in population history, Mexico and the Caribbean.* (Berkeley and Los Angeles, 1971).

26 See Kenneth F. Kiple, 'Dimensión epidemológica de la esclavitud negra en el Caribe' in *La influencia de España en el Caribe, La Florida y la Luisiana (1500–1800)* (Madrid, 1983), and *The Caribbean slave: a biological history* (New York, 1984).

27 The term *pieza de Indias* can lead to confusion. Fiscally, and only in the second half of the seventeenth century, it meant a young unmarked slave measuring seven *cuartas* or quarters of a Spanish yard. Here it is not used in that sense, but to describe a slave who was fit for work regardless of age, height or defects. On this topic, see Vilá Vilar, *Hispanoamérica*, pp. 186–93.

28 The document was written by a captain from Seville, Fernando Silva Solís, who claimed to have a slaving concession in the years immediately following the Portuguese rebellion of 1640. Although only the parts which pertain to the Caribbean are quoted here, the document refers to all of America, and can be found in AGI Indiferente General 2796. It has been published fully in Enriqueta Vilá Vilar, 'La sublevación de Portugal y la trata de esclavos', *Ibero-Amerikanisches Archiv*, 2/3, (1976), pp. 175–7. In this article some criticism is made of the figures.

29   Eric Williams, *The Negro in the Caribbean* (Washington, 1942) p. 83.

30   See the introduction to Richard Price (ed.) *Maroon Societies* (New York, 1973).

31   In 1578 the thirty free mulattos in Panamá asked to be exempted from paying the tribute. AGI Panamá, 40.

32   Mellafe, *Breve historia*, p. 113.

33   The polemic engaged by Tannenbaum, Elkins, Freyre and Klein, on the one hand, who maintained that under the Spanish model of colonization slaves were better treated, and on the other hand, Williams, Harris and Davis, who emphasize the similar nature of slavery as a system of economic exploitation, has not come to an end yet. This discussion is dealt with in Eugene Genovese, *Esclavitud y capitalismo* (Barcelona, 1971), p. 24.

7

Native society and the European occupation of the Caribbean islands and coastal *Tierra Firme*, 1492–1650

Neil L. Whitehead

Introduction

The Caribbean, which here is taken as equivalent to the old Spanish administrative region of the *Audiencia de Santo Domingo*, including the littoral region known as *Tierra Firme*, was the initial scene of the encounter between Europe and the Americas. As such its native populations were the first to negotiate the new political and economic realities which the Europeans imposed, as well as to endure the ecological and demographic consequences of that arrival.

In the islands of the Caribbean these processes were brief and brutal as in the Greater Antilles where the native population had all but disappeared within a few decades; but they were longer lasting and more convoluted in the Lesser Antilles whose inhabitants offered stout resistance to a succession of colonial powers. By the same token, the impact of the Europeans on the native societies of *Tierra Firme* was often locally disastrous but also allowed for more extended interactions to develop, like those seen in the Lesser Antilles. This situation produced a wide range of novel political and economic responses on the part of the native population, which displayed a highly-variable continuity with pre-Columbian times. Arguably none of the societies of the Caribbean region that were extant in 1492 survived unscathed, for, even where contacts were not direct, the impact of the Europeans on regional trade and alliance systems was fundamental, inducing change amongst groups well before they even encountered the invaders. Such a pattern of effect outrunning its cause is most evident in the spread of European epidemic diseases, which did not just prove lethal to biologically pristine populations but also encouraged a rapid and widespread migration away from the epicentres of disease dispersion. However, it is not sufficient to explain all population loss from given locations by this means and, as we shall see, the consequences of the introduction of European disease differed greatly between the densely-packed Maya settlements and the more scattered settlements of other regions. On the islands the virulence of diseases was enhanced by the physical circumscription of the native population, but this did not preclude migrations by sea, towards the southern continent.

Within this general context the first encounters with the natives of the islands loom largest in the historiography of the region and in the ethnological schema of subsequent anthropologies, both colonial and modern. This has resulted in a situation where those initial observations that the Europeans made of the native population have become enshrined in the general literature concerning the Caribbean region, and most notably in the *Handbook of South American Indians*[1] as well as in the (recently re-issued) classic account of *The Early Spanish Main* by Carl Sauer.[2] This has had the result that our perceptions of the native Caribbean are heavily prejudiced by the distinction, first made by Columbus[3] between the fearsome *caribes* (Caribs) of the Lesser Antilles and the tractable *aruaca* or *guatiao* (Taíno)[4] populations of the Greater Antilles; this fallacious distinction being generalized ultimately across the whole of the northern part of the continent.

Recent scholarship on the native population of the Antilles[5] has begun to make good that deficiency, but its tenacity partly stems from the historical reason that this ethnological dualism was directly adopted into Spanish colonial law,[6] such that Caribs were legally defined as any and all natives who opposed Spanish occupation in the Caribbean. As a result Caribs were discovered on *Tierra Firme* as well as the islands and the colonial logic of directly enslaving those who could not be brought within the system of *repartimiento* (a forced distribution of native lands and peoples) was widely applied.

Thus, the type of native societies the Europeans encountered strongly conditioned their political responses. The initial diplomacy exercised towards the *caciques* (kings or chiefs) of Española, or the necessary diplomacy shown on the Yucatán peninsula, strongly contrasts with the summary military invasions of Puerto Rico or Trinidad and the Venezuelan littoral, which were the early hunting grounds for slavers seeking labour to replace the wasted population of the Greater Antilles. In such situations ethnological expectations and definitions became critical political factors, as is shown in the great debates between Las Casas and Sepúlveda concerning the humanity and rationality of the New World population.[7] But these ethnological definitions were also responsive to the unfolding needs of the emergent colonial system and, for example, in the case of the Caribs it was finally necessary for the Spanish Crown to despatch a special legal mission, under the *licenciado* Rodrigo de Figueroa, to make an evaluation as to the Carib nature of the native populations of the Caribbean islands and Venezuelan littoral.[8] Figueroa's depositions of 1520 indicate that this process was highly political, in that populations were assigned to the Carib category in a way that served the interests of the planters and slavers of Española.[9] Figueroa's classification was therefore only tangentially related to ethnological issues, principally the practice of 'cannibalism'. This is shown both by the fact that populations that were previously Taíno could become Carib[10] and by Figueroa's own usage of the term *caribe*, in which the eating of human flesh was only one of the criteria he cites for so classifying a population.[11]

In such a context the native population was itself polarized around the question of how to meet and deal with the European invaders, some favouring appeasement, others confrontation, but no single strategy was successful over time and actual responses were often highly variable, even within the same village or longhouse. In short, the encounter with Europe was a fundamental disjuncture in native patterns of historical development and it is the nature of that disjuncture and the new historical trajectories that were born of that encounter that are considered here. In order to explain these developments a narrative of external contacts with the Europeans will precede an examination of the internal effects these contacts had on Amerindian modes of life and thought.

The islands

It is well known that Columbus first sighted the islands of the Caribbean in October 1492, but it is perhaps less appreciated that within eight years the Spanish Crown had sent a Royal Governor, Francisco de Bobadilla, to try to stabilize the nascent colony on Española because Columbus, his family and their opponents had all but destroyed the indigenous population in a series of brutal military campaigns, against both indigenous opposition and the dissenting Spanish factions.[12]

The critical moment in these events was a large-scale military confrontation in 1495 between the Europeans and the natives of the valley of Maguá (or La Vega Real), the largest and most densely-populated native province on the island. Here, barely two hundred men faced the combined forces of the principal *caciques* of Española, numbering tens of thousands of warriors. However, the military technology and organization of the Europeans, which included armoured cavalry, steel weapons, guns and attack dogs, utterly devastated the native warriors whose leaders were captured and tortured to death. Out of this destruction the native leader Guarionex emerged to mediate European demands for food, labour and, above all gold. But by 1497, following famine and the first outbreaks of epidemic disease, this appeasement ended when Francisco de Roldán induced rival chiefs to support his opposition to the Columbus family, and Guarionex was won over to the cause. However, Bartolomeo Columbus forestalled this opposition by a night attack on Guarionex's villages to seize the rebel *caciques*, most of whom were then executed.

Guarionex himself was allowed to live, but functioned essentially as a tool of the Columbus family until his death by shipwreck *en route* to Spain in 1502. In fact by 1500 most of the complex native polities of Española had ceased to operate and, following Ponce de Léon's conquest of Puerto Rico in the early 1500s, the complex societies of the Greater Antilles had effectively collapsed.

The few native survivors of this first decade or so of European occupation were therefore incorporated into the burgeoning colonial settlements of the region and the need for their labour answered by the importation of black Africans as slaves. It is open to question as to what percentage of the aboriginal population had either fled the Greater Antilles or had died there, but the overall consequence, as the colonial processes that initially unfolded on Española repeated themselves in Cuba, Jamaica, the Lucayas and Puerto Rico, was the complete dispersion and disappearance of the native element.

This was particularly true of Puerto Rico, which was nearest both physically and culturally to Española, and where Juan Ponce de Léon first led an expedition of reconnaissance in 1508.[13] However, although native resistance on the island itself was short-lived it was fierce, being also supported by Caribs from the Lesser Antilles. The continuing attacks on the Spanish in Puerto Rico throughout the sixteenth century (see below) may thus be directly related to a wider alliance among native populations dispersed and driven out by Ponce de Léon's initial occupation of the island.

No such resistance was encountered on the Lucayas, the most northerly of the Caribbean islands, and the population there,[14] which lacked some of the natural refuges available to the inhabitants of the larger islands, was simply 'harvested' by slavers during the period 1509–12.[15] The subsequent 'discovery' of Florida by Ponce de Léon might, therefore, be rightly characterized as little more than '…an extension of slave hunting beyond the empty islands…'.[16]

Few records have been left concerning the occupation of Jamaica, which was initiated by Diego Colón and completed by Juan de Esquivel in 1509. According to Las Casas[17] the natives were not evangelized and were put to hard labour in the production of foodstuffs, cloth and hammocks. As a result, when the new governor, Francisco de Garay, took over from Esquivel in 1515, the Royal Factor, Pedro de Mazuelo complained of the tiny number of natives left on the island, and their total disappearance within a couple of years was confidently predicted.[18]

Although Columbus had surveyed the coast of Cuba during his first voyage, official interest did not manifest itself again until 1508 when the then Royal Governor of Española, Nicolás de Ovando, sent Sebastián de Ocampo to circumnavigate the island – rumours of gold quickly followed.[19] In 1511 a licence to occupy Cuba was given to Diego Velázquez de Cuéllar, a veteran of the brutal combats on Española. Cuéllar assembled 300 troops on the south-western peninsula of Española and was then joined on Cuba by troops fresh from the conquest of Jamaica, as well as a further contingent from Española. This latter contingent included the future Indian apologist Bartolomé de Las Casas for whom this was to prove a critical experience in the formation of his negative views as to the European treatment of the native population. With brutal efficiency the two parties of invaders had overrun the island completely by March of the following year.[20]

These rapid conquests in the Greater Antilles contrast strongly with the situation that unfolded on the Lesser Antilles, which became a refuge not just for native populations, but also for the *cimarrónes*[21] (escaped black slaves). In this way Puerto Rico emerged as a southern frontier of Spanish settlement in the Caribbean islands, with the Lesser Antilles only being occupied during the seventeenth century by Spain's imperial rivals, the French, Dutch and English (see Chapter 5). During this hiatus between the end of new Spanish colonization and the onset of the French, Dutch and English occupations, the native populations of the Lesser Antilles were able to take advantage of their position on the main shipping lanes between Europe and America to practise a profitable trade with the European vessels that stopped to replenish their drinking water and supplies after the Atlantic crossing.[22] Relations with the Spanish were still usually hostile and the farms and ranches of Puerto Rico were frequently raided by the Caribs, whom it was suspected held not just African and European captives (including the son of the governor of Puerto Rico) but also a vast treasure of gold and silver taken from wrecked and plundered shipping. The issue of the Caribs, therefore, remained a preoccupation of the Puerto Rican colonists and evidence continued to be collected as to their lawlessness and 'cannibalism' in the hope of persuading the Crown to permit the slaving of the Lesser Antilles.[23] But Spanish imperial ambition had turned its attention to the wonders of the Incan and Aztec empires, as well as the rich plunder that was to be had all along the Central American isthmus (see below), and the struggle with the *caribes* little troubled Spain, until they made alliance with the French.

Following their expulsion from Brazil, the French redoubled their efforts to gain a settlement in the Caribbean, which project began in earnest by the 1630s, principally on Martinique and Guadeloupe.[24] In a similar manner the English, partly stimulated by their expulsion from Surinam in the 1660s, joined the scramble for islands in the Lesser Antilles, centring themselves on Barbados and St Lucia. In most of these locations the fate of the native population was the same and despite initially peaceful contacts, the Caribs were driven out or marginalized. On St Vincent and Dominica, however, the occupation of the islands was fiercely contested on all sides and the native population was alternatively courted by the French and English rivals. This meant that native political autonomy persisted into the eighteenth century since they had become valuable allies in the inter-colonial rivalry that beset these tiny islands.[25]

In the event, and only following a full-scale war in the 1790s, the English carried out a mass-deportation of a large part of the indigenous population of St Vincent, which had thoroughly mixed with *cimarrónes* to form the 'Black Caribs',[26] leaving only a remnant population of 'Red Caribs'.[27] The indigenous population of the island of Grenada, which had been settled by a mixture of native groups from the islands and adjacent continent, was progressively abandoned by the *indigenes*, as well as by the French who nominally claimed it as their colonial possession. However, it was never developed as a plantation colony or as a trading entrepôt until it was taken over by the British in 1760, at the same time as St Vincent and Dominica were seized. On Dominica the independence of the native population has endured until the present day, but this was at the price of a close and often disastrous involvement in the inter-colonial rivalries of the seventeenth and eighteenth centuries.[28] In this sense the Dominican Caribs show a long history of close adaptation and opposition to the Europeans and their successors in the Caribbean, with the result that many of the cultural and social features that were a product of European intrusion into the Caribbean islands and *Tierra Firme* are to be seen in microcosm in the history of the native population of Dominica.

Tierra Firme

Physically proximate to the Lesser Antilles and culturally integrated with them were those regions that the Europeans referred to as the Pearl Coast, Paria and Trinidad. Although all these locations had been seen by Columbus in 1498, only the Pearl Coast was exploited initially, following the information gathered during the armed reconnaissances of Alonso de Hojeda and Cristobal Guerra.[29] With the discovery of the vast pearl fisheries off the island of Cubagua in 1512, European interests centred on the Venezuelan coast, rather than Trinidad, and it was not until 1531 that any sustained attempt was made to occupy and explore Trinidad and the Orinoco river. Eventually both these locations were simultaneously occupied by Antonio de Berrio at the end of the sixteenth century.[30]

In this intervening period the status of the native populations as *caribe* or *guatiao*, was closely debated. In this context the classificatory exercise of Figueroa (see above) is revealed as deeply political. For example, Trinidad was declared Carib in 1511, but that decision was reversed, following the intervention of Las Casas, in 1518.[31] This decision was itself reversed again in 1530, in order to facilitate the occupation of Trinidad by Antonio Sedeño. In a similar way, the initial favourable classification of the native populations in the vicinity of the Cubaguan pearl fisheries as Taíno was reversed in 1519 once commercial extraction of the pearls had got under way.[32] In the period between these decisions it was the hapless Lucayans (see above) who supplied the majority of Amerindian slaves for the fisheries. This hiatus in the onset of Spanish exploitation of the local populations also allowed the foundation of the first Franciscan monastery in the New World at Cumaná, as well as a Dominican mission at Chirivichi.[33] But these pacific contacts were not to last and in 1519 the activity of the slavers re-commenced. The native response was decisive, the religious foundations were destroyed and the Spanish settlements besieged, but the Spanish reoccupied the region in 1522, waging a deadly war *a fuego y sangre*.[34] Thereafter followed a period of virtual anarchy during which various *doradistas* vied for access to the fabled wealth south of the Orinoco from their bases in the Cumaná and Trinidad. The pearl fisheries themselves had been exploited to the point of near exhaustion by 1540 and the once flourishing town of Nueva Cadiz was virtually abandoned. Even as new pearl beds were opened up off the island of Margarita, the lure of those discovered in the Gulf of Panama proved far stronger. Along the Venezuelan coast the rule of the missions was gradually re-established, but only with the support of a series of military campaigns, most notably that of Juan de Orpín in the 1630s which definitively established Spanish dominance in this region.[35]

The native networks of gold trading that the *doradistas* so eagerly hoped to intersect, ultimately connected both the Caribbean islands and the western coasts of *Tierra Firme* to the heartland of the Colombian sierras.[36] It was here that the dreams of encountering an *El Dorado* were indeed realized[37] and the occupation of the coastal region in order to gain access to those gold-working cultures was correspondingly brutal.

Uniquely in the history of Spanish colonialism, the first substantial occupation of the Gulf of Venezuela region was carried out by Germans under licence from the Spanish Crown. Ambrosio Alfinger, Jorge Spira, Philip von Hutten and Nicolas Federmann were the principal *conquistadores* who initiated this enterprise, under the auspices of the House of Welser merchant-bankers, who were creditors of the Spanish Emperor Charles V. Alfinger was chosen to be the first governor and arrived at Coro in 1529, where the existing Spanish governor, Juan de Ampués, deferred to the authority of the newcomers.

Initial reconnaissance by Alfinger was to the west and the regions around Lake Maracaibo. In subsequent years the valley of the Río Magdalena was penetrated and the true wealth of the native cultures uncovered; Alfinger's final expedition returning to Coro at the end of 1533. Alfinger was then succeeded by Jorge Spira (known in German sources as George Hohemut) who pushed into the region to the south, there garnering reports of a fabulous land called *Meta*, but losing many men before his final return to Coro. During his absence Nicolas Federmann, Spira's lieutenant, lead an unauthorized *entrada* also to the south. He crossed some of the major rivers that ultimately drained into the Orinoco basin and at length managed to ascend the *cordillera* to his west and enter the plains of Bogotá. However, he found that he had been beaten to this objective by an expedition approaching from the Magdalena valley, led by Jimenez de Quesada.

Last in this line of German adventurers came Philip von Hutten. He spent four fruitless years in journeying from Coro across the great *llanos* of Colombia and Venezuela in search of the fabled lands of *Meta* and *El Dorado*, only to be hacked to death with a blunt machete on his return journey to Coro at the behest of his rival, Juan de Carvajal, founder of the Venezuelan city of El Tocuyo.[38]

This long succession of adventurers left a violent mark on the native societies they encountered.[39] When the coastal Venezuelan territories became the direct responsibility of the Spanish Crown once again, the new administration of Juan Pérez de Tolosa found a population chastened and resentful at the treatment they had received from the *doradistas*.

Nonetheless, Spanish occupation crept out inexorably from these early coastal enclaves, southward into the *llanos* of Orinoco and westward along the Venezuelan littoral towards the Gulf of Urabá and the province of Darién. In the next few decades the cities of Borburata, Barquisimiento, Valencia, Trujillo, and, in 1567, Caracas itself were founded.[40] From these slender beginnings the province of Venezuela and the Captaincy of Caracas rapidly grew in economic significance. By 1600 up to 45 ranches were established in the *llanos* and by the mid-seventeenth century some 75 per cent of exports to Spain were of cattle hides;[41] much of this having been achieved through the forced labour of the native population.[42]

Further to the west, the information that had been gathered on the voyages of Guerra and Hojeda and led to the discovery of the Cubaguan pearl fisheries, revealed also the existence of the Caquetío and Wayú (Goajiro) who occupied the region around the Gulf of Venezuela. Over time the Wayú in particular were to develop an active accommodation with the

Europeans, based on their skill as cattlemen, and as traders with the imperial rivals of Spain, especially the Dutch and English. This legacy, similar to that of the *caribes* of the islands, has also preserved their autonomy from the Venezuelan state and given them a reputation for hostility to outsiders that persists right up to the present day.[43]

Exploration of the Gulf of Venezuela region also indirectly led to the discovery of the Gulf of Urabá and the province of Darién by Juan de la Cosa and Rodrigo de Bastidas in 1500–01.[44] The return to this region was almost immediate and the native town of Urabá was captured and looted in 1504 by Juan de la Cosa.[45] There were many indications here of the rich gold-working cultures of Colombia, particularly the Sinu. However, the slaving activities of the Guerra brothers to the east, around Cartagena, and the subsequent foray by Alonso de Hojeda into this region in 1505, as well as Cosa's own attempts to take slaves during his return from Urabá, produced yet again a legacy of hostility to further European intrusions.

The Spanish Crown, in order to regulate the occupation of this region, issued two concessions. One was to cover the area to the west of Urabá, the other to the east. The former concession was named Veragua, following the usage of Columbus who had first sighted the region during his fourth voyage, and was given to Diego de Nicuesa. The latter region was known as Urabá, following native usage, and given to Hojeda, with Cosa as second in command.

Just as was the case in the occupation and exploitation of the Pearl Coast, the natives of the coast west of Cartagena were declared to be Caribs, thus opening the way for a summary military conquest and a seizure of the population as slaves. However, the martial abilities of the natives were considerable and Juan de la Cosa himself was killed, along with another seventy of the Hojeda expedition, on attempting their landing at Cartagena. The survivors were saved by the arrival of Nicuesa's fleet, *en route* to Veragua. The Spanish then fortified a position at Urabá, from where a series of plundering raids were conducted into the interior. But Hojeda himself, still suffering from his wounds received at Cartagena, returned to Española, leaving the nascent colony in the charge of Francisco Pizarro, later *conquistador* of Peru. The Spanish held on in Urabá for a few more months but then abandoned the site in favour of the native town of Darién in the land to the west, occupied by the Cuna who initially proved more tractable to their purposes.

Nicuesa, meanwhile, had landed in the next native province beyond Darién, called Careta. Here the expedition split into two groups but as Nicuesa pushed ahead he became lost, while the slower party tried to fortify a position on the Río Belén, following the earlier example of Columbus. But they were eventually forced to evacuate, having rescued the remnant of Nicuesa's group. A second expedition the following year achieved little more than to confirm the undesirability of European occupation in the eyes of the native population of the region – the Cuna, Guaymí and Sumo.

These initial acts of possession had done little to establish the Royal concessions of Urabá or Veragua. It was the pragmatic actions of Vasco Nuñez de Balboa, in illegally taking command of the survivors of the Hojeda and Nicuesa expeditions, that allowed the Spanish to forge ahead with the project of colonization from their base of Santa María, founded on top of the native town of Darién in 1511. Balboa proved an altogether more able strategist in regard to the native population and was able to use local rivalries to his advantage. The fruits of this policy were a more stable food supply and a firmer political basis for the control and exploitation of the hinterland, particularly the gold-rich chiefdom of Dabeiba. But perhaps his greatest prize was the sighting of the 'South Sea' (Pacific Ocean) on 27 September, 1513.

In response to this momentous discovery, as well as the rising fortunes of the Spanish in Veragua and Urabá, the two concessions were united and re-named Castilla del Oro with Royal authority being vested in Pedrarias Dávila. This was to prove a total disaster. Contemporary records are unanimous in their description of the brutality of Dávila's governorship towards the Amerindians, even in the case of Las Casas and Oviedo y Valdes, otherwise at odds in the matter of the European treatment of the native population. At the beginning of the sixteenth century, Oviedo[46] estimated the native population of the Panamanian isthmus region to have been over 2 million. By 1607 the *Audiencia* of Panama was reporting a desolate and impoverished scene, and the dominant cultural group, the Cuna (then known as the *Cueva*), were reduced to a fraction of their original population, many also having retreated away from their previous coastal and downriver locations. This utter devastation of the native population was also dramatically reflected in the changed ecology of the coasts and immediate hinterland, which was overgrown with thick forest by the mid-sixteenth century where once the savannas and fields of native agriculture had dominated.[47] Like the remnant *caribes* of Dominica and St Vincent (see above), the Cuna also adapted to the presence of large numbers of fugitive black slaves and provided alliances for the French and Scottish colonies that existed in Darién from 1690–1757. In contrast the other major grouping of this isthmian region, the Guyamí, though also initially withdrawing away from the anarchy of the coastal region, were brought into missions in considerable numbers during the latter part of the sixteenth and early part of the seventeenth century.

In considering the fate of the native populations in the northernmost areas of the Veragua region it is important to note that the impact of European colonialism on native society came full circle here, in that the post-contact culture of the Miskito, Sumo and Paya was significantly influenced by that of the 'Black Caribs', who were transported here by the British in the

1790s (see above). So too, the specialized military organization of the Miskito seems to have been a legacy of their close alliance with the English planters and woodcutters who settled the Nicaraguan and Honduran coastline in the early seventeenth century, as was the re-development of hierarchial social organization from the wreckage of the Spanish *entradas*.

In closing also the cycle of narration that has taken us from the north-ernmost islands of the Caribbean, through the Lesser Antilles and west along the Venezuelan littoral to the Central American isthmus, we come finally to the Yucatán peninsula and the borderlands of the Maya. The story of the first encounters and conquests of the Maya cannot properly be told here but do provide an opportunity for reflection on the larger processes of colonial occupation that are sometimes hidden in the details of successive combats with natives and intrigues among their would-be *conquistadores*.

Although Columbus may have encountered a trading canoe that carried goods for Maya markets during his final voyage in 1502, it was not until 1517 that a specific expedition was launched, from Cuba, under the leadership of Francisco Hernández de Córdoba. The destination was vague but the intent, to seize slaves and gold, was clear. Instead of going south towards the rela-tively known coasts of the isthmus they headed due west and so quickly came upon the Yucatán peninsula. From their ships they could sight a great town and so their hopes were duly high as to the rewards they might glean. However, at closer quarters their progress was less direct and the Spanish party suffered serious losses at the hands of this Maya outpost which was possibly forewarned of their intent, if not the actual voyage.[48] In the event, further hostile encounters along the coast of the peninsula, especially at Campeche, decimated the Spanish expedition and Córdoba himself died of his wounds a few days after they had struggled back to Cuba. But the reports of gold obliterated memories of the disastrous aspects of this encounter and lead instead to an immediate second attempt on the peninsula, under the command of Juan de Grijalva in 1518.

For their part, the Maya also seem to have been chastened by that first encounter with Córdoba, and Grijalba was met with offers to trade. Significantly he was also urged onward along the coast, being assured that even greater treasures lay in other places. And so it was that in practice, fol-lowing the initial example of Hernando Cortés, whose fleet was preparing to sail from Cuba at the point of Grijalva's return, over the next decade the Spanish concentrated on the Aztec empire in the hinterlands. The rest of the Yucatán peninsula was left relatively unscathed, except for the port of Cozumel which proved a convenient point for ships to refurbish *en route* to Mexico.

However, following this hiatus, Francisco de Montejo received a licence for the pacification of the Yucatán peninsula in 1526. But Maya settlement patterns meant that there was to be no city of gold in the interior, and the coastal villages, rich and populous though they were, had represented the best pickings on the peninsula. Also, unlike their Aztec neighbours, but much like the other peoples of the *Tierra Firme* littoral, Mayan political organization provided no easy path to colonial control, being relatively amorphous with sovereignty in political matters usually located at the level of the individual settlement.

As a result, by 1535, the Spaniards had abandoned the peninsula. It was re-occupied in 1540 but by a group of men more content to pursue a longer-term profit from the labour of the natives, rather than in expectation of plundering golden treasures. Nonetheless, the effects of initial contacts had already taken their toll among the Yucatán Maya and internecine strife, famine, and introduced diseases had resulted in a general collapse of political authority and a corresponding decline in agricultural and economic productivity. Direct Maya responses to the Spanish re-occupation also involved the destruction of their subsistence base and their holy places – having defended their land they now appeared to destroy it rather than cede it to the colonizers. As with the Wayú, Guaymí and the Cuna, some of the remnant population permanently melted away into the forests and swamps of the southern part of the peninsula, but some also came back to re-occupy the coastal villages. Here they were easily incorporated under Spanish control, but not before a last 'rebellion' in 1546 which was firmly extinguished.

On the back of this pacification the missionaries began their evangelization and most notable among that company was to be Diego de Landa, Bishop of Yucatán from 1571–9. Landa was both a great scholar and great destroyer of traditional Maya thought and belief. He burned all the books and sacred objects he could uncover, yet left an invaluable testimony to the culture of the sixteenth century Maya in his own work *Relación de las cosas de Yucatán*. Thus, the continuity of Maya culture was largely extinguished by the Spanish occupation, though the nineteenth-century rebellion of the Maya descendants against their white masters, known as the 'Caste War of Yucatán', serves to remind us that the trauma of that conquest remained, and still remains, a potent force in the historical consciousness of native American peoples.

Internal consequences

Having outlined the initial manner of the Amerindian encounter with the Europeans it now remains to try and trace the effects of these often violent occupations on Amerindian life-styles. Discussion will consider three spheres of change: the sociopolitical, the economic, and the cosmological and religious. However, despite the complexity and variability of the processes of European occupation, as well as the wide diversity of native cultures and polities that the Europeans encountered, recent theoretical work in anthropology suggests that the categories that need to be employed to explain and analyse these processes are relatively few.[49] By using the concept of a 'Tribal Zone', that is a physical and conceptual area of interaction that emerges as expanding state formations encounter a range of indigenous organization, we are able to classify the myriad of differing forms of encounter in a way that brings out some of the regularities of the colonial process from the native point of view.

The Tribal Zone can be characterized as that shifting region that stretches out from the points of European entry into the, as yet, uncontacted hinterlands. As we saw in Chapter 5, it should be emphasized that the activity of the Europeans is often felt well within this area before any *direct* encounters occur. In the Caribbean, as elsewhere, this happened most obviously through the spread of European diseases, such as smallpox and measles, to which the native population had no resistance. Although there is still extensive debate on the timing and severity of epidemics outside of the Maya region there can be little doubt that this was a significant factor in inducing new kinds of social and political organization. Dramatic population losses, through either war or disease, provided the demographic context for the emergence of new leaders and new visions of how Amerindian people might respond. For example, the emergence of the Caribs in Orinoco as a significant political force in the eastern Caribbean region, as well as reports of the appearance of prophetic leaders among them, can be related to the physical extinction of a number of élite families that had previously ruled the lower Orinoco.[50]

In a wider sense also the longer-term implantation of alien flora and fauna upset existing economic relationships as well as changing ecological practices. For example, as the Spanish began systematically to penetrate to the south of the Venezuelan littoral the many thousands of head of cattle they brought with them negatively affected indigenous species, and signalled an attempt to lessen their initial dependency on Amerindian-supplied foodstuffs.[51] Indeed, the supply of foodstuffs, as well as fresh water and wood for shipbuilding, was a constant feature of early relationships between Amerindians and Europeans. For example, the supply of *aru* (manioc flour) and fresh water to the pearl-fishing colony on Margarita in the early sixteenth century engendered extended alliances between the Spanish and certain native groups – principally *aruacas* (Lokono) from the Guyana coast[52] – which heavily influenced the pattern of European and Amerindian settlement for decades to come. In like fashion, the Caribs of the Lesser Antilles, particularly Dominica, were repeatedly visited by ships in the last stages of the Atlantic crossing, seeking to replenish their food, water and wood supplies.[53]

In a similar fashion the introduction of metal tools by the Europeans was an opportunity for Amerindian leaders to reform political traditions as the possession and distribution of such favoured items was the source of significant political authority. The European colonizers also used the exchange of metal tools in a political fashion, trading with those Amerindian leaders who were tractable to their designs, excluding others who were more troublesome.

Of particular significance to European influences on Amerindian ecologies was the way the supply of metal tools allowed the more extensive practice of slash-and-burn agriculture.[54] Both the supply of foodstuffs to the Europeans and their slaves, as well as the ability to become economically autonomous from the more sedentary and established chiefdoms, were powerful reasons for the adoption of slash-and-burn modes of horticulture and so became the economic context for the emergence of new political leaders referred to above.

The trade in metal tools also had significant impacts on native ecological practices, since the efficiency of cutlasses and axes permitted the extensive clearing of forest for slash-and-burn horticulture. It also permitted a commerce in cut wood which, like the supply of processed dyes, animal products such as jaguar pelts, live birds and various gums and resins, were facets of a burgeoning Amerindian-European economic relationship.

Economic relationships, like the trade in foods, metal tools and forest products, thus strongly affected native ecological practices and resource usage. But they were also used to foster close political relationships with selected Amerindian leaders and to influence autonomous native societies in a variety of ways.

In political terms the mere presence of Europeans could spark latent conflicts. As the Spanish occupied the Venezuelan coastal region in search of gold their *entradas* to the south left a trail of destruction that radiated out, upsetting the existing relationships between the various native polities, provoking migrations away from the points of contact and causing secondary conflicts among the native population. A good example of this process was the migration of the 'ancient rulers' of Trinidad, the Yao, down the Atlantic coast almost as far as the mouth of the Amazon. Here they settled amongst an extant population but were unable to re-establish their political authority and were repeatedly raided by local groups. Even alliance with various English and Dutch expeditions failed to preserve them and they disappear from the historical record altogether by the mid-seventeenth century.[55]

Similarly, as the Spanish moved into the Yucatán peninsula they became aware of the existence of two shipwrecked Spaniards who had been living amongst the Maya for some six years.[56] Theirs was not, therefore, the 'first contact' that the Maya had with the Europeans and we can only guess at the consequences of this for subsequent Mayan political strategies towards the Europeans.

Similar examples can easily be found throughout the history of the European occupation, which was often tentative and episodic away from the regions of Mexico, Peru and the Greater Antilles. However, a regularity of effect as a result of even these tentative attempts at colonization, does emerge. Principal among these was the *tribalization* of extant native socio-political structures. Such tribalization essentially consisted in the formation of increasingly closed and endogamous social groups and often the develop-ment of hierarchical political authority expressing the emergence of new ethnic divisions.

At issue were usually native strategies for dealing with external inva-sion. The analysis of Maya or Aztec responses to the Europeans would only partly fit the model of the Tribal Zone referred to above.[57] But it is most rele-vant to understanding native responses when applied to the wider Caribbean region.[58] Essentially the term *tribalization* becomes a shorthand for express-ing the unity of effect that European contact induced. We have already seen how this operated in that part of political life concerned with leadership, and how ecological and economic factors could reinforce these tendencies. At the level of the family household further consequences can be traced.

Marriage and kinship relations, where they did not actually incorporate Europeans and, later, Africans, certainly altered in their structure and quality in a number of ways. For example, marriage exchanges as part of the indigenous political process were quickly altered by the changing political conditions. Stable patterns of exchange between élite families, as well as established exchange patterns between tribal clans or moieties rapidly broke down, as in the case of Española, Puerto Rico and the Lesser Antilles.[59] The role these types of exchanges had in cementing both local and regional rela-tionships therefore ceased or were supplanted by new ones. A good example of this process would be the emergence of intense patterns of intermarriage between the Amerindians of the Antilles and the mainland. Although it is unlikely that there were no such exchanges in pre-Columbian times, the history of the island Caribs is particularly marked by the intense relationships they developed with the Caribs of Orinoco. Given that the Orinoco Carib were themselves *par excellence* a group that had their origins as an apolitical force in the conditions of European contact, the specifically colonial context of this pattern of marriage alliance seems undeniable.

At the interpersonal level we can certainly trace a change in quality of kinship relations directly to the effects of European intrusion. The category *poito* in Carib kinship terminologies now designates a range of statuses: son-in-law, trade client/partner, servant, or slave. But the roles of client and slave seem to have been greatly expanded as the Europeans introduced a commercial trade in Amerindian war captives, as well as taking Amerindian women and children as domestic servants. Alongside this the enhanced trading opportunities, in metal goods, slaves and guns, for those favoured by Europeans meant that the category of trade client (sometimes with the connotation of debtor) was a prevalent means of forming political solidarity and dependency by the new wave of Amerindian leaders who supplanted the ancient élite.

But it is in the sphere of military behaviour and institutions that the effects of occupancy of this Tribal Zone can be at their most dramatic and immediate. As will be appreciated from the narrative given above of European intrusion into the Caribbean, the historically compelling reason for this is that warfare and plunder were often the primary form of interaction between would-be colonizer and colonized. Although, as outlined above, the effects of trading relationships, especially where this involved steel tools or guns, could have an equally profound effect on native autonomy and sociopolitical organization in the longer term. But the consequences for the native population of a rising tide of military conflict were not always negative, in that many native groupings acted as 'ethnic soldiers' or 'martial tribes'; that is mercenaries recruited on the basis of their tribal loyalties. In this way the Caribs and Miskito became military specialists fighting without regard to the putative distinction between native and colonizer.[60]

One might, therefore, make the following anthropological distinctions among the political trajectories of native groups in the Caribbean for the period we have been considering, in order to summarize the regularities in the various forms of Amerindian-European contact:

1 Groups that emerged mainly as a result of the European presence and their situation in a Tribal Zone, e.g. Caribs, Miskito, sometimes called 'colonial tribes'.

2 Groups that were aboriginally powerful, exemplifying chiefdom-style political incorporation of many villages, but who i) failed to survive the new conditions of initial European occupation and so were reduced to 'tribal' status by direct military campaigns, e.g. the Cumanagoto and Warao, or ii) did make such a successful transition, e.g. the Cuna, Wayú and Guaymí, but were nevertheless tribalized as a consequence of their wider involvement with the Europeans.

3 Groups that emerged as an indirect consequence of the European presence, being the end result of a series of relocations and changing marriage exchanges in the hinterland, but often without any direct contact until the seventeenth or eighteenth century.

This latter category was non-existent in the coastal and island locations we have been considering but certainly includes groups who are sometimes treated as having existed untouched since 1492, such as the Yanomamo or Ye'cuana of the Venezuelan Amazon.

In each of these cases specific ethnic identities were influenced by the rhythm of expansion and contraction on the part of the colonial states in this region, regardless of a group's geographical distance or relative isolation from these states. In this sense no modern native groups can be seen as exemplifying pre-Columbian patterns of existence, as has sometimes been the assumption of the ethnographers and archaeologists.

These kinds of sociopolitical distinctions are also reflected in the way in which ethnic identities were ideologically derived. In the first case political authority derived largely from competence in trade and war, kinship boundaries becoming commensurately negotiable as both 'clients' and 'captives' (*poitos*) were tribally incorporated. In the second case, and befitting those groups who displayed the most complex polities at contact, political authority originally derived from some form of dynastic social charter or genealogical positioning and kinship boundaries were correspondingly inflexible as a result. But as European pressure persisted such groups came more and more to approximate to those in the first case. In the third case political authority emerged from positioning in exchange relationships, both marital and economic, within the surviving indigenous political economy of the region, *tribalization* thus being only indirect and tenuous.

In sum, the European occupation provoked demographic collapse, predation from slavers, repeated immigrations and wide-scale amalgamations of previously independent groups throughout the whole of northern South America, and the Caribbean region in particular. In turn these forces provoked a fundamental reorientation of patterns of ecology, marriage and inter-group relations which had the overall effect of *tribalizing* indigenous life-styles. This meant an increased isolation between different ethnic communities, once a phase of amalgamations had ceased, an end to many long-range trading relationships and a shrinking of the demographic base of political leadership. This continuing process effectively produced the kind of small-scale, linguistically homogenous and endogamous social grouping which is familiar from the more recent ethnographic record. However, it is now clear that the historically contingent nature of this style of tribal organization was intimately linked with the European occupation.

It remains to suggest how Amerindian thinking and cosmology reflected these radical processes. In general terms the advent of missionary work, within a few years of the first arrival of Columbus, most obviously challenged existing categories of Amerindian thought. But the fact that the missionaries were not mere purveyors of ideas, being actively and openly supported by the military capabilities of the *conquistadores*, put this exchange of ideas on a thoroughly inequitable basis. Since the élite of native political leaders often derived their authority from putative divine genealogies, or from arcane procedures for intercession with the spirit world, the political conquest was inevitably inseparable from the spiritual one – as the Spanish themselves so clearly enunciated.

It is all the more remarkable then that 'conversion' to Christianity remained an uncertain process, evidenced more in the acceptance of the temporal power of the church and the political and economic influence of the missionaries, than in a respect for their spiritual authority. Indeed, it was not until the nineteenth and twentieth centuries that significant syncretic religious idioms emerged, the native spiritual traditions being vital up to the present day, even in those areas that were in the forefront of the first attempts at conversion.

Principal amongst these traditions is *shamanism*, by which practice those adept or skilled in techniques of trance, vision, prophecy and song, directly encounter the denizens of the spirit world. Obviously it was this class of native spiritual leaders that was most directly attacked by missionary endeavours but, given the fact that *shamanic* practice in these regions is essentially open to those who can master the techniques, it did not offer up an institutional target for religious extirpation as did the temple and ancestor cults of the Aztec, Maya or Inca.

Certainly the European invasion prompted all kinds of specific vision and prophecy as native leaders struggled to explain and control the unpredictable consequences of a European encounter. But, unlike in Peru or coastal Brazil, no millennial tradition emerged, not least because the autonomous persistence of native society was so severely curtailed in the Caribbean context. On the Lesser Antilles, for example, vigorous *shamanic* practices are recorded down to the present day, but they did not underwrite a particular movement of opposition to the Europeans. In this way the tribalization of native political and economic structures was reflected in the cosmological sphere by a shrinking role for the *shaman* in the ordering of political decision making which now largely fell to the warriors. Rather, the *shaman* becomes a figure associated with curing, healing and the symbolic ordering of change through mythic narratives. Though even in these more limited roles, the authority of *shamanic* vision was compromised by the succession of epidemics that swept most coastal and island societies, as indigenous theories and beliefs about death and contagion were proved inadequate or irrelevant.

Something of the way in which the Europeans were incorporated into native thought may be understood from their common designation as *paranaghiri* (spirits from the great water). Although there has been much speculative writing about the extent to which the Europeans may have been prefigured in native thought – either as returning culture-heroes, such as *Amalivaca* in Venezuela or *Viracoa* in Peru and Ecuador, or as fulfilments of specific prophecies, as for the Aztec and Maya – most assimilations of the Europeans proved to be far more pragmatic. For example, around the 1590s, Caribs in Trinidad and Orinoco were stirred by the apocalyptic visions of one of their number who, claiming the authority of *Wattopa* (spirit of fire), prophesied the liberation of the Amerindians from the oppression of the Spanish through the imminent military intercession of the Dutch and English. The pragmatism of this vision is underlined when we remember that it was at precisely this moment that Walter Raleigh was arming the Trinidad natives, following his capture of the Spanish governor, and searching the coast of the Orinoco and the Guianas in search of an entrance to *El Dorado*. His open appeal for alliance with the Amerindians was thus culturally translated into the vision of this Carib seer.

In representational terms the artistic expression of the Amerindians was very much altered by the European hunt for gold and silver. Native gold-working seems to have effectively ended at the point of European arrival and only persisted in the most marginal regions of the Caribbean until the end of the sixteenth century – partly explaining the frustrations of the search for *El Dorado* in Orinoco. In short, knowledge of the sources of gold or of the locations of artifacts became highly dangerous knowledge as the Spanish did not scruple at torture and execution in order to discover its whereabouts. Certainly native leaders specifically enjoined their followers to withhold such information and invented tales of great dragons that guarded the golden ores in order to discourage the curious.[61]

In a less tangible way the native experience of radical difference in styles of dress, habits of speech, technologies and ethical belief provoked reflection on the meaning of cultural identities, just as it did for the Europeans. If the reported words of various Amerindians are to be believed then it would seem that they were no less active in debating the significance of the encounter with the *paranaghiri*, and, just as the Europeans themselves were divided in many ways over the import of this new world, so too Amerindians were eager to travel to Europe and learn of the context from which the invaders sprang.

The real inequity in this experience stems from the European con-sciousness of their relative unity as 'Christian' and in their initiation of the encounter with the peoples of the native Caribbean. Amerindian responses were confined to reacting to those colonial initiatives and were not organized by a common cosmological or ideological order. As such the inequity of understanding is obviously symptomatic of the inequity of all colonial rela-tionships. But the vigour, inventiveness and endurance of native strategies for dealing with the European conquest clearly demonstrate the sober reality of historical process and consciousness amongst these historiographically hidden peoples.

NOTES

1   See I. Rouse, 1948.
2   Carl O. Sauer, 1966.
3   Varela, C., ed., 1982, pp. 31, 100.
4   The term *taíno* as an ethnic ascription, although derived from native termi-
    nology (de Goeje, 1939), was only coined in the nineteenth century by
    C.S. Rafinesque (1836), lending a spurious authority to the ethnographic dualism
    of the early Spanish accounts. A number of other terms, such as *ciboney,
    ciguago, bohio, aïtij, boriqua,* as well as the titles of *caciques,* occur in the early
    sources and may have carried ethnic implications. This chapter will not examine
    the dynamics of these latter ascriptions, but will follow some of the conse-
    quences of those associated with the term *caribe.* However, the ethnic plurality
    of the '*taíno*' is implicit in the discussion that follows. Rouse's (1948a, 1948b,
    1986) use of the terms '*ciboney*' and '*arawak*' to refer to successive phases of
    native occupation in the islands prior to an assumed '*carib*' invasion, and
    Taylor's (1977) use of the term '*Taíno*' to refer to the remnants of native lan-
    guage repertoire from Hispaniola, represent more subtle forms of this dualism:
    an issue that is directly addressed in Whitehead, 1993. It is therefore to be
    regretted that usage of the term continues in more recent works (Keegan, 1993;
    Rouse 1986; Stevens-Arroyo, 1988; Wilson 1990).
5   P. Hulme and N.L. Whitehead, 1992; J. Sued-Badillo, 1978; N.L. Whitehead,
    1994b.
6   CDI (1864–84), 31, p. 196; P. Delgado, 1970.
7   A. Pagden, 1982.
8   CDI (1864–84), 1, pp. 377–85; 11, pp. 321–7.
9   J. Sued-Badillo, 1978, pp. 86–9; and see below.
10 CDI (1864–84), 1, p. 382.
11 *Ibid.,* 1, p. 380.
12 F. Fernández-Armesto, 1992, pp. 133–52; S.M. Wilson, 1990, pp. 74–110.
13 CDI (1864–84), 31, pp. 283–7.
14 See W.F. Keegan, 1993.
15 CDI (1864–84), 31, pp. 438–9.
16 C.O. Sauer, 1966, p. 160.
17 B. de Las Casas, 1875, Book II, chapter 56.
18 CDI (1864–84), 1, p. 258.
19 *Ibid.,* 31, p. 388.
20 *Ibid.,* 32, pp. 369–72.
21 The term *cimarrón* appears to derive from the Spanish *cima* ('summit' or 'top
    part') since the escaped slaves often sought refuge in the relatively impassable
    hill and mountain ranges that often lie beyond the coast throughout this region,
    both on the islands themselves, as well as in *Tierra Firme.*
22 P. Hulme and N.L. Whitehead, 1992, pp. 45–80.
23 *Ibid.,* pp. 38–44.

24   *Ibid.*, pp. 83–9.

25   *Ibid.*, pp. 89–168.

26   There has been a confusing array of names applied to the surviving native inhabitants of the Antilles and substantive scholarly debate still continues as to correct usages and the significance of various orthographic renderings (see note 1). Suffice it to add here that these *caribes* of the islands were *not* Carib in the linguistic or cultural sense, being in fact Arawakans like their extinct cousins of Puerto Rico and Española. As was indicated in the introduction to this chapter this lamentable confusion has resulted from the fact that historians and anthropologists alike have uncritically borrowed the categories of colonial occupation.

27   P. Hulme and N.L. Whitehead, 1992, pp. 169–231.

28   *Ibid.*, pp. 231–354.

29   L.-A. Vigneras, 1976, pp. 48–63.

30   P. Ojer, 1966.

31   B.de Las Casas, 1875, III, p. 390.

32   E. Otte, 1977.

33   G.F. de Oviedo y Valdes, 1959, pp. 20–4; B. de Las Casas, 1875, II, pp. 18–45.

34   N.L. Whitehead, 1988, pp. 73–7.

35   M. de Civrieux, 1980, pp. 55–135.

36   A.S. Nagy, 1982.

37   N.L. Whitehead, 1973b.

38   J. de Oviedo y Banos, 1885, Book III, ch. 3.

39   *Ibid.*, Books I–III.

40   *Ibid.*, Books IV, V.

41   E. Arcila-Farias, 1946, pp. 77–8.

42   See *ibid.*, 1957.

43   B. Saler, 1988, pp. 35–8.

44   B. de Las Casas, 1875, Book II, ch. 2.

45   G.F. de Oviedo y Valdes, 1959, Book XXVII, chapters 1–4.

46   *Ibid.*, Book XXXIX, ch. 10.

47   W. Denevan,. 1992a.

48   I. Clendinnin, 1987, p. 8.

49   R.B. Ferguson and N.L. Whitehead, eds, 1992.

50   See N.L. Whitehead, 1988, 1994.

51   *Ibid.*, 1988, pp. 30–2.

52   P. Ojer, 1966; N.L. Whitehead, 1994a.

53   See P. Hulme and N.L. Whitehead, 1992, pp. 45–80, plate 9.

54   W. Denevan, 1992b.

55   See R. Harcourt, 1613.

56   I. Clendinnin, 1987.

57   See R. Hassig, 1992.

58   See N.L. Whitehead, 1992.

59   J. Sued-Badillo, 1994.

60   See N.L. Whitehead, 1990a, 1990b.

61   N.L. Whitehead, 1990c.

8

The city in the Hispanic Caribbean, 1492–1650

Alfredo Castillero-Calvo

Form, ideology and content of the Hispanic city

The work of city-building carried out by Spain in the Americas was one of the most spectacular and effective achievements of spatial organization, political administration, and utilization of material resources ever seen in the New World.

The city was probably Spain's major instrument in its domination of the new territories and the most powerful civilizing mechanism which the nation employed in its great hemispheric enterprise. It was certainly the Spanish state's most effective ideological instrument of domination. The city secured Spain's advances, concentrated the population and prevented its dispersion through the vastness of the continents, made the dissemination of Hispanic values and their imposition on the subject peoples more effective, assured administrative efficiency, broke down the territories into political and economically exploitable districts while according these territories the necessary functions, and, finally, established the architectural patterns whose urban shapes and outlines gave symbolic expression, in a most persuasive way, to the presence of the empire's authority.

The essential fact, however, is the instrumental nature of the city as part of a larger, coherent, imperial schema. Seen in this way, Hispano-American cities arose as a result of a basically teleological plan, and they became a powerful tool in the exploitation and domination of the new territories. Some of them, such as the *flota*-posts of Havana, Cartagena and Panamá,[1] arose as the seat of the regional government, with commercial and service-oriented functions. Others were born as inter-regional communication links; this was the case with Buenos Aires, Montevideo and Guayaquil. Still others, such as Tunja, in Colombia, were agro-administrative centres. Some were military posts, for example, Portobelo, Cartagena, Havana, San Juan (Puerto Rico) and St Augustine (Florida). Some were mining centres, such as

Potosí, Zacatecas and Guanajuato. Other, more modest, cities were founded as frontiers of the missionary advance; examples of these are the Jesuit mission towns of Paraguay, established in the seventeenth century and remaining until the expulsion of the Order in 1767, and the mission towns which appeared well into the eighteenth century along the coast of California and the banks of the San Antonio River in Texas.

Spain's systematic and consistent effort to concentrate the New World colonizers in urban nuclei and prevent their dispersion into the rural wilderness responded to a policy of state clearly resolved upon since the initial stages of the Conquest. The explanation for this fact lies in the rational nature of the nascent monarchic state. The Hispano-American city arose as an expression of a political intentionality, an ideological conception of power, which in this case is the power of a centralizing state. That is why the function of the city, as visualized in the nascent state's plans, was to agglutinate, organize, control (and thus to act as a hub in a network of communication and transport), to preserve royal power, to foster unity, and to buttress and secure the empire's dominance. Thus, from the very beginning of the Conquest, the act of populating the city is an eminently political act, burdened with ideology. The urban mentality signifies ideology in all of Spain's possessions in the Americas, and the urban nature of the colonies becomes one of their fundamental characteristics. The study of the city is, then, essential to an understanding of the social, economic, and political phenomena of the New World, and to a comprehension of the way in which New World mentalities were formed.

This brings us to one of the great differences that separate English colonization from its Spanish counterpart, and it is important to stress this contrast. The urban policy, or mind-set, characteristic of Spanish culture was absent from English colonization in the New World. The difference is fundamental. In the English colony it is only as an exception that we find a pre-established plan for the city – or it will appear much later, as in the case of Kingston, Jamaica, which was planned by John Goffe in 1692 as a replacement for the capital of the island, Santiago de la Vega, which had been destroyed by an earthquake. In none of the 'four migratory waves' of colonization in North America, to use the recent classification by David H. Fischer[2] – whether the Puritans of New England, the aristocratic Anglican group in Virginia, the Quakers of Pennsylvania, or the emigrants from the England-Scotland border who came to America late in the eighteenth century and were pushed into the continent's back country – do we find government, or state, regulation of the spatial ordering of the settlements, at least not as a premeditated nor ideological action by the British Crown. Nor was there ever an impulse toward planning (as mentioned above) that was sponsored by a centralizing state. The regularity of the grid-like layout of William

Penn's Philadelphia is an exception to this rule, but Philadelphia was an attempt to render into brick and mortar a religious Utopia. It was the realization of the City of God, not a city-building project sponsored or conceived by the British Crown, and its founding occurred in 1682, more than a century after the city-building experiments of the Spanish colonies had reached their maturity. Colonial society in North America was eminently rural; its élites lived in luxurious mansions erected in the midst of vast plantations, much like the great country estates of England, which they were, of course, trying to imitate. Monticello, Mount Vernon, Mount Claire, the mansions of the Carters, the Berkeleys, or the Kenmores, to mention but a few, were typically set upon prominences with splendid views of the great rivers of the Tidewater: the Potomac, the Rappahannock, the Patapsco, the Delaware, the York and the James. In these northern colonies there were no Quitos, no Cartagenas or Havanas, much less such magnificent metropolitan centres as Mexico City, Lima, Puebla or Potosí. With the possible exceptions of Philadelphia, New York and Baltimore, the remaining cities of the northern continent – Boston, New Haven, Plymouth, Williamsburg, Yorktown, Fredericksburg, Annapolis, Alexandria – were 'small towns' in comparison with the vice-regal capitals and dozens of lesser provincial capitals, not to mention many cities of second or third rank, in the colonial Latin America of the same period. This is true whether one compares their architectural and urban values, their populations, or, more importantly, their influence over their surrounding regions.

The importance acquired by the city in the Spanish American colonies gave colonial society an eminently urban character, since the city was where most of the active forces of society were concentrated, and the place from which the rest of the colonial territory was ruled. The cities were the dominant economic poles, and were the centres of political, religious and cultural activity. From the beginning, the populating of the hemisphere rested upon an urban base, and wherever one looks, the city was the launching point from which colonization spread. The discovery of America resulted not only in a true biological revolution, transforming the hemisphere's rural landscapes with its massive introduction of plants and animals from the Old World into the new, but also in an 'urbicultural revolution.'

In the New World, the city – as concept and as intentionality – played a powerful binding, nucleating role, and was of extraordinary social and political significance. In the city the central power's organs of expression were concentrated; from the city the spatial organization of the colony was instrumented, and thus coherence and unity were given to the discontinuities created by the immense distances. Cities acted as the nodes of intercommunication which ensured regions' mutual survival and cohesion. They made royal power and state control effective so that the city of the Indies was the great instrument of state by which unity was forged out of multiplicity. These considerations explain why the great colonizing machinery of the New World rested upon an urban base. It was there, in the city, where bureaucracy – power – had its headquarters, where most of the colonists were quartered, where the dominant classes lived, and where the Church did its catechistic work.

Yet until only a few years ago the urban history of Latin America had been neglected, perhaps because of the prevalent and long-standing perception that the colonies were largely rural. The pioneering studies by Juan A. García of Argentine (*La ciudad indiana*, 1900) and Jorge Basadre of Peru (*La multitud, la ciudad y el campo en la historia del Perú*, 1920) dealt, respectively, with social and institutional questions and with the relationships between city and country, but these were isolated efforts which had virtually no imitators at the time. It was, in fact, the formal or physical aspects of the city which attracted the attention of the international academic community, and since the 1940s it has been the chessboard design, the central plaza, and the great civic, religious, and military monuments which have occupied scholars' interest. Since the 1960s, thanks probably to a combination of the stimulus furnished by new cultural policies aimed at the conservation and restoration of monuments, scholars' growing access to an ever richer mass of documentary and bibliographic material, and historians' increasingly profound knowledge of many aspects of the period, both in Europe and Latin America, the range of interest in subjects for study has widened greatly, and to the theme of the merely formal aspects of the city have been added others of no less importance.

At first, there was a flood of articles and books discussing the tradition of the chessboard layout of cities in the Western world, from Hippodamus of Miletus through the Roman *centurazione* and the French *bastides* to the city-building experience in Spain at the end of the *Reconquista*. For that aspect of my study I have drawn on the excellent collection of articles in the *Boletín del Centro de Investigaciones Históricas y Estéticas* published by the Universidad Central de Venezuela under the editorship of Graziano Gasparini. Since then, there have been numerous studies dealing with the ideological contents underlying the urban phenomenon (Gabriel Guarda, Richard Morse, José Luis Romero, and others[3]) and with the significance of the city as part of the ecological environment (Jorge Enrique Hardoy and Roberto Segre, for example[4]). Authors such as Francisco Domínguez Compañy have carefully analysed as many as 37 charters (*actas de fundación*) of Latin American cities and have reinterpreted the significance of the charter.[5] Others have studied specific aspects of the urban landscape (plazas, streets, services), and we are seeing an ever greater number of empirical studies of individual cases (and especially of major cities such as Marco Dorta on Cartagena and Aníbal Sepúlveda on San Juan) and of groups of related cities.[6] All of these impressive efforts have contributed in an important way to clarifying the issue of the colonial city.

Some ideas which enjoyed a degree of acceptance in the past have now been superseded or are beginning to be abandoned, such as the idea of the influence of Renaissance Italian radial plans after Filarete, Scamozzi, Alberti, and others, and of the influence of the grid-like layout of such great pre-Columbian urban centres as Tenochtitlán or Cuzco.

Even some problems that were considered resolved, such as that of the 'classical' grid model which for years was thought to be repeated monotonously as a standardized pattern throughout all the Spanish colonies, have been proved to have passed through a long and hesitant process of experimentation, and authors such as Hardoy maintain that it was not until perhaps 1527 that the pattern was actually 'set' once and for all. Although the orthogonal, or grid, plan was characteristic of the process of city-building in the Spanish New World, there have proved to be abundant exceptions, depending upon the topography of the locale (mountains, escarpments, etc.), the location's own character and history, and the talents of the city's founders with respect to city planning.

Three major lines of hypothesis have survived. One of these links the geometric regularity of the grid model with the existence of a strong central (and centralizing) state, and sees the model as the expression of a higher imperial design: the chessboard would then be the emblematic expression of the will of the Spanish state, the outward sign of its intention to impose symmetry and order upon its colonial dominions. The paradigm of Spanish city-building in the Americas might be found in Spain itself, in the encampment of Santa Fe founded in 1491 by Ferdinand and Isabella for the final siege of the kingdom of Granada. The builders of Santa Fe were no doubt inspired by sources such as Vitruvius, the influence of whose works, passing through the Roman *castra* and other urban manifestations (such as the French *bastides* which were established in the north-western part of the Iberian peninsula), no doubt brought the classical tradition, dating back to ancient Greece, to Spain. The regular quadrangular plan, therefore, was heir to a long historical line, which had reached its maturity during the Classical period, wavered a bit (though never died out) during the Middle Ages, and experienced a brilliant (and modernized) resurgence during Spain's great work of city-building in the Americas. George Kubler, Erwin W. Palm, Gabriel Guarda, Leonardo Benévolo, Jorge E. Hardoy, Graziano Gasparini, Damián Bayon, Pedro Lluberes, and Ramón Gutiérrez, among others, have discussed this subject extensively.[7]

Another hypothesis maintains that many of the first founders, relatively crude men of little culture, could hardly have been familiar with such authors as Vitruvius, and must have lacked the specific knowledge to design an urban plan in conformity with the classical model – that is, with a regular geometric outline. If they used the rectilinear grid it was not because they were harking back to theoretical models or because they were versed in the classical tradition of city design or because they were conscious of the laws and precepts governing the subject. Their solutions to the layout of cities were empirical; they followed what appeared to them to be the easiest and most practical order. The chessboard was 'natural', and it permitted an ordered distribution of lots and spaces which favoured the founders. That is, the chessboard gave ample space to the central plaza and sufficient land for government buildings, monasteries and convents, and churches. And in so far as the terrain of the area allowed, the grid design made unlimited orderly expansion possible, as the city would continue to be governed by the original rectilinear plan, no matter how large it grew.

This 'naturalness' and even 'spontaneity' might, however, also be an explanation for the frequent cases of irregular layouts, wherein the city's 'design' is quite imperfectly symmetrical. There exist a few plans from the early years of the Conquest, and these recall the layout of medieval cities, with their narrow, twisting streets, more than the classical rectilinear model. These plans might, in fact, support the arguments of those who believe that the first efforts at constructing cities were spontaneous and totally pragmatic, and not underlain by the notion that a city's geometric regularity might emblematically represent the central power of the Spanish state or that the imperial will to conquer the new territories might be expressed in the order and symmetry of the urban landscape. The founder of cities would, then, be unaware of the ideological content of the urban geometry – though this unawareness does not necessarily imply a parallel lack of recognition of the significance of the city-building enterprise itself as an instrument for assuring domination of the new territories, since these are two very different 'aware-nesses'. The city as idea, as rationalization for the act of conquest and domination – that is, as an instrument of the empire's will to conquer – would, then, apparently be widely recognized by those first founders.

Finally, there is the hypothesis that in the last analysis the decisive element in city planning was that the idea of the city was deeply rooted in Hispanic cultural traditions. Gabriel Guarda,[8] Richard Morse,[9] and others have widely argued this interpretation. Morse recalls that the shape of the city which Spain imported into the New World was consistent with certain medieval Spanish treatises, which in turn owed much to St Thomas Aquinas. Guarda maintains that the Spanish statutes for colonization that were based on Vitruvius were less generally cited than those of Aristotelian/Thomistic inspiration. The ideological substrate of these latter ordinances made the founding of each city a liturgical act, by means of which the new occupied territories were sanctified. As Morse says, 'more than a mere exercise in cartography, urban design was the vehicle for a transplanted social, political, and economic order and exemplified the "mystical body" that was central to Iberian political thought.'[10] According to this thesis, then, the shape of the city obeyed less of an aesthetic or functional criterion than a social philosophy. This explains why taking possession of new territories (as well as founding new cities) was almost invariably accompanied by a courtly ritual whose purpose was to sacralize the act, as shown in the detailed account contained in Bernardo de Vargas Machuca's *Milicia y descripción de las Indias* ['Warfare and Description of the Indies'], published in 1599, and also in the preambles to several New World charters. These documents give witness to the fact that the founding of a city contained deep religious meaning. The founder was conscious not only of the political significance but equally of the transcendent spiritual significance of the courtly ritual he enacted.

Thus, the discussion of the phenomenon of the city has become much more complex than simply tracing the genealogy of the rectilinear grid. The various lines of hypothesis summarized here contain undeniable truths, and although at first glance they might appear to contradict one another, they are actually mutually complementary.

During the long years of the *Reconquista* in Spain, one finds that in the practice of the founding of cities and the occupation of new territories, as well as in the surviving official documentation, there is a line of virtually unbroken continuity that makes abundantly clear that the city embodied a cultural value deeply rooted in the Spanish people – or at least in the power élites of that people – and that this value was almost never abandoned.

We know that most of the Spanish settlements founded during the *Reconquista* followed political and economic objectives established by royal authority. Furthermore, the Spanish Crown had always been partial to the rectilinear grid, whose advantages had been proved over the centuries as the urban design most effective in safeguarding conquests, defending the territories seized from the nations of Islam, and launching new advances from those outposts. One of the essential functions of the city was consolidating control and domination of the occupied territories. In many cases the cities were actual fortresses, erected to protect crops and other economic activities in the neighbouring region. The French *bastides* – descended from the Roman *centuraziones* – were the model for this type of settlement, and they began to appear from at least the ninth century,[11] thanks in part to the enormous influence that France, as a Christian ally in the *Reconquista* of northern Spain, exerted. Historians have pointed to the continuity of these models, and have called attention to the writings of the Catalonian Frances Eiximenic, whose fourteenth-century treatise titled *El Crestía* presents a plan for what would be an ideal city, one which much resembles a French *bastide*. This treatise is also highly reminiscent of classical theories of urban design.

On the eve of the discovery of America, three cities were founded in Andalusia: Puerto Real (1483), Baeza (1489) and Santa Fe (1491). These cities were carefully planned by Spain's King Ferdinand and Queen Isabella, and may be considered undeniable antecedents for the New World city-building that came soon after, under these same monarchs. According to studies carried out by Eladio Lapresa Molina,[12] the model for Santa Fe was Briviesca, a small city in the northern peninsula whose layout was very similar to that of the French *bastides* of the Carolingian period. Erwin Walter Palm suggested several years ago that these newly-founded cities, and especially Santa Fe, were the models that inspired the cities of the Spanish Americas.[13]

Another persuasive piece of evidence is the *Carta Puebla de Puerto Real* [the 'Charter of Settlement of Puerto Real'], by means of which Ferdinand and Isabella gave instructions to be followed in the city planning of that settlement.[14] The importance of this document is that it throws great light on the legal and city-planning precepts of the day. In it we find collected all the rules, regulations and guidelines that governed the founding and construction of cities at that time. These show us the 'ideological' content that underlay the phenomenon of the city, the prevalent criteria for the selection of the site, and the significance of the city in the process of occupying new territories. The document alludes to the fact that cities were fundamental to defence and communication, and stresses the monarch's responsibility to situate cities where they best suit his or her royal plans. According to these instructions, the site finally chosen should possess certain ecological advantages, such as a large, safe harbour, fertile soil for agriculture, planting trees and orchards, raising livestock, and growing grapes, abundant drinking water, etc. The *Carta Puebla* also contains instructions as to the way the city should be governed, guidelines for rewarding the founding residents and indications of their duties and rights, and finally, suggestions as to the distribution of lots and spaces within the city, for example, the location of the church, government buildings, streets, the central plaza, the amount of land to be given over to common areas (for use generally by the poorer classes, and for grazing cattle and goats, cultivating kitchen gardens, and the like).

When these instructions are compared with those given barely thirty years later to Pedrarias Dávila (see below), or with the charters of New World cities, the first thing one notices is the extraordinary resemblance in their content, suggesting an unbroken line of continuity. There is such close affinity between the concepts of urban planning that clearly date to before the discovery (including the legal guidelines set forth by the royal authority for the founding of Puerto Real) and the instructions for settling the new territories that followed the discovery, that it is almost impossible to deny their close kinship.

It is obvious, then, that at the time of the discovery there existed a clear 'idea' of the city, and indeed even an 'urban ideology'. This was not, as we have seen, simply a formal idea, a purely morphological model with ecological prescriptions for types of use and infrastructural systems or hierarchized instructions for cutting up the urban fabric. Such ideas are present, of course, and their genetic link can be traced back to remote periods of Western civilization. Spanish (or more specifically, Castilian) culture borrowed, and shaped to its own ends, certain characteristic features of this long tradition. The elements of the grid or chessboard, used in the time of Pericles by Hippodamos of Miletus, the Roman construction of encampments and cities with their characteristic orientation by compass-points (the 'castramentation' systematized by Vitruvius, and Vegetius, author of *Instituta Rei Militaris*), and the prescriptions for urban sanitation given down since the times of Aristotle, came into Spain through St Thomas Aquinas and the *Partidas* of Alfonso the Wise (or Learned). They were collected in the fifteenth century by Rodrigo Sánchez de Arévalo in his *Suma de la política que fabla como deben ser fundadas e edificadas las cibdades e villas* ['Summary of the Policy Which Speaks of How Cities and Towns Should be Founded and Built'].

The city-founding process in the Caribbean

Thus there had been a long process of maturation of urban thought by the time, in the ultimate stage of the *Reconquista*, that Ferdinand and Isabella built the cities of Puerto Real, Baeza and Santa Fe. And it was under these monarchs that the founding of cities was begun in the Caribbean, where both the commercial and military objectives for the islands' cities were very similar to those for the cities in the southern Iberian peninsula. By 1503 there were five towns on Hispaniola, and by 1508 ten more had been founded on Hispaniola alone, while in that same year Ponce de León was founding Caparra in Puerto Rico and the settlement of Cuba was under way. In 1510, with the founding of Santa María de la Antigua del Darién, the first settlements on the American continent *per se* were begun. By 1571, according to the report of Juan López de Velazco, there were more than two hundred existing towns and cities in the Americas, not counting the enormous number which, having once been founded, were abandoned.[15] Thus the somewhat tentative experiment of settling the New World, which exploded in all directions when the conquest really began, gave Western culture the opportunity to apply its much-refined city-building expertise with an intensity, and at a speed, never before known. This process became, in the New World, the depository of an urban technology of long tradition, and was an accumulation of the entire Western tradition of the science of cities.

Yet while the idea of the city was present from Columbus's first voyage (even though the first settlement was in fact a fort, called Fort Navidad, founded in 1492), it is obvious that the Castilian Crown did not at first have a clear plan for constructing cities in its new possessions. It would take years, in fact, for a clear, coherent plan to be developed for the colonies, whether one considers the urban aspects of that plan or the overall issue of colonization. The establishment of the first colony on Hispaniola, Isabela, which was founded by Columbus himself on his second voyage, not only made the island a base for further exploration, first throughout the Caribbean and then onto the continent, but also meant that the city-building experience gained there would serve as a direct model for the subsequent settlement of the New World. From Isabela onward, Columbus ordered forts to be built in the interior of Hispaniola, in order to explore and conquer the island. That was how Santo Tomás, Magdalena, Esperanza, Santiago and Concepción de la Vega arose, some of which later became urban centres. After these, Santo Domingo was founded on the south coast of the island, on the eastern bank of the Ozama River, and from there the new governor of the island, Nicolás de Ovando, in turn moved the city in 1502 to the western bank, where it was to remain, as the new capital of the realms of the Indies. Thus, with Isabela in the north and the new capital in the south, a north-south axis was created, with settlements such as Santiago, Concepción de la Vega and Bonao in between. This schema is the first example in the New World of a reorganization of geographical spaces in which the city is the articulating factor.

There has been much discussion as to whether Columbus, educated, as we are informed he was, in an urban culture distinct from that of Castile, had the same concept of settlement as the members of the Isabelline court. We have been reminded that the sites Columbus founded seem based more on the model of *factorías* or *feitorías* (that is, centres with purely commercial functions which would be relatively self-contained within their own urban environment, according to the pattern which Portugal had used in Africa and which Columbus was very familiar with) than on the Castile-León model, according to which the city is an instrument of political domination of a territory. At any rate, Columbus' governance of these lands was soon ended, and after the brief Francisco Bobadilla administration of 1499–1502 and the arrival in that last year of the new governor-general of the Indies, Nicolás de Ovando, with his 2500 new colonists, urban policy was controlled entirely by the Crown. It is important to stress that in the instructions which the Crown gave to Ovando for insuring the colonization of the Crown's new possessions in the Indies, concrete directives are included for establishing urban centres on the island:

> *Porque en la Isla Española son necesarias de se facer algunas pobla-ciones e de acá non se puede dar en ello cierta forma, vereis los lugares e sytios de la dicha Isla; e conforme a la calidad de la tierra e sytios e gente allende de los pueblos que agora hay, fareis facer las poblaciones e del número que vos paresciere e en los sytios e logares que bien bistos vos fuere.*

[Because on the Island Hispaniola some settlements are necessary to be made, and from here it is not possible to impart shape to them, look to the places and sites of said Island; and according to the quality of the land and the situations and the people in addition to the towns which now exist, have the settlements made, the number of which as you may think fit and in the places and upon the sites which you deem best.][16]

These are the first city-planning instructions for the New World. As we can see, they are extremely vague, but it is important to note that colonial policy already considers the founding of cities to be a necessary element in the consolidation of the new dominions. Ovando faithfully obeyed the royal commands, and he ensured the effective control of the island. By 1516 fifteen towns had been established: Salvatierra de la Sabana, Verapaz, Lares de Buahaba, Puerto Real, Puerto Plata, Santa Cruz, Salvaleón de Higüey, Santo Domingo, Azua and Villanueva de Yaquino, all on the coast and San Juan de la Maguana, Buenaventura, Concepción de la Vega and Bonao in the interior.

The geographical distribution of the cities clearly obeyed a plan for exploiting the island. The plan was based on two fundamental concerns, the production of subsistence supplies and the exploration for gold. To deal with these concerns the *encomienda* system was adopted for organizing work in the fields and mines.[17] The *encomienda* was supplemented with the *conuco*[18] for some food production, mainly the growing and processing of cassava, which, used for bread, would soon supplant wheat as a staple and thereby be a decisive factor in the expansion of the conquest into the continent.[19]

The implementation of these economic plans and the adaptation of indigenous agricultural technologies, in addition to the founding of cities, profoundly altered the organization of space on the island, and the effects of this on the population were irreversible. The population literally disap-peared, and the plains of Hispaniola were invaded by cattle and swine, which in the space of a few years had reproduced amazingly, to a degree much greater than island needs – even the needs of the fleets of ships that stocked up for their expeditions to neighbouring islands – required. In 1508 the chronicler Peter Martyr announced that there were so many cattle on Hispaniola that the residents were pleading that no more stock be sent from Spain. This fact is significant, for it not only demonstrates the success of the colonial enterprise and the obvious control that the colonists exerted on the island, but also shows that Hispaniola was now prepared to launch from its shores expeditions of conquest to neighbouring lands and islands. It is not without significance, then, that in 1508 Ovando sent Juan Ponce de León off to conquer Puerto Rico, in 1509 he sent Juan de Esquivel to Jamaica, and in 1511 he sent Diego Velázquez to Cuba, while in 1508 preparations were begun, through the expeditions of Alonso de Ojeda and Diego de Nicuesa, for the conquest of the continent. For the experienced *conquistador* – a Velázquez, for example – the causal relationship between sufficient supplies and plans for territorial expansion must have been amply clear. This connection between supplies and expansion, I believe, must have been 'lived experience' that hardly needed discussion. This view is supported by the famous *Carta de Relación* written by the conqueror of Cuba to the Emperor in 1514:

> *Esta isla es mui fructífera i podrá proveer de pan a la tierra firme. Los puercos que se trajeron se han multiplicado hasta treinta mil; además la isla es mui a propósito de toda navegación.*

> [This island is most fruitful, and will be able to provide bread to the continent. The swine which were brought here have multiplied to the number of thirty thousand; the island is, besides, most fit for any sort of navigation.][20]

Two years later Cuba would be ready for the Mexican offensive, as Hispaniola had been ready for the offensive to the other islands and the continent. According to Bernal Díaz del Castillo, most of the supplies were in the form of pork and cassava bread, since there were not yet sufficient beef cattle (which did not begin to be abundant in Cuba until 1538). Supplies were gathered first for the Francisco Hernández de Córdoba expedition to the Yucatán in 1517, then that of Juan de Grijalba in 1518, and finally those of Cortés in 1519 and Pánfilo de Narváez in 1520.

Stressing the importance of food supplies in this phase of the conquest does not reduce the speed, or the success, of the operation to this single factor. The depopulation of the islands (due among other things to war, forced labour and disease), was coupled with the need to remedy the scarcity of manpower. The search for labour, first in the 'Lucayas' (or the Bahamas), later in the Guanajas Islands of Honduras, then off the coasts of

Urabá and Cumaná (Venezuela), and finally, around 1527, in the Yucatán and Pánuco, was one of the elements which spurred on the expeditions into new territories. Some authors, however, prefer to attribute the expansionist impulse to the need to find new deposits of gold, as those deposits being exploited began to run dry. One reads, then, of 'gold cycles', as though to imply that the rate of speed of the conquest was determined by exploration for gold. I believe there is still much to be studied, and at greater depth, in this period, in order to determine what factor or factors were decisive in each case. What is beyond question is that one of the great brakes to the conquest was the scarcity, and sometimes total lack, of foodstuff, and conversely, an abundance of such supplies immediately opened up new options for conquest and expansion. Without food, the conquest was simply going nowhere. The absolutist Spanish state's great schemes of power, all the institutional and ideological machinery, the great missionary promise glimpsed by the Catholic Church, the impulse to realize in mortar and stone the city-building policies of the empire, were but houses of cards when the *conquistador* came face to face – as he frequently did – with the truth that the vast dominions, sometimes overflowing with precious minerals, pearls and jewels, were unable to supply his basic physical needs. This was perhaps one of the fundamental considerations of the conquest, but historians have given little attention to the subject. Yet such was the case in Hispaniola, and later in Puerto Rico, Cuba, on the continent and elsewhere. In this respect, the model of Hispaniola would be paradigmatic.

The pattern of colonization on Hispaniola would be repeated faithfully on each of the conquest's new fronts, especially on the islands, where the situation was so similar to the original model. This fact should not surprise us, since virtually all the leaders of these new enterprises had received their training, as it were, in the Dominican campaigns. Ponce de León and Esquivel took part in the conquest of the eastern part of Hispaniola, where they founded the town of Salvaleón del Higüey in 1505, and Ponce de León constructed a famous stone house there in the shape of a fortress (still standing). This building is believed to resemble closely the house he built later in Caparra, the first capital of Puerto Rico. Velázquez captained the campaign in the western part of the island, where he founded Verapaz (in Xaragua), Yaquimo, San Juan de la Maguana, Azua and Salvatierra de la Sabana. Ojeda and Nicuesa were well-known scouts on the island, and it was on Hispaniola, as one would expect, that most of their army was recruited for their explorations in Urabá and Veragua. Balboa, the conqueror of Darién and founder of Santa María and Acla, had been an obscure colonist in Salvatierra de la Sabana.

One of the most prominent characteristics of the colonizing process was the establishment of coastal cities. Obviously cities were located on coasts in order to facilitate sea connections, essential not only to commercial intercourse and supply lines (and the problem of supplying ships and men during this phase of the conquest was literally a question of life and death) but also to defence. In every case it was far easier to send or receive re-inforcements within the coastal area should an emergency arise. Towns located inland were few, and though they were necessary for the articulation of the networks of communication, supply, and defence, and for controlling the area, they did not enjoy the same favour as the coastal nuclei. On Cuba, five of the seven cities founded by Diego de Velázquez in the sixteenth century were coastal cities, or located near the sea: Baracoa (1512), Puerto Príncipe, Trinidad and Havana (all 1514), and Santiago de Cuba (1515). Only Bayamo (1513) and Sancti Spiritus (1514) were inland. But Cuba is such a narrow island that the sea is never very far off.[21]

On Jamaica the first settlements founded were Villa Diego and Melilla, in 1508. In 1510 Sevilla del Oro was founded to serve as the capital. All these towns were located on the north coast of the island. Shortly afterwards, to the south, there appeared Oristán, which was also near the coastline. These were all transitory settlements which quickly disappeared. In 1524, due to Sevilla's unhealthy location, the new governor, Francisco de Garay, moved the capital to Santiago de la Vega (today Spanish Town), on the western bank of the Cobre River. According to a 1582 description, this was the only populated city on the island. One after another the settlements were founded on the coastline, or very near it. Santiago de la Vega was later to lose the honour of being the island's capital to Kingston, another coastal town, however, due to its strategic position it continued to be an important naval and ocean-trade centre.[22]

In Puerto Rico, San Juan's more advantageous naval position decided the question of the move of the seat of government from Caparra to San Juan. The rest of the major colonial cities of Puerto Rico, with the possible exception of San German, were also located on the coast.[23]

Finally, on the isthmus of Panama, for many years the only settlements which prospered were Santa María de la Antigua and Acla, both coastal cities. Later, when the 'Panama plan' took on permanence – first in order to launch the colonizing offensive into Central America and Peru, and later as a transit zone for Peruvian silver and as a centre for imperial transport and commerce – virtually all the settlements founded were either on the coastline or near it: Panamá (1519), Nombre de Dios (1520), and Portobelo (1597) were predominantly harbours and terminus cities for trans-oceanic shipping. Natá (1522) remained, like many of the first towns of Hispaniola, very near the ocean, and also close to the alluvial plain (as were Higüey and Caparra), and was followed by Concepción (1559), Los Santos (1569), La Filipina (1572), Penonomé (1573), Remedios (1589), Montijo (1590) and Alanje

214

(1591). These were almost all the towns or settlements founded by Spaniards on the Isthmus during the sixteenth century. The only exception was Santa Fe (1558), which was located in a mountain pass halfway between Natá (founded as a centre of grain storage and cattle for the isthmus) and Concepción (a mining centre), in a strategic position for linking the production of foodstuffs to the gold-mining region.[24]

There was, then, unquestionably a pattern of settlement, established since the time of the colonization of Hispaniola, in which we see clearly-evidenced concerns about the ecology of the area of the founded city and about the possibility of economic exploitation (nearness to agricultural and cattle production, availability of communications, travel, and shipping facilities, nearness to mining centres, etc.). Hispaniola also set the pattern for the architectural and city-building guidelines that were followed on all the nearby islands and in the colonization of the continent, for example, the fortress-residences of Ponce de León. On Hispaniola, the fortress of Concepción de la Vega and the Homenaje tower in Santo Domingo with its battlemented walls and round towers, undeniably inspired by medieval castles, were the models for La Fortaleza ('The Fortress'), which was and still is the governor's house in San Juan, Puerto Rico, and for La Fuerza castle in Havana. The gothic tracery of the Santo Tomás (today San José) church in San Juan follows the pattern set by the cathedral in Santo Domingo.

But it is in the urban landscape, its layout and design, that the model is most obvious. As early as 1955, Erwin Walter Palm suggested that although the original plan for Santo Domingo was not a fully-developed example of an orthogonal, or grid-like, layout, still, according to the chronicles of the time, the city had been conceived as following a quadrangular design, and was perceived as doing so by contemporaries.[25] To that effect, the words of Fernández de Oviedo, written in 1524, have often been quoted:

Esta es una ciudad nueva, bien planeada, que ha de servir de modelo a todas las ciudades de América fundadas en aquel tiempo.

[This is a new city, well planned, which shall serve as a model for all the cities of the Americas founded in that time.][26]

Bishop Alejandro Geraldini, who visited the city twenty-five years after its founding, wrote:

Quedé admirado de ver tan ínclita ciudad ... porque sus mismas calles anchas y rectas, que con ellas no sufren comparación las calles de Florencia.

[I marvelled to see such an illustrious city ... for its wide, straight streets, which outstrip the streets of Florence.][27]

And indeed the regular rectangular pattern, with a plaza whose centre is occupied by the cathedral, can be clearly seen in some early sixteenth-century engravings, such as that made to illustrate Sir Francis Drake's attack on the city. In truth the pattern is not strictly regular, but that is the case too with other early cities, such as Cartagena. Still, it is clear that the idea of rectilinearity is there, and if not observed strictly in this case, it was not followed scrupulously in many other New World cities of much later date, either, at a time when there did exist much more precise and detailed rules and regulations governing the pattern to be followed.

Certain writers hesitate to accept the orthogonal nature of the early city plan, and have downplayed the importance of contemporary texts, as, for example, with Hardoy. Others have attributed the irregularities to the influence of the mental image of medieval cities (Marco Dorta for Cartagena, for example), still others to the lack of more precise regulation. But it may be that the irregularity was owing either to the lack of good surveyors, who when the city was being founded failed to lay it out with sufficient regularity, or to the fact that as the city grew and new buildings were constructed, they were sometimes not positioned in accordance with the regular lines of the original layout (if the layout had been traced at all). Thus, the streets gradually curved and twisted, or at least lost what original rectilinearity they had possessed. Also, when the old houses were rebuilt, on the original lots, the original layout may have been perpetuated as the builders were unable to change the old physiognomy. The risk of losing regularity also increased in sites at some distance from the city centre – that is, from the place where the original plan had been laid out. Houses that grew up outside the centre would generally have been those of the humbler classes, and sited without great attention to rules or aesthetics.

The Hispaniola model was, indeed, formally proposed for the founding of cities in Puerto Rico, and in 1505 the Crown issued the first guidelines for the city planning of that island, with the following orders to Ponce de León:

> ... *que vos, llegando el dicho Vicente Yañez Pinzón a la dicha isla de Sant Xuan, señalaréis a donde los dichos vecinos puedan poblar una villa o dos u tres o quatro, de cada cincuenta o sesenta vecinos; más si más hubiere y veréis ser más necesario y complidero, y útil y priovechoso a ellos; y que en el repartimiento de las caballerías, y tierras y árboles, y otras cosas de la dicha isla, se haga según de la forma y manera que se han fecho y facen en la dicha isla nombrada Española...*

[... that thou, upon the arrival of the aforesaid Vicente Yañez Pinzón at the aforesaid island of Sant Xuan [Puerto Rico], shalt indicate where the aforesaid residents may settle a town or two or three or four, one for each fifty or sixty residents; more if there should be more[;] and thou shalt see that he obey my wish, and thou shalt give him the time that for this thou seest to be most necessary and convenient, and useful and beneficial for them [the residents]; and that in the division of the horses, and land and trees, and other things of the aforesaid island, it be done in the form and manner in which [it has] been done and that they still do on the aforesaid island named Hispaniola....][28]

These instructions are rather more detailed than those given to Ovando in 1502, and in that respect are a step forward. Yet one still notices the adherence to the model of the *Carta Puebla de Puerto Real*. There is no specific mention of the shape or outline of the city, though other issues related to city planning are dealt with: the estimated size of the population (one-quarter that of Puerto Real, due to Puerto Rico's lack of population), the distribution of land, and the royal power as the ultimate authority.

The imprecision of the instructions left the colonizer ample freedom to choose the site on which to found the city, nor were the instructions clear as to what the settlement's physical or functional characteristics were to be. It is clear that unfamiliarity with the conditions to be encountered in the New World, whose character was only beginning to emerge, encouraged the Crown to leave many of the final decisions concerning the settling of the country in the hands of the *conquistador*.

There is, after this, a long interim period until 1513, when the Crown sent Pedrarias Dávila [Pedro Arias de Àvila] instructions for the settlement of Castilla del Oro – probably the first instructions in the New World specifically regulating the founding of settlements. They demonstrate, in fact, a great advance over the instructions for Hispaniola and Puerto Rico, but it is obvious that they are based on the experience gained in the settling of those islands, especially in Hispaniola. The instructions contain suggestions as to the nature of the site and its compass orientation, thoughts as to the healthfulness and distribution of lots, and they are the first to contain city-founding regulations which themselves had been arrived at by following a plan. Here is the key fragment:

... habéis de repartir los solares del lugar para facer las casas y éstos han de ser repartidos segund las calidades de las personas, e sean de comienzo dados por order; por manera que, hechos los solares, el pueblo parezca ordenado, así en el lugar que se dejare para plaza, como el

lugar en que oviere la iglesia, como en el orden que tuvieren las calles, porque en los lugares que de nuevo se hacen dando la orden en el comienzo, sin ningun trabajo ni costa quedan ordenados, y los otros jamas se ordenan...

[... thou shalt apportion the lots of that location in order to construct houses, and these lots shall be apportioned according to the condition of the persons, and shall be given in order from the beginning; so that, the lots being divided, the town shall appear orderly, both in the place given for the plaza and in the place where the church shall be built, and in the orderliness that the streets shall obey, for in those places that are built *ex novo*, when order is given from the beginning it is with no labour or cost that they are orderly, while the others [those built without this imposed order from the beginning] are never rendered so...][29]

Though these are concrete instructions with respect to the orthogonal plan, they are still so excessively general and vague that the city's founder, basing his work on them, might have some difficulty in designing a rigorously square-angled plan on the 'classical' model. And yet there is evidence that the cities founded by Pedrarias Dávila in Panama did in fact follow a strictly orthogonal design.

In an attempt to explain this, I have referred in other articles[30] to the fact that Pedrarias Dávila – who had taken part in the founding of Santa Fe in Granada and must have been well aware of the monarchy's intentions, since he was an experienced courtier and was sent to the New World as the King's personal representative – probably required no further instructions. He knew what he had been sent to do, and how to do it. And founding cities, as part of the grand imperial scheme, was surely one of his main objectives. His 'correct interpretation' of these instructions suggests that, in spite of their vagueness and omissions (or perhaps *because* of their vagueness and omissions), Pedrarias Dávila was aware of, and a participant in, Spain's profound historical experience in the discipline of city-building. We find this same vagueness in the *Carta Puebla de Puerto Real* and in the instructions for the settlement of Hispaniola and Puerto Rico. Ovando, like Ponce de León and Pedrarias Dávila, took part in the founding of cities in southern Spain at the end of the *Reconquista*. And like Pedrarias Dávila, Ovando, thanks to his experience and the nature of his mission, was an ideal interpreter of the royal design. These men, imbued with the imperial ideology and handpicked to carry it to fruition in the new colonies, would only have needed a hint and they would have set to work. In fact, the most important thing was not that the plan should be strictly and unvaryingly orthogonal, but that it should be more than a display of surveying skill. What was asked of Ovando, Pedrarias Dávila and Ponce de León was that the city's layout be the vehicle by which the ideology and values central to Spanish political thought be communicated. These principles, as I have stated, had followed a long course of maturation from their beginnings in Aristotelian thought, through their readaptation by St Thomas Aquinas, down to Alfonso the Wise, and they clearly underlay the instructions given to the settlers and their leaders.

In Pedrarias Dávila's armada travelled the *alarife*[31] and 'good geometer' (in modern terms, surveyor) Alonso García Bravo, who probably took part in the design of the city of Panamá, as Woodrow Borah and Richard Konetzke have suggested.[32] Through a sort of *curriculum vitae* titled *Información de Méritos y Servicios* presented by García Bravo, we know that he was 'the *alarife* who designed the city of Mexico' and that he had accompanied Hernán Cortés in his New Spain campaign, even laying out the first design for Veracruz and later that of Antequera.[33] García Bravo's case is interesting not only because he was to become one of the most prolific city planners in the New World, apparently doing his job well, but also because he was the first to put into practice the Instructions of 1513. This he did first on the Isthmus of Panama, perhaps by 'redesigning' the original design of Santa María de la Antigua, perhaps also by taking part in the design of Acla and other settlements such as Fonseca Dávila and the Anades which Pedrarias Dávila ordered to be founded in Darién. He also worked under the direct orders of Pedrarias Dávila, and therefore must have refined his perception of the ideal city model to which the Crown aspired.

No archaeological studies have been done of the Panamanian cities of those years. The first Panamá was not on the shoreline, although its true location is not really known. A very short time after its founding, and still in the time of Pedrarias Dávila (although the exact date is unknown), Pedrarias ordered the city to be moved to the site now known as Panamá Viejo. In turn, this city was abandoned after its destruction by Henry Morgan in 1671. The original Nombre de Dios disappeared when it was moved to Portobelo in 1597, and the only settlement of that era still in existence today is Natá, but its original plan has not yet been fully studied. Nevertheless, the only two designs for the old Panamá – that by Juan Bautista Antonelli in 1586 (in the Naval Museum in Madrid, and very little known) and that of Cristóbal de Roda in 1609 (which has been reproduced many times) – both show a city laid out with considerable regularity, its central plaza flanked by the cathedral and the *cabildo*, or town hall. However, in the 1586 layout several streets are notably twisted, and although the design does resemble a chessboard, the regularity is far from strict. It was not until Roda's plan that the design was perfected. Here, the regularity is clear, and this characteristic is easily visible in the ruins that can still be seen today. Acla was abandoned entirely in 1559, and no one has yet studied it – in fact, its location has never been authoritatively determined – but the chronicles clearly mention its central plaza, on whose scaffold Pedrarias Dávila ordered Balboa's head to be cut off. According to Fernández de Oviedo, the edict authorizing the sale of Balboa's property after his death, which had been nailed to the scaffold in the middle of the plaza, was bitten by a horse and torn off. When referring to Santa María la Antigua, Oviedo also makes a clear reference to its 'plaza'.

Another important piece of evidence is the charter, or *acta de fundación*, of Natá. The other charters for the cities of Panama have been lost, as have those of most colonial cities in the New World. Natá's is therefore of great importance: it is a document, like the charters of Acla, the original Panamá and Nombre de Dios, drawn up under Pedrarias Dávila's orders. This means we can assume that this particular document gives reliable witness to the procedure followed in the founding of these other cities as well. In it, the grid design is expressly detailed. We are told that the assignment of space for lots, plaza, street-grid, etc., was carried out *'por la orden y manera que por la traza que yo hice de la dicha ciudad y pueblo parecen señalados y trazados'* ['in the manner which my plan of the city indicates'] and then, in order that there is no doubt as to the layout, concludes that 'said design of said town is as follows... ,' by which we are clearly told that the map or layout of the town was attached to the charter as an appendix.[14] Domínguez Compañy has concluded, after a study of twenty such charters, that reference to a chessboard layout *per se* is rare, though the image is present indirectly in the documents.[35] There are cases, such as that of the city of Mendoza in Argentina, whose charter is accompanied by a plat map, and Natá is one of those exceptional cases, though unfortunately the layout has been lost.

The grid design of Veracruz was, as noted earlier, another design of Pedrarias Dávila's and Cortés' architect Alonso García Bravo. The exact layout of the original Veracruz by García Bravo is not known, but the Aztec capital was already basically grid-like in layout, though the streets to the east and north of its central plaza did not fully conform to that geometry, and Cortés did not want to alter its plan too much, in order to preserve the palaces of Montezuma. However, as Manuel Toussaint says, Antequera is a perfect example of the layout of streets in a chessboard plan, with the cathedral and principal edifices of government centred on the main plaza.[36] By about 1520 the quadrangular plan had begun to be applied throughout New Spain.

The grid design is, then, part of a generalized 'manual' which, though not set forth in strict rules and regulations, was surely in the mind of the founder, at least in general outline. The Instructions to Pedrarias Dávila were repeated in the orders given to the Hieronymites for regulating the indigenous settlements of Hispaniola. They are repeated again in 1521 with Francisco de Garay's *capitulaciones*, or pacts, for the conquest and colonization of the province of Amichel in Mexico. And finally, there is a virtually verbatim repetition of the 1523 Instructions in the documents sent to Hernán Cortés in his new post of Governor of New Spain (Cortés having been, until 1511, a scribe in Hispaniola, where he must have become familiar with the regularity of the city plan, as Palm has pointed out).[37] The repetition of the clauses of the Instructions to Pedrarias Dávila show, then, that this was a pattern linked to widely-shared mental constructs.

But it was not until the issuance of the *Ordenanzas de Descubrimiento, Nueva Población y Ocupación de las Indias* ['Ordinances for the Discovery, New Settlement, and Occupation of the Indies'], which were signed by Philip II of Spain in 1573, that the first rigorous instructions for the 'chalkline', rectangular layout of cities were definitively set forth, i.e. the characteristics and arrangement of the streets, plazas and buildings and the selection of cities according to the functions they were expected to carry out, etc. This body of regulations was to prevail for the rest of the colonial period; it is reproduced almost word for word in the 1683 *Recopilación de Leyes de Indias*, or Code of the Indies. Into these regulations is gathered all prior experience of city-building, from the vague instructions to Ovando to the more detailed ones to Pedrarias Dávila, and including practical lessons learned from the more than two hundred cities founded up to that point. In fact, the 1573 *Ordenanzas* only ratify and assign specific regulations to the guidelines for colonization and city-building which the founders had been following since the very beginnings of the conquest, and for which the examples of Hispaniola and the Instructions to Pedrarias Dávila were the great models. By 1573, in fact, the major cities and virtually all the capitals of the current nations of Latin America had already been founded; so had virtually all those of the Hispanic Caribbean, most of the vice-regal and provincial capitals of New Spain and Peru, and many of the cities which acted as district and provincial government seats from Santa Fe, New Mexico to Buenos Aires, Argentina. Thus, the great experiment of city-building in the Americas had been carried out without a rigorous body of rules and regulations, as this explicitated 'building code' did not appear until virtually all the most important work had been accomplished.

By the time of the *Ordenanzas*, the sense of hierarchization in the use of urban spaces had been clearly defined. The two hundred or more experiments in founding cities had been assimilated and brought to the new legislation, and these new laws were to be applied with the greatest rigour possible to future city-building projects. Many cities had been abandoned and others moved two, three, or more times, and changing circumstances had modified the function of many of them, especially in the Caribbean, when the campaigns against Mexico and Peru between 1520 and 1530 displaced the conquest's centre of gravity toward the continent. The 1573 *Ordenanzas*, and a century later the Code of the Indies, present us with a finished city-planning 'manual' in which, at least in theory, very little is left to the whim of the founder or to circumstantial factors.

This may be seen in the cities founded after 1573. The new cities are oriented to the cardinal points of the compass, as in the Roman city-camps, and the axial design unrolls from the central Plaza Mayor, symmetrically organizing the orthogonal plan and the distribution of lots and buildings: the church or cathedral, the *cabildo* (or building of the City Council), the houses of the powerful, the Casas Reales,[38] the convents and monasteries of the religious orders that might be attached to the town, other smaller plazas, and as one approached the periphery, the houses of the humbler classes. When the new city had military functions and was founded with a defensive wall about it, the gates in the walls would open onto the main streets to form symmetrically laid out axes, and this layout further accentuated the rectilinearity of the city's plan. A magnificent example of this design is the new Panamá, founded in 1673 as a walled military city; its rigorous symmetry, its central Plaza Mayor, its absolutely rigid orthogonality, and the axial layout of its streets and gates made it a 'classic' model of a New World city. But one must remember that Panamá was denominated *primada*, or 'major'; it was the capital of the district, with its own *Audiencia* (the territorial court or tribunal), and the seat of the bishopric.[39]

Other cities founded *ex novo* after 1573, however, such as Portobelo and St Augustine, sometimes yielded to the exigencies of topography. This was in spite of their role as defensive settlements, and in spite of the fact that their construction was in the hands of military engineers who were familiar with the rules and regulations for laying out cities and who in their professional capacities should, more than anyone else, have respected the *Ordenanzas*. These two cities lack that regular, strictly-ordered grid design that was called for in the 'rulebooks', and their city blocks are irregular in both shape and dimension. Instead of a square grid, we find that the city blocks are elongated, that the cities have two or three longitudinal streets and two or three cross-streets. Their plazas are not central, as the norm calls for. In both cases, too, the small size of the city and the nature of its site – St Augustine on a small, narrow peninsula bordered by three rivers running into the ocean and Portobelo virtually pushed into the sea by the mountain at its back – forced its builder to depart from the rules and to lay out the city longwise, fitting it as best might be to the available site. In Portobelo the parish church was not on the main plaza. That place of honour was taken by the famed customs house, where money was taken in during the city's renowned fairs, and by the building known as the *Casa de la Negrería*, or slave house, where the offices of the slave trade were located and where slaves arriving by shiploads from Africa were kept until they could be sold off and distributed through the Central American isthmus and the colonies of the Pacific. This siting apparently symbolized the importance of these institutions to the city, whose *raison d'être* was trade, and their importance to the empire generally.[40]

In St Augustine the church did not face the central plaza, but had its back to it, in order to avoid the noise produced by the soldiers of the garrison.[41] This is probably the reason for the location of the church in Portobelo, as well, which is far from the customs house and the slave house and generally removed from the area of greatest animation during the famed trade fairs of that city.

Much the same thing occurred in Cartagena, although that city was founded long before the time of the *Ordenanzas*. But when, between 1577 and 1579, the original cathedral (of wood and rattan) was replaced by one of stone, the church was built not on the Plaza Mayor but 'alongside the buildings of the *cabildo*, with one of its sides opening onto a small plaza immediately beside the other [plaza]', as Marco Dorta relates.[42]

But the founding of cities involved many other problems besides their layout and the distribution of their spaces for hierarchized uses. One city might look quite different from another depending on its role (whether it was a military, trade, administrative, mission, communications-link, inland or coastal, mountain or plain, cold-clime or tropical, rainy or dry, cattle-raising, mining, or framing town, etc., or a combination of these), and depending also on the predominant construction materials – palm thatch, wood, cement, stone, coral, etc. In Portobelo, St Augustine, Havana, Cartagena and San Juan the presence of great fortresses of stone, in some cases true leviathans of military architecture such as the Morro fortresses of San Juan and Havana or the fortress San Felipe de Barajas in Cartagena, and their imposing walled perimeters, are the dominant note. In other cities it is the convents and monasteries that dominate the urban landscape, for within populated nuclei no larger than 150 acres (sixty hectares, or less than one-quarter of a square mile) one might find eight or ten religious buildings, from modest hermitages and cathedrals to large monastic complexes. Panamá Viejo is a good example of these 'monastery cities'. But when this city was abandoned and moved to its new and final location, it was the military note that predominated, and in the documents which have been preserved that relate to the site-plans and plans for the move, it is clear that the concern for perimeter walls and the nature and distribution of bulwarks and other defensive constructions take precedence over all other aspects of the city.[43]

The city's social hierarchization

Legislation for the city clearly reflected the values of a rigidly hierarchized society. There was to exist in principle a close relationship between the spatial distribution of buildings and the residence patterns of the settlement's citizens. The centre of the city – its main plaza, called the *Plaza Mayor* or *Plaza de Armas* – was the nucleus of privilege *par excellence*, and from it there radiated outward the further hierarchical levels of buildings and residents. On the central plaza one would find the residences of the city's most important citizens, at a little further distance out, the residences of those of an intermediate class, and on the periphery, the masses – poor Spaniards, mulattos and mestizos, and, in some cities, *barrios* solely for Indians. One of the essential actions taken in the founding of cities was this socially-hierarchized spatial distribution. Often, in this regard, authorities cite the 1513 Royal Instruction to Pedrarias; paragraph seven of that document reads as follows:

> ...*habéis de repartir los solares del lugar para facer las casas, y estos han de ser repartidos segund la calidad de las personas, e sean de comienzo dados por orden; por manera que hechos los solares, el pueblo parezca ordenado... asimismo se han de repartir los heredamientos segund la calidad e manera de las personas, e segun lo que sirvieren así les creced en heredad y el repartimiento ha de ser de manera que a todos quepa parte de lo bueno e de lo mediano, e de lo menos bueno, segund la parte que a cada uno se le hobiere de dar en su calidad; e porque los primeros que allá pasaron con Hojeda e Nicuesa e Enciso han pasado mucho trabajo e fambre e necesidad, a Hojeda e a ellos se les ha de face mejoría en repartimiento, a el como a Capitán, e a ellos como a vecinos en el lugar que esta fecho.*

> [...thou shalt apportion the lots of the place in order to build houses on, and they shall be apportioned in accordance with the quality of the person, and they shall from the beginning be given out in order; so that when the lots shall have been divided, the town shall appear orderly ... likewise shall the farms be given out in accordance with the quality of the person, and in accordance with their service let their farm be larger, and the apportionment shall be done so that every person receives a share of the good land and the middling land and of the less good land, in accordance with the part that to each person shall be given in his quality; and because the first men that went to that place with Hojeda and Nicuesa and Enciso suffered much work and hunger and need, the apportionment to Hojeda and the rest shall be improved, to

him as Captain, and to the others as to residents in the place that is meet.][44]

The principle of class, while at the same time the intention to reward the first settlers, is very clear. For Pedrarias this latter intention meant favouring Balboa's companions over his own. In the founding of Panamá (which occurred within a few months of the order for Balboa's decapitation), it was highly unlikely that the city would be laid out in accordance with the royal orders. Pedrarias did, as Oviedo tells us, exactly what he pleased.[45]

In the 1573 *Ordenanzas de Descubrimiento*, these hierarchizing principles were expanded and made more precise; rules were given for the proportion to be observed between the size of the lot and the importance of the individual, and specifying that the same criterion should be used for the apportionment of arable land and pasture. But as I have pointed out, these dispositions came at a bad time, when most of the city-building in the Americas had already been accomplished, and so they were probably applied only in a very limited way. (Here, as in other instances, the case of new Panamá was an exception.) Based, as I have mentioned, on the century's accumulated experience, the orders or 'instructions' were more than anything an attempt to 'fill certain institutional voids and to contribute to the Spanish experience certain techniques of settlement of a decidedly feudal origin.[46] However the case may be, there is no doubt that at this time not only was the parcelling out of lots 'performed in all important cases, but also speculation had stepped in to correct, increase, and reorder the intentions of the *conquistador* society.[47]

Although the 1681 *Recopilación de Leyes* repeats almost verbatim the 1573 *Ordenanzas*, the later codification is more a formalist idealization of what a New World city should be (according to urban schemata based above all on the needs of the empire) than an effective instrument to be imposed upon reality. Each city, depending upon its ecological and economic conditions and the dynamics of the social forces working within it, produced results that often eluded control by the norms for founding cities. Evidence of this can be seen, for example, in the desacralization of the plazas, which while reserved by law for certain privileged uses were in practice converted into noisy, smelly market places. Another indication is the process by which urban centres fell to the level of shantytowns, with their proliferation of stores and craftsmen's workshops. In Panamá, Cartagena and Havana, the architecture of important buildings (those, for instance, near the main plaza) tended to include a mezzanine-storey, and this space was often rented out to tailors, blacksmiths, carpenters and barbers. Finally, there is the absenteeism of the élite class, which became ever more likely to spend most of their time on their out of town properties. This tendency reordered the relative value of 'hinterland' *vis-à-vis* that of the urban centre. Of course, these were general tendencies.[48] What is needed is a study of how and when these processes occurred in the various New World cities.

Again, the city of Panamá is an interesting example. In the original, older city, many buildings had the mezzanine-storeys described above. Important citizens occupied the principal houses near the plaza and rented out the building's mezzanine to an artisan who might live there with his family. The lower storey might also be rented out for a shop or a grocery store where a bustling (and none too select) clientele would congregate. This image of overcrowding is typical of the mid-seventeenth-century city.

There is very little known, through lack of documents, about the spatial distribution of the various social groups in Panamá. We do know that the underclasses, especially of blacks and mulattos, lived on the periphery of cities, in slums. These were the areas least affected by the fire caused by Morgan's attack in 1671, and during the next three years, until the city was moved to its new site, it was in the huts of these slums where most of the city's residents found shelter. Significantly, the construction of the new city gave the élite class the opportunity to recover the city's symbols of social stratification and to utilize the urban space as an expression of power. Two facts help to prove this: the façade of the new houses and the exclusion of the non-élite population from the new city centre.

With respect to housing, the new city inherited from the old its verticality, its mezzanines, and, probably, its running balconies. But there the resemblances end; the innovations are actually more significant. The lots of the old city were considerably more generously proportioned than in the new city, though the frontages were narrow. The average frontage for all houses standing at the beginning of the seventeenth century was 1.9 *lumbres*, less than eight metres or about 26 feet; the average frontage for the principal residences was approximately 12 metres or about 40 feet, very seldom 15 or 16 metres, 50 feet or so. The contrast with new Panamá is striking. There, the frontages of the principal residences often reached 30 metres (100 feet) or more. Was this the result of a new conception of urban space? Had experience shown some need to broaden the housefront? If so, what experience had it been? Or was it perhaps a symbol of power, showing to the populace as a whole what sort of man owned this building, and offering some idea of the kind of luxury that might be found inside? This intention could be more easily realized, perhaps, by broadening the façade of the house than in any other way. But in order for this to occur, there had to be, first, an élite interested in flaunting its wealth or its power, and, second, enough space in the city for this new model of construction. These two requirements were met in the new Panamá.

In the old Panamá it had probably not been until late in the sixteenth century, after several generations of settlers, that a ruling élite had actually begun to define itself, and by that time many of the early lots had been subdivided, making it virtually impossible to aspire to a house with a broad façade. Moreover, there is evidence that the concept of space for housefronts was conditioned not solely by rational and objective factors such as the lots' frontage dimensions, but was also a mental construct based on Peninsular precedent. A plan, in the abstract, designed for the city of Portobelo in 1600 may illustrate what I mean. Though the plan was drawn first on paper, so that frontages might be as large as anyone desired, none the less all the lots have frontages of less than three *lumbres* (12.3 metres, or approximately 40 feet). When the *oidor* Losada Quiñones built the edifice known as El Taller in the new Panamá (the building on whose lot the Presidential Palace now stands), his neighbours protested its exaggerated size: its façade measured six *lumbres* (some 25 metres, or more than 80 feet). The traditional, archaic (perhaps even medieval) model had doubtlessly created visual habits that it was hard to free oneself from. If the residents of a city clung to this older model it was because it was part of their idea of what a city was and should look like, and because it represented deep-seated sociocultural values held by them. In order for this new modality to be accepted, not only did people have to change the way they viewed the urban space; the very structure of the city had to be subjected to profound change, as well.

This opportunity was offered in Panamá when it was founded for a second time. Losada Quiñones' precedent, in spite of some initial resistance, was soon followed. Thus, the new shape acquired by dwelling places (whose wide façades not only made them more comfortable and elegant, but also allowed the rich and/or powerful to use this front elevation, as never before, as a means of expressing their social standing) brought to the local urban culture an architectural modality previously unknown, one which was to make the city something very different from what it had been before. There is no doubt that this was a novel change, even perhaps revolutionary. The width of the house front became emblematic; it acquired ideological significance. The houses of the rich and powerful were no longer simply residences, they were now a visible manifestation of their owners' power and fortune.

In addition, the new city, which unlike the old was verging on an extreme of exclusivism, began to take on the character of an unquestionably élitist space. In the urban materialization of the new Panamá there are two fundamental things that immediately strike one: first, the city's segregative and excluding nature, for the city threw up a wall against the outside,[49] and second, the number of lots sought within the protection of the walls. These aspects are, of course, closely linked. They strongly suggest that the walled city was conceived to shelter only the white minority, and that indigents and the coloured masses were banished to the slums. It hardly seems coincidental that the number of lots within the walls should total approximately three hundred – that is, just enough to accommodate the population of white residents. Can there be any doubt that it is for those white citizens belonging to the local élite that the *numerus clausus* of the lots is destined? In that measured, orderly, rigidly structured city, number is also a political referent, apportionment an act of dominance. Given that throughout the seventeenth century the population of colour had always been a certain threat, feared because of its growing number (as evidenced in many, varied documentary sources), a wall would be not simply a defensive bulwark against some outside enemy, it might also be a barrier against internal danger, and thereby acquire deep social significance. It was, in all its consequences, a premeditated action of which the central power was surely aware.

Nothing better suited the empire's traditional urban policy than an élitist city such as new Panamá. Even setting aside considerations of hierarchical ordering of the urban spaces, and the emblematic and political nature of the city, for the Crown it was essential to have a complicity and alliance among the colony's privileged classes. Consubstantial with the absolutist policy then in vogue was the notion that an oligarchy dependent upon royal favour should be strengthened and encouraged to grow. Thus the state protected those privileged minorities by creating a wide range of institutional procedures and mechanisms. In this way, in intimate collaboration with the local élites, the number of lots within the walls was limited from the outset and the wall which separated the slum from the city *per se* was erected. Nor was the rigorous limit set randomly. From the outset, it was clear that the needier classes would be excluded from the city. The lots were expensive, and quickly became more so; add to this high city taxes which were only applied within the walls, and a doubly impenetrable barrier is thrown up to the poor. Negroes and mulattos were banished without compunction to the unprotected areas on the other side of the wall, whose gate was closed at nightfall. Thus the wall came to signify a socially dividing, excluding barrier marking the boundary between the privileged and not-privileged. This technique was undoubtedly a type of urban prophylaxis, inspired by prudence and as such, astutely preconceived. In yet another way the city served as an instrument of social and economic domination, exogenously imposed through the complicity and participation of local élites.

So the new Panamá was born out of an attempt to give concrete shape to a rigid social segregation. The city enclave became a socially privileged space, an exclusive place into which only the elect 'fit', quite literally. The new city was a political triumph for the ruling class, an unprecedented action by which this class was able comfortably, smugly and confidently to employ architectural codes that allowed them to be recognized for what they conceived themselves to be, and this was in turn possible because of the harmonious collaboration between imperial power and its local counterparts and representatives. That was why the political 'meaning' of the urban model that was employed in the Americas served both to consolidate the institutions of imperial power (by externalizing that power's intention to extend itself through perpetuity) and to confirm the stability of the élites and their pre-eminence over the rest of society. Élites could not have been unaware of the architectural (and other, more broadly urban) codes by which the Crown attempted to manifest the essence of its political aims. On the contrary, these élites were the Crown's best agents, because it was through these symbolic manifestations that the élites found their identity and the justification for their privileges.

It is not surprising, therefore, that it is within the walled enclave of the city, reserved by the élites for themselves, that the greatest concentration of symbolic components may be found and the architectural and urban-space rules achieve their greatest semantic value, their greatest connotative charge. In the slums those codes are diluted, faded, and barely perceptible. There is a lack of geometrical rigour in the layout of the space outside the walls, an absence of centrality around which the rest of the space is organized (though this is not suspected, perhaps, until much later, with the Santa Ana church and its adjoining plaza, though even there the plaza did not conform very faithfully to the prescribed canons). The lack of rigour in the outlying space can be seen also in the absence of buildings with hierarchized functional attributes. This is in clear contrast with the élitist city where such buildings did exist, as the churches, convents and other civil and military structures of any walled city amply attest. The slum was, then, a defective copy of the model of the city found within the walls. This latter space was the hierarchized urban space *par excellence*, because it was there that the founders and residents faithfully transcribed the system of signs programmatically imposed by the empire and enthusiastically adopted by the local élites.[50]

Construction materials

Construction materials varied widely from one area or location to another. In some places, such as Portobelo, San Juan, Havana, Trinidad and Panamá, wood was excellent and abundant, and was used for door and window frames, beams, balconies and their railings, balusters, doors, windows, stairs, the capitals of support posts, the uprights themselves, carved ceilings and parquet floors, and braces. From Cuba 'excellent mahoganies, ebonies, and *lignum vitae* and ironwood trees'[51] were sent to the Escorial to be processed. And throughout the colonial period, cedar, *lignum vitae*, mahogany, mangrove, *níspero* (sapodilla), and *cocobolo* (sometimes known as granadilla wood, *Dalbergia retusa*) was sent to Lima, a city almost totally without forest resources. The sawmills soon were solely in the hands of a few wealthy men, and the lumber business, not only for shipbuilding but also for construction, prospered in places such as Havana and Panamá. In Panamá, by 1607, there were seven sawmills and several shipbuilders, and in a city as small and recently founded as Portobelo frigates and even larger boats were being built by 1606.[52]

These factors made wooden construction predominant in the areas noted, though other reasons also came into play. Until the end of the sixteenth century and beginning of the seventeenth, many of the cities of the Caribbean were almost entirely of wood: their churches, Casas Reales, *cabildos*, and the houses of the powerful were all built of wood. It undoubtedly would have been more economical to build in wood than in stone or cement, since apparently it was easier to find carpenters than masons and other craftsmen necessary for stone and cement construction, and therefore carpenters' salaries were lower. In Panamá, for example, a fairly complete census of the urban population in 1607 indicates that in the list of manual crafts, including 144 professionals, there were thirty-two carpenters, two blacksmiths, two chairmakers, and eleven caulkers, but not a single mason or stonecutter. Wood craftsmen alone totalled forty-five, which represented 31 per cent of the total manual professionals.[53]

Another factor was the cost of tools. Tools lasted much longer in carpentry than in stonecutting or masonry, and since the iron needed for the manufacture of tools and implements was not yet mined and processed in the Americas, but had to be imported from Europe, any work which consumed tools rapidly was more expensive. In Cuba, and especially in Havana, carpenters achieved extraordinary mastery of their craft, and turned out beautiful, finely-detailed work – lattices, grillwork, capitals and brackets, ceilings, etc. – in the *mudéjar* or arabesque (or 'Moorish') style that might still be found in Spain after the Moors. They had at their disposal not only 'the finest woods in the world' but also experience gained in their work as shipbuilders, 'whose techniques [are] very much like those of fine woodworkers.'[54] Some of the work of these superbly talented woodworkers is among the 'highest examples of wooden ceilings ever built', in the words of Joaquín E. Weiss.[55] In more provincial Trinidad, surrounded by rich forests, the woods of the bully or bulletwood tree, mahogany, and oxhorn bucida (hard, resistant, beautiful woods) were widely used in construction. One can still see, and admire, colonial houses in Trinidad, famed for the beauty of their woodwork. Some incredibly hard woods were even used for hinges and for what, in stone, would be foundation stones used to prevent wood pillars from rotting if sunk into the ground; some of these wooden marvels still exist. It is perhaps due to the abundance of noble woods in Trinidad that stone and masonry construction did not become widespread there until the end of the eighteenth century.[56]

In Nombre de Dios, Panamá and Portobelo, too, wood construction predominated until far into the seventeenth century. The accountant Peinado de Aguirre informed the Crown in 1537 that in Panamá there was an almost total lack of lime (chalk) for cement, that there were no stonecutters, and that if there had been, they would be so expensive that they would charge 'two *castellanos* [a gold coin] and meals per day'. According to Peinado there was need for a fortress in Nombre de Dios, but though there was good quality stone and one could obtain lime, there were no stonecutters or masons there, either.[57] When this city was destroyed by Sir Francis Drake in 1596, the survey of damages showed that only one of the city's 50 houses was of brick, the others being of wood or simple *bohíos* (rustic huts) of clay and wattles.

In the 1570s and 1580s several accounts state that in Panamá, then a town of some 250 to 300 inhabitants and some 300 dwellings, 'all the houses are of boards and wood' or 'of wooden boards roofed with tile', not to mention being 'small and mean', even that of the bishop, which was falling down, and the Casa Real and *cabildo*, likewise in very bad condition. A royal decree forbade both the construction of new wooden or shingle houses and the repair of those that existed, 'unless they be made of stone and *tapiería*,' but the owners of sawmills appealed and things went on as before.[58] In 1586 Juan Bautista Antonelli mentions the existence of 350 houses, 'all built of wood', including the Casa Real. This picture had hardly changed by the beginning of the seventeenth century when there were 332 houses with 'garrets' or 'attics' [i.e., of more than one storey'], all roofed with tile, most with mezzanines, plus 40 small houses and 112 thatch or wattle *bohíos*. 'The houses', Antonelli adds, 'are all of wood, save eight, which are of stone: the Audiencia Real building, the *cabildo* of the city, and six private homes', plus three more 'that were of stone up to the garret', that is, up to the second storey. Even the cathedral was of wood.[59] This slow drift towards more durable construction increased. Although wooden construction continued to predominate, by 1640 there were beginning to be more and more buildings 'of stone and masonry', according to Juan de Requejo Salcedo, schoolmaster, in his '*Relación sobre Panama*'. By this year the city had some 700 houses, of which about 'twenty were of stone, cement and brick.'[60] In one generation, barely twelve new masonry houses had been built.

This phenomenon was repeated in Portobelo. In 1600, three years after the city's founding, there were only '40 houses of inhabitants, 30 built well of wood, boards, and roof tiles of varying quality, such as the church-hospital, the House of Commerce, *cabildo*, and the other eight or ten houses are of easy and inferior construction, and all, I estimate, will occupy less than 160 *lumbres* [65.6 metres, or 214.4 feet] of 15 feet and rear of 8 feet,[61] and I would estimate clay-and-wattle huts outside the main body of the city to be almost the same number again.'[62] In 1606 we are given a detailed description of the city:

> *Dentro de la traza de la ciudad hay 50 casas sin los edificios públicos, que son la iglesia mayor, el convento de la Merced, el Hospital Real, las Casas Reales y el Cabildo. Estos y todo el edificio de las casas de la ciudad, son de maderos gruesos estantes sobre fundamentos de piedra, las paredes principales y las medias de tablas, los techos cubiertos con tejas. Todas las casas son altas con bodegas en lo bajo, entresuelos y mucho ventanaje, por el calor grande de la tierra. Algunas casas se han comenzado a labrar de piedra y ladrillo, y se halla de mejor vivienda. De esta suerte hay cinco hasta ahora, las dos del todo de piedra y ladrillo hasta el techo, y las tres hasta el primer suelo.*

[Within the plan of the city there are 50 houses, without the public buildings, which are the main church, the convent of la Merced, the Royal Hospital, the Casas Reales, and the *cabildo*. These and all the construction of the houses of the city are of thick timber posts on stone foundations, the main walls and those inside of boards, the roofs covered with tiles. All the houses are tall, with store rooms below, mezzanines, and many windows, on account of the great heat of the country. Some houses have begun to be made of stone and brick, and are found to be better dwellings. Of this sort, there are five up until now, two entirely of stone and brick up to the roof, and the other three up to the second floor.][63]

But decades later, following the same pattern as in Panamá, the main buildings had begun to be built of masonry, as was the case of the Hospital de San Juan de Dios, completed about 1623, the parish church begun in 1624, and the customs house begun in 1630.[64]

In Portobelo the fortifications were at first excessively burdensome and time-consuming to build. The engineer in charge, Juan Bautista Antonelli, tried to use basalt rock, which turned out to be too hard to work; it took the workers a great deal of time to cut it, apart from the stone ruining their tools. After much government pressure, Antonelli was obliged to seek alternative materials, and the solution was a kind of coral 'stone' he found on nearby beaches. This rock turned out to be ideal for the buttresses and for the masonry in general.[65] From that time on, coral predominated in all important construction projects in Portobelo. It is found in the customs house, in all the fortifications, in the churches, and in the most important houses. And Antonelli later transferred this experience to the other Caribbean settlements to which he was sent to raise defensive walls or build fortifications, and where he found this material in abundance: Cartagena, Havana, San Juan, Santo Domingo, and so on.

A further difficulty lay in finding good materials close by for roof tiles, bricks and lime; the further materials had to be transported, obviously, the more expensive construction would be. For the projects in Portobelo, lime, bricks and tiles were carried by sea from Cartagena, and always at a high price. In St Augustine, lime was made from oyster shells, and was used from a very early date in the construction of the characteristic flat roofs [*azoteas*] of the houses. This type of lime was also employed for the whitewash used on the plaster walls. Oyster shells would later be common in construction of all kinds in Florida. At first, virtually no other material was used – the exception being clay-and-wattle construction – until Pedro Menéndez Marquez discovered good-quality stone in 1580; still, this 'cockleshell rock' was found only within a limited area and transporting it was very costly relative to the funds available to the colony. But the first building of lime and cement was not constructed in St Augustine until the early seventeenth century. This building is considered the 'first residence for Europeans which used stone in what is today the United States.'[66]

In Portobelo the customs house, or counting house, though such an important edifice, was at first and continued for decades to be of wood, and it was not until the 1630s that the beautiful piece of architecture designed by the *alarife* Cristóbal de Armiñán was built. In spite of the extensive alterations which it later underwent (especially the redesigns and repairs carried out in 1764 by the engineer Manuel Hernández), this is basically the same building that still stands in Portobelo today.[67]

In Cartagena, too, there was great difficulty at first in finding durable materials for construction. The first settlers complained in 1538 that the island on which the city was located 'is all swamps and wastes of sand, and in the entire city and harbour there is not one house of stone and what the inhabitants live in are houses of thatch and canestalks and wood and palm fronds, which are like huts in Castile.'[68] A series of fires soon showed the need to upgrade the building materials, but in 1569 most of the houses were still of wood, and it was not until the last third of the sixteenth century that construction of stone houses accelerated.[69] By 1582 one resident declared that most of the houses were 'of stone, with roof tiles and *azoteas* [flat roofs].'[70] A more reliable witness confirms this detail four years later, by stating that 'the houses of the city are all, almost, of stone.'[71]

This is the same general picture we find in Santiago de Cuba. In 1538 the Fidalgo de Elvas, a Portuguese nobleman accompanying Hernando de Soto on his Florida campaign, wrote:

La ciudad de Santiago tendrá 80 casas, grades y bien repartidas; las más tienen las paredes de tablas y están cubiertas de heno; algunas hay de piedra y cal, cubiertas de teja; tienen grandes corrales, y en ellos mucho árboles, diferentes de los de España.

[The city of Santiago has, I estimate, some 80 houses, large and well distributed; most have walls of boards and are roofed with hay [i.e., thatch]; some are of stone and cement, roofed with tiles; they have large enclosures, and in them many trees, different from those of Spain.][72]

The lack of certain construction materials, and the scarcity and sometimes total lack of good workmen, especially in smaller cities, made importing certain goods essential. Among the most important of these was iron, which was obviously used for latches, nails, bolts and pins, locks, etc., and which came in 'sheets' or grids' and would have to be worked by local smiths, who were very well-paid and much sought after during this period. The lack of skilled stonecutters often forced the colonies to import certain pieces of carved or worked stone, such as brackets and supports, coats of arms, capitals, friezes, the piers of arches, doorways, doorjambs, etc. One example of this is the architectural fragments found in New Seville, Jamaica, testifying to the early (c. 1530) introduction of the *plateresco*, or Spanish baroque style into the Caribbean. Another is the coat of arms found in the Fuerza castle in Havana, which was carved in Seville about 1579. There are many other specimens of carved stone in churches and convents, and even the private homes of the wealthy, which may still be seen in Havana.[73]

We find, then, a pattern throughout the Caribbean. Until perhaps the middle of the sixteenth century, relatively fragile edifices of somewhat precarious durability, and built of relatively humble materials, predominated. These were hut-like constructions of clay-and-wattles, thatch, or similar materials. They were succeeded by wood construction, and in some places, by the 1670s or 1680s, by masonry. This is the case, for example, in Cartagena and Havana, where masonry was used extensively, though it is not the case in all cities, as we have seen in Panamá and Portobelo. The exception to all this, of course, is the stonework and masonry of military fortifications and defensive walls surrounding some cities. Most of these fortresses and walls, in Portobelo and Chagres, Cartagena, Havana, San Juan, Santo Domingo and St Augustine, were constructed between 1680 and 1700 under the direction of Juan Bautista Antonelli.

The only city which departs from this regional model is Santo Domingo, to which, beginning with Columbus' second voyage, a number of *alarifes*, master builders, and stonecutters arrived. These men were to give Santo Domingo a very different look from that of the other cities of the Caribbean. Several foremen and master builders arrived later with Ovando, and they played a role in the construction of the Homenaje tower and the stone residences on Las Damas street. Another shipment of master stone-cutters and *alarifes* arrived in 1510. Juan de Herrera of Seville and Orlando de Bretendón of Bilbao were the two leaders of the crew, which consisted of eleven further artisans and craftsmen. Between 1512 and 1516 the first true architects (as opposed to the *alarifes* mentioned above) arrived, Rodrigo de Liendo and Luis de Moya, this latter man to oversee the work on the cathedral. And other artisans and craftsmen would continue to arrive in later months and years.[74] Nothing comparable occurred in the other major cities of the Caribbean of that time. As a result, by the first decade of the sixteenth century there began to be many buildings of stone and mortar in Santo Domingo, as ordered by the Crown in 1506. The presence of Bishop Alejandro Geraldini, a man imbued with the spirit of the Renaissance, was a determining factor in this process, although by the time he arrived the city's physiognomy had already begun to reflect the impression made on it by the artisans. In his *Itinerario*, which he wrote in Latin, Geraldini described the capital of the New World in these enthusiastic words: 'I marvelled to see such an eminent city, founded but the brief span of twenty-five years, for its buildings are as tall and lovely as those of Italy.' And the chronicler Fernández de Oviedo himself, passing through the city in 1524, wrote in his *Historia General* that 'of Santo Domingo I say that with regards its buildings, no town of Spain, not even Barcelona, outshines it.'

Filled with Renaissance energy, Geraldini breathed new life into the construction of the city, and he encouraged such works as the first cathedral in the Americas, which was built by the Andalusian master builder Luis de Moya. This cathedral, of basically gothic design, perhaps influenced by the cathedral at Seville, replaced the former building, which had been of *bajareque*, a kind of cane-and-mud adobe, with a timber structure. The new design combined gothic arches and tracery with Isabelline decoration, the Moorish design of the presbytery, and the *plateresco* of the portal façade, as though it was trying to symbolize the adaptation to the New World of the sum of aesthetic values brought by Hispanic culture to the hemisphere, that is, the Americanization of Hispanic architecture.[75]

The cathedral was followed by the Santo Domingo church, which is another summation of gothic-like elements turned to baroque intentions; the convent of San Francisco, famed for the rope-like decoration which symbolizes the order's habit (a symbol repeated on the façade of the 'Casa del

Cordón' or 'House of Rope', whose name was taken from the motif); the hospital of San Nicolás de Bari, built between 1533 and 1552, 'whose cruciform design has linked Diego Angulo Iñiguez to the designs of the hospices of Ferdinand and Isabella'; and finally, the splendid castle of Diego Colón (1510–14), which was to be copied by Hernán Cortés for his palace in Cuernavaca, and which served as a model for the magnificent suite of sixteenth-century residences we can still admire in Santo Domingo today: the Casa de Osorio, the Palace of the Audiencia, the Casa de Francia, the Casa del Cordón, the residence of Francisco de Tostado, and others, all combining late gothic and early Plateresque design.[76]

Nevertheless, beginning in 1509 the centre of gravity began to shift away from Hispaniola towards other areas of the Caribbean, and by mid-century, regional hegemony had moved entirely to Cuba, or rather to Havana, which became the great port-city linking the most important routes connecting the continent with the Peninsula. Hispaniola was rapidly de-populated, and although Santo Domingo retained a degree of importance due to its status as the capital of the island, its significance as an urban centre entered a period of decline. In the last two decades of the sixteenth century the military outposts of the empire – especially Havana, San Juan and Cartagena – began in their turn to acquire greater and greater import-ance from the point of view of city-building, and with the influx of stone-cutters, masons, carpenters, lathe operators, and other artisans brought from Spain to carry out the numerous military construction projects these fortified settlements required, qualified craftsmen were suddenly available in these cities to a much greater degree than ever before. As a result, the urban and architectural landscape notably improved, and this period coincided with what might be called a boom in masonry construction, and a consequent total change in the cities' physiognomy.

The urban infrastructure

In the urban infrastructure of most of the cities, public works such as bridges, cisterns, aqueducts, roads for communication with the hinterland, piers, docks and other harbour constructions were necessary for the very survival of the settlements.

In general, Caribbean cities were very poorly provided with springs and clear rivers for their inhabitants' water supply. One of the exceptions was Portobelo, whose springs of 'delicate and crystalline' water, rising in the high mountains near the city, were soon channelled down to the town through stepped cisterns, such as the one which can still be seen beside the original fort of Santiago de la Gloria. Another fortunate city was San Juan, whose San

Antonio spring, located at one end of the little island-peninsula on which the city was founded, and beside the bridge of the same name, was a permanent object of concern on the part of the authorities. But unlike these, cities such as Santo Domingo, Santiago de Cuba, Panamá, Cartagena and St Augustine had to turn to costly and not always convenient solutions for their water supply.

Panamá and Cartagena were dotted with cisterns that collected rainwater; these helped to meet at least the most pressing need for water for domestic use. But the cisterns were only useful where (or when) it rained. In Santiago de Cuba the average rainfall is far below the rest of the island, since the city is on the south coast of Cuba, on the leeward side of the Sierra Maestra mountains, and the trade winds deposit their moisture in the mountains before they reach the city. Travelling from Baracoa to Santiago, says Levi Marrero, is like 'travelling from the jungle to tropical steppes.' To solve the problem of lack of water, several projects were proposed. One, in 1609, consisted of a *noria*,[77] or Persian wheel, near Santa Ana la Vieja, to take up water from a subterranean river. This project, however, though backed by the *cabildo*, turned out to be a swindle. In a second project, according to a 1745 source, water from a stream located two leagues from Santiago was brought to the city through a sort of aqueduct or canal consisting of 'very thick, strong walls made of cement and brick' and paid for by a bishop of the city. But this project failed to solve the problem of Santiago's perennial lack of water.[78]

In Cartagena several projects were proposed for bringing water to the city from Matute Creek, near Turbaco, but none materialized. Unlike other cities in the hemisphere, Cartagena never had a source of water within the city. The solution was cisterns, which by 1795 were estimated to number no fewer than 237. The area of the city known as San Diego changed its name to 'Jagüeyes' (*jagüey* being the Taíno word for 'cistern') to celebrate the abundance of gathering-pools within its area.[79] In several cities in Puerto Rico cisterns were so common that many *barrios*, or areas within a larger city limit, go by the name of '*Jagüeyes*'.

Another settlement without springs or other sources of water and, like Cartagena, riddled with cisterns, was Panamá. One can still see, in the ruins of Panamá Viejo, cisterns everywhere. The most remarkable, containing several vaulted chambers, was that of the convent of La Concepción. Toward the outskirts of the city, on the road to Portobelo, a great well, known as La Reyna, was dug. In the 1630s President Enrique Enríquez attempted several public works projects in order to improve conditions for the city, among them construction of a trench which would resolve the problem of the terrible scarcity of drinking water, but with his death the project was abandoned. So far as its known, nothing similar was ever done, or even attempted, afterwards. In Panamá Viejo the shortage of water became so acute that during the summer the wealthy would send their slaves to bring water from the distant Chagres River, some 30 kilometres (20 miles) from the city. But for the rest of the year, according to a 1610 source, drinking water was 'brought from a creek half a league away; a ewer of water [was] sold for half a *real*.'[80] In the new Panamá the situation was no better, and there was virtually no house without its own cistern. The only spring nearby, called El Chorrillo, 'The Barest Trickle', was several kilometres away in the foothills of Ancón Peak, where even early in this century laundresses would go to wash clothes and water sellers to collect water which they carried in large earthen jugs on horse- or muleback to sell in the city. Given this situation, and considering the risks of a siege without sufficient water for the defenders, a gigantic cistern was built on the bulwarks of the fort named Chiriquí (known today as Las Bóvedas, 'The Vaults'), and a hydraulic system, still there today, was rigged in a series of vaulted chambers. These precautions were also taken in Portobelo, where there are still cisterns of various sizes in the fortifications built during the eighteenth century.

In Havana the solution for supplying water was the Zanja Real (the 'Royal Ditch' or Canal), the most important hydraulic project realized in Cuba during the colonial period. As its name indicates, the Zanja Real consisted of a ditch or canal which transported water from a distant source (the Almendares River) to various points in the city. Begun in 1566 by a master builder named Calona, and completed in 1592 by Juan Bautista Antonelli, it was a source of water for irrigation and for human consumption for both the city and the ships anchored in Havana harbour, as well as serving as a power source. It ran through three Havana neighbourhoods, along the street named after it and De Dragones Street, and forked into two smaller channels, one passing alongside the plaza on which the cathedral stood, the other ending on the dock at the end of Luz Street. Later, smaller channels were dug to supply Havana's hospitals, convents, monasteries and public fountains, and little 'dribbles of water' were also granted to individuals for farms and industries. The Royal Canal was some eleven kilometres, or almost seven miles, long, had a trapezoidal section, and was walled with stone. It could carry 70 000 square metres of water per day, and it was the only aqueduct in Havana until the construction of a second one under Ferdinand VII in 1835.[81]

Lack of water, combined with the existence of a source of water on the other side of the Ozama River, was the motivation behind the move of Santo Domingo in 1568. This well, which took water from the wheel-driven *noria* of San Francisco, was under the direction of Rodrigo de Liendo, who built it in the 1540s. But the San Francisco system was insufficient for the needs of the city. Upstream, a 'masonry fountain' had also been built at some point (it existed in 1538), but it too was insufficient, and by the seventeenth century, due to the poor quality of the water it took up, it was apparently abandoned, and was not reopened until sometime in the early eighteenth century. Because of the chronic scarcity of water, from as early as 1531 there had been suggestions for projects that would bring water to the city from the Havana River, some 20 kilometres, almost 15 miles, distant, but by 1568 nothing had been done. Rodrigo de Liendo was also given the job of building a bridge, which would also serve as an aqueduct, to cross the Ozama, but nothing came of this project either.[82] In fact, during the colonial period not a single bridge was built over the Ozama.

One should stress that with the exception of Havana and its canal, lack of water was a general characteristic of Caribbean cities, and it was not until the early twentieth century that the first modern aqueducts began to be constructed. In old colonial cities whose better years are well behind them – such as Portobelo – no aqueducts have been constructed to this day. Though little research has been done on the subject of supplying water to Caribbean cities, what is known suggests that although there was no lack of proposed projects, such as the ones I have mentioned here, most never materialized, and the solutions actually put into practice were quite unsatisfactory.

Another important aspect of urban infrastructure was bridges. In any modest city, no matter how small, for example, Panamá, Portobelo, San Juan and Caracas, numerous stone bridges would be built. Some were most impressive, generally of one arch, though three-arch spans, such as that built in Caracas over the Anauco River, were not unheard-of. By the eighteenth century Caracas had no fewer than five bridges spanning the numerous creeks and rivers that surrounded the city.

In some Caribbean cities the history of bridges has been intimately linked to the history of the city from the very beginning. There are many documents on a number of these bridges, and this abundance indicates the importance the bridges had for the growth and development of the cities. The history of San Juan, for instance, is closely linked to the San Antonio (formerly Aguilar) and Martín Peña bridges, built in about 1519 when the capital was moved from Caparra to San Juan. At first, the importance of the bridges was tied simply to the need to link the small island-peninsula on which San Juan was situated to the rest of the island. But the Aguilar Bridge (whose name, María de los A. Castro says,[83] was given it in honour of its builder) soon took on military importance, since it was the logical access route for an attack from the south. A watch-tower was built and a strong guard posted on the San Juan side of the bridge, thus from about 1647 onwards the bridge became known as Soldiers' Bridge. But soon the Martín Peña Bridge also became militarily important, or potentially so. At first these were simple pontoon bridges, and on two illustrated maps drawn in 1575 (attributed to Juan Escalante de Mendoza) and 1579 (by Juan Ponce de León II) one can see that they are still wooden bridges, but it is believed that by

1598 the San Antonio bridge was of stone.[84] Throughout the colonial period both bridges underwent a number of extensive reconstructions. The 1784 design for the Martín Peña Bridge by Juan Francisco Mestre, a masterful engineering project of nine arches, is understandably famous. These two bridges were essential not only for supplying the capital and maintaining its links to the larger island but from the point of view of defence as well. They achieved glory in several famous episodes of Puerto Rican military history.[85]

In Portobelo nine small bridges were erected over the little rivers that criss-crossed the city, and some are still standing today.[86] In Panamá four were built, two small ones in the centre of the city, and two outside it: El Rey, of one large arch, and El Matadero, of one smaller arch. The El Rey bridge crossed the Gallinero River, linking the city with the road to Portobelo, and it was under intensive use during colonial times for transporting Peruvian silver and for giving access to the eastern cattle-raising plains. The Matadero bridge, over the Algarrobo River, linked the city with the road that led to the Chagres River (which also had a great deal of commercial traffic) and with the agricultural and cattle-raising area to the west. Their dates of construction are not known, but we do know that El Matadero was standing in the early seventeenth century. In 1626, in order to build El Rey, a 20 000 peso fund was established from taxes collected, and the bridge was standing by 1630. Its builder was Cristóbal de Armiñán, the *alarife* who built the customs house of Portobelo.[87] El Matadero took on military importance, too, when Antonelli pointed out that it was the logical access route for an attack on Panamá from the Chagres (it was, in fact, from that point that Morgan attacked in 1671). Beside El Matadero, therefore, on the city side, Fort Navidad was built, the only military construction of stone in the old Panamá, and whose function was similar to the guard house protecting the San Antonio bridge in San Juan.

From a very early date the strait of water that separated Cartagena from the island of Getsemaní, which was the first land area into which the city spilled over as it grew, was crossed by a bridge. This was one of the first public works carried out in Cartagena, and its construction was begun in 1539. The need for the bridge was summed up by someone who said that it was:

> *cosa muy necesaria para la contratación desta tierra, porque esta cibdad está aislada con el mar y unas caletas della que la cercan y con esta puente ay entrada y salida a esta ciudad y para la contratación de la tierra y para llevar y traer ganado al pasto della.*

> [very necessary for the trade of this land, for this city is isolated by the sea and the coves from the sea that surround it, and with this bridge

there is entrance into and exit from the city and for the trade of the land and in order to bring in cattle from and take cattle out to its pastures.][88]

This bridge was a 'firm' (*massissa*) piece of work, 'with two arches', and was considered to be 'as necessary as the bread that is eaten here.'[89]

NOTES

1 Here and throughout, with an accent over the á for the city of Panamá, as distinguished from the country which has no accent. [Trans. note.]
2 David H. Fischer, *Albion's Seed: Four British Folkways in America* (New York: Oxford University Press, 1989).
3 See notes 8 and 9 below for Morse and Guarda. Romero's work is *Latinoamérica: Las ciudades y las ideas* (Mexico City: Siglo XXI, 1976).
4 Cf. the several articles by these authors in *Boletín del Centro de Investigaciones Históricas y Estéticas* (Caracas: Universidad Central de Venezuela).
5 Francisco Domínguez Compañy, *Política de poblamiento de España en América: La fundación de ciudades* (Madrid: Instituto de Estudios de Administración Local, 1984).
6 Enrique Marco Dorta, *Cartagena de Indias, puerto y plaza fuerte* (Cartagena: A. Amado, 1960); Aníbal Sepúlveda Rivera, *San Juan: Historia ilustrada de su desarrollo urbano, 1508–1898* (San Juan: Centro de Investigaciones CARIMAR, 1989). These works have been my main sources for Cartagena and San Juan, respectively.
7 This debate may be followed in the *Boletín del Centro de Investigaciones Históricas y Estéticas* (Caracas: Universidad Central de Venezuela).
8 Gabriel Guarda, *Santo Tomás de Aquino y las fuentes del urbanismo indiano* (Santiago, Chile, 1965); 'Tres reflexiones en torno a la fundación de la ciudad indiana', in Francisco de Solano (ed.) *Estudios sobre la ciudad iberoamericana*, (Madrid: CSIC, 1983).
9 Richard Morse, 'The Urban Development of Colonial Spanish America', in Leslie Bethell (ed.) *The Cambridge History of Latin America, Vol. II (Colonial Latin America)*, (London: Cambridge University Press, 1987), pp. 67–104; 'Introducción a la historia urbana de hispanoamérica', in Francisco de Solano, *op. cit.*, *Las ciudades latinoamericanas* (Mexico City: Sep-Setentas, 1973), pp. 96, 97.
10 Morse, R., 'Urban Development', p.69.
11 Pierre Lavedan, *Les villes françaises* (Paris: Vincent Fréal, 1960).
12 Eladio Lapresa Molina, *Santafe: Historia de una ciudad del siglo XV* (Granada: University of Granada Press, 1979).
13 Erwin Walter Palm, *Los monumentos arquitectónicos de la Española*, 2 vols., Ciudad Trujillo, Santo Domingo, (Dominican Republic: Universidad de Santo Domingo, 1955).
14 The text of this document was published in its entirety by Antonio Muro Orejón in 'La Villa de Puerto Real, fundación de los reyes católicos, 1483,' *Anuario de Historia del Derecho Español*, Vol. XX (1959), pp. 746–57.
15 Juan López de Velazco, *Geografía y descripción universal de las Indias* (Madrid: Atlas [Biblioteca de Autores Españoles], 1971).

16   Spanish text in Pedro Torres de Mendoza (ed.) *Colección de documentos inéditos relativos al descubrimiento, conquista y organización de las antiguas posesiones españolas de América y Oceanía sacados de los Archivos el Reino y muy especialmente del de Indias* (Madrid: n.p., 1864–1884) Vol. 31, pp. 13–14. (Hereafter referred to as CODOIN.)

17   In the *encomienda* system the use of Indians as labourers was granted to the Spanish colonists by royal decree. The Crown decided how many Indians the founding settler or subsequent colonist would receive, and the colonist could use them in agriculture, mining, etc. as he saw fit. The Indians were not slaves to the colonist, yet so long as they continued to live on the land included in the *encomienda* they had to serve him. [Trans. note.]

18   The *conuco* was a plot of land which the Indian inhabitant cultivated for his own use. The Indian would supply his wants from this plot, which he would cultivate 'on his own time', and he might sell any surplus he produced. [Trans. note.]

19   I have dealt with this subject in the following articles: 'Los orígenes coloniales de la agricultura y la ganadería en Panamá, s. XVI', *La Prensa* (Panama City), 'Suplemento Cultural', 20 November, 1986; 'Niveles de vida y cambios de dieta a fines del período colonial en América', *Anuario de Estudios Americanos* (Seville) No. XLIV (1987); 'Subsistencias y economía en la sociedad colonial, el caso del istmo de Panamá, ss.XVI–XVII', *Revista de Historia* (Universidad Nacional de Costa Rica, School of History, 1989).

20   The Spanish text of the *Carta de Relación* is reproduced in its entirety in Levi Marrero, *Cuba: Economía y sociedad*, Vol. I. (San Juan, P.R.: Editorial San Juan, 1972), pp. 231–3.

21   For more information on the activities of Velázquez in Santo Domingo and Cuba, *cf.* Levi Marrero, *op. cit.*, Vol. I, pp. 105ff. Velázquez, in fact, is perhaps Ovando's best pupil: on Hispaniola alone, he founded five towns, and between 1512 and 1515 he founded seven more in Cuba.

22   For Jamaica see H.P. Jacobs, 'The Spanish Period of Jamaican History', *Jamaican Historical Review*, iii, No. 1 (1957); Francisco Morales Padrón, *Jamaica Española* (Seville: n.p., 1952); C.V. Black, *Spanish Town* (Spanish Town, 1960); William B. Goodwin, *Spanish and English Ruins in Jamaica* (Boston: Meador Publishing Co., 1946); David Buisseret, *Jamaica from the Air* (Barbados: Caribbean UP, 1969). For an excellent summary of the patterns of settlement in this initial phase of the conquest of the Caribbean, cf. Franklin W. Knight, *The Caribbean: The Genesis of a Fragmented Nationalism* (New York: Oxford University Press, 1990), Second ed., pp. 30ff.

23   Adolfo de Hostos, *Historia de San Juan, ciudad murada* (San Juan: Institute of Puerto Rican Culture, 1983). Cf. also Aníbal Sepúlveda, *op. cit.*, Chapter 2.

24   Cf. my studies *Estructuras sociales y económicas de Veraguas desde sus orígenes históricos, siglos XVI y XVII* (Panama City: Editora Panamá, 1967); *La fundación de la Villa de Los Santos y los orígenes históricos de Azuero* (Panama City: Dirección Nacional de la Cultura, 1971); *Políticas de poblamiento en Castilla del ro y Veragua en los orígenes de la colonización* (Panama City: Imprenta Universitaria, 1972); *Fundación y orígenes de Natá* (Panama City: Instituto Panameño de Turismo, 1972).

25   *Op. cit.*

26   Fernández de Oviedo, *Historia general y natural de las Indias*, five vols, (Madrid: Atlas [Biblioteca de Autores Españoles], 1959).

27 Bishop Alejandro Geraldini, *Itinerario por la regiones subequinocciales* (Santo Domingo, D.R.: Editora Caribe, 1977).

28 CODOIN, Vol. 31, pp. 310–11.

29 CODOIN, Vol. 1, No. 39, pp. 284–6.

30 Especially in 'Ideología de la ciudad: Panamá, ciudad primada', *Revista Nacional de Cultura*, Nos. 20–21 (Panama City, January 1981); and 'La fundación de Panamá Viejo: Móviles y conflictos', in *La Prensa* (Panama City), 'Enciclopedia de la Cultura Panameña', August 1985.

31 This craft, and its title, has no modern equivalent. It may be thought of as combining the knowledge and skills of an architect (self-taught) and a master builder, or overseer. [Trans. note.]

32 Woodrow Borah, 'La influencia cultural europea en la formación del primer plano para centros urbanos que perdura hasta nuestros días', in *Boletín del Centro de Investigaciones Históricas y Estéticas*, No. 15 (Caracas, February 1973). Richard Konetzke, *Historia Universal Siglo XXI, América Latina, II, La Epoca Colonial*, Vol. 22 (Madrid: Siglo XXI de España Editores, 1965), p. 40.

33 'Información de méritos y servicios de Alonso García Bravo, alarife que trazó la ciudad de México', published by Manuel Touissant with an introduction (Mexico City: Imprenta Universitaria, 1956).

34 I have published the complete certificate in *Fundación y orígenes de Natá, op. cit.* F. Domínguez Compañy reproduces this document in his work cited above.

35 Domínguez Compañy, *op. cit.*, pp. 82–3.

36 See Toussaint's 'Introduction' to García Bravo's 'Información de Méritos'.

37 Palm, *op. cit.*, Vol. 1, p. 72.

38 The *Casas Reales* or Houses of the Crown, were the extension of royal authority to the colony. They generally contained the offices of the monarchy's deputy or representative (the royally-appointed mayor or governor, etc.), the gaol, and a military barracks for the soldiery. Meetings of the town countil (the *cabildo*) might also be held here in some cities. [Trans. note.]

39 I discussed this subject for the first time in my book *El casco viejo de Panamá y el convento de Santo Domingo* (Panama City: Impresora de la Nación, June 1981).

40 Cf. also my articles 'Portobelo: Apuntes para un libro en preparación', in *Revista Patrimonio Histórico* (Panama City: Instituto Nacional de Cultura, 1980), Vol. 2, No. 1; 'La arquitectura civil durante la época hispana: Los edificios de gobierno', in two parts, *La Prensa*, 'Enciclopedia de la Cultura Panameña', Jan. and Feb. 1986; 'La vivienda colonial en Panamá: Arquitectura y calidad de vida', in two parts, *La Prensa*, 'Enciclopedia', Feb. 1986; 'La aduana y contaduría de Portobelo', *La Prensa*, 'Suplemento Cutltural', Jan. 22, 1987.

41 My best source for information on St Augustine in this article has been François-Auguste de Montequin, 'El proceso de urbanización en San Agustin de La Florida, 1565–1821: Arquitectura civil y militar', *Anuario de Estudios Americanos*, XXXVII (Seville, 1980).

42 *Op. cit.*, p. 89.

43 Cf. my *El casco viejo, op. cit.*; 'Ideología de la ciudad: Panamá, ciudad primada', *Revista Nacional de Cultura*, Nos. 20–21 (January 1984); 'Panamá Viejo', *La Prensa*, 'Enciclopedia de la Cultura Panameña', August 1985; 'Los puertos y el movimiento portuario de Panamá Viejo', *La Prensa*, 'Enciclopedia', September 1985; 'La sociedad colonial, la formación de las estructuras', *La Prensa*,

'Enciclopedia', September 1985; 'El casco Antiguo de la ciudad de Panama', *La Prensa*, 'Enciclopedia', September 1985.

44   Angel Altolaguirre y Duvale, *op. cit.*, p. 39.

45   Gonzalo Fernández de Oviedo, *Historia natural y general de las Indias*, Madrid: Atlas (Biblioteca de Autores Españoles), 1959, Vol. III, Chap. 4.

46   Pedro A. Vives, 'El Ambito del Imperio en la Ciudad Colonial, ¿Unn Función desestructuradora?', in Francisco de Solano (ed.) *Historia y futuro de la ciudad iberoamericana*, Madrid: Consejo Superior de Investigaciones Científicas, 1986, p. 55.

47   *Ibid.*

48   I first came across this insight in Pedro A. Vives, *op. cit.*

49   One must remember that the new city was born as a walled enclave, and that in the ordering of the city, military purposes prevailed over all others.

50   I first developed these ideas in 'Ideologia de la Ciudad', cited above, note 30. I have expanded them in my recent study titled 'Arquitectura y Sociedad. La Vivienda Colonial en Panamá', *Humanidades*, Third Series, No. 1, Univ. of Panama, December 1993, and in my book (in press) *Arquitectura, urbanismo y sociedad. La vivienda colonial de Panamá. Historia de un sueño*, Panama: Fondo Cultural Shell. In these latter two works, I deal with housing and dwelling places as the architectural expression of the ideals of the colonial Panamanian élite.

51   Joaquín E. Weiss, *La arquitectura colonial cubana, siglos XVI/XVII* (Havana: Instituto Cubano del Libro, Editorial de Arte y Literatura, 1972), p. 17. Cf. also Levi Marrero, *op. cit.*, vol. II, pp. 121 ff.

52   'Relación de la Audiencia y Ciudad de Panamá, año 1607', published in M. Serrano y Sanz, (ed.) *Relaciones histórico-geográficas de América Central*, (Madrid: V. Suárez, 1908), p. 171; cf. also 'La ciudad de Panamá, 1610', in 'Descripción corográfica de algunos lugares de las Indias, sacada de informaciones que están en las Secretarías del Consejo, año 1610', in CODOIN, Vol. IX, pp. 79–108; 'La ciudad de Portobelo, 1610', in the same collection; 'Descripción de la ciudad de San Phelipe de Puertobelo, sacada de Relaciones de los años 1606–1607', folios 125–53, unpubl. original in Biblioteca Nacional, Madrid; ms. 3064.

53   Relación de la Audiencia', *ibid*,

54   Joaquín E. Weiss, *op. cit.*, pp. 84–5.

55   *Ibid.*, p. 84.

56   Yolanda Aguirre, 'La villa de Trinidad', in *Arquitectura Cuba* (organ of the National College of Architects of Cuba), XXX, No. 332, n.d.

57   Biblioteca de la Academia de la Historia, Madrid, Muñoz Collection, Vol. 81, f. 128, 'Carta al Emperador', Nombre de Dios, 11 December, 1537.

58   Archivo General de Indias (hereafter AGI), Seville: Panamá 11, 'Carta del Obispo de Panamá al rey', 15 May, 1571 (this letter states that 'the town is of 300 houses'); AGI Panamá 13, 'Carta de la Audiencia al rey', 12 April, 1579; AGI Panamá 30, 'Instrucciones y Memorial de la ciudad de Panamá sobre cosas que pide', 16 May, 1580; AGI Panamá 13, 'Carta al rey del Fiscal Diego de Villanueva Zapata', 12 December, 1581; AGI Panamá 13, 'Carta de la Audiencia al rey', 25 April, 1583.

59   'Relación de la Audiencia', *op. cit.*

60   Printed in *Relaciones histórico-geográficas de América Central*, *op. cit.*, pp. 20, 40, 54.

61   While these dimensions are clear in the original, the text itself seems to be garbled, as they do not 'add up', [Trans.]

62   AGI Patronat 256, 'Relación y discurso que hace el Cap. Miguel Ruiz Delduayen, Alcalde Mayor de la ciudad de S. Phelipe de Po. y Comisario de las Fábricas de la dicha ciudad de Portobelo', Portobelo, 22 March, 1600.

63   'Descripción de la ciudad de San Phpe. de Portobelo, sacada de relaciones de los años 1606–1607'. Biblioteca de la Real Academia de Historia, Madrid, ms. 3064.

64   On the hospital and the church, documentation may be found in AGI Pamana 48.

65   Antonelli complained that 'the stone is very, very hard, of dreadful quality, and in all this region there is not another, and a stonecutter with a great deal of labour works a building stone, one vara [0.84 m., or about 33 inches] square, per day, and many cannot complete one' (AGI Panama 44, 'Bautista Antonelli al rey', Portobelo, 15 July, 1597). On the same subject, cf. AGI Patronato 256, 'Relación de las costas que parece a Hernando de Montoya, aparejador mayor [chief foreman] de las fábricas de Portobelo que tendrá la de la obra que se propone para el San Felipe', Portobelo, 29 March, 1600. On the good qualities of coral, cf. 'Descripción de Portobelo de 1606–1607', *op. cit.*; there we read that it 'is a stone which has been discovered underwater, which they call reefs, very soft to work and of very little weight, almost like pumice stone: once worked, it forms a skin and hardens, and artillery is stopped by it, does not split it or have any effect whatever; it is mixed with lime, and a certain red clay, and it sets and hardens most powerfully.' Santiago castle was made entirely of coral, and according to my calculations in this fortress alone more than 33,000 tons of coral were used. With regard to this subject, in July 1990 I prepared a 'Documentary Report on the Extraction of Coral for the Colonial Edifications of Portobelo' for a team of marine biologists from the Smithsonian Tropical Research Institute of Panama.

66   François-Auguste de Montequin, *op. cit.* Cf. also Jean Parker Waterbury, *The Oldest House, Its Site and Its Occupants 1650 (?) to the Present* (St Augustine: The St Augustine Historical Society, 1984).

67   I have dealt extensively with the subject of the Customs house in 'La arquitectura civil durante la época hispana, los edificios de gobierno', in two parts, *La Prensa*, 'Enciclopedia de la Cultura Panameña', January and February, 1986; and 'La Aduana y Contaduria de Portobelo, *La Prensa*, 'Suplemento Cultural', 22 Jan, 1987. E. Marco Dorta devoted a chapter of his book *Estudios y documentos de arte hispanoamericano* (Madrid: Real Academia de la Historia, 1981) to the Customs house, as well.

68   Cf. Marco Dorta, *op. cit.*, p. 26.

69   *Ibid.*, p. 27.

70   In tropical or semi-tropical countries, an *azotea* is a common architectural feature, while the excellencies of what must be designated in translation as a 'flat roof' may be lost on those who live in English-speaking latitudes, where snow, to mention just one problem, makes flat roofs actively undesirable. Here, two implicit considerations make the detail of a flat roof 'important' to the chroniclers: first, hard, durable materials such as cement are required to build a flat roof that will remain in place; the weight of rain, for instance, will bring down a poorly-built flat roof, or one made of inferior materials; wood will rot

where rain stands. There could be some pride, then, in having a good flat roof. Second, *azoteas* furnished a cool place to sit or even sleep on hot nights, and so were seen as rather luxurious 'improvements' to house architecture; this feature had been inherited, in Spain, from the Arabs, as the Spanish word with its Arabic etymology shows, and soon had become a distinctive feature of Mediterranean architecture. Thus, the flat roof would indicate that the level of 'civilization' in the colony was rising. [Trans. note.]

71   *Ibid.*, p. 53.
72   Quoted by Levi Marrero, *op. cit.*, Vol. I, p. 152.
73   Cf. Joaquín E. Weiss, *op. cit.*; Erwin Walter Palm, *op. cit.*, Vol. I, p. 200; William B. Goodwin, *op. cit.*, pp. 162–3.
74   Eugenio Pérez Montás, *Casas coloniales de Santo Domingo* (Barcelona, n.d.), pp. 23–4; Palm, *op. cit.*, Vol. I, pp. 87 ff.
75   Cf. Ramón Gutiérrez, *Arquitectura y urbanismo en Iberoamérica* (Madrid: Ediciones Cátedra, 1983), pp. 14–15.
76   *Ibid.*, p. 14–17; E. Pérez Montás, *op. cit.*, pp. 23–62; Palm, *op. cit.*, Vol. I, pp. 50ff, Vol. II, pp. 99–112.
77   This was a wheel-driven 'pump' which lifted buckets of water up through a well-shaft to the surface; it had much the same design as a waterwheel, except that the buckets used to raise the water were attached to rope or a chain, and the motive power was provided by horse, mule, ox, etc. [Trans. note.]
78   Cf. Levi Marrero, *op. cit.*, Vol. 3, p. 61.
79   Cf. E. Marco Dorta, *Cartagena*, pp. 10–13.
80   CODOIN, 'Descripción de la Audiencia de Panamá, 1610.'
81   Cf. Joaquín E. Weiss, *op. cit.*, pp. 16, 20, 57 and 58.
82   Cf. Erwin W. Palm, *op. cit.*, Vol. 1, pp. 172–4.
83   Maria de los Angeles Castro, *Arquitectura en San Juan de Puerto Rico (Siglo XIX)* (Rio Piedras: UPR Press, 1980), p. 18.
84   *Ibid.*, p. 31.
85   Cf. M. de los A. Castro, *op. cit.*, and also Anibal Sepúlveda Rivera, *op. cit.*, pp. 70 and 72.
86   AGI Panamá 139, 'Carta del Cabildo de Portobelo al Rey sobre la falta de proprios' (Portobelo, 5 May, 1725).
87   AGI Panamá 31, 'Esteban Tofiño a nombre de la ciudad de Portobelo, contra la ciudad de Panamá, en súplica a la Audiencia de Panamá', n.d., prob. 1626.
88.   Cf. Marco Dorta, *op. cit.*, p. 38.
89   *Ibid.*

9

INTELLECTUAL, ARTISTIC AND IDEOLOGICAL ASPECTS OF CULTURES IN THE NEW WORLD

Gustavo Martin-Fragachan

CONQUEST AND COLONIZATION

Introduction

An analysis of the development of the intellectual, artistic and ideological aspects of the cultures of the new societies which arose in the Caribbean upon the first contact between Europe and the New World depends necessarily upon an understanding of the ideological schemata brought to the lands of the Americas by the discoverers and *conquistadores*. Of equal importance is the study of the intellectual systems which existed among the Amerindian and African societies which helped to make up these new societies. One must note, however, that due mainly to the forced acculturation to which the Amerindian and African inhabitants were subjected, the presence of cultural elements from those societies was not always explicit, but in many cases hidden or disguised, and one tends to encounter logical forms of thought rather than phenomenal expressions of culture. Thus the traditional approach, tinged with experimentalism, by which anthropology, ethnology, history, and the other 'social' disciplines have confronted the problem of acculturation, will be seen in this chapter only in terms of the tangible or visible aspects of cultures.

Seen from a phenomenal standpoint, it can be suggested that the work carried out by Europeans in the New World, especially during the first years of contact, would seem to be not so much a process of discovery as an invention or creation of a different reality. It was structured mainly through an objectification of the Europeans' own ideological and intellectual *Weltanschauung*, which while serving as an explanatory model led almost inevitably to a confirmation of their own ghosts, myths, dreams, hopes and fears.[1]

Alternatively, in structural terms, the categories *discovery, invention, creation, contact, encounter,* and all the other terms employed with explanatory intentions tend to become meaningless, since they lack the analytical value achieved when the implicit dimension of cultures is treated. It is this latter perspective which will be discussed in this chapter.[2] An attempt will be made to examine a series of mental structures which began to take shape in the sixteenth century and which explain the development of the intellectual, ideological and artistic dimensions of Caribbean culture, dimensions which have very particular characteristics.

We are all aware of the problem presented research by the sources of this period. The reports or *cartas de relación,* the royal letters-patent, the pacts or *capitulaciones,* the royal orders or *Requerimientos,* the chronicles, personal relations, and other documents, implicitly bear the stamp of a markedly Castilian-Aragonese view of what was happening. Evidence from the aboriginal groups, who lacked writing, was limited mainly to archaeological remains and interpretations (generally biased in one way or another) made by *adelantados,*[3] *conquistadores,* travellers and chroniclers. None the less, it is important to acknowledge that from the fifteenth century on, two currents of thought regarding the New World panorama began to distinguish themselves: one, steeped in racial and ethnic prejudice; the other, an Edenic vision, rife with idealizations, which became a true *apologia* for primitivism. These two views continued for centuries, and continue still into our own times, influencing the history of ideas not only in the New World but in the Old World as well.

The structural analysis suggested here takes as its given a vision of the *criolla* or 'creole' culture[4] as gradually evolving from the moment of the first contact, and does not take that culture as simply a syncretism of concrete contents, by which tangible cultural expressions are integrated and reintegrated, adapted and readapted, on the basis of general economic, political, or historical processes (though this view has meaning and scientific validity), but rather assumes a view of these newly-emerging cultures as the introduction of new institutions, beliefs and cultural practices into models of thought different from the European models. But even from this perspective, there remains the problem of the essential European-ness of the logical schemata brought to the New World by the *conquistadores,* for we must not forget the influence (to some degree decisive) which such cultures as the Arab and Judaic exerted upon these men.

The structure of relations with Muslims and Jews in Europe was tinged with many ambiguities; there were intermittent periods of peace and times of conflict, even war, depending mainly on the commercial interests at stake at any given moment. This way of conceiving one's relationships with the 'other', meaning in this case Jews and Muslims, produced a complex of attitudes and institutions which was transported to the New World.

European-ness, if I may be allowed to speak of it in some pure form, or at least the European-ness seen in the Spain of their Catholic Majesties Ferdinand and Isabella, was deeply shaken by a series of tremors coming from at least two quarters at once: supporters of a decaying feudal system, with their quiet courtliness and forced exculpations; and the defenders of a return to Greco-Roman roots. This latter position may be seen in chroniclers such as Fernández de Oviedo and Bartolomé de Las Casas,[5] whose works are filled with comparisons between Amerindians on the one hand and Greeks, Romans and Jews on the other. These chroniclers also constantly quote from or allude to Virgil, Pliny, Seneca and Cicero in order to give voice to their impressions.[6]

Christopher Columbus himself was a victim of these contradictions. He was more than familiar with the Italian and Mallorcan portolan maps which, when used with the compass, allowed ever greater precision in navigation. He was imbued with the new seamanship, or art of navigation, brought to Spain by the Arabs, and with the latest notions of geography. He was widely read in cosmology and astrology (especially Ptolemy's *Almagest*) and in the writings of Alfonso XII the Wise (or Learned, as some have it). He possessed the abilities of a true navigator, was expert in the use of instruments, and he was aware of the superiority of the caravel, Latin rigging, and the stern rudder.[7] Yet at the same time the Admiral's mentality retained a certain medieval cast, which took concrete form in a belief in some aspects of fantastic geography (mermaids, giants, the earthy paradise, monsters and mythical beasts), a certain mysticism, the somewhat millenarian spirit that had inspired the Crusades, and a nostalgia for the time of the knightly romance.[8] Although Columbus was a poor and non-noble sailor, his hopes were fuelled not only by 'gold fever' to some degree but also by the tradition of *hidalguismo*, that particular brand of Spanish chivalry which had been pervasive from the time of La Mesta, a powerful society of sheep-breeders with pastoral tendencies and aristocratic aspirations. Furthermore, it has been said that books such as *Amadis of Gaul* and *La Historia del Caballero Cifar* further inflamed that chivalric spirit. We must not forget, in this regard, that on several occasions the Admiral toyed with the idea of putting the gold of the Americas at the disposal of a Christian reconquest of Jerusalem.

This 'Quixotism' (of the kind severely criticized by Cervantes) no doubt had its foundations, as Pierre Vilar points out, in 'the territorial and religious view of expansion, more than in commercial and economic ambition', and this emphasis marks a difference between the plans and achievements of Spanish conquest and those carried out by other European nations, including Portugal.

Given the questionable European-ness of Spain, then, the idea of the supposed relative superiority of the white cultural element becomes difficult, to say the least, to sustain, and generates a mirage which follows us down to our own times. The formalism of the European cultural contribution and the questionability of its essential European-ness, combined with the lack of 'objective' data on much of the process, underscore how problematic is any attempt at historical reconstruction of the process by which the cultures of the Caribbean were shaped, especially with regard to the first century of their development and to their ideological, intellectual and artistic aspects, for which few data exist. And even within the documentary evidence certain contradictions, such as between the captains' diaries and ships' logs on the one hand and the *cartas de relación* on the other, are patent. In the first documents we find descriptions of riches, in an attempt to justify the efforts at exploration, while in the latter, upon which the 'official history' is constructed, we find characteristics both of strong realism (the harshness of the climate, the savagery of the aborigines, the unhealthiness of the tropical nature are recurrent topics) and an extreme of fantasy tricked out in an epic, heroic style belaboured with semantic transformations by which Indian leaders are metamorphosed into kings, the second tier of leaders into knights, their thatched huts or *bohíos* into palaces, their canoes into Ganges rafts, their corn or maize into Italian millet.

To all this is added the difficulty represented by the epistemological perspective of a long historiographic tradition[9] which insists upon constructing theories and extracting conclusions almost exclusively from the standpoint of sensible phenomena and under the paralysing assumption that the observer is ideologically and intellectually free of contamination. Nor should we neglect to mention here the indigenous-privileging, folkloric, or 'local colour' tendencies of one school of anthropology, which generally overlooks the methodological imperative that in the definition of a country's or region's ethos, universal culture in general should be taken into consideration.[10] Likewise, we must not fail to consider the habitual treatment of the ideological, intellectual, and artistic aspects of culture, wherein these aspects appear as a simple epiphenomenon of the material conditions of a society or as an extension of natural mechanisms of adaptation.

These observations imply that we need to reconsider the cultures of the Caribbean from their very origins forward, not only from the point of view of their external manifestations (their concretion in beliefs, myths, rituals, customs, technologies, styles, usages, instruments and tools, and any other human product) but also by means of a study of the forms of thought which make possible both the emergence of these sensible or tangible elements and their organization into a whole which is endowed with meaning or significance. This overcomes the explanatory limitations of the traditional concepts of 'acculturation', 'transculturation', and 'conflict of cultures'. In this respect, the analysis of the perception and representation of certain values is more pertinent than a study of their intrinsic and 'objective' value.

We see, then, that the cultures of the Caribbean were, from their very beginnings, true cultures of the crossroads, wherein besides the undeniable syncretism of external contents, we find the juxtaposition of forms of thought or, perhaps more commonly, the organization of imposed cultural features within a logical model or schema which is alien to those imposed features. Using concepts from contemporary semiotics, we would talk about the adoption of the signifiers but not of the imposed signifieds. This last idea is related to the effort expended by the subject societies toward developing forms or mechanisms of cultural resistance that are hard to perceive, both for the dominators and for the researchers who uphold that epistemological view I have already criticized above. Even the stigmatizing characterizations of things 'Indian' or 'American' (in the continental sense of the word) seem to carry within themselves that contradiction implied by an acceptance of their external expressions, along with a rejection of the logical and symbolical order within which one attempts to categorize (or pigeonhole) them.[11]

The signification of 'Caribbean'

Taking all this into account, then, we arrive at the signification of the term 'Caribbean', which is so filled with ambiguities and contradictory evaluative yardsticks. All the intellectual, ideological and artistic components which arose at the moment of this 'multi-cultural encounter' were marked by the ambivalent and hybrid nature of all that occurs or exists in the New World. The construction of one of the possible paradigmatic chains of Caribbeanness leads us to 'cannibal',[12] to barbarity, heresy and savagery, to sodomy, incest and anthropophagy. This first line of descent, privileged in the personal relations and graphic representations initially made of the New Lands,[13] rests as much on the writings of Amerigo Vespucci, in which he relates his experience with the Tupinamba, as on the information given by the Taíno Indians themselves, native to the Greater Antilles, about the cannibalism of their neighbours the Caribs. The opposite paradigmatic chain leads us to the 'noble savage' and the perception of the indigenous peoples, in general, as generous and innocent, of indigeneity as synonymous with generosity and innocence.[14]

With respect to the subsequent evolution of this contradictory view, Ileana Rodríguez says the following:

It is upon these foundations that the image of the exploited race is built, an image employed by mestizo literature of the following cen-

251

turies. The image emphasizes the survival habits that a cunning, alert, intelligent personality develops, using tricks and ruses and lies. This is the personality of the animals in the Nicaraguan tales of Tío Coyote and Tío Conejo.[15]

In large part this personality model reproduces the European view of the Indian as embodying a dichotomy between words and actions, between stated morality and real behaviour, and it helps stiffen the normative religious, axiological and institutional formalism that gives particular meaning to the new ideological and intellectual structures that arise in the Caribbean. Withdrawal, duplicity, hypocrisy, a degree of passivity – all defence mechanisms – might be explained on the basis of this view. One might even go so far as to suggest, as some have done, that this inward-turning implies a rebirth and a true expectancy of what is insinuated.

The superposition of cultural expressions imposed upon logical schemata or mentalities which were 'other' produced intellectual, ideological and artistic dimensions of culture that are essentially baroque. The readaptation of these imposed cultural features and complexes, generally expressed paroxistically (so that the dominator might see the acceptance), allowed those most essential, most immutable, and least permeable aspects of culture (logical schemata, *Weltanschauungen*, or, in other words, the ultimate ends of culture) to survive. Thus, the 'New World baroque', understood in this way, was a counterculture, or a 'resource of countermodernity'.[16]

One might suppose that this cultural complexity was also influenced by the relatively unstructured or unsystematized character of the new beliefs, practices and institutions brought by the colonizers, which I believe led in turn to the façade-like nature of Caribbean societies, since to some degree they were little more than bridges for the arrival of persons and the dispatch of merchandise and provisions to Central and South America.[17] This implied a constantly temporary character, which prevented (much more than on the continent) the formation of structured cultural systems. This permanently provisional nature of Antillean society fuelled myths, intellectual frameworks and ideological schemata, endowing the Ante-ilhas with a certain air of *mysterium tremendum* in which at one and the same time we find a taste for adventure and a fear of the unknown. This archetype is an intellectual and ideological element of the first importance in the new cultures being forged.

Contradictions between conquest and colonization

Institutional and judicial formalism is also susceptible to being explained by reference to the obvious opposition between the Code of the Indies, first promulgated in Burgos in 1512 and which embodied the centralizing and imperial ambitions of the Peninsula, and the harsh reality of the New Lands, this last element combined with the local hungers of the *conquistadores*. This confluence establishes in the daily life of the Americas, once and for all, the primacy of the military over the colonial law formulated in Spain.

The contradictions between the various conceptions of conquest and colonization,[18] behind which there also doubtlessly lurked personal interests, were to be seen from the earliest years of the process. We see Christopher Columbus propounding the Portuguese-Genoese model of *feitorías* which had been successfully put into effect in Africa and which contemplated a mercantile-military predominance; other characteristics of this model were the payment of tributes and 'ransoms', a slave trade for the markets of the Mediterranean, and a strict prohibition of private appropriation of the labour of the Indians. On the other hand, we find the model which has been called the Castilian-municipal model,[19] defended in Hispaniola by Governor Nicolás de Ovando and the *alcalde-mayor* Francisco Roldán.[20] This model had been used in Granada in the war against the Moors. In Hispaniola it encouraged *vecinos*[21] to settle around a *cabildo*, or town council, and depended upon the private use of an indigenous labour force. The system was institutionalized under a system of *encomiendas*,[22] land distribution, and peonage. This model, with adaptations such as the so-called 'white *caciques*',[23] was at last imposed initially on Hispaniola, but subsequently was used in the Greater Antilles and throughout the continent.

The *conquistadores* spirit of adventure[24] was fuelled by several factors:

1   The difficult conditions of life in Europe, especially for certain kinds of people – Jews, *mudéjares* (Spanish Muslims),[25] murderers and other prisoners – who preferred to go off in search of new experiences than to die on inquisitorial bonfires or in the prisons or streets of the Old World. To these considerations one should add that in the case of nobles, the law of primogeniture sometimes figured large in their desire to try the New World.

2   The lure to the European imagination represented by the stories of such travellers as Marco Polo, and the consequent creation of a whole fantastic geography based on travellers' tales.

3   The exacerbated optimism of the first chronicles, written at or just after the initial contact with the native peoples of the Americas. These chronicles were charged with an ideology, borne with the discoverers and colonists wherever they went, that was filled with dreams, hopes and fears. And this 'everyday ideology' was one of the intellectual and ideological systems used by the *conquistadores* to try (at least at first) to understand those beings, cultures and societies which their

uncomprehending eyes beheld. Nor was this fantastic ideology ever to abandon us – it fuelled a long intellectual tradition whose contemporary expressions in literature and art are known as 'magic realism'.

This everyday ideology, the Spaniards' 'natural' way of looking at the world, was based in large part on centuries of wars, plagues, famines and religious schisms. A dark and sombre wind had blown and was blowing still through Europe. Among the many menaces to Christianity were the Turks, the various Antichrists,[26] the Bleemy, the Maelström, gryphons and other monsters, Amazons and mermaids, the antipodes, baboons, cholera, witch hunts, heretics and Jews, and the *danse macabre*. But out of this horrific and terrifying climate there always emerged some hope, and this is the other side of the coin of the everyday ideology: men believed in Parousia (the Second Coming) and even, on a more concrete level, the discovery of the Garden of Eden on earth, which in turn implied a return to a Golden Age, prior to original sin.[27] The European, moved by the need (apparently a constant of the human spirit) to confirm his dreams and fantasies, projected onto the New World all these images, both positive and negative.

The European was also moved by a kind of frontier spirit. As Guillermo Céspedes del Castillo quite rightly points out, the New World was for them 'the new frontier'. On this new frontier,

> men who had depended on a massive institutional and ideological schema ... suddenly began to act on their own, without any of the institutions that traditionally governed them, or any of the social structures which for centuries had made them feel subordinate, dependent, protected in their daily lives.[28]

This situation is even more succinctly expressed in the famous phrase *'Dios está en el cielo, el Rey en Castilla y yo estoy aquí'* ['God's in heaven, the King's in Castile, and I'm here']. Here, that is, with the tools available to me for interpreting and trying to change this reality before me. Those tools are none other than a frankly medieval mind-set: the vision of the Crusades, the struggle against the infidel, nomadic sheep-herding carried on for years in the plains of La Mancha, and the forays on the frontiers of the Muslim Empire to steal and loot whatever one could find.

The relative independence of the first *conquistadores* and colonizers is also touched on by other authors:

> [It] might be said that though the Iberian monarchies took an interest (a financial interest) in the recently discovered lands, they did not share in

the risks implied from the outset by the exploration, exploitation, or initial occupation of those lands – risks confronted by the merchants, sailors and adventurers who acted, in practice, with a wide margin of autonomy *vis-à-vis* the empire's organs of power. Thus, the dynamics of the initial encounter were ruled, in essence, by the complexes of interests and motivations of its principal protagonists, interests and motivations inscribed within the more general framework of the Iberian Crown.[29]

The *conquistadores'* spirit of adventure, according to Peter Martyr, is common to the entire Spanish people:

Van a construir en La Española una armada nueva para pasar con ella a aquellas regiones y levantar una colonia, y no le faltará quien le siga, porque toda esta nación española es tan amante de cosas nuevas, que a cualquier parte que, sólo por señas o con un silbido se la llame para algo que ocurra, de seguida se dispone a ir volando; deja lo seguro por esperanza de más altos grados, para ir en pos de lo incierto.[30]

[They are about to build on Hispaniola a new armada, to go with it to those regions and raise a colony [the reference here is to Chicora and Vásquez de Ayllón's party]; and there will be no lack of those to follow, for this entire Spanish nation so loves new things, that wheresoever they are called, whether by waving of hands in a sign or by whistling, and told that something is occurring, immediately they rush to see; they leave certainty and safety, and in hope of higher things, go off into uncertainty and danger].

Settlement and society

The plan on which the first cities of the Americas were modelled, according to Céspedes del Castillo, was that of the ideal medieval city, or *urbe* (see Chapter 8 for Hispanic city-building). Ruggiero Romano and Alberto Tenenti state that 'in the first years and throughout the sixteenth century, these "cities" were simple agglomerations, more than anything else, in which a rural character clearly continued to predominate'.[31] But we know that Columbus himself bore in his mind the idea of fortified cities like the Spanish *urbes* of the Middle Ages; this was the model that was followed in the construction of Isabela and the fortress named Santo Tomás, in the region of Cibao. These communities began to be called *villas* in order to distinguish

255

them from the *pueblos* (the more usual name of a small town or settlement) of the Indians. On 16 September, 1501, Governor Ovando received instructions to found 'a number' of these communities, and seven years later the Crown granted coats-of-arms to fifteen *villas* on Hispaniola. In the case of Cuba, we find that the 'Pacificator' Diego de Velázquez had founded seven villas by 1515. These included Santiago de Cuba, which was to become the capital and seat of government of the island.

On 22 July, 1497, before his third voyage, Columbus received authorization to distribute parcels of land and to grant them as private property to the colonizers. The beneficiary of this grant was obliged to remain on the property and work it for four years. Excluded from the distribution were those lands on which gold was found, as these would be the property of the Crown. A similar provision was made for the production of the wood called brazilwood. These exceptions, however, were never observed, and the real distribution of land was made on the basis of the existing Indian *pueblos*. These distributions originated in the need to appease Roldán and his mutineers, who had refused to acknowledge the authority of Christopher Columbus and his brother, the *Adelantado*.

In his book *Obra dominicana*, Pedro Henríquez Ureña gives the dates of the foundation of these first cities, which in his view are 'European' in nature. First there was Isabela, in 1494, though it was abandoned a short time afterwards, then Santo Domingo, the oldest of the original cities still in existence today, was founded by Diego Colón in 1496. Henríquez Ureña goes on to say that 'by 1505 there were seventeen European-style settlements on Hispaniola, not counting the isolated fortresses'.[32] San Juan, Puerto Rico was founded in 1508, Santiago de Cuba in 1514, Havana in 1515, San José de Oruña on the island of Trinidad in 1592. On the coasts of South America, Coro was founded in 1527 and Nueva Córdoba (later Cumaná) in 1562.

Of foremost importance in the transplantation to the New World of European culture were churches, monasteries and convents. With regard to this aspect of the colonizing process, Henríquez Ureña says the following:

> The religious life began with the erection of churches; within a short time came the monasteries. The first of these was the Franciscan monastery founded in the city of Santo Domingo in 1502, followed in that same city by the Dominicans in 1510 and the Mercedarians (the Brothers of Mercy) in 1514. Some time later came the female orders. And beginning in the year 1504 the Vatican determined to erect bishoprics.[33]

With the establishment of monasteries began formal education: the first school was founded on Hispaniola in 1505 by the Franciscans. In 1513 the

Spanish Crown ordered that Latin be taught to some select Indians of the Antilles. In 1538 the College of the Dominican Order in Santo Domingo was authorized to call itself the Universidad Santo Tomás de Aquino, and in 1540, in that same city, the Universidad de Santiago de la Paz y Gorjón was founded. These centres of study followed the model of the universities at Salamanca and Alcalá de Henares, with their four 'faculties' and obligatory use of Latin, except in the study of medicine.

Returning to the European's spirit of adventure, we find that this adventurousness, fanned by utilitarian zeal and spiritual fantasies, contrasts with the passivity and indolence imputed to the natives by such chroniclers and interpreters as Padre José de Acosta, Gonzalo Fernández de Oviedo and Juan Ginés de Sepúlveda, who gave examples of such phenomena as an absence of sexual appetite in the indigenous male, physical proof of which is offered by his near-hairlessness. In contrast, the aboriginal woman, repressed or unsatisfied for centuries, throws herself into the arms of the European male. From these ideas a new ideological archetype with many ramifications emerges, achieving the status of 'theory' some time later in Buffon. The Caribbean cultures were permeated with that image of the poor, raped, indigenous mother, whose points of congruence with the voluptuous and sexually-pleasuring female are unclear, coupled with a denial of any reference to the paternal side, in which passivity and resignation are internalized. Ideological attempts to avoid these stigmata resulted in a cowardly activism which depended upon a certain contextual morality and a very specific conception of honour, both values finding concretion in the famous phenomenon of '*machismo*'.

Here, as in many other cases, writers of the time divide along the lines of the contradictory signifieds they attribute to the same signifiers. Thus sexual passivity or activity in the Indian female are seen differently by Fernández de Oviedo and Las Casas. While for the first, the indigenous females were 'the most lecherous and dishonest and libidinous women seen in these Indies or anywhere',[34] for Las Casas the women 'obeyed their husbands greatly, for by their nature all these people, more than any nation of the earth, respect their elders, the wives their husbands, the children their parents, the servants their masters, the subjects their kings'.[35] The opinion that won out in the long run would be Fernández de Oviedo's, and it would make the voyage to the New World, especially to the warmer zones where women supposedly would have the same heat as the climate, much more attractive.

The Indians' essential sexual innocence runs parallel to their sexual passivity and their existential resignation, and that would link them to the idea of childlikeness. This is why it made sense to create the so-called *pueblos* of Indians, in which the native peoples were subject to privileges and tutelage generally accorded minors. The work of colonization, and especially evangelization, was understood in terms of 'up-bringing'. Transculturation and resocialization implied a movement on the part of the indigenous peoples toward adulthood, in which journey they are led by the hand by the European father. I believe that this paternalism is also internalized as an archetype. Still, once more we see the polysemic nature of the images: what for some is innocence is for others simple stupidity. The drama of New World ideology lies precisely in this constant ambivalence, to which Francisco Morales Padrón refers when he states that:

> The Spaniard soon pondered these beings of new pigmentation. The Hispanic ideology ran in two channels: for some they were 'noble savages'; for others, 'filthy dogs', as though they were Saracens. The Indian's nature, like the problem of just titles, entailed a long process of discussion. People discussed his capacity to live in accord with Spanish customs and to receive the Catholic faith. In the vehemence that resulted from these discussions, the Crown inclined toward a middle ground and adopted a paternalistic attitude, regulating the Indians' existence as though they were minor children. Their rationality was acknowledged, and it was believed that their backwardness was the fruit of sin or the Fall, not of some natural inferiority, as the Europe of the seventeenth century would claim.[36]

The geography of the Caribbean

The wickedness or ignorance of the aborigines, their indolence and passivity, contrasted with the beauty and exuberance of nature. The initial descriptions of the geography of the Caribbean are filled with this lush nature, the idea of which fosters the possibility of finding in these lands the Earthly Paradise, and legitimates the colonial enterprise to the royalty and commercial houses of Europe. These geographical descriptions constitute the first literary genre of the New World, and came to serve, moreover, as an instrument of international law. In the reports sent back to Europe, as mentioned earlier, there was a mixture of perceived reality and fantasy – vivid fantasy, and in one sense no less real than 'reality'. But once more, the 'factual' won out, and away from the Edenic vision there was a shift to the profoundly critical, which would reach its zenith in the eighteenth century. Among many other things, it was argued that there was too much water, and that this condition favoured rot; that animals did not grow satisfactorily; that lions (feminized, as the men also were) had no manes; that birds' songs were grotesque, as they imitated the inaudible voices of the aborigines; and that there were too many cold-blooded animals (reptiles and insects). Queen Isabella herself expresses opinions as to the quality of the trees and men in the Indies:

> *Bien que se escriba de un dicho que dixo la Catholica Reyna, doña Isabel de la calidad desta tierra é gente della; porque con este dicho tan grande é natural philosophia acabaré de fundar mejor lo que dixe de suso, expresando las causas por donde nunca han de faltar trabajos á los que governaren en las Indias. E lo que dixe aquella serenisima Reyna fué aquesto: Quando el primero almirante, don Christobal Colon, ovo descubierto estas Indias, estando un dia dando particular razón al Rey é á la Reyna de las cosas de estas partes, dixo entre otras cosas o particularidades, que los árboles en esta tierra, por grandes que sean, no meten hondas debaxo de la tierra sus raíces, sino poco debaxo de la superficie. Y assi es la verdad, porque allende de aquella corteza ó temple que tiene la superficie del terreno (que puede ser medio estado ó poco mas), poquissimos y raros árboles llegan las raíces un estado de hondo; porque alli adelante o antes hallan la tierra seca é calida quanto mas ahondan; y cómo en lo alto está húmeda, en aquello poco se sustentan los árboles é se extienden é se multiplican é esparçen tantas raíçes o mas que tienen ramas; pero, como es dicho, no entran en lo hondo de la tierra … Despues que la Reyna le ovo escuchado, mostró averle pessado lo que avia oido, é dixo estas palabras: En esa tierra donde los árboles no se arraigan, poca verdad y menos constancia avrá en los hombres).*[37]

[Well it is written of a saying spoken by the Catholic Queen, doña Isabel, of the quality of this land and the people of it; for with this saying so great, and natural philosophy, I will make better founded that which I said above, stating the causes by which there will never be a lack of work for those who govern in the Indies. And what Her Most Serene Highness said was the following: When the first admiral, don Christopher Columbus, had discovered these Indies, one day giving particular arguments to the King and to the Queen of the things in those parts, he said among other things or particularities that the trees of this land, however large they may be, do not put their roots deep down into the earth, but rather a little distance under the surface of it. And this is true, because beyond that covering possessed by the surface of the earth (which may be half an *estado* [something over five feet] or a bit more), very few and uncommon trees put their roots one *estado* deep; and since higher up [*e.g.*, on the surface] the ground is humid, in that little [earth] the trees maintain themselves and spread and multiply and put out as many roots or more than they have branches; but, as is said, they do not go deep into the earth. And after the Queen had heard this, she seemed to weigh what had been told to her, and spoke these words: In this earth where the trees do not put down roots, little truth and less constancy will be found in the men.]

In his *Refutación de Las Casas*, Bernardo Vargas insisted on the unhealthfulness of the new lands. This condition was due to their humidity, the heavy vapours that emerged from the ground, and the lack of entry for sunshine caused by the thickness of the upper vegetation in the jungle. All these things made people less than good and hardworking. There is, then, a parallel between nature and its characteristics on the one hand and mankind and human society on the other.[38] This archetype lasted through the years, and established a close relationship between heat and humidity on the one side and underdevelopment and a 'natural tendency' toward dependency on the other.

But the nearness to nature allows other sorts of conjectures, as well. Life in nature constitutes an ideal for the classical world; the buccolic life may constitute a valid ideological reply to the miseries brought by progress. This proximity to nature explains the Renaissance revalorization of the feminine, which is already a given in the New Lands, bringing about new ideological and intellectual derivations touching upon the primacy of the affective over the rational, a reading which implies the absence of any sort of logic of the emotions.

The day-to-day ideological structures of the European, as I have said, are fed by numerous beliefs, myths and legends. The reports concerning the Asia of the Khans (and more concretely the empire of Kublai Khan), stories of the kingdoms of Cipango (located on the maps of the time on the same latitude as the Canary Islands) and Cathay (situated some thousand miles from Cipango) and other fabulous lands filled with treasures and great marvels – information brought to Europe, as I have mentioned, by Marco Polo and other travellers – served as a crucible for the European imagination,[39] which forged a vast fantastic geography. In this geography we find fabulous areas and things such as the lands of Prester John, King Solomon's mines, the province of Ophir, the region of the Amazons, the land of Ararat, the land of Gog and Magog, the *zona perusta* or region of the Second Coming, the Mare Tenebrosum, the fountain of eternal youth, and the Earthly Paradise, generally confused with *El Dorado*, the Land of Gold. In spite of the fact that Gil Eannes and Alfonso Baldaya, sailing for Prince Henry of Portugal, had destroyed a good deal of this mythical geography in 1434–5 when they sailed south of Cape Bojador (*Caput Finis Africae*),[40] thereby demonstrating that in spite of common belief, those mysteries were not to be found there, the arrival on the shores of the New World revitalized belief in their existence, and almost all these 'things', especially that land of *El Dorado*, were sought for on the New Continent.

When Columbus arrived in the New World in 1492, he thought he knew everything essential for his Asiatic venture. He believed he was in Cipango (Japan), and believed that from thence to the lands of the Great Khan was a journey of ten days. On 1 November he assumed he had reached 'Quinsay' (now Hang-zhou) in 'Catayo' (Cathay) and that he must also be near the Golden Chersonese (on the Malay Peninsula). When he heard the word *cibao*, the natives' word for the place, he identified it with Cipango, and when he heard something about the 'Canibs' who attacked the Cibao natives, he says that 'it is no other thing than the people of the Great Khan, who must be very near here, and will have ships and come to capture them, and as they do not return they believe they have been eaten'.[41] As Tzvetan Todorov has said, 'an overdetermined world must of necessity be an overinterpreted world as well'. Still, after these Asiatic dreams evaporated, the quest for the land of *El Dorado* continued throughout the New World: from the larger islands the search moved to the smaller ones, and then to the so-called Pearl Coast, to Darién (Panama), Trinidad, the Meta River in modern Colombia, Santa Marta (also Colombia), the Orinoco River, the Marañon River in Peru, and thence ever onward.

The myth of *El Dorado* was born in the Caribbean, even though its future was to be tied to the Continent. From very early on, information given by the indigenous people to Columbus encouraged a belief in its existence, proof of which, they claimed, he could see in the greatness of the treasure of the Taíno *cacique* Caonabo, the 'Lord of the Golden House'. This treasure was transported by the Admiral to Spain. Thus,

> gold defined the direction which the exploration and conquest was to take, guided the inquisitive glances of the newly arrived, and determined or at least influenced what they saw, and finally measured and quantified the nature of the dialogue 'question and reply' between the European and the aborigine.[42]

Some of the roots of the formation of the *El Dorado* myth lay in the interests of the financial establishment in Europe; the gold fever was fed by tales such as that of the mysterious island from which Solomon extracted the gold and silver for the building of the Temple in Jerusalem. This island was located, according to Columbian fantasies, in the middle of the Atlantic.

The military nature of the conquest

The military nature of the conquest is also an indisputable fact. The Europeans possessed a technology of war far superior to that of the native peoples. The thunderous noise of the firearms alone, plus the very presence of horses, were in and of themselves weapons of great psychological power. If to this we add the use of steel swords, crossbows, spears and lances, harquebuses and such artillery weapons as lombards, culverins, and the so-called ('slings'), not to mention trained dogs used to hunt down the Indians, we see the disadvantage of the native peoples.

In terms of military tactics, we also find, as Manuel Beroes reminds us,[43] a clear European superiority. The tactics of the Indians, based on hand-to-hand combat at close quarters or in ambushes, were soon learned and neutralized by the Europeans. Thus we see that:

> [the] Iberian groups, soon becoming aware of this fact, exploited it to their own favour by applying techniques based either on the fundamental and growing employment of cavalry and artillery on suitable terrain, that is, in open fields, or on the constant mobility of their troops and action either by individuals or small groups on difficult terrain, for efficient use of those resources. In the first case, as the indigenous contingents, disposed in regular closed order, were attracted into the open field, [the cavalry and artillery] could decimate them and even scatter them with only artillery fire and charges by the horsemen, without committing their infantry to a frontal attack which might in other circumstances be difficult if not unfavourable. The work of infantrymen being simplified in this manner, they could then enter into combat under conditions assuring a victory virtually won in the initial phase of it. In the second case, when fighting on rugged terrain or in thick vegetation, the rapid dispersion into open order, upon being ambushed or attacked, avoided the concentration of enemy power upon a single point, rendering nil, because of the scant ability for manoeuvring shown by the indigenous military contingents, the possibility of being surrounded, and thus opening the alternative of forcing a transfer of the combat to a setting more favourable for the effective employment of cavalry and/or artillery.[44]

Nor should one minimize the role played in the conquest of the indigenous populations by the *conquistadores* and colonizers taking advantage of long-standing conflicts between the indigenous groups themselves.

The native peoples' rebellion against their subjection took several forms. Besides armed confrontations with the Europeans, these peoples also committed mass suicide or fled into the wilderness of the mountains or jungles. Those who fled were called *cimarrónes*, and entire communities of *cimarrones* grew up, called *palenques*, from which attacks were launched against the Spanish dominators.

Religious domination and scholasticism

In spite of the importance of domination by military means, the value of the missionary to the New World enterprise is undeniable, and this missionary element takes us into another line of argument: the argument for religious domination. The missionary spirit contains a contradiction, expressed in the fact that while there is a recognition of the spiritual aspect of the indigenous peoples' lives, there is at the same time a disdain for their culture. This culture particularizes the indigenous peoples, makes them different from other men, while evangelization, on the contrary, seeks universalization; it believes in the universality of moral standards. The missionary spirit was institutionalized (perhaps even sanctified) in the Seville Council of 1478, in which the Crown and the episcopate agreed that the reform of the Spanish Church would be effected without outside intervention, even from Rome. The encounter with the settlers of the New World became the occasion for a true theological renewal. This was accompanied by heated debates such as had not taken place when Africa was discovered and conquered. What would later be known as anthropology, too, had its origins in this process of contact with the new societies, encounters with diverse cultures and different men in the New World, as one can see from the numerous documents written by dozens of missionaries.

The religious ideology constitutes another of the important intellectual tools employed to try to explain the 'American reality'. But this ideology was not homogeneous, either; here there were also confrontations and collisions between those who clung to medieval theological tradition, the defenders of Scholasticism, and the founders of Humanism,[45] which fed mainly on Erasmian ideas. Romano and Tenenti have the following to say on this subject:

> In the late fifteenth century, Christianity, though profoundly trans-formed from what it had been in preceding centuries, was still the only spiritual and mental framework in Europe. Within it, divergent forces, contradictory tendencies, were stirring, but none of them did away with it, or pretended to do away with it, in radical terms ... Meanwhile, the collective sensibility in large sectors was adrift. An example of this is the wide diffusion of the practice of magic. By its nature, magic is

extremely close to many cult practices defined as Christian though in truth no less superstitious.[46]

Conflicts between the Dominicans and the Franciscans were a clear expression of these different points of view. While for the Franciscans 'the gunpowder used against the infidels is incense that rises up to God', for the Dominicans, beginning with the famous sermon by Padre Montesinos in Hispaniola in 1510 (p. 89), the conquest was permeated with brutality and the institution called the *encomienda* was devoid of all humanity. And these conflicts are in addition to the influence of Protestant religious ideology in the region, which would make itself felt as early as the sixteenth century. Still, 'the idea triumphed that orthodox Catholicism and Spanish solidity were identical'.[47]

Early on, Erasmian ideas began to filter into the Americas. According to Fernando Pérez Memén,[48] this was due to a series of circumstances among which one might single out the influence of the Dutch humanist on Cardinal Ximénez de Cisneros, who was the most important leader of the renewal of religion through the inclusion of the ideas of Christian humanism (for which he founded the university at Alcalá, sponsored a polyglot Bible, and reformed the mendicant orders). Cardinal Ximénez' admiration for Erasmus was shared by many other important persons, among them Archbishop Manrique, who held the position of Inquisitor-General, Archbishop Fonseca, Bishops Cabrero and Ruiz de Virués, and Fernando Columbus, Christopher Columbus' brother. The Emperor, Charles I of Spain, himself was knowledgeable in the works of Erasmus, and the book *Institutio Principis Cristiani* (1516) was written at the request of the young future-emperor's tutors.

As Pérez Memén says:

Faced with the spread of Lutheranism, as Deive notes, some Spanish humanists saw Erasmianism as a liberal alternative by which orthodoxy, and in fact the political unity of the Holy Empire, might be saved, from which [supposition] one might infer that humanistic thought conditioned important decisions by the Emperor. And the Emperor's Indies policy was [indeed] under the influence and determination of intellectuals and courtiers who were sympathizers of the Dutch thinker.[49]

With regard to the Caribbean, we can see that Erasmian thought was widespread in Hispaniola during the sixteenth century, and especially during the 1530s. Erasmus' books were widely disseminated at this time, and the speeches of Padre Carlos de Aragón were filled with the Erasmian, and therefore anti-scholastic, style. Pérez Memén even sees traces of Erasmianism in Fernández de Oviedo.

The death of the Inquisitor-General, the rise of the Counter-Reformation, and the Emperor's abdication were the starting points for the crisis suffered by Erasmianism in Spain. Erasmus' ideas began to be forbidden, and followers of Erasmianism were tried. This occurred in the New World, too: Padre de Aragón, an Erasmist, was tried in Spain and forced to make a public retractation, then locked in a monastery for the rest of his life; the poet Lázaro Bejarano, Governor of Curaçao (Isla de los Gigantes), was accused of proposing, under the influence of Erasmus' *Enchiridion*, that the Bible be personally interpreted by every man; the Mercedarian Friar Diego Ramírez was also sentenced to refrain from preaching for six years, to refrain from public confession, to refrain from saying mass for six months, and to refrain for life from printing books of theology.

Another intellectual and ideological instrument often used in the colonial process was the philosophy of Aristotle. Aristotelian ideas were frequently employed by Las Casas and the Dominicans, generally against medieval theological dogma, and this use implied a certain Renaissance tendency in these men, though its full flowering still lay in the future. The introduction of Aristotelian thought into Europe had come late, for it dated to only the thirteenth century. Scholasticism had undertaken to reconcile Aristotelian geography and anthropology with Christian ideas. But there were those contradictions of expression, so Aristotle was employed in an attempt to legitimize antagonistic opinions, signifieds, and concepts. Thus, for example, we find, particularly in Sepúlveda, the use of Aristotelian ideas of hierarchy. In his *Democrates alter*, whose printing Las Casas managed to suppress, Sepúlveda posits that hierarchy is necessary in order to guarantee 'the empire and domain of perfection over imperfection, strength over weakness, supreme virtue over vice'.

As for Las Casas, even though he was inscribed within the Scholastic tradition, he tried to support his egalitarian beliefs against Aristotelian ideas of hierarchy:

> In this let us send Aristotle packing, for from Christ, who is eternal truth, we have the following commandment: 'Thou shalt love thy neighbour as thyself'. Although in fact he was a great philosopher, he was not worthy by way of his lucubrations to arrive at God through a knowledge of the true faith.

Such Lascasian statements as the foregoing are perhaps what have led many writers, such as Manuel Giménez Fernández, to think that Las Casas proceeded by great moral intuition, though the doctrines he postulated lacked a logical or rational basis. In any case, in spite of all, Aristotelian thought was a kind of general equivalent to which theological, anthropological and legal disputes were referred. Even when most of these controversies took place in the Old World, I believe they are important to note here because of the ideological and intellectual repercussions they had on the New World in general, and the Caribbean in particular.

In Spain, Aristotle was to be used in arguments about the problem of the Indians' soul and employed to define the degree of their primitivism or barbarity, and he was to enlighten minds as to the appropriate methods of conquest in each case.

Perhaps the central Aristotelian notion employed was that of the 'citizen' or resident of the *polis*. For Aristotle, the *polis* was natural, and man an animal made naturally for life in the *polis*. The residents of the *polis* were distinguished from the non-residents by a series of traits: they possessed a nuclear family, they had governors and magistrates, they engaged in commercial activities, they had writing and a medium of exchange, and they maintained a permanent relationship with the divine, among other features. Many pre-Columbian societies possessed these cultural traits ascribed to the Greek 'citizen', but the contents underlying the manifestations were different from those known to European civilization. Thus, for example, there were attempts to measure the rules of kinship – alliance and filiation – that prevailed among the classificatory systems in aborigine groups by the ideas and categories of descriptive systems. The idea of an individual with several mothers or fathers, numerous siblings, a large number of children, or the possibility of marrying several women (within which what today would be called first or second degree of kinship) were shocking, and sounded like promiscuousness to most Europeans.

The distinction Aristotle drew between the development of virtue in the various latitudes was also important. That is, Aristotle stated that the peoples who live in cold regions, even when they may have much bravery and courage, lack intelligence and ability, so they are free but unable to give their life a political organization within which to maintain that freedom. Contrariwise, peoples who live within the heat of Asia are skilful and intelligent but lack courage, which makes them live always under the yoke of slavery. The Hellenic peoples, on the other hand, by living in an intermediate region, are able to join skilfulness with courage, which allows them to reconcile good government with freedom. Paradoxically, however, in the quest which many explorers launched for *El Dorado*, the heat of the equatorial circle was a factor to be taken into consideration, for there existed a theory of the determining influence of the sun, the 'will' of that stellar body, on the development of gold. Many writers, such as André Thévet, Joannes Boemus and José de Acosta, repeated these ideas.

THE SIXTEENTH-CENTURY CARIBBEAN ECONOMY

As mentioned earlier in this chapter, reconstructing what occurred in the sixteenth-century Caribbean is made difficult by, among other factors, the almost total lack of documents or testimonies from the indigenous peoples themselves. Many chroniclers and travellers tell of some of the cultural features which they found in the societies of the Greater Antilles, which were populated mainly by Arawak-language groups. Thus it is commonly said that their political organization was on the basis of *cacicazgos* (*cacique*-ships, one might say in English) of greater or lesser importance, a system in which there was a specific territorial division and in which the payment of tributes to other tribes was very common. Societies were stratified. At the peak of the pyramid were the *caciques*, with *caciques* of a second order beneath them, functioning as sort of district leaders.[50] Under these came the nobles (sometimes known as *nitaínos*), then the people of the communities, and then, in the lowest place, the slaves or *naborías*. Many of these *cacicazgos* were hereditary through the maternal line, and it was not unheard-of for women to occupy these leadership positions; one example of a *cacica* was the famous Anacaona of Hispaniola.

In the Lesser Antilles, with the exception of Trinidad, the Bahamas, Barbados, Curaçao and Isla Margarita, the inhabitants belonged to the Carib-language family. It was from these islands that Indians were taken by the Spaniards as slaves to the larger islands; this was done after they were declared 'cannibals'.

Food

The aboriginal economy on these islands was based on the production of tubers and root vegetables, principally *yuca* or cassava, *camote* or sweet potato (after the Spaniards, known as *batata*), and *age*, another sort of sweet potato. The most common method of cultivation was slash-and-burn, with the division of land into *conucos* or small parcels, and rotation of fields, leaving some uncultivated for one or a number of years. The ground was worked with mattocks. Another common agricultural implement was the *macana*, a swordlike tool. There were also axes, picks and planting sticks. The loosened and aerated soil would be piled into hillocks, by which the effects of erosion might be lessened. Peter Martyr even mentions the existence of irrigation systems on Hispaniola.

There are reports of Caribbean communities on the coast of the continent which were said to divide labour along gender lines. The women would be in charge of the agricultural work and the preparation of food, especially rootstarch bread and cornbread, while the men hunted and fished.

In the farm fields of the islands, peanuts, beans and tubers were the main crops. Corn was known in Cuba and on the continent. Outside the fields were plantings of cotton and tobacco – *cohib* – and *bixa*. There is some possibility that these plants grew wild, since there are no descriptions of how and where they were actually planted.

Bowls and other containers were made from gourds. Tobacco, genip or genipap, and certain mineral pigments were used as dyes for decorating the skin. The plant the natives called *cohibá* (the modern 'tobacco') was used to make a narcotic powder called *cohoba*. Along the coasts of Central and northern South America, men chewed a leaf which was probably also tobacco. There were many fruit trees, especially the *mamey* (the mamee or mamey-apple) and the *anón* (the soursop or custard-apple) on the islands, and the pineapple and guava on the continental coasts.

The diet of the Taínos and other indigenous groups was rounded out with foodstuffs that they gathered and the product of their hunting and fishing. There were many varieties of fish and land animals (small mammals such as the *hutía* or *jutía*, which the Spaniards called hares or rabbits, and reptiles such as the iguana). Along the continental coastline there was a wider range of animal life, including deer, peccaries, and other larger mammals such as the tapir. On the other hand, domestication of animals was unknown in the Greater Antilles, and the keeping of fowl for food was rare. Only the Caribs of the lesser islands and the Caribbean coastline of Central and northern South America appear to have possessed domesticated ducks and geese. Still, on his first voyage Columbus himself took note of the fact that many birds migrated to these latitudes in the wintertime, among them many geese and ducks, and that these were hunted by the Indians. There were also many doves, parrots and other such birds. In Cuba and Jamaica birds were hunted by an ingenious system of swimmers hiding under large gourds.

The most common hunting tools were a short wooden spear with a fire-hardened point, the *macana* or sword-like tool, and wooden clubs. On the continent, larger mammals were hunted by groups of men who beat their prey into corrals, nets or traps.

Columbus and Las Casas mention the presence on Hispaniola of small dogs that did not bark; these were edible, and were bred either to be eaten or used in hunting to scare up prey.[51] The Spaniards called them 'mute dogs', *perros mudos*. These 'little dogs', which the Spaniards also used for food during the great starvation of 1494, quickly became extinct. Besides the uncontrolled action of men, the introduction of true dogs and swine, many of which quickly became wild, hastened the extinction of much Antillean fauna.

The most common hunting strategies were nets made of cotton cord or palm-fibre and cords with hooks of bone or tortoiseshell attached. Hobbles were often used. In Cuba there were fresh and saltwater fish hatcheries. Las Casas gives a description of one of these:

> ... *es tanta la multitud de pescado que en él hay, mayormente lizas, que tenían los indios dentro del mismo puerto, en la misma mar, corrales hechos de cañas hincadas, dentro de las cuales estaban cercadas y atajadas 20, 30 y 50 000 lizas, que una de ellas no se podía salir, de donde con sus redes sacaban las que querían y las otras dejábanlas de la manera que las tuvieran en una alberca o estanque.*[52]

[Great is the multitude of fish, most mullet [*lizas*], which there is, and which the Indians have within the very harbour, the very sea, in corrals [traps] made of staked reeds, within which there were 20, 30 and 50 000 mullet trapped and held, that not a one of them might escape, and from which their nets took out those they wished and the others they left there so that they had them in a reservoir or tank.]

For fishing the Indians also used a plant called *barbasco*, probably *Serjania inebrians* or a relative. The leaves of this plant had narcotic properties, and it grew along the riverbank or lake shore; it would be tossed into the water to stupefy the fish. They also employed a technique called *cuabeo*, which consisted of bringing a lighted torch near the water at night so that the fish might be attracted to it and easily caught. All these foods were complemented by conch and other shelled molluscs, by sea turtles and turtle eggs, and by sea cows or manatees.

In other areas of the Caribbean, such as in the Isthmus of Darien, cassava bread was unknown and corn bread was its substitute. Wine was also made of corn and other fermented fruits, its flavour enhanced with spices. The Indians of the Antilles, on the other hand, did not know alcoholic drinks.

Food was preserved in various ways, such as by smoking and salting meat and fish.

On the continental coasts there is evidence of exchange and barter, and of true fairs or markets to which products from various regions would be brought for sale or trade. Blocks of salt from Araya, and pearls, were important items in these trading activities. There were also ceramic and gold objects brought from the interior.

The use of cotton and palm-fibre cloth is attested to by many reports. Cotton fabrics were used to make hammocks and clothing. Cotton was also used, as I have indicated, for making hunting and fishing nets.

269

Various woods, many of them very fine and hard, such as mahogany and tropical cedar, were commonly used in making canoes, or *almadías* as the Spaniards called them, after the raft-like boats known from India. These excellent hardwoods were also used for the low ceremonial seats called *duhos* and for platters, trays, and containers of great beauty, such as those known to have been possessed by Anacaona. Gold was the only metal the native populations worked, and it was worked either in pure form or as the alloy known as *guanín*. Gold, skin dyeing, ceremonial masks and woven belts were used for both decorative and religious purposes.

Housing

The Indian houses, called *bohíos*, seem to have been bell-shaped, and the first mentions of them compared them, at least in their shape, to the large Arab tents called *alfaneques*. They had two doors and a smoke stack. They were multi-family dwellings, though those who lived in them considered themselves all related. The usual *pueblo* would consist of a group of twelve to fifteen *bohíos*, though other larger settlements of as many as 50 dwellings existed, with populations upwards of one to two thousand inhabitants.

Las Casas gives a more or less detailed description of the way these dwellings were constructed:

> *Los vecinos de esta isla Española y de estas islas concercanas y parte de tierra firme hacia la costa de Paria, y en otras muchas partes, hacían sus casas de madera y de paja, de la forma de una campana. Estas eran altas y muy capaces, que moraban en cada una de ellas diez y más vecinos. Hincaban los palos gruesos como la pierna y aun el muslo en rededor, medio estado en el suelo y los ataban con ciertas correas como raíces, que arriba dijimos llamarse bejucos ... Sobre aquellos primeros palos ponían al través y cruzados otros muchos delgados y muy atados con aquellas raíces, y de estas raíces y cortezas de árboles teñidas con tinta negra, y otras desolladas que quedaban blancas, hacían lazos y señales o follajes como pinturas por la parte de dentro, que no parecía sino que eran de otra hermosa y pintada material.*[53]

[The residents of this island Hispaniola and these islands nearby, and part of the continent toward the coast of Paria (Venezuela), made their homes of wood and straw, in the form of a bell. These were tall and very spacious, and there lived within one of them ten or more residents. They would pound tree trunks as thick as the leg or even the thigh around, one-half *estado* into the ground and thick, and all of them would come to tie it above, where they would tie them with certain belts like roots ... called *bejucos* (a word now current in Spanish, meaning 'vines'). Upon those first trunks they would lay through and across others, much thinner, and tied tight with those roots, and from these roots and the bark of trees dyed with black ink, and others (barks) (which they) flayed and which turned out white, they made knots and signals or bits of foliage like paintings on the inside, which seemed to be nothing but another lovely painted material.]

At the centre of their *pueblos* or settlements there were rectangular spaces where they celebrated their assemblies, meetings, and the festivals they called *areytos*. In these spaces, which were called *bateys*, they also held their ball games, the practice of which was widespread throughout the islands and the continent.

Population and ethnography

In many regions assigning ethnic labels is difficult because the Europeans used relatively simplistic classificatory criteria. Thus, all hostile groups were called Caribs, even when they were not, as seems to be the case on the Costa de las Flechas of what is today Colombia. This distinction (or lack of it) seems to be owing to Columbus himself, who always kept in mind the possibility of extracting some profit for himself out of enslaving the Caribs.

There are also difficulties in trying to establish the exact number of settlers in 1492 in what today we known as the Caribbean region. While Rosenblat calculates a population of 100 000 inhabitants for Hispaniola, Las Casas mentioned some 3 000 000, and Professors Cook and Borah of the University of California, Berkeley, taking into account the testimonies of Columbus and his companions, the calculations done for the distribution of the Indians in 1514, and their own mathematical model, estimate the population of Hispaniola at 8 000 000 at the time of Columbus' arrival. Frank Moya Pons gives a figure of 377 000 persons for Hispaniola. Rosenblat also give estimates for the population of the main islands of the Caribbean: Hispaniola, 100 000, Cuba, 80 000, Puerto Rico, 50 000, Jamaica, 40 000, and the Lesser Antilles and Bahamas, 30 000. We lack reliable data on the population of the Caribbean regions of Central America, Colombia and Venezuela.[54]

It is believed that the settlement of these islands began in approximately BC 5000, with the first waves of settlers of the Greater Antilles arriving

271

just 2000 years before our era. These were initially populations of the group of the so-called independent languages, which were later displaced by members of the Arawak language family, who, in turn, were hunted and harassed by peoples speaking the Carib language.

Most of the population of the Greater Antilles spoke the Arawak language. Exceptions to this general rule were the hunter-gatherer groups found in the western part of Cuba and the Ciguayos and Macoryxes of Hispaniola. In the Lesser Antilles most people were of the Carib family.

As I have said, in order to go a bit further in these ethnographic analyses, it is perhaps necessary to make a theoretical generalization that does not allow us to consider certain concrete aspects of the particular cultures in their diversity but which does, in return, make it easier for us to reconstruct the intellectual and ideological framework of the societies. This generalization is that these societies and cultures could be seen under the model of tribal society, a statement which is undeniable in the case of the Taínos, among whom there existed the figure of a confederation of tribes. This theory is also applicable to the African groups transported to the Americas as slaves: their cultures in Africa were eminently tribal. It suggests, therefore, a close relationship between the logical mental structures of the New World indigenes and those of the African slaves.

The characterizations of tribalism that have been attempted have been undertaken also from the standpoint of the phenomenal criteria I criticized earlier. Moreover, while the structural specialization of current industrialized societies makes it relatively easy to delimit the economic, political, social, legal and ideological spheres, it is very difficult to delimit those spheres in the case of tribal societies. This in turn presents us with the need for more holistic or all-inclusive epistemological and methodological criteria. Thus, in analysing the rational structures of this type of society, we will speak, for clarity, of economic, political, kinship, magico-religious structures, etc., as though these were autonomous domains.

One first important factor in classifying the tribal society is constituted by the fact that in these societies people use a logic of the concrete.[55] The capacity for abstraction, therefore, is not well developed. The terms used for the construction of ideological systems are concrete: animal and vegetable species, astronomical and meteorological phenomena, cultural and natural objects. The gods and other spirits are endowed with the same virtues and defects as human beings. Therefore, the idea of God and the Catholic saints was accepted, but endowed with a special significance which removes them from their original context. A good example of the misunderstandings which might result is an anecdote about Bartolomé

Columbus, the Admiral's brother, who once caught some Indians burying Christian images:

> This act was interpreted by the Spaniards as an outrage, a true profanation of Christian symbols, when in truth it was common practice among the Taínos to bury images of their idols in the fields in order to guarantee a good crop.[56]

José Juan Arrom relates an anecdote told by Fray Pané in which having converted a family to Catholicism, he left them a group of figures of saints for them to worship:

> And it happened that, the friar having gone, six Indians arrived, took the images and carried them away. And Pané added: When these had left the altar-place, they threw the images to the ground, and covered them with earth, and then urinated upon them, saying: Now your fruits will be great and good. And this because they buried them in a planted field, saying that the crop that had been planted there would be good.[57]

Another fact important to note in the construction of this 'science of the concrete' is that this worldview generally makes use of metaphors that establish a series of equivalences between elements located on different planes of societal and individual existence: macrocosm and microcosm are thus united. In other words, beings and objects are given a multiplicity of significations which derive from their insertion into numerous chains of similarity or contiguity. This brings elements which apparently have no features in common into a whole endowed with meaning. Thus, in the previous quotation, we see a sympathetic yet at the same time contaminating magic at work, for the presence of gods within the earth guarantees the growth of the plants and a good crop. Therefore, we should not be surprised at the fact that the indigenous peoples and the African blacks situated the cultural traits imposed on them by Europeans within new chains of signifieds with new meanings, 'denaturalizing' them and creating the appearance of a perfect acculturation. Roger Bastide makes the following observations about this issue:

> The syncretism cannot be explained in any other way: in principle it is no more than a 'mask' which allows the naive race of masters to believe that the blacks are celebrating the 'Christian mysteries' in their own way, that is, singing and dancing before the [figures of] saints, while in truth they are worshipping the *orisha* or the *vodún* ... The

syncretism is explained in this case by the isomorphism of the two religions in which we see a single God and a whole corps of intermediaries between Him and man. This makes the name of the saint no more than the white name of the same entity that the blacks worship under its African name.[58]

In this societary model commercial economic rationality is totally absent. In fact in many indigenous languages the concept of work did not even exist.[59] The production of excess was limited, and with that there was an attempt to restrain competition and to keep the emergence of higher regulatory units within certain limits. There was even talk that the Taínos (who belonged to the Arawak linguistic family) celebrated their *areytos* or large festivals in order, in part, to consume all the excess that had been produced, in a phenomenon that reminds us of the potlatch so well known to anthropologists and ethnologists. At the same time, this helped avoid the waste of what we would today call the labour force. It is quite probable that subsistence commodities were excluded from the exchange system, so that exchanges were carried out, at least within the tribe, on the basis of sumptuary goods (*guanín*, for example), which generally had a certain sacredness about them. All this explains the presence of a very moderate rhythm of work, though increased to gravely serious extremes with the introduction of the *encomienda* system, which many writers take as the main cause of the extinction of the native peoples and the depopulation of the Antilles.

Other writers, such as Guillermo Céspedes del Castillo, are inclined to think that the greatest destructive effect lay in infectious or contagious diseases, which were one mechanism of domination. In that vein, Céspedes says the following:

> The decimation of the aboriginal population ... began very soon on the lands of the island of Hispaniola with illnesses caused by soil and water contamination (1505), when the Spaniards brought together a large number of natives and concentrated them at the site where the gold was panned in order for them to extract the gold-bearing sand. This pollution brought on true epidemics of dysentery, etc. But the most serious time was when the infectious and contagious diseases of the Old World arrived, which began very soon also, and which from 1518 onward not only accompanied the *conquistadores* and settlers, but actually preceded them. In truth, all the horror and destruction attributed to the conquest, I would daresay 95 per cent of it, at least, was the horror and destruction relating to the bacterial aspect of this ecological revolution wrought by the arrival of the Europeans in the New World.[60]

This 'exchange of bacteria' was noted from the earliest days of the conquest and colonization. The Europeans contracted such diseases as syphilis and brought with them diseases such as measles, the first great epidemic of this illness occurring in 1518.

The problem of the physical extinction of the indigenous peoples grew so serious that by 1518 reports were indicating that in the case of Hispaniola there were only 11 000 natives left, and that it was calculated that they too would be dead in three or four years.

Diseases also lent themselves to an important ideological use: they were generally seen as divine punishment. They were the fury of God wreaked upon the Indians who would not submit to His faith. They were also seen as an expression of divine anger against the Europeans and the abuses they committed against the indigenous peoples. The presence of this *ira Dei*, this 'heavenly chastisement', was to constitute another archetype whose psychological effects were very important not only on the cultures of the Caribbean but across all the rest of the continent as well, acting as it did as a mechanism of social containment and individual resignation.

From the point of view of the indigenous economy, the role played by social distance was very important. Social distance defined the rules of exchange, in which reciprocity was of utmost importance. Gifts given by the indigenous peoples to the first Europeans had this meaning. Reciprocity even bound the chiefs, leaders, or *caciques* with respect to their subordinates. This feature defined a part of the economic and political culture present in Caribbean societies.

The Taíno religious systems

José Juan Arrom has analysed the Taíno religious systems in some detail, basing his work mainly on the chronicles written by Fray Ramón Pané, who in speaking of the Taínos' supreme deity says that 'they believe that he is in heaven and is immortal, and that no one can see him, and that he has a mother but has no beginning, and is called Yócahu Bagua Maórocoti'.[61] These Arawak terms translate more or less as 'the spirit of the cassava and the sea which had no masculine forebear', that is, who was not born of man. This supreme being lived through several avatars which saw him be frog, manatee, serpent, and other animals beneficial or harmful to crops.

Of this supreme being it was said that he warned the *cacique* Cáicihu about the coming of the Spaniards. Once more, the anecdote is told by Pané and quoted by Arrom:

275

*Y a aquel gran señor, que dicen que está en el cielo, según está escrito
en el principio de este libro, hizo Cáicihu un ayuno.... . Y dicen que este
cacique afirmó haber hablado con Yacahuguamá, quien le había dicho
que cuantos después de su muerte quedasen vivos, gozarían poco tiempo
de su dominio, porque vendría a su país una gente vestida, que los
habría de dominar y matar, y que se morirían de hambre. Pero ellos
pensaron primero que éstos habrían de ser los caníbales, mas luego,
consideraron que éstos no hacían sino robar y huir, creyeron que otra
gente había de ser aquella que decía el cemí. De donde ahora creen que
se trata del Almirante y de la gente que lleva consigo.*[62]

[And to that great lord, who they say art in heaven, as it is written in
the beginning of this book, Cáicihu made a fast ... And they say that
this *cacique* declared that he had spoken with Yacahuguamá, who told
him that all of those who were alive after his death would enjoy but a
short time in their domain, for there would come to their country a
clothed people who would dominate and kill them, and that they
would starve to death. But they [the Indians] thought first that these
would be the cannibals, though later, they realized that these did
nothing but rob and run away, so realized that that race spoken of by
their *cemí* (the deity) must be another race. And therefore they now
believe that this is the Admiral and the men he brings with him.]

The deity, according to Pané, has a mother, and she is known by many
names: Attabeira, Mamona, Guacarapita, Iiella and Buimazoa. The translation
of this name seems to be 'mother of the waters'. Arrom sees this divinity as
linked to the tides, the moon, and menstruation. He also connects her with
the three stones which the *caciques* wore around their necks, and which
served the following functions: one was for good crops, another for allowing
women to give birth without pain, and the third for making the sun come
out or making rain during droughts.

In addition to these spirits there are the gods of the sun and the rain,
which emerged from a cave located in the country of the *cacique* named
Mautiatihuel, the 'Lord of the Dawn'. These were two *cemíes*, the twin brothers Boinayel and Márohu, the 'Lord of the Dark Serpent and the Clouds' and
the 'Lord of the Cloudless Sky'. The so-called tearful *cemíes* were also part of
the cult of Boinayel. Boinayel and Máhoru were, then, the gods of rain and
the sun, and a third cult was devoted to the serpent rainbow.

Arrom details the existence of other deities such as the 'Lady of the
Winds', who might call on two auxiliary spirits, the 'Lord of the Region of the
Dead', the dog god, and the *cemí* Baibrama, used by the shamans in their

healing ceremonies. In the oral literature of a religious nature, the cycle of the four twins, the probable sons of Mother Earth, plays an important role.

The presence of these *cemíes*[63] among the Taínos suggests the possibility of the existence of totemic systems in which a homologous relationship was established between the various social groups and the beings or natural objects, as among these spirits there were such deities as natural phenomena, family spirits, personified gods, geographic accidents, etc. Therefore, culture and nature mutually included one another. However, unlike the African cults, the phenomenon of hermeticism is not suggested here. Previously, on the contrary, the Taíno religion was characterized by the permeability of myths and beliefs, to the degree that both Christ and the saints were easily incorporated into the pantheon of *cemíes*. The interest in gold demonstrated by the Europeans, added to their military success, led some to suggest the possibility that even gold might be a *cemí*. Thus,

> Hatuey [a *cacique*] proposed that the Indians themselves should worship the Christian god gold in an *areyto*, so that he [gold] might intercede for them with the *conquistadores*, and at last proposed that this god be thrown into the bottom of the river, so that the Christians might not find him, and when they tired of looking, leave his lands – this argument intriguingly correct, though too late.[64]

The Taíno *cacique* Caonabo planned to use the Christian *cemíes* gold, tin and copper in a war he was preparing against the conquerors. Cassá says that this *cacique* believed that the bell at Isabela was a *cemí* that talked.[65] This shows us that any object or being might become a *cemí*, within a religious schema of great permeability.

It is generally thought that the magico-religious beliefs and practices of the aboriginal peoples had no influence on their conquerors. The persecution carried out against the native cults makes research into this question difficult. Still, it does not seem unreasonable to conjecture that Spaniards may have taken part clandestinely in the *areytos* and in consultations with the shamans, or *behiques*. We must not forget that beyond its external forms, the Spanish sense of religion was permeated with mysticism, superstition and Muslim cultural traits, and that divination and omens had great importance. This might have led to the sort of multiplicity of signifieds which were a feature of the religious ideology of the Caribbean, in which a visible or explicit 'Catholic' code coexists with other beliefs that endow the Catholic signs with a new significance and that are kept at underlying or implicit levels of the society. It is even probable that the first use made of tobacco by the Spaniards themselves was for divination. We should not forget that all of these elements were latent in the mentality of the Europeans, repressed only by religious intolerance and dogmatism.

Kinship relations

From the standpoint of the kinship relations[66] present in the aboriginal societies, the most important feature, apart from the existence of classificatory systems, is linked to the pre-eminence of matrilineal filiation. Some writers even speak of the importance achieved by matrifocality. There was payment of a dowry for the marriage, and the sexual division of labour seems to have been established. The insertion of the Spaniards into this model strengthened this phenomenon of the paternal absence and added an entire ideology based on the Mediterranean concept of honour, whose structure, in simplified terms, is the following: seek to possess material goods in order to possess persons. This panorama was rounded out with the idea of the existence of a social distance which generated a contextual morality. Thus, while the women close to an individual (mother, daughter and wife) are sacred, other women are not. This ideology of honour also implies the predominance of the social sanction over the normative or legal sanction. We are once again up against the idea of a normative and institutional formalism which leads to the existence of a double ideology: the explicit one, which holds to this normative façade, and the implicit one, which is backed by different value systems. I believe that this normative and institutional formalism was a distinctive feature of the intellectual and ideological culture of the Caribbean.

With regard to the family formalism, I find that the following quotation from Jean Benoist illuminates the question quite well:

> Numerous studies of the Antillean family have showed the considerable difference between the normative context enunciated in each case and the behaviour actually performed. A double system is observed, in which the stable nuclear family, united by marriage and admitted as a general model, coexists with a devalorized model characterized by the weak cohesion of the cohabitational unit, the instability of the unions, and successive or simultaneous polygyny ... Under these conditions, given the expressed norm of marriage, a constellation of behaviours is developed which centre on the 'matrifocal' family.[67]

The external structures of indigenous kinship relations were altered. From very early on, unions began to be entered into between Spanish men and Indian women. The absence of white women was a cause of this phenomenon. Mixed marriages were authorized by the King in 1501 and the Governor of Hispaniola, Nicolás de Ovando, supported the legalization of concubinage. However, the Spaniards preferred to maintain this kind of relationship or contract marriage with white women, even if they were prostitutes, whose activities were legalized in 1526. The Indian women, aware of their inferiority, began to employ a series of artifices in order to whiten their skin. Much the same thing happened later with negro men and women and with mestizos as well, giving rise to what were known as 'pure blood' trials. This fact had important repercussions both on ideologies and on the forms of self-perception and self-esteem developed in the Caribbean.

Kinship had great importance in the tribal societies, for it was on the basis of kinship, for example, that one inherited property, that distribution was made of the means of production and the excess of production, that one occupied a position in the social organization of production, and that one obtained political or administrative positions and achieved social prestige. Therefore, the centre of tribal strategy was the reproduction of the society through the preservation, at all costs, of the webs of alliance and filiation. In the Caribbean, kinship was centred mainly on consanguinity, which was generally in conflict with the fluidity and dynamism of the rules that governed residency.

The economic and political experiments in the Caribbean were tinged by the influence of these kinship patterns, and above all by the creation of new modes of alliance, among which *compadrazgo* and *padrinazgo* had special importance. In these relationships, parental, religious and economic links were joined. Thus, the intellectual, ideological and artistic dimensions became much more difficult to separate from other aspects of the culture, such as the material aspects.

Myths and the concept of time

The earth, as I have mentioned, was considered by the native peoples of the region to be a female entity, and in one of the myths that was most widespread among the Taínos and the Arawak peoples of the continent, there is the notion that both the sun and the moon are offspring of the earth, an idea which expresses a geocentric and even ethnocentric conception of the universe and which is not far distant from the prevailing European notions about this subject. We find this ethnocentrism most deeply rooted in the Carib groups, in which the factor conferring identity and at the same time humanity is the language. Thus I believe that the famous 'Hana Karina Rote', or 'only we Caribs are men', is the explanation for the anthropophagy of the Carib group: the person who does not speak our language is not a man, he

279

or she is an animal, a being located in a position symmetrically opposed to the gods on the social continuum, and therefore edible.

The concepts of time held by the indigenous peoples, in which the paradigmatic also comes into play, are important. Through these time concepts, a cyclical, recurrent, closed history is constructed, and this history is structured in such a way that any out-of-the-ordinary event is perceived as an omen or presage, and this, in turn, perceived as a law which will inevitably be obeyed. Unusual events, therefore, were absorbed and interpreted in the light of a pre-existent intellectual and social ordering. Thus, the present was subordinated to the past, which is covered with the mantle of the mythic, while prophecy functions into the future. But myth and prophecy are equivalent; the future is conceived in terms of a repetition of past events. Thus the shamans, seers and *behiques* became the historians of these societies. The cyclic nature of time was also an ideological and intellectual constant in the emerging societies. With regard to this, Tzvetan Todorov says the following:

> The individual's future is ordered by the collective past; the individual does not construct his future, his future is revealed to him; thus the role of the calendar, omens, auguries. The question that is characteristic of this world is not, as it was among the Spanish *conquistadores* or the Russian revolutionaries, the praxeological question 'what to do?', but rather the epistemological question 'how to know?'.[68]

As unknown signs emerged they had to be assimilated by means of the models of thoughts which were at hand. Thus, just as the Europeans made use of their intellectual structures – filled, as I have noted, with the contents of their everyday ideology, including Aristotelian ideas and Christian beliefs and dogmas – the aborigines also applied their own tribal models, endowing the invaders with divine nature or thinking they were simple animals, being terrified by the horses,[69] the dogs, and the gunpowder, debating the immortality of the new arrivals. Several times Fernández de Oviedo mentions this clash of signs, this is one such occasion:

> There a horse died ... and he had him buried secretly ... so that the Indians might not see it or know that the horses were mortal, which [the horses] they fear greatly, for they had never seen any of them there [before].[70]

On another occasion the Indians made an empirical test, to see whether the Spaniards died or were immortal, and in this test they drowned a man named Salcedo.

And when they confirmed that they [the Christians] are mortal, in the way I have said, they made it known to their *cacique*, who each day sent other Indians to see if Salcedo [the dead Spaniard] got up, and still doubting if he was being told the truth, he himself determined to go and see, until several days had passed, and they saw that sinner [Salcedo] much more spoiled and rotten. And thence they took heart and courage for their rebellion.[71]

THE AFRICAN INFLUENCE

Now we must touch upon the role of the intellectual, ideological and artistic structures that entered the new cultures of the Caribbean by way of the peoples brought here from Africa. The beginnings of the European slave trade in Africa were linked to the Portuguese, who began this hateful practice in the first half of the fifteenth century, after having rounded Cape Bojador and reached the Ouro River. The slaves, often turned over to the white men by rival tribes in exchange for various kinds of goods, came from many different regions. The figures on the number of slaves transported to the New World are not known exactly, and in fact are wildly contradictory. The Jesuits, for example, state that during the sixteenth century 12 000 slaves left Angola each year, 7000 from the Congo, while Bastide points out that the *Enciclopedia Católica* talks about a total of 12 million slaves transported from Africa to the New World, a figure which cannot be proven.[72] Other figures state the presence in Santo Domingo of 12 000 blacks and 5000 whites in the year 1546. In 1568 there were said to be 20 000 blacks. As for the *cimarrónes*, the escaped slaves, the data we possess today indicate that there were between 2000 and 3000 in Santo Domingo in 1542. But none of these figures would seem to conform to reality, and writers such as Curtin question them. Still, for more exact information on this question, we refer the reader to the chapter by Enriqueta Vilá Vilar in this volume.

This is what Joseph Ki-Zerbo has to say about these new inhabitants of the Caribbean:

The black man, already upon his arrival a slave, was stripped of his name, separated from his family and his neighbours in his community. He fell into the anonymity of servitude, and the rotation and rapid dispersion of the labourers subjected them to such a degree of atomization that they became objects, sunk in absolute isolation and alienation. From that moment onward, they lacked all social referents.[73]

281

The daily life of the first slaves

Descriptions of the life of these first slaves indicate that they lived in collections of huts, appropriating the construction techniques and materials of the Indians in building their own *bohíos*. With regard to the first black settlements, Manuel Moreno Fraginals says that:

> it must be kept in mind that when they arrived in the New World, most of these Africans were not integrated into organically created and developed demographic complexes. On the contrary, they were taken into uninhabited areas where they were formed into homogeneous labour groups, under absolute individual control, and set to work in agriculture or mining. Or they were incorporated, under the same strictures, into a production unit of the same kind which was already in existence.[74]

Many of the dwellings were constructed using a system of labour organization that included *cayapas* or gangs of workers working together, forms of cooperation which involved communities working together for an individual who would in turn be obliged to lend his contribution in building houses for the other members of the community. Supervision generally was in the hands of a white overseer and one, or several, black bosses. Some slaves managed to become artisans and craftsmen, plying the trade of shoemaker or carpenter, or selling water, or sometimes even becoming a gang foreman.

Children were brought up in special houses, called in Cuba *casas de criollitos*, where they were cared for and fed by a nanny or nursemaid. Women, who were always fewer in number than men, were also occupied, either at farm labour or domestic chores, and we should not forget that in many cases they were also obliged to provide sexual services to their white 'masters'.

Clothing was scarce, and was regulated by legislation. It consisted of one suit of clothing per year (called the *esquifación*), its component or components varying according to region. Generally the slaves were not given shoes. The food was good,[75] especially when there were places in which the slaves were allowed to cultivate their own small plots of land (*conucos*) whose products they could themselves consume. On the sugar plantations a great taste for sugar was acquired, and this brought on a parallel taste for salt:

> This was another result of the work on the plantations. Working all day in the sun, or in the high temperatures of the boiler sheds, the slaves eliminated all the salt through their pores with perspiration, and required a daily supplement of sodium chloride.[76]

282

For their aches and pains and illnesses the slaves continued to practise their known therapeutic formulae, such as herbs and poultices, and in these lay the origin of what is today known somewhat pejoratively as *curanderismo*. A slave's life expectancy was from five to seven years.

Diversions and entertainments were allowed only on Sundays and certain special days related to feast days of the Catholic Church. From early on, the feasts of Corpus Christi, St Peter and St John (San Pedro and San Juan) were celebrated, with the addition of dances, musical instruments and African masks.

Besides the rebellions which inevitably occurred (as in the sixteenth century Wolofs' rebellions in Puerto Rico and Santo Domingo), other forms of opposition to the power of the white men were suicide, self-mutilation, sabotage, and the killing of whites. Of special interest in this regard are the communities of escaped black slaves, the *cimarrónes*, also called *cumbes* or *quilombos*, in which there was an attempt to reconstruct the conditions of life the men and women had known in Africa. Another form of passive resistance was what Germán Carrera Damas has called *ladinismo*, or cunning, and which he defines in the following way:

> This passive resistance, as a form of rejection of oppression and a way of channelling the trauma of a slave's life, was manifested in simulated obedience in which one did nothing or as little as possible of what was ordered, or did it badly or half-heartedly, and exercising a degree of violence against the instruments of production. This tradition of *ladinismo* – faking tasks, which basically were either not done or done badly, incompletely, or imperfectly – has had serious repercussions on current black social groups, since it formed negative modules of labour behavior.[77]

In the Caribbean there came to be many freed slaves, as well, called *horros*. These and their families little by little occupied the peripheries of the cities and took up work that whites and mestizos considered beneath them. These freedmen were allowed to form councils, *cabildos*, which included foremen or captains. From these early organizations came *cofradías*, or 'guilds', which had their centres in churches and which not only allowed certain magico-religious expressions to survive but served as centres of mutual aid and support. These guilds in turn became tied to certain religious sects that emerged later.

African beliefs and practices

It is important, especially from the phenomenal point of view, to respect the distinction between African culture and 'black' culture. This difference leads us to the still-unresolved problem of the originality of the beliefs and practices of the Africans brought to the New World. This is a key issue for arriving at the logical moulds or structures that define the African contribution to the formation of the ideological, intellectual and artistic dimensions of culture in the Caribbean.

As for the study of the ideological and intellectual structures of the Africans, we should point out that the observations made earlier as to the pre-eminence of a concrete and metaphoric mode of thought[78] among Amerindian tribal groups seem to be applicable also in analysing the African modes of rationality. This concrete thinking does not distinguish between the sensible, tangible dimensions of the world and the intellectual dimensions, nor between the material and immaterial dimensions, nor between the objective and subjective aspects of reality.

In attempting to draw an equivalence between the logical and intellectual structures of Africans and Amerindians, I do not pretend to make an evolutionist comparison or a functionalist assimilation of diverse cultures, but rather to understand their structural character, as it is this, more than folkloric observations, that allows us to gauge the true contribution made by Africa to the Americas. Once again, we face the difficulty of studying cultures in which it is not easy to abstract theoretical categories from phenomenal forms. Still, one example of what we are suggesting here is found in the linguistic acculturation achieved in the Caribbean, for European grammatical contents were from the beginning ordered by the logical principles of African grammars, as has been shown by the interesting work of Richard Allsopp, cited in the bibliography at the end of this book.

The relatively small capacity for abstraction may be illustrated by the virtually ineffable nature of African categories, which allow one to think about, and carry out a synthesis of what for traditional Western philosophy are contradictions or oppositions. Moreover, these ineffable elements are in the things themselves, they are their unity, or, better yet, their essence. One must make clear that this is not a question of animating forces superimposed upon beings or external to objects. Perhaps this very relative difficulty of abstraction implies the necessity to endow the non-living with life and to assign it virtues and defects similar to those of humans. We might even suggest that the great importance of trances and possessions in African religions derives from this necessity to think of and experience everything in concrete terms.

African anthropology suggests a continuity between the living and the dead. It is important to make clear that for this line of thought '"existing" and "living" are not the same thing. The dead do not live, though they exist'.[79] Ancestors constitute a higher social category whose responsibility it is to guarantee the fertility of the earth and of men. The spirits are beings, they possess life. They once dwelt in a body and probably will one day do so again, so they can be reincarnated in a child. In discussing Yoruba *orisha*-worship, Miguel Barnet says the following:

> *Orisha*-worship is linked to the notion of a family: a family of numer-ous members who are all the offspring of one forebear, a family which comprises the living and the dead. The *orisha* would in principle be a deified ancestor who when alive established ties which guaranteed him control over certain forces of nature, such as thunder, wind, fresh or salt water. He might also be able to perform certain activities such as hunting, metalworking, and understanding the properties of plants and how to use them. The power, or *eché*, of the ancestor-*orisha* would, after his death, give him the ability to embody himself for a time in one of his descendants during a phenomenon of possession brought on by the *orisha* himself.[80]

Alongside these essential spirits, people had a multiplicity of souls. When one of these souls was stolen, a man might become ill with certain diseases. The theory of multiple souls was introduced by Africans into the Americas, as were a series of funerary practices and especially that of 'dancing' the dead person so that he or she might lose the way back should he or she wish to return.

The greatest disgrace for an African lay in not leaving offspring, for posterity guaranteed that the person would be remembered. A dead man or woman was more or less strong depending upon the number of descendants he or she possessed. The greatest curse that could be dealt a person was wishing him or her not to have children. The childbearing abilities of women were a strategic element of first importance, and an infertile woman was con-sidered highly polluting. Those responsible for this infertility were the deceased members of the family. Therefore, the family's relationship with the dead was signified by great ambivalence: the dead were rewarded with offer-ings (often food, which is a means by which they could be imagined as alive) if they gave abundant crops and many children, or they were punished if they did not.

The ancestor cult, according to Joseph Ki-Zerbo, had a certain eschato-logical and redemptive sense to it for the slaves that were brought to the Americas:

> The ancestor cult, so characteristic of the religion of the Africans, for whom the dead were not alive yet did exist with greater force than here below, acquired in the context of slavery a significance which

reached the sublime: the dead, now free of the tyrant-master's rod, would make, it was believed, in a reverse direction, the infernal voyage across the Ocean; sailing without bonds back to the beloved continent, they would be reunited with the venerated world of their own ancestors, there beyond the 'big water', 'in the land of the Guinea'.[81]

Where the accommodation of external European customs to the African mode of rationality is most palpable is in religion. God and the Catholic saints were assimilated without great strain into the pantheons of the various religions brought from Africa. Catholicism made its own adjustments to African beliefs, and yet most people think the opposite. Let us look once again at what Miguel Barnet has to say in this regard:

In the natural and spontaneous process of syncresis, which took place when the first African established the equivalence between his deities and the Catholic saints, Yoruba features determined the conditions of that equivalency. Forced by the repressive imposition of the Catholic Church, which in frequent historical periods recognized none but its own pre-eminence, the black African produced one of the most complex sociological phenomena in syncretizing his deities with the Catholic saints.[82]

The saints were treated as though they were in very close kinship to man. If they were good to men and kept some promise or granted some favour they were given rum and special food, or taken up and danced with. If not, they were punished by being left outside in the rain, or tied up, or not given drink or food, etc.

The exception to this syncretism is perhaps the case of the secret societies, such as the *ñáñigos* of Cuba, which tended to preserve in more or less pure form the beliefs and practices of Africa. Many of these societies even hid themselves behind the façade of the guilds, which, as I have noted, were organized around the figure of a saint. All of this was motivated mainly by the terrible religious persecution the blacks were subjected to, and out of political reasons as well. Much the same thing happened in the *cimarrón* settlements where there was an attempt to reconstruct and also maintain intact the myths and rituals the Africans had brought with them.

For the African, the diverse living beings, unlike men and objects, did not in themselves possess movement. It was men, or the dead, that conferred the ability to move, and that did so through the intellect, which in turn was connected to the word. This explains the importance possessed by the verb as a giver of movement. Also, heard words possessed greater wisdom than spoken ones, so the sense of hearing had pre-eminence over the other senses. Rhythms and harmonies were favoured over forms and contents. Therefore, many Afro-American magico-religious beliefs were related to the granting or theft of names, to good and evil words that might be spoken, to the effectiveness of the vehemence with which spells and formulae were uttered, to the signatures or magical traces of the spirits. With regard to the importance of names, Leovigildo López has said the following:

> It is said that no *briyumbero* writes his complete signature, for if he did someone might use it to do him harm. According to informants, the saint is found in the signature; that is, when a *briyumbero* traces out his signature, the saint comes into it. Thus one might assume that when a *briyumbero* writes his signature he thinks that he himself is potentially to be found there and that therefore anyone who possesses that signature may do as he will with his [the signer's] person.[83]

There is no doubt that we might speak of the arrival in the New World of different systems of religion, quite complicated from the point of view of ritual, with rich pantheons and an extensive hierarchy of priests and priestesses. These are not, as one can see if one studies them with some care, purely magical beliefs and practices, but complex religious systems. Among these systems one sees:

1 Osha Lukumi, *orisha*-worship, which is of Yoruba origin and which evolves into *santería*.
2 Abakwa, which comes from the Calabar groups, and which evolves into the *ñáñigos*, with its two varieties, the *efor* or *efok* and the *efi* or *efik*.
3 Vodú or Vodún, which originated in Dahomey among the Fon.
4 Orula or Orúnmila, which later became linked to *santería* also.
5 The group originating in the Congo, the Mayombe cult, with its Palo Monte or Palo Mayor order, and which joins *santería* by way of the members of this order.

This latter group's most characteristic expression is the cult of the dead.

The common beliefs and features of these religious systems are the following:

1 There exists a spirit or life principle shared by both the living and the dead, both beings and objects, both men and nature.
2 The vital principle may be controlled by the name.

3 There is the presence of a very large group of spirits (as many as 400 *orishas* in Nigeria) which control every movement of any being or thing in the universe.

4 Great importance is given to ancestors or the dead.

5 There is a pre-eminence of rituals of possessions, with states of ecstasy and adorcisms.

6 Decisive importance is given divination as a means of controlling human and natural forces.

The stereotype of the negro contained other important elements, many of them constructed out of degraded and degrading views of these religious systems. Thus, the negro was tied to witchcraft, to black magic. Even the Indian feared African witchcraft. Once again, there is a paradigmatic chain in which

negro = night = death = witchcraft = moon = devil/demon

until finally one comes to the last term, 'evil'.[84] The *cimarrónes* took advantage of this paradigm to surround their settlements with a halo of mystery that kept their pursuers out. To this stereotype one might add that of the archetypes of the 'black Apollo' and 'black Venus', with their attributes of ardour and voluptuousness. With respect to these latter stereotypes, Manuel Moreno Fraginals makes the following observation:

> The tremendous disproportion of men to women created a tense climate of repression and a sexual obsessiveness that were expressed in a thousand ways: tales, games, songs, dances ... The pathological sexual obsession that tinges the world of the black men and women of the Americas did not originate in the physiological or cultural conditions of the African, [however,] but in the subhuman plantation system ... Slavery deformed the slave's sexual life, and racists justified the deformations by inventing the myth of the sadistic sexuality of the black man, the immorality of the black woman, and the lechery of the mulatto woman. And all this independent of the fact that in urban nuclei, and in the single household, the sexual life was the link by which women improved their economic conditions.[85]

For traditionally oral cultures, rhythm plays a determining role, and if to that we add the fundamental role played by fecundity, we find rituals of similar magic expressed in dance, in which there is a mimesis or representation of the actions that comprise the sexual conquest to the point of orgasm. Among the best-known dances was the *maní* or 'peanut', the *makuta* or *kisomba kia ngóngo*, the *palo* or *garabato*, to name just a few. It has been said that these dances were secularized when they arrived in the Americas, becoming in fact virtual 'orgies' in which even whites participated. The famous *rochelas*, or 'shindigs', derived from these. Among African musical instruments, besides the drums with their different tones (the *minas, curbetas, rechonchos,* etc.), there were the marimbas, marimbolas, maracas, and other membranophones and idiophones. But returning once more to structural analysis, I believe that the importance of the religious aspect lies in a logical order underlying the mere external secularized or folklorized expressions of it.

I have already pointed out the presence of a particular kind of 'economic rationality' in tribal societies, in which the economic sphere, in the strict sense, is closely tied to non-economic factors such as kinship, politics, magic and religion. Africans shared this vision of the economic sphere, contributing models of the social organization of labour based on cooperation and reciprocity among family groups and lineages. The same thing occurred with the rules for the distribution of property and of the products of labour, in which the parental and magico-religious components play a role of first importance. With regard to this point, however, there is a controversy between those who think that this is a question of traits which are typical of African tribes, on the one side, and those on the other who believe in processes of adaptation to the new conditions of life imposed in the Americas. The same occurs in studying some of the characteristics of kinship systems, such as simultaneous polygamy, successive polygyny, matrifocality, and matrilineality, and even in studying music.

THE DEVELOPMENT OF STRUCTURES OF THOUGHT AND VISION

It is true that there is a more or less exact time at which the initial encounters between Europeans and the native American peoples took place in the Caribbean.[86] The dates given for each case are the following: Hispaniola area (Santo Domingo), 1492–1508; Cuba region, 1492–1516; Puerto Rico area, 1493–1516; Jamaica area, 1492–1516; and the continental region of Venezuela and north-east Colombia, 1498–1570. Exactness with respect to the definitive implantation of ideological, intellectual and artistic structures of thought and vision, however, is much more difficult to achieve, for the theories, myths, styles, motivations, ideas, prejudices, idealizations and stereotypes, among the many elements which go to make up those structures of thought and vision, have neither a date of appearance nor a time of disappearance in the same way that instruments and tools, techniques, and other components of the material culture have.

The territories which were little by little conquered were governed, at least in theory, from Santo Domingo, where a vice-royalty was created that functioned from 1526 onward. However, this power was more formal than real, and it is in the day-to-day life in the various regions that 'governance' may be found. This is the typical example of the coexistence of two rationalities: one normative, institutional and explicit, and the other implicit and valorative.

There has been much discussion of the total, or almost total, extinction of the indigenous cultures of the Caribbean, especially their religious, artistic, intellectual and scientific dimensions. I believe that this is a half-truth, for the truth is that what disappeared were most of the sensible, palpable, tangible (or phenomenal) aspects of those cultures, while the logic of thought that formed them and gave them meaning remained. This logic of thought, this *Weltanschauung*, served to order the new contents imposed by the Europeans. In addition, some aspects of the visible culture survived as 'folkloric' remains.

It is unquestionable that certain material beliefs and practices had considerable influence on the formation of new intellectual, ideological and artistic structures. For example, the practice of 'ransom', by which mirrors, beads and needles were exchanged for gold, pearls and precious stones, left a very important ideological impression which took concrete form in the internalization of a contextual morality and the spirit of 'quick-wittedness' in economic exchanges. Equally important in the formation of a world-model was the use of the mechanisms of political, military and religious domination which has been discussed in the previous pages. All these mechanisms of domination were 'answered' by the development of forms of submissiveness which played an important role in the intellectual, ideological and artistic dimensions of culture in the Caribbean.

Furthermore, it is also unquestionable that necessity led many colonizers to depend in large part on the means of transport, patterns of consumption, and certain technological elements of the indigenous people. Among the latter we might mention housing, forms of light river and sea transport, mechanisms for preserving and cooking or otherwise processing food, medications, systems of orientation within the unknown territories, interpreters and translators, etc. From these 'tools' there arose a certain effective ambivalence toward the indigenous people, and this is one aspect of the intellectual and ideological structures of the Caribbean culture.

But let us try to analyse in terms of its concrete and visible manifestations that which emerged in the Caribbean from the point of view of the intellectual, ideological and artistic aspects of the culture of these new societies.

Architecture and city-building

From the point of view of architecture, we find that there was a tension in the New World between what was called the 'style of the period' and certain personal yearnings, a tension generally resolved in favour of the characteristic anonymity of the first. Spanish architecture, however, was less influenced by prototypical architectural tendencies than other European nations, and this allows a small door to open into the realm of the personal. In Hispaniola one might point to the architectural work of Rodrigo de Liendo, to whom the building of the Iglesia de las Mercedes is attributed, as is the Iglesia de San Francisco as well as the building of the Bastidas Chapel in the cathedral.

Liendo's architectural solutions to certain problems of forms and contents categorize him as a sort of pre-baroque figure. According to Palm, his personal expression is seen most clearly in the apse of the Iglesia de San Francisco. There, one can see an attempt to achieve a unity of the contradictory forces represented by on the one hand the particular architectural vocabulary of the late Middle Ages and on the other the expression of the sentiments of community revitalized by the Italian Renaissance. In this attempt, the forms are the bearers of a new signified, which links Liendo's art to the style of the Counter-Reformation.

Thus, the religious architecture of the sixteenth-century Caribbean is signalled by a combination of styles, producing what Henríquez Ureña has called the 'Isabelline style' in honour of Queen Isabella of Castile.[87] Thus, for example, in the monasteries and convents we find gothic expressions in the body of the churches alongside Renaissance elements in the portals. The richness of the portals contrasts with the rigid austerity of the convent churches, leading Palm to say that 'thus there is another expression, on the soil of the Americas, of the clash between gothic tendencies and the "Romanesque" which is so familiar in the Spanish ecclesiastical architecture of those decades'.[88] Here one sees why there has been an inclination to speak of sixteenth-century Caribbean architecture in terms of an anticipation of the Spanish baroque. These baroque tendencies are still more marked in the interiors, where medieval expressions, which refused to accept the Renaissance secularization of content, coexist with forms which have lost their metaphysical meaning. These are the oppositions which make themselves felt later, and with greater forcefulness, in the so-called 'Seicento'. It is more than probable that the strange and allegorical contents which make up the point of contrast with the structures and forms were fed by representations forged in the New World. It is even possible that indigenous artisans and craftsmen worked on the decoration of churches and cathedrals.

Students of the aesthetic theories behind New World colonial architecture, especially Palm,[89] see the significance of the movement in the fact that it allowed a fusion between structure and ornamentation. This movement constitutes that 'emotional boldness of the baroque', which places Liendo, as we have seen, in the next century.

There has been much debate over the problem of the presence of Islamic or *mudéjar* elements in the sixteenth-century architecture of the Caribbean. These elements are perhaps clearest seen in Cuba, where there still stand residences with coffered ceilings constructed of elaborately worked corbelled beams and rafters. Manuel Toussaint offers photographs of these characteristics, and gives as reasons for their employment the climatic conditions of the country and the presence of fine and odorous woods.[90] Still, the most important manifestations of *mudéjarism* in Cuba are the ceilings of the churches of Santa Clara, Santa Teresa and Santo Domingo, which were constructed after the sixteenth century.

There are a few examples of this sort of architecture on Hispaniola, also. Thus, for example, the fortress called the Tower of Homage (*Torre del Homenaje*), built by Governor Ovando and resided in by the vice-roy, Diego Colón, seems to correspond in many ways to this style. Diego Colón's *alcázar*, or castle, shows many 'Moorish' traits, such as archways, windows with ogee-arch closures, and coffered ceilings. Even the cathedral in Santo Domingo incorporates certain Muslim expressions, such as its Moorish arches and its battlements. These same elements are also present in the Las Mercedes church. In the monastery in Santo Domingo there are geminated or paired windows, and the doors of the sacristy show *mudéjar* influences.

As another important component of the Spanish architectural legacy to the New World, one should mention, in addition to religious architecture, the military construction of forts and fortresses. Forts began to be built by Columbus himself, on his first voyage, and out of such materials as wood. By the sixteenth century, however, many larger fortresses were being built at the major, and most strategic, ports across the Caribbean. For these constructions, the Spaniards drew on the knowledge of such important engineers as Antonelli. The typical pattern for a fortress was the following: it would be built of stone, rubble, or rock, and cement, with four unequal faces and four bulwarks at the corners. Often, some of the faces would be surrounded by a low protective wall, and those which faced the land were generally bordered by a moat. Inside, there were magazines for weapons and powder, barrackrooms for the troops, a chapel, and emplacements for cannon.

We have already mentioned the cities and houses built by the *conquistadores* and colonizers. Let it suffice here to point to Philip II's *Ordenanzas de Descubrimiento, Nueva Población y Ocupación de las Indias* [Ordinances for the Discovery, New Settlement and Occupation of the Indies], issued in 1573, and especially the rules established for the choice of sites for cities:

> *Para haber de poblar, así lo que está descubierto, pacífico y debajo de nuestra obediencia como en lo que por tiempo se descubriere y pacificare, se guarde el orden siguiente: elíjase la provincia, comarca y*

tierra que se ha de poblar teniendo consideración que sean saludables, lo cual se conocerá en la copia que hubiere de hombres y mozos de buena complexión, disposición y color y sin enfermedades, y en la copia de animales sanos y de competente tamaño, y de sanos frutos y mantenimientos; que no se crien cosas ponzoñosas y nocivas, de buena y felice constelación, el cielo claro y benigno, el aire puro y suave y sin impedimentos ni alteraciones y de buen temple, sin exceso de calor o frío, y habiendo de declinar, el mejor que sea frío.[91]

[In order to settle, both that which is discovered, peaceable, and under our sway and that which for some time may be discovered and pacified, the following order shall be kept: the province, region and land to be settled shall be chosen by taking into account that they be healthful, and this shall be known by the abundance there may be of men and youths of good complexion, disposition and colour, and lack of disease, and in the abundance of healthy and good sized animals, and of healthy offspring and maintenance; by the fact that poisonous and noxious things do not there grow, with good and happy climate, the sky clear and benign, the air pure and soft and without impediments or alterations, and of good temperature, neither too hot nor too cold, and having to decline [?], best if it be cold.]

Moreover, there were to be springs of water for human and animal consumption and for irrigating the crops. There should be woods or forests to provide building materials and firewood. The settlers were exhorted to seek out relatively high ground. For the coastal cities, it was recommended that there not be tides at noon or sunset.

As for the layout of the cities, Philip's orders specified that the town square was to be the axis and starting point for the city, and that it should be located near the docks in the case of a port city or in the centre of the town in the case of the interior. The plaza was to be rectangular, and from it four streets should radiate out. The corners were to be set at the four cardinal points of the compass. Both the plaza and the four main streets would have arcades, which were considered important for the merchants and traders who might come to the cities.

Even before 1573, however, people had been building cities in the Caribbean. These were constructed on the medieval model of the city (a model with Greek and Roman influences) and without taking into account, in many instances, the more or less 'scientific' criteria for their siting. The materials used in building houses were, besides the native woods, rubble masonry, palm thatch, and mud or adobe. Their locations tended to be near Indian *pueblos* or where there was presumed to be gold.

Music

With regard to music, one must point out that polyphonic music flowered in the Caribbean from a very early date, and was generally linked to religious ceremonies. Polyphonic music had come into the Iberian peninsula in the twelfth century, its first manifestation being in the Codex Calixtinus, which was probably written in about 1137. Other codices in which polyphonic compositions appeared were the Codices of Huelgas and Toledo and the *Libre vermell*; there were also other compositions of the *Ars antigua*. On the peninsula, therefore, there already existed a taste for this type of music, which had been supported enthusiastically by Charles V, who brought a choir of musicians, directed by Adrián Picard, to Spain. These *capillas*, which consisted of cantors from all the monasteries of the Jeronymite order, continued to exist under the rules of Philip II and Philip III, and from thence were brought into the New World.

Many musicians came to the Americas, among them the cantor Porrás and the *vibuelista* Alonso Morón as well as the famed 'Ortiz the musician', who played the *vibuela* (the precursor of the guitar) and the viola and taught dancing. Nor should we neglect to mention the Cuban mestizo Miguel Velázquez, who studied in Seville and Alcalá de Henares, where he learned to play the organ and studied the rules of the Gregorian chant, or plainsong.

A choir was created in Baracoa, Cuba in 1528, and for this choir

> no person may be presented unless he be skilled and learned in music, at least in the plainsong; [and for this choir] the cantor shall take the lectern and teach the servants of the church to sing, and shall order and correct and amend those things which pertain to choral singing, and in other things, and this shall be done by himself and not by third persons.[92]

In these choirs persons of different races and social positions mixed. In spite of the criticism that blacks were allowed to participate in these activities, inter-racial musical groups prospered, due mainly to the scarcity of performers. The small orchestra formed by the Seville bass-viol player Pascual de Ochoa and the black freedwoman sisters Micaela and Teodora Ginés merits special mention. Teodora composed the famous piece 'Son de la Má Teodora', based on an Estremaduran romance; Alejo Carpentier has reprinted the lyrics and music.[93]

In Carpentier's opinion, the profusion of this last type of music, the romance, is very significant, and he mentions especially the Estremaduran version of the Romance de Gerinoldo. Carpentier believes that the widespread diffusion of this romance was due to the illiteracy of many *conquista-*

dores, who kept the events of the romance alive in their memories through the rhyme.

Musical instruments employed by these European musicians were the organ, the sackbut, the *vihuela*, the viola, the harp, the dulcimer, the flageolet and fife, and the bass viol. The incorporation of African instruments such as the *güiro* (a dried gourd which was scored and played with a scraper to make a percussive rasp) was met with scandal.

Some indigenous musical compositions were recovered, to a degree, by adapting Christian lyrics to the *areytos*. This, however, was not the rule, and the *areyto* dances and songs were generally considered pagan, and hence undesirable. Gonzalo Fernández de Oviedo described one version of a Hispaniola *areyto*, and Alejo Carpentier quotes this description in his book:

Tenían estas gentes la buena y gentil manera de rememorar las cosas pasadas e antiguas; eso en sus cantares y bayles, que ellos llaman areyto, que es lo mismo que nosotros llamamos baylar cantando ... E por más extender su alegría e regocijo, tomábanse de las manos algunas veces, e también otros trabábanse brazo con brazo, ensartados o asidos muchos en rengle (o en corro así mismo), e uno de ellos tomaba el oficio de guiar (o fuesen hombre o muger), y aquél daba ciertos pasos adelante e atrás, a manera de un contrapás muy ordenado; e lo mismo (o en el instante) hacen todos, cantando en aquel tono alto o baxo que la guía los entona, o como lo hace e dice, muy medida e concertada la cuenta de los pasos con los versos o palabras que cantan. E así como aquél dice, la moltitud de todos responde con los mismos pasos e palabras, e orden; en tanto que le responden, la guía calla, aunque no cesa de andar el contrapás. E acabada la respuesta, que es repetir o decir lo mismo que el guiador dixo, procede encontinente sin intervalo la guía a otro verso e palabras que el corro e todos tornan a repetir; e assí sin cesar les dura estos tres o quatro horas y hasta que el maestra [sic] o guiador que les danza acaba su historia, y a veces les dura desde un día hasta otro.[94]

[These people had the good and kindly manner of recalling past and ancient things, that is in their songs and dances which they call *areyto*, which is the same as we would say dance while singing ... And to further extend their happiness and delight, they would take one another by the hand sometimes, and also other times link themselves arm in arm, joined or tied many together into a line (or a circle likewise), and one of them would take the job of leading (whether man or woman), and that one would take certain steps forward and back, in the fashion of a very orderly *contrapás* (a Catalonian dance); and at once (or soon) all would do the same, singing in that high or low tone that the leader might intone, or as he did while calling out, very modestly and in concert, counting the steps with the verses or words they sing. And as he speaks, the multitude of them reply with the same steps and words, and order; as soon as they reply, the leader falls silent, though he does not stop dancing the *contrapás*. And when the reply is done, that is repeating or saying the same as the leader spake, then the leader proceeds without interval immediately to another verse and words which the circle and all in turn repeat; and so on, without cease this may last three or four hours, and until the master or guide who leads them in dance completes his story, which sometimes lasts from one day until another.]

As we can see from this description, the *areyto* was able to keep alive many of the tribe's traditions by means of repetition and the mnemonic properties of rhyme. This was very important for peoples who did not possess writing, as in the case of the Taínos and the various societies discovered on the continent. The musical instruments employed by the indigenous peoples were the tuned drums, rattles and *fotutos* or conch and other shells.

As for African influences on Caribbean music, we find that while they were considerable, it is hard to speak today of the influences on the sixteenth century. Besides the dances and singing performed on Sundays and feast days, it is probable that the so-called labour chants (for harvest, milling and grinding, milking, etc.) and cradle songs or lullabies were also present from the beginning.

European and indigenous technology

Along with medieval beliefs and practices such as fantastic geography and anthropology, Europeans brought the true scientific and technical knowledge of the Renaissance to the Caribbean. But during the period we are examining we should perhaps consider instead how European science was forced to modify and expand its conceptions of botany, zoology, astronomy and geography. Still, one should not fail to note the attempts that were undertaken to adapt domestic plants and animals to the American soil. Likewise, it is important to consider the development of technologies in which European and indigenous knowledge was fused, as one can clearly see in certain agricultural and metallurgical techniques.

Also, from the point of view of technology, one should note the new nutritional techniques and habits that were developed. Besides the Europeans' adoption of new foods such as corn, cassava bread, cassava itself, and other tubers, we find that they also adopted, according to Nitza Villapoll,[95] such food-preparation techniques as *sofrito* (preparation of the seasoning base for food by sauteing onions, peppers, etc.), *fritanga* (frying foods in large amounts of fat; today we might call this deep-frying), and *pilado* (husking grains by pounding in a mortar).

Education, writing and art

Education, as I have indicated, was linked to the religious orders, the Franciscans being the first to establish a school. This was in Santo Domingo, in 1502. The Dominicans founded their own school in 1510, and were followed by the Mercedarians. A public school was founded by Bishop Ramírez de Fuenleal in the 1520s.

The first university, the Universidad de Santo Tomás de Aquino, was founded in 1538 with the same privileges as the universities at Salamanca and Alcalá de Henares. In 1540 another university opened its doors; in 1583 its name became the Universidad de Santiago de la Paz y de Gorjón. These universities were comprised of four 'faculties', on the model of the medieval university that had been followed in Spain: Theology, Law (civil and canon), Medicine, and Arts (the trivium: grammar, Latin, and rhetoric and logic; and the quadrivium: arithmetic, geometry, music and astrology). Instruction was in Latin, with the exception of the faculty of Medicine.

I have referred to the existence in the sixteenth century of a line of philosophic thought that attempted to resolve various dilemmas presented mainly by the new discoveries. Among these problems were that which opposed humanism to Christianity and that which was posited in terms of incorporating the indigenous peoples into 'civilization', an act which would entail the destruction of their cultures. Augusto Salazar Bondy suggests that:

> there is a rich depository of philosophical meditations on the humanity of the Indian, the right of making war on the indigenous peoples, and the just title to the Americas; this is certainly the most valuable aspect of sixteenth- and seventeenth-century thought. Thanks to this issue, Scholasticism at times achieved a vitality and immediacy; those times were when it touched upon the problem of existence in the recently conquered world and in the thick of the process of colonization, which at that time meant adaptation to Hispano-European models. But basically, philosophical meditation, even that which took up the 'American issue', was carried out from a Spanish point of view. There was not, and perhaps could not have been, especially at the beginning of the colonial period, anything resembling a New World focus *per se,* a

corpus of doctrine which responded to the motivations of the men of this continent.[96]

This reaffirms what I have previously noted, that the Spaniards evaluated the New World 'reality' with the intellectual and ideological instrument they possessed at that moment. These mental tools, as I have said several times, were filled with profound and unresolved contradictions. Salazar Bondy himself states that the Spaniards employed a conservative and anti-modern mentality.

With respect to the first books published in the Caribbean, Fray Cipriano de Utrera's work *Los primeros libros escritos en la Española*[97] mentions the following: the *Diario de Colón*, Padre Pané's *Escritura*, Fray Pedro de Córdoba's *La doctrina cristiana para indios*, Bishop Alessandro Geraldini's *Itinerarium*, Las Casas' *Apologética histórica de las Indias*, Fernández de Oviedo's *Historia general y natural de las Indias*, plus Dr Chanca's *Carta* (1493) and Fernández de Oviedo's 1526 *Sumario de la natural y general historia de las Indias*.

Among the secular authors we find besides Dr Chanca (a true detractor of New World nature in general and the Indians in particular) Juan de Echagoyan, who produced a *Relación de la Isla Española* which was sent to Philip II in 1568. There were also Lorenzo Bejarano and the physician Dr Juan Méndez Nieto, who wrote *Discursos medicinales*.

From an early date several genres of literature flourished in the Caribbean. Poetry, generally based on octosyllables and hexasyllables, was very popular. The first well-known poet was Bishop Alessandro Geraldini, an Italian humanist who wrote one work, the *Voyage to Subequinoctial Regions*, in Latin using Sapphic and Adonic verse forms. Another important poet was Lázaro Bejarano, an Andalusian accused in 1558 of being an Erasmist. Almost all Bejarano's work has been lost, though we still have three epigrams and two five-line stanzas from his *Purgatorio del amor*, a satire aimed at the important personages of the city.

Among the native writers we might take note, in the sixteenth century, of Juan de Castellanos, the poetesses Elvira de Mendoza and Leonor de Ovando, the professors Francisco Tostado de la Peña and Cristóbal de Llerena. Llerena, author both of plays which were performed in the churches and other, comic, works which sought to keep the faithful entertained, was the author of the first play performed in the New World, a one-act farce that satirized the government establishment. It employed but two characters, the comic character or *gracioso* and the fool or idiot, as was typical of this sort of popular drama.

With regard to the decorative arts, we find that in painting, the first artists arrived at the very commencement of the discovery and conquest, and were brought to the New World mainly in order to decorate churches. Diego Pérez arrived with the ships of the discovery itself. Juan Pintor arrived in Santo Domingo in 1500, Diego López in 1501, J. Sánchez is known to have died in Santo Domingo in 1510, Alonso de Arjona arrived in 1511. As for woodcarvers, Pedro Vélez arrived in 1511, Alvaro González in 1513, Juan de Mendoza in 1531, and Pedro Calderón in 1539. Other painters that soon arrived were Alonso Rodríguez in 1538, Marino de la Torre in 1548, Ximón in 1552, Cristóbal Moreno in 1553, Diego del Valle in 1557, Alonso Callejo and Francisco Fernández Estrada in 1585, Juan de Salazar and Alonso Dávila in 1586.[98] We must remember that the custom of the time, in which works of art were not signed, has left many works anonymous.

Unlike that which occurred in music, people of colour were not allowed to study painting; this included Muslims and Jews. Queen Isabella herself ordered Francisco Chacón, the Royal Censor, to be certain that 'no Muslim or Jew be so audacious as to dare paint the face of the Saviour or His glorious Mother, or any other saint of our Religion'.[99]

The favourite subjects of painting were religious in nature, especially Nuestra Señora de la Antigua de la Catedral de Santo Domingo, Nuestra Señora de la Antigua de la Catedral de la Vega, figures of San Telmo, Santiago Apóstol, the evangelist San Juan, and Nuestra Señora de Altagracia de Higüey. Among the non-religious subjects we find paintings which allude to the discovery and conquest. One famous painting was of the 'Vision of the Virgen de Las Mercedes', based on a miracle related by Antonio del Monte y Tejada and quoted by Rodríguez Demorizi. In the following words Del Monte tells of the battle of Vega Real (Hispaniola) and the miracle that occurred there:

> The battle of La Vega Real and its traditional episode, the miraculous vision of Las Mercedes, on the Holy Peak, brought about the birth, in the area nearby, in the days of Columbus, of the opulent city of Concepción de la Vega, of magnificent edifices of brick, the fort, and the Church. Made a bishopric in the dawn of the sixteenth century, given a coat of arms in 1508, and whose temple, in which the new mass of the most celebrated Padre Las Casas was celebrated, [this city] was praised in the following way by the Dean of La Concepción in a letter of 2 December, 1547: 'A Cathedral Church as good as there are in Castile, and so well served that in the Indies there is none that surpasses it ...' Destroyed by the earthquake of 1562, its inhabitants formed a new city on the banks of the Camú River, taking with them what they could save from the catastrophe, and nothing less than the painting of La Antigua, brought by Columbus, according to tradition, perhaps, the painting arrived at the continent in most remote years, which is still preserved.[100]

González Fernández de Oviedo may even be considered an artist, or at least a draftsman, so Rodríguez Demorizi says. For having been a friend of Leonardo, Berruguete and Mantegna, Fernández de Oviedo liked to illustrate his works so that the reader might better understand them.

As for sculpture, besides the altars and doors of the cathedrals and churches, there are some sepulchres, such as Geraldini's in the Santo Domingo cathedral, and saints' images, many brought from Europe and whose presence in the New World was haloed with miracles and legends, such as the famous Maracaibo Christ, which merit mention.

It is in what has been called the religious syncretism of the time, the nutritional habits, and the language, that the fusion of cultural elements of varying ethnic groups is most reflected. In the religious cults we find that Catholic beliefs and practices are mixed with others derived from the indigenous peoples and from the various African cultural groups brought to the New World. These combinations produced the syncretic expressions known as *santería* and voodoo (*vodún*).

As I have said, culinary syncretism occurs from the very earliest days of the conquest. Indians contributed cassava bread, cassava itself, sweet potatoes, and many fruits. Corn, even though initially rejected by the Spaniards, was in time adopted as a foodstuff. For their part, the Spaniards brought wheat, olives, ham and bacon, celery, endive, and cattle and sheep. Africans brought both foodstuffs and new ways of preparing and cooking food. The combination of all these elements produced a culinary tradition preserved until our own days.

In the sphere of language, we find that Spanish was enriched with words and expressions belonging to all the different African and indigenous groups with which it came in contact. Spanish words such as *hamaca, huracán, cacique, bohío, canoa, bahareque, caoba, caney* and *batey* are Taíno and Carib words. *Mondongo, ñame, quimbombó, curbeta,* and *cumbe* are African in origin. The African influence is also seen in much oral literature, especially in the stories of Tío Tigre and Tío Conejo, much like the Uncle Remus stories told by slaves and well-known in the southern United States. Certain retained non-European grammatical forms are also important, such as some brought from Africa. Richard Allsopp cites the work of Douglas Taylor to discuss the survival of these grammatical forms:

> If there was continuity in the use of a grammatical system, everything seems to indicate Africa as the place of origin of that system – probably not in any African language *per se* but more probably in some Afro-Portuguese pidgin.[101]

The survival of these grammatical forms (the reduplicative structure, for example), over and above the semantic level of the words contributed by the various European languages, is proof of what I have been calling the survival of logical forms of thought.

Conclusion

Culture cannot be reduced, as I have been stating, to its sensible aspects, and much less so if one examines its intellectual, ideological and artistic dimensions. Behind the phenomenal expressions of culture, a whole world of thoughts, motivations, stereotypes, prejudices, idealizations, etc. is hiding, and many times these elements are not verbalized or explicitated. Over and above these phenomenal expressions of European culture, present in the New World from the first moment of the discovery, it is important to take into account the structures or the logic of thought that allowed those contents brought by Europeans to be ordered. It is there that, from my point of view, we find the key to understanding the Caribbean cultures. All the contents brought to the New World by the Spaniards were ordered by a rationality or logic of thought which was not consubstantial with those contents. This recourse, known today as 'antagonistic acculturation',[102] served to allow the Caribbean societies to maintain more or less intact their logical or mental schemata. All this produced the baroque cultural forms in which European signifiers coexist with Amerindian and Afro-American signifieds. In my view, this is the most distinctive trait of the cultures which were born in the Caribbean within the new societies that were formed.

But out of the discovery and conquest of the New World, there also occurred changes in ways of thinking in Europe. I have pointed out that in zoology, astronomy and botany the New World forced profound revisions of the concepts and taxonomies of the Old World. But over and above this, I believe that Joan Bestard and Jesús Contreras' thesis is correct, which states that in 'the years immediately after the "discovery", the Americas, or better, the Indies, had not yet broken altogether with medieval, biblical and Aristotelian assumptions, or even with the fantastic and marvellous beliefs of the preceding centuries'.[103] The first study of the societies, customs, men and nature of the New World was done in accordance with patterns inherited from the Middle Ages, in which the fantastic and marvellous prevailed. It was not until twenty years after the discovery that Europeans confirmed to themselves something they had only suspected: the Indies were a new continent. This second discovery forced them to invent a whole new complex of theories that could give a new interpretation to what they had found. Among other things, a great push was given to the creation of museums and 'cabinets', or collections of exotic objects. By the mid-sixteenth century Europeans had gone from the idea that these were peoples without law to another, by which it was seen that they were ruled by custom, and that these customs determined their moral behaviour.

The spiritual repercussions of these discoveries, according to Romano and Tenenti,[104] are many:

1 A breach is made in the equivalence of *oikoumene* and *christianitas* that had prevailed since the High Middle Ages (as Romano and Tenenti note, '*christianitas* is irremediably reduced to Europe alone').

2 As a consequence, theories of a polygenetic origin of mankind begin to gather strength, contradicting the dogmas given down by St Augustine.

3 As a consequence of this last phenomenon, the missionary impulse begins, though this impulse entails serious contradictions, mainly concerned with the notion that 'the end of the world will coincide with the conversion of the entire world to the one true faith'.

4 The possible theological solution to this problem is suggested by Francisco de Vitoria, who proposes a return to a natural order based essentially on experience.

With this change of course comes, even as early as the sixteenth century, the use of the comparative method, by which there is an attempt to define the nature both of the Americans and of their customs. These comparisons were always made between the Indians and 'other' barbarians described by such writers as Strabo, Pliny and Herodotus. For example, in Fernández de Oviedo we find numerous comparisons between the Amerindians and the Thracians, Scythians and Ethiopians. All this led to a sharpening of certain controversies, such as those between the defenders of the chronology of the world set forth in the Bible and their opponents, between the monogenists and the polygenists, between the defenders of ascending evolution and the defenders of decaying evolution, etc. In time, all of these debates would be turned to the case of the New World, and would enrich the contents of the intellectual, ideological and artistic dimensions of its new societies.

NOTES

1 This was the case until at least the mid-sixteenth century, and the process was carried out through the extension of many medieval customs and beliefs. As Bestard and Contreras put it in their work *Bárbaros, paganos, salvajes y primitivos, una introducción a la antropología*, 'Christopher Columbus apparently felt

no discomfort, or stupefaction, or even doubt or surprise, when he came in contact with the New World aborigines' (p. 35).

2 My theoretical and methodological approach is inscribed basically within structural anthropology. This school posits that beneath phenomenal reality there is a structural or logical dimension which orders and gives meaning to the phenomena of what is called the sensible (visible, tangible, etc.) world. Thus, it is my view that the cultural contents brought by the Europeans are ordered according to logical frameworks or schemata of pre-existing thought.

3 *Adelantado* was a title bestowed on the leader of an expedition; he would be empowered to govern whatever lands he discovered and conquered. The title was also used for governors of provinces and territories. [Trans.]

4 I am adopting here the distinction established by Ileana Rodríguez between a *criolla* culture, in which the Spanish element predominates, and a 'creole' culture, in which the dominant note is indigenous or African. I recognize, however, that this distinction is based on tangible cultural components. Cf. I. Rodríguez, *Primer inventario del invasor*, (1984), p. 20.

5 Pietro Martire d'Anghera (an Italian, 1457?–1526, diplomat for Ferdinand and Isabella, dean of the cathedral of Granada, historian and chronicler of the royal family, and known throughout Spanish history as Pedro Mártir de Angleria, now in English [and throughout this essay] as Peter Martyr) used references to the Greco-Roman roots of Europe in order to ironize the deeds of the *conquistadores*.

6 This, in spite of declarations such as 'Who can doubt that gunpowder against the infidel is incense to the Lord?' and other comments charged with xenophobic and racist sentiments.

7 Columbus had also read Marinus of Tyre, Aristotle, Strabo, Pliny, Seneca, Mandeville, Marco Polo and Pierre d'Ailly. He was greatly impressed by D'Ailly's idea, in *Imago Mundi*, of the relative ease with which one might arrive at the shores of Asia by sailing westward. However, this 'Columbian circle' school of thought has been called in question by Juan Gil in the introduction to his edition of *El libro de Marco Polo anotado por Cristóbal Colón*, wherein he indicates that it was not until 1498 that Columbus possessed a library containing all the books mentioned above. Gil shares the opinion of Peter Martyr when Martyr 'accuses our sailors of being ignorant of Cosmography.'

8 Francisco de Solano states in this regard that 'the crucial moment for the knightly romance was the period from 1501 to 1550, precisely the period during which most of the great Spanish conquests of the Indies were reported. One hundred and fifty-seven editions were printed during those years, counting both original romances and reprints' (*El conquistador hispano*, (1987), p. 28).

9 This historiographic tradition has been widely questioned by researchers such as Germán Carrera Damas (q.v.). in his article 'Diez puntos sobre la enseñanza de la Historia de Venezuela', *Revista Tierra Firme III*, No. 11 (Caracas: July–September 1985).

10 By this I mean that most anthropological theories or writing lacks an 'anthropologicity' which takes into account the particular characteristics of a culture while at the same time inscribing them within a more universal concept of Culture, with a capital 'C'.

11 Given this, I believe that the current cultures of Caribbean nations may be explained not only by the presence of cultural features or complexes deriving

from various ethnicities, but also, and primarily, by the ordering of those features and complexes into a totality which lends them coherence, and which corresponds to what I have been calling 'logical structures of thought', 'rationality' or '*Weltanschauung*'. This system is not visible, it underlies visible and conscious cultural manifestations, and uncovering or unveiling it should, from my point of view, be the true objective of anthropology in Latin America.

12 Juan Gil, mentioned above, states that this term apparently originated on Columbus' second voyage, in a bloody fight with the native people of Guadaloupe, which Columbus identifies with the island of Necuveran, described in Rodrigo de Santaella's translation of *The Book of Marco Polo*, where Marco Polo speaks of men who 'live like beasts and eat human flesh'. Cf. Gil, Chapter CXIV.

13 Cf. Ricardo Alegría, *Las primeras representaciones gráficas*, 1978b.

14 This idyllic vision was fuelled by Columbus himself, who, beginning in 1501, attempted to present himself under the image of a providential man, the precursor of the Second Coming; he did this in a work which announces the imminent conquest of Jerusalem, the beginning of the Empire of the Last Days, and himself as a true *Christo ferens*. To justify his vision, Columbus makes abusive use of biblical texts.

15 Ileana Rodriguez (1984), p. 116.

16 Georges Balandier (1975), p. 75.

17 'Thus, from the island of Hispaniola between 1508 and 1510 there departed groups ("enterprises", *empresas*) which went to Cuba, Borinquen (Puerto Rico), Castilla del Oro, *Tierra Firme* (the continent; specifically, the Atlantic coast of Colombia), and Jamaica, and in 1527 the group which passed on to *Tierra Firme* (the region of Venezuela) and founded Coro; from Cuba did so that which in 1519 went to New Spain; from Jamaica, those which in 1510, 1520, and 1521 attempted unsuccessfully, due to resistance from the indigenous base, install themselves in the region of Pánuco (New Spain) ...' (Beroes, (1982), pp. 62–3).

18 In spite of the fact that in some readings, such as those of Manuel Beroes, Germán Carrera, and others, there is stress on the primacy 'of the expansionist tendency of European capital, a process in which Spain and Portugal were the principal actors during the fifteenth and sixteenth centuries' (Beroes, (1982), p. 40).

19 This model had been imposed in Spain through the formation of the Holy Brotherhood, made up of *corregidores* or local leaders. These men owed their allegiance to the Crown and were therefore opposed to the aspirations of local nobility. It was through *fueros*, or privileges and exemptions granted a city or province, that the municipalities achieved a degree of autonomy.

20 This Roldán was later to rise in mutiny against Columbus, which led Peter Martyr to say the following of him: '*Roldanus quendam Ximenun facinerosum*' (quoted in Morales Padrón, (1981), p. 145).

21 While this word can mean nothing more than 'inhabitant' or 'resident', during the colonial period and after it also meant 'head of household' in the sense of 'land-owning', or 'tax-paying' head of household. Here, it no doubt has some of both meanings, as one assumes a 'household' would settle. [Trans.]

22 The assignment of a number of Indians to a settler; the assignment was not hereditary, and so was not 'slavery', but the Indians were expected to work for the settler. The settler was not granted land with the *encomienda*, just 'employees'. [Trans.]

23 The term used for Spaniards who penetrated the kinship structures of the indigenous peoples through unions with *cacicas* (female leaders) or the daughters of *caciques* (the male leaders). These unions would have put the Spaniards in a very privileged position from the standpoint of political control and social dominance within these communities. This phenomenon was limited to Hispaniola.

24 This spirit of adventure has been questioned by several writers, among them Francisco de Solano, who in his article titled 'El conquistador hispano, señas de identidad' says that 'the Conquest was, on the contrary, the work of soldier-colonists of a mature age, an age when there is no room for thoughtlessness, or frivolity, or the impulses that belong to a younger man and that would justify a passion for adventure and a great curiosity to know the unknown' (Solano *et al.*, p. 24). But in that same book, Guillermo Céspedes del Castillo's article 'Raíces peninsulares y asentamiento indiano, los hombres de la frontera' reasserts the *conquistadores* spirit of adventure.

25 As his working definition of *mudéjar*, Manuel Toussaint gives the following: 'A *mudéjar* is the *moro* [Moor, or worshipper of Islam] who, peacefully rendered subject to the Christians, continues to follow his own [religious] law' (1). These, then, were those Muslim Arabs who lived in Spain after the Reconquest, and maintained the characteristics of their literature, art, music, and architecture. [Trans.]

26 For some, even the discovery of the New World could be interpreted as a prelude to the Apocalypse. Thus the Huguenot Theodore de Bry posited the existence of a paradisal, original innocence among the American indigenous peoples, and said that their postponed Fall had at last been precipitated by the Spanish Conquest, supported by the Pope. 'Before the Second Coming, there must be a purge of the diabolic condition generated by Spain, [and this will be] effected by the establishment of Protestants in self-sufficient communities: producers and consumers of ordered and inbred foodstuffs.' Cf. Boon, (1989), p. 62.

27 In Peter Martyr's *De Orbe Novo Decades* (1525) there is, in spite of indirect reporting which uses such statements as 'they tell' and 'it seemed to them', much of this idyllic vision.

28 Guillermo Céspedes del Castillo (1987), p. 39.

29 Manuel Beroes (1982), p. 43.

30 Quoted in Alberto M. Salas (1986), p. 57.

31 Ruggiero Romano and Alberto Tenenti (1974), p. 190.

32 Pedro Henríquez Ureña (1988), p. 293.

33 *Ibid.*, p. 297.

34 Quoted in Roberto Cassá (1974), p. 142.

35 *Ibid.*

36 Francisco Morales Padrón (1981), p. 329.

37 Quoted in Gonzalo Fernández de Oviedo y Valdés (1851), IV:I, p. 100.

38 This is a recurrent theme during the Middle Ages as it is in later periods as well. It may be found in such authors as Pierre d'Ailly, Haly, Boemus, Thévet, and others.

39 Thus: 'The world of Columbus was not that which he saw with his eyes, but that which he wanted to see, the world of Ptolemy, Pierre d'Ailly, and Marco Polo. The Ante-ilha or Fore-Isle which medieval cartography located in the Atlantic took on the plurality of the Canaries, Azores, and Baleares, and then

became the Antilles. On his first voyage, Columbus thought he saw mermaids (in actuality, manatees or sea-cows) and he identified the island Matinino [now Martinique], inhabited, according to the Indians, solely by women, with the Amazons' (Morales Padrón, (1981), pp. 115–16).

40 That *alterum Orbem* was believed to lie at 'the antipodes', that is, in the southern hemisphere. This belief had been criticized by Augustine in *The City of God*, and even denounced as heretical, for the inhabitants of those regions, if they existed, would necessarily have to be descendants of Adam.

41 Quoted in Carl Ortwin Sauer (1984), p. 46.

42 Ileana Rodríguez, p. 21.

43 Manuel Beroes (1982), pp. 76ff.

44 *Ibid.*, pp. 78–9.

45 A Humanism which embodied a great paradox, for the idea of a universal man assumes the death of all 'exotic' and particular expressions. Neither philosophy nor the so-called 'social sciences' have been able to recover from this dichotomy to this day.

46 Ruggiero Romano and Alberto Tenenti (1974), p. 216.

47 Pierre Vilar (1987), p. 45.

48 Fernando Pérez Memén (1987), pp. 101ff.

49 *Ibid.*, p. 203.

50 It was said that the *cacique* Behechio once called more than 300 *caciques* together, upon the occasion of honouring Governor Ovando. Cf. Sauer (1984), p. 84.

51 Quoted in Carl Ortwin Sauer (1984), p. 96.

52 Quoted in Jesús Guanche (1983), p. 89.

53 *Apologética*, Chap. 46.

54 All these figures have been taken from Arellano, (1987), pp. 23–5.

55 Claude Lévi-Strauss calls the savage mind the 'science of the concrete'. Cf. Chapter 1 of *The Savage Mind* (1966).

56 Quoted in Fray Juan Manuel Pérez (1984), p. 15.

57 José Juan Arrom (1975), p. 23.

58 Roger Bastide (1982), p. 67.

59 Even in Castile, manual labour was absolutely devalorized.

60 Guillermo Céspedes del Castillo (1987), p. 48.

61 José Juan Arrom (1975), p. 19.

62 *Ibid.*, p. 42.

63 There were certain triangular stones which were also considered *cemíes*. These, Arrom says, were buried in order to bring fertility and abundance in the harvest.

64 Roberto Cassa (1974), pp. 221–2.

65 Among the Africans we also find the idea of the existence of a spirit of the drums who speaks through them.

66 Including both alliance (for example, rules or prescriptions for marriage) and filiation (bloodline relationships).

67 Jean Benoist (1987), p. 93.

68 Tzvetan Todorov (1987), p. 95.

69 Many indigenous peoples believed that horse and rider were a single being. Cf. Bernardo Vargas' *Refutación de Las Casas*, p. 172.

70 Constantino Láscaris (1970), p. 30.

71 *Ibid.*, p. 32.

72 Roger Bastide (1969), p. 11.

73   Joseph Ki-Zerbo (1980), p. 323.
74   Manuel Moreno Fraginals (1987), p. 15.
75   I respect Moreno Fraginals' conclusions. He says that 'it was food which met dietary, administrative, and even psychological requirements, for its plenty produced a certain degree of satisfaction', pp. 24–5.
76   *Ibid.*, p. 25.
77   Germán Carrera Damas, in Moreno Fraginals (ed.) (1987), p. 40.
78   With regard to this metaphoric use of thought, it is worthwhile to stress the assignment of human qualities or defects to the various animal species; this is a distinctive feature of African children's stories.
79   John Hanheinz (1970), p. 127.
80   Miguel Barnet (1983), p. 169.
81   Joseph Ki-Zerbo (1980), p. 326.
82   Miguel Barnet (1983), pp. 176–7.
83   Leovigildo López, 'Las firmas de los santos', quoted in Miguel Barnet (1983), p. 221.
84   In Venezuela one of the synonyms for demon is *mandinga*, the name of the members of an African ethnic group.
85   Manuel Moreno Fraginals (1987), p. 21.
86   Manuel Beroes (1982), p. 39.
87   Pedro Henríquez Ureña (1988), p. 307.
88   Erwin Walter Palm (1974), p. 136.
89   *Ibid.*, p. 144.
90   Manuel Toussaint (1946), p. 19.
91   Quoted in Graziano Gasparini (1956), pp. 48ff.
92   Alejo Carpentier (1972), p. 23.
93   *Ibid.*, pp. 41ff.
94   *Ibid.* p. 28.
95   Nitza Villapol (n.d.), pp. 329ff.
96   Augusto Salazar Bondy (1969), p. 23.
97   Quoted in Pedro Henríquez Ureña (1988), p. 207.
98   All these names and dates appear in Emilio Rodríguez Demorizi (1966), pp. 41–2.
99   Quoted in Emilio Rodriquez Demorizi (1966), p. 45.
100 *Ibid.*, p. 68
101 Richard Allsopp in Manuel Moreno Fraginals (1987), p. 138.
102 Georges Devereux (1974), pp. 240ff.
103 Joan Bestard and Jesús Contreras (1987), p. 99.
104 Ruggiero Rumani and Alberto Tenenti (1974), pp. 179ff.

10

THE CARTOGRAPHY OF THE CARIBBEAN, 1500–1650

David Buisseret

Introduction

Since maps are found in almost every culture, it is very likely that the pre-Columbian peoples of the Caribbean also composed them, whether as carvings on rocks, as arrangements of sticks, or as drawings in the sand. Indeed, we know from the log of Columbus that the Lucayans were able to explain to him the position of adjacent islands by sand-drawings; later, in Europe, two of them were able to set out the general position of the islands using beans on a table. However, no material remains of this pre-Columbian map-making have yet been found, and perhaps none has survived. For practical purposes the cartography of the Caribbean begins with the arrival of Columbus.

Before the end of the first decade after 1492, manuscript maps had been drawn showing the outline of the Greater and Lesser Antilles with some accuracy, and during the early sixteenth century, when the Spaniards were still centrally interested in the area, increasingly accurate maps were produced. However, the conquest of Mexico in 1519, and the subsequent diversion of Spanish attention from the islands, meant that the pace of this active initial phase was not sustained. For the rest of the century attention would be focused on the mainland, and as always cartographic development followed the main area of political and economic interest.

From 1520 to 1650 we shall therefore find only minor improvements to the general image. In this work the Spaniards continued to predominate, working out of Seville, where since 1508 they had had a navigation school that was the envy of the other European powers. As ships' masters returned from overseas voyages, they had to report to the pilots and cosmographers of this school (housed in the *Casa de Contratación*), who then accurately entered all well-founded geographical observations on the master map or

Padrón Real. This master map was also used to equip outgoing mariners with appropriate detailed maps.

The Spaniards had developed this cartographic system by following the example of the Portuguese, who during the fifteenth century had worked out their own master map or *padrao real.* However, the Portuguese were relatively uninterested in the Caribbean, concentrating on Brazil and the Far East instead. Neither Spain nor Portugal had printing presses capable of producing large, detailed maps, which is why most of their cartographic innovations reached the restricted reading public only through the printers of Germany, Italy and the Low Countries. The German printers were particularly prominent between 1501 and 1520, when the outline of the Caribbean was first being established. Later on, in the 1550s and 1560s, French cartographers of the Dieppe School also compiled manuscript maps of the Caribbean, and towards the end of this period we find West Indian maps in the first maritime atlas published by an Englishman, in Robert Dudley's *Arcano del Mare* (Florence, 1647).

The early Spanish manuscript maps showing the Caribbean are widely scattered throughout Europe, often still in the princely archives to which they were originally sent. On the whole they have survived well, for they were generally drawn on vellum, using natural inks, and were from the start prized as precious objects even when their geographical information had long been made out of date. Printed maps are surprisingly abundant even from the sixteenth century, for they too commanded a good price from the start, and also tended to be carefully kept even when they became outdated.

Islands in the 'Ocean Sea'

The first surviving European map of the Caribbean islands was drawn about 1500 by Juan de La Cosa, who may have accompanied Columbus on his second voyage in 1493–4, and subsequently made other transatlantic voyages (Plate 9). This map shows the islands of the Caribbean with remarkable accuracy, naming Cuba and 'Española' and some of the smaller eastern islands. To the west lay *terra incognita*, upon which La Cosa placed the image of Saint Christopher (Columbus thought of himself as 'the Christbearer'). To the north La Cosa daringly sketched in a coast from Florida (as yet undiscovered) to the 'sea discovered by the English' up by Newfoundland; to the south he showed some of the coast of what would be South America. Over the whole Caribbean area fly the flags of Castille, for this region lay within the region assigned to that Crown by the Treaty of Tordesillas (1494).

Technically, the map of Juan de La Cosa comes straight out of the medieval portolan chart tradition. The eastern half of the map, not shown on Plate 9, delineates Europe and Africa in the way that had become common from about 1300 onwards. The coastlines are well observed, and territorial allegiances are shown by flags, just as they are on the New World half of the map. There is a gross difference in scale between the two halves, for the New World is shown as being much larger than it should be, and within this half of the map certain features, like 'Isla Fuerte' off the South American coast, are in turn shown at a very large scale. This was in accordance with the medieval practice of giving a larger scale to those elements of the map that the cartographer wished to emphasize.

Subsequent maps tended to retain the scorpion-like shape of Cuba, and in many cases to misinterpret the eastern chain of islands, which La Cosa had shown so well. Thus in 1506 Francisco Roselli of Florence engraved a world map by Giovanni Matteo Contarini, of which a single copy survives in the British Library (Plate 10). Here the 'Terra de Cuba', 'Jamaica' and 'Insula hispaniola' are marked, with a Latin inscription noting that 'these are the islands which Master Christopher Columbus discovered for the most serene King of Spain'. Immediately to the west of these islands lies 'Zipagu', Marco Polo's Japan, itself situated some way eastward of the coast of Asia.

This image of the world, with the Caribbean islands floating in the 'Ocean Sea' not very far off the coast of Asia, survived until Vasco Núñez de Balboa sighted the great Southern Sea, or Pacific Ocean, in 1513. After that time cartographers like Martin Waldseemüller guessed that there might be a thin ribbon of land separating the Caribbean from the Pacific, but it was not until 1519 that Alonso Avarez de Pineda sailed around the eastern shore of the Gulf of Mexico, confirming that it was an enclosed basin.

Thus as late as 1519 the anonymous cartographer who composed the superb 'Miller' atlas, still in ignorance of Pineda's voyage, offered a blank region west of Cuba (Plate 11). However, by then the shape of Cuba had been fully grasped, and the size and position of the other Caribbean islands much more fully appreciated. From Trinidad at the end of the chain we can follow the names around: Dominica, Guadeloupe, Saint Croix, San Juan (Puerto Rico) and so forth. This map is a summary of Spanish knowledge of the Antilles, in the period before the mainland came to be known and exploited.

This is also a fine example of the way in which maps can transmit images of natural history and of everyday life. The woods and creatures at the top left of the plate seem to come out of the Edenic phase of European reporting of their New World, while the figures at the lower left convey a lively impression of the indigenous activities of hunting and digging for gold.

The closing of the Gulf (1519–30)

Pineda's voyage is unusual in that the resultant manuscript map has survived. He had set sail from Jamaica in 1518, touched land in western Florida, and lingered for a while at the mouth of the Mississippi River, marked as the 'Rio del Espirito Santo', or River of the Holy Spirit, a name which it retained for some decades. The expedition eventually came to grief on the Mexican coast, but the map which survived from it showed not only the Gulf coast but also the Yucatán peninsula, in much their correct proportions.

During the ensuing decade, the Caribbean Sea and the Gulf of Mexico were delineated in many maps of the Seville school, of which about a dozen have survived. The latest of these is the map drawn by Diogo Ribero about 1532, now preserved in the ducal library at Wolfenbüttel. This map is more detailed than most of its predecessors, but it resembles them stylistically. Major geographical regions are shown in bold print. The 'Golfo de la Nueva España' is the Gulf of Mexico, and the 'Islas de las Lucayas' are named for the Indian inhabitants, who by this date had mostly perished. The two 'tierras' or lands in North America are named for the Spanish entrepreneurs who had been trying to settle them, Lucas Vasquez de Ayllón of Hispaniola and Francisco de Garay of Jamaica.

Other features are shown in smaller characters beginning with 'La Bermuda' out in the Atlantic Ocean. Among the Bahama Islands 'Guanahani' is conspicuous; it was the site of the Columbus landfall. The Greater Antilles are rather grossly shown, but the Lesser Antilles appear in considerable detail, mostly with the names that survive today. Reading from the north we have 'Las Virgines', 'Anegada', 'Sombrero', 'Anguila', 'S Bartomomé', 'Labarda' (Barbadu), 'Antigua', 'Dominica', 'Guadeloupe', 'Matenino', 'S Lucia', 'S Vicento', 'Barbados', 'La Granada', 'Tobago' and 'La Trinidad', the latter with the 'Boca del Drago'. There is also much detail on the northern coast of South America and in Central America; however, the west coast of Mexico had not yet been plotted in 1532.

This map represents the end of the first phase of Caribbean map making, which had been almost exclusively the work of the Spaniards. They had taken the medieval art of portolan chart making, and applied it to a new continent. The result was maps that gave a good enough idea of the outline of the land and sea, but were as yet useless for long-distance navigation, since they did not take into account the sphericity of the earth; that problem would not be solved until the advent of Gerard Mercator's projection, after the middle of the century. One medieval form survived for a while, and that was the *rutter*, or set of sailing directions. Such a description, known as the *Espejo de Navegantes*, was compiled by Alonso de Chaves about 1530, and forms an interesting check on the cartographic evidence.

Some geographical concepts were expressed not in maps or rutters, but in texts like those published by Peter Martyr (c. 1457–1526), Gonzalo Fernández de Oviedo (1478–1557), and Amerigo Vespucci (1454–1512). Martyr's *De Orbe Novo*, taking the form of letters written over many years, was widely translated and gave Europeans their earliest impression of the Indies; it also included a map. Oviedo's *De la Natural Historia de las Indias* (Toledo, 1526) included many plates, and covered not only geography but also natural history, making its author the first systematic natural scientist of the New World. Vespucci has become a somewhat shadowy figure, because of the doubt surrounding two of the voyages that he claimed to have made. But the *Letters* that he published in the early sixteenth century, often with plates, also played their part in forming the geographical concepts of the Europeans.

The Antilles delineated, 1530–1650

After 1519 the Spaniards were much diverted by their expansion into Central and South America, so that during the next hundred years the area would be most innovatively mapped by other Europeans, including the French, Dutch and English. As early as 1520 there had been French expeditions to Brazil, and the mariners of Dieppe, on the English Channel, were in the vanguard of overseas expansion. They represented the maritime arm of trading interests that reached back to the great mercantile centre of Rouen, and from there in some cases to the merchant families of Italy and Germany.

From about 1540 onwards the cartographers of the 'Dieppe School' began producing manuscript maps and atlases of the world, on which the Caribbean was well shown. These mapmakers began by copying the Spanish and Portuguese chartmakers, but eventually developed distinctive maps of their own. One characteristic example of their work has an elegant flowered border and lively scenes. Indians are shown mining gold in South America under the gaze of a Spaniard carrying a musket.

There is an imaginary group of islands to the east of Tobago, but the islands are otherwise well delineated, following Spanish models. During the 1550s French ships probably began to penetrate the Caribbean, and there were French expeditions to Florida in 1562 and 1564. The maps of the Dieppe School thus came to include more details about the West Indian islands, which were particularly well shown in Guillaume le Testu's *Cosmographie Universelle* of 1555, now at the Ministère des Armées in Paris.

From the middle of the sixteenth century onwards, large printed maps of the world began to appear, often showing the West Indies in some detail. They were printed in the Netherlands, Germany or Italy, since Spain lacked

312

presses large enough for this task. Thus in 1544 Sebastian Cabot published his world map at Antwerp, followed most notably by those of Abraham Ortelius (also at Antwerp, 1564) and Gerard Mercator (Duisburg, 1567). It is hard to make any estimate about the original diffusion of these large world maps, since they often hung on walls, and were destroyed once they became shabby and outdated.

Philip II, who came to the throne of Spain in 1556, greatly encouraged cartographic activity of all kinds, and during the 1570s was in part responsible for the extensive mapping of Spain's overseas possessions. In 1577, indeed, he sent out a general order for his administrators to compile and send back to Spain reports accompanied by maps, and in response to this request about 100 such maps, or *pinturas*, were made, and were sent back to Spain as part of the *relaciones geográficas*. Alas, if any *pinturas* were made for the Caribbean, none seems to have survived.

The information contained in the *relaciones geográficas* was summarized in a series of maps by the royal cosmographer López de Velazco, eventually published by Antonio de Herrera in the *Décadas* (Madrid, 1601–1615). Plate 12 shows the map describing the *Audiencia* of Española from this series, which contained a general world map and thirteen subsidiary maps. This 'Description del Destricto del Audiencia de la Española' is not particularly innovative or even very accurate, but it does form part of a remarkable cartographic project. Only the Spanish Crown at this time would have been capable of producing a uniform set of fourteen maps showing all its overseas possessions, for only the Spanish Crown had been able to develop and to some extent control so massive an effort of colonization.

As the century wore on, the Spanish Caribbean became more and more vulnerable to French, Dutch and English attacks, but these raids, a sort of marine banditry, did not lead to any striking cartographic developments. The general image of the Antilles remained as it had been established in the 1520s, for the pirate bands lacked the skill and inclination to produce their own charts, though of course they used Spanish charts when they fell into their hands. It was not until the eighteenth century that the European powers began to operate in the Caribbean with huge naval fleets, for which the so-called 'Admiralty charts' were indispensable cartographic tools. With the composition of the Admiralty charts, every part of the Caribbean came under close scrutiny and was mapped with hitherto unknown care and precision.

The earliest precursor of these general sea atlases was the *Spieghel der Zeevaert* (in English, *The Mariner's Mirror*), published by Lucas Waghenaer at Leiden in 1584–5. This contained only charts of the coasts of Europe, but eventually led to such publications as the *Dell' Arcano del Mare* of Robert Dudley, published at Florence in 1647. One of the Caribbean maps in the *Arcano* shows the islands with great clarity and detail, and located in roughly their correct positions. As far as the West Indies are concerned, Dudley's work marks an important point. It was composed when the Caribbean was still a Spanish lake, before the major incursions of the other European powers. It made no basic improvements over the early models, but it did provide a detailed map in *printed* form.

Over the ensuing years, the islands would be mapped in detail and their relative positions much more accurately established by naval surveyors. During the eighteenth century, navigational instruments achieved an accuracy hitherto unknown, and the development of an accurate chronometer allowed the precise plotting of longitude. Moreover, developments in the art of printing meant that large atlases could be produced relatively cheaply, and frequently revised in the light of fresh observations. The Admiralty charts introduced a form of chartmaking that has survived virtually unchanged down to the present day.

Individual island maps

It was a remarkable feat, given the complexity of the geography, to have established the general location of most of the Caribbean islands as early as 1520. However, this early work was carried out by marine cartographers, using techniques originally developed to map the Mediterranean with portolan charts. There was no comparably excellent tradition of land cartography, which is one of the reasons why the detailed internal mapping of the islands lagged behind. After 1520, too, the islands' importance to the Spaniards was much reduced, so that any motive to produce detailed topographical maps of them had almost disappeared.

Among the Greater Antilles, it was 'Hispaniola' that received most attention. In 1509 the pilot Andrés de Morales produced a map of the island that traced its outline with considerably accuracy, and showed the fourteen town sites already established by the Spaniards. This map has along its bottom edge a scale running from 0 to 190, but its purpose is not clear. About seven years later some unknown cartographer produced a manuscript map of the island, now bound into a copy of Peter Martyr's *Décadas* preserved at the Library of the University of Bologna. This map has a considerable advantage over the version of 1509. It is in colour, with the hills picked out in green, the plains in brown and the rivers in blue. The towns are marked in much the same way as on the Morales map, but they now number sixteen. In short, we have here a striking image of the island at the height of its importance during the first phase of Spanish expansion, before it became chiefly important as a base of operations for the ventures in the rest of the Americas.

About 1545 the Spanish cosmographer Alonso de Santa Cruz compiled his *Islario General*, now preserved at the Bibliotheca Nacional in Madrid. This work is in effect a geography of the world known to the Spaniards, and has accompanying maps. The one of Santo Domingo is rather unsatisfactory, in that it offers a stubby outline less accurate than those of the maps of 1509 and 1516. But the accompanying text is remarkably full, and read in conjunction with the map offers a good idea of the extent of Spanish settlement at the time.

After 1540 there was a long period of stagnation in the cartographic representation of Santo Domingo. It did appear as a single map, 'Hispaniola Insula', in the *Descriptionis Ptolemaicae Augmentum* published by Cornelius à Wytfliet at Louvain in 1597, but this map represents a regression on the early versions, as does the *Mapa de las Islas de Santo Domingo y de la Tortuga* published at Mexico City by Montemayor de Cuenca in 1658. For a fuller and more accurate delineation of the island we have to await the early eighteenth century, and the emergence of French Saint-Domingue.

Much the same pattern of development holds for Cuba. Here the early settlement was less intensive; Santa Cruz, for instance, allots to Cuba less than a third of the space assigned to Santo Domingo. As we have seen, on the earlier general maps the island had a scorpion-like shape, but this had been corrected by about 1520. The map of Cuba in the *Islario General* of Santa Cruz is a masterpiece, astonishingly accurate for the north coast and deficient only in the exaggerated length it gives to the south-east coastline (Plate 13). Eight settlements are shown, and there is an attempt to delineate the mountains in green. The map of 'Cuba Insula' in Wytfliet's *Descriptionis* of 1597 marked no improvement on the work of Santa Cruz, which would not be surpassed until the maps of the French cartographers of the late eighteenth century.

Jamaica was even less well served than Cuba. It did appear in the anonymous world map accompanying the edition of Peter Martyr's *Décadas* published at Seville in 1511, but this was in very gross form. Surprisingly, the version offered by Santa Cruz in his *Islario General* was not very much fuller, perhaps because the island depended not on the Spanish Crown, but on the Columbus family. Spanish cartographers only began to make relatively full maps of Jamaica after the English invasion of the island in 1655.

The same neglect is found for Puerto Rico and the Lesser Antilles, which were, after all, peripheral to Spain's military concerns throughout this period. In about 1614, it is true, Nicolás de Cardona did provide maps of the islands in his 'Descriptiones geographicas e hydrographicas de muchas tierras y mares del Norte y Sur en las Indias' of 1614, but these were remarkably crude for the period, as the map of Barbados shows (Plate 14). As in the case of the Greater Antilles, we have to await the period of greater interest by the other European powers to find more detailed and accurate maps.

315

The mapping of cities

As we saw in Chapter 8, Spanish culture in the Old World was primarily an urban culture, inheriting from the Roman Empire a political and economic structure based on the towns, and so quite different from the feudal rural societies of northern Europe. It is therefore not surprising that in the New World their towns were from the start relatively fully mapped, sometimes in response to the requirements of the Code of the Indies concerning town planning, and sometimes as part of some fortifications project.

During the first half of the sixteenth century these plans were often drawn in a more or less improvised fashion by officials on the spot. However, towards the end of the century, with the rising menace from French, Dutch and English pirates, the Crown began to send out highly-qualified engineers, who mapped the cities of the Spanish Caribbean in the course of preparing for their fortification.

One of the earliest of these engineers was Bautista Antonelli, who came to the West Indies in 1581. Antonelli was a member of an engineering dynasty, which originally came from the region of Rome. We do not know where he was trained, but the accuracy and elegance of his work suggest that he was acquainted with the latest techniques of his time. He worked at Santo Domingo, Havana, Cartagena, Veracruz, San Juan, Portobelo and Panamá, leaving plans of many of these places. Plate 15 shows his plan of Santo Domingo, drawn in 1592. Two alternative lines of fortification are shown, enclosing the urban area within which the main monuments are precisely sited, though without any indication of the streets. A scale in feet completes this document, which would have been an essential tool for planning the re-fortification of the city.

By the end of the sixteenth century the Spanish Crown no longer had to rely on engineers from abroad, but had produced able engineers trained in the peninsula. One of these was Cristóbal de Rojas (c. 1555–1614), who was born in Toledo and became a professor at the Mathematic Academy established by Philip II at Madrid in 1582. Rojas worked all over the peninsula, and his son(?), also named Cristóbal de Rojas, visited many sites in the Caribbean. In his plan of Havana, drawn in 1603, there are two alternative lines of fortification, and an explanatory cartouche by the scale bar. This cartouche contains key references to 24 points in the city, including the main churches and hospitals, the governor's palace and the major elements in the fortifications.

Six years later, Rojas drew a plan of Panamá which is even more impressive in its coverage. This time it takes in not only the city and its streets, with the fortification on the spit, but also the adjacent countryside. It does not appear that Rojas envisaged any fortifications for the town on its land side; certainly it fell into the hands of Henry Morgan in 1671 with relative ease. After his pirates had finished sacking and burning the site, there was little choice but to move to a new one, and 'Panamá Vieja' soon became ruinous.

In 1592, as we have seen, Antonelli had proposed two possible fortification schemes for Santo Domingo (Plate 15). Either would have been very costly, but it looks from a plan prepared for Governor Antonio Ossorio in 1608 as if the cheaper one was chosen. This elegant plan, with its scale and orientation sign, shows not only the line of fortifications but also the pattern of streets, which is in conformity with the recommendations of the Code of the Indies for Spanish colonial towns. Most of the plan is drawn planometrically, as if seen directly from above, but here and there prominent features are sketched in elevation.

After the burst of work for two decades each side of 1600, the major Spanish sites of the Caribbean tended merely to be maintained in their existing state – no easy task in view of the constant depredations of the climate. Some plans were drawn during the 1630s and 1640s, but these were often inferior to those produced in the days of Rojas and Antonelli. It was as if the general decline of Spanish power was felt even in the maps of her engineers. Towards the end of the century fine maps again came to be drawn, as the influence of Bourbon Spain more and more infiltrated the peninsula.

Conclusion

In the Caribbean as elsewhere, cartography closely reflected both political needs and technological possibilities. The skilled marine cartographers of Seville found their talents most fully exercised during the early decades of Spanish expansion, producing accurate maps of the Caribbean at the period when it was at the centre of Spanish preoccupations. Later, the best work came to be done by Frenchmen of the Dieppe School, and then by the Dutch and English.

Although the detailed mapping of the islands tended to be neglected during the sixteenth century, the great cities that were the nodal points of the Spanish empire came to be mapped in great detail, as part of the attempt to protect these vital ports from attack. At the height of that effort, the Crown was able to call upon the services of remarkably able engineers, whose plans remain crucial evidence for those interested in the historical reconstruction of the great Spanish cities of the Caribbean.

NOTES

Manuscript sources

Many of the great world maps associated with the cartographers of Seville are scattered throughout European collections. For other material, however, three Spanish depositories are very rich:

1   The *Archivo General de Indias* at Seville holds many maps abstracted over the centuries from the *legajos* (or 'bundles') which held the administrative correspondence from the colonies.

2   The *Biblioteca Nacional* at Madrid has in its departments of maps and of manuscripts much material collected over the centuries both from the Crown and from private individuals.

3   The *Archivo General de Simancas* contains many maps abstracted from the non-colonial correspondence of the Crown. These maps are often useful in tracing the early careers of persons who later worked in the colonies.

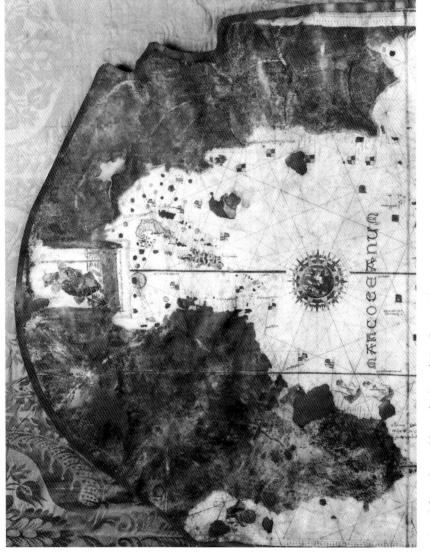

9 Detail from the world map by Juan de La Cosa, c.1500

10 Detail from the world map by Giovanni Matteo Contarini, 1505

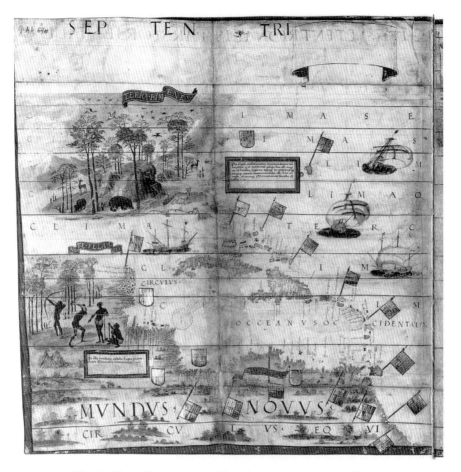

11 Detail of the Caribbean from the map of the Atlantic Ocean in the 'Miller' Atlas, 1519

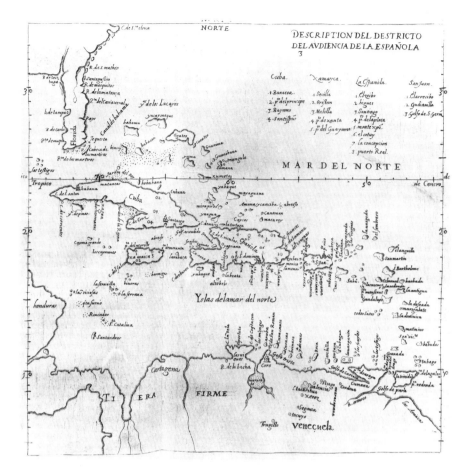

12 Map showing the Audiencia of Española, from the *Decadas* of Antonio Herrera, Madrid, 1601-15

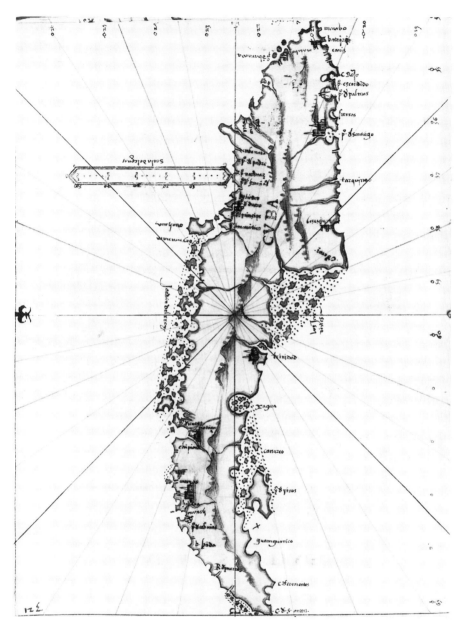

13 Cuba, from the *Islario General* of Alonso de Santa Cruz, c.1546

14 Barbados, from the *Descripción geográphica* of Nicolás de Cardona, 1592

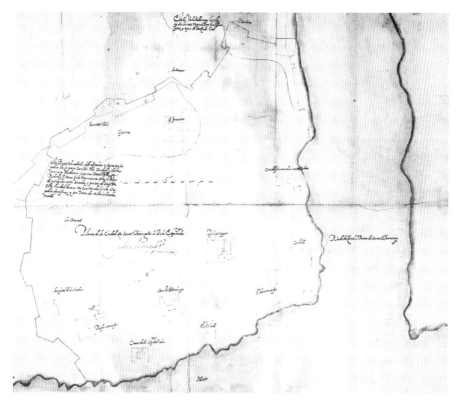

15 Plan of Santo Domingo by Bautista Antonelli, 1592

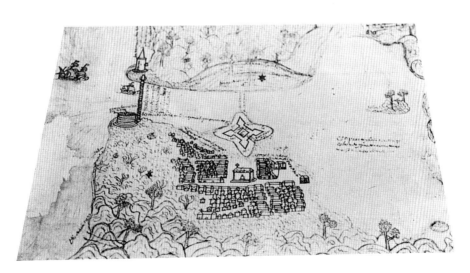

16 A plan of Havana by Cristobal de Rojas, c. 1603

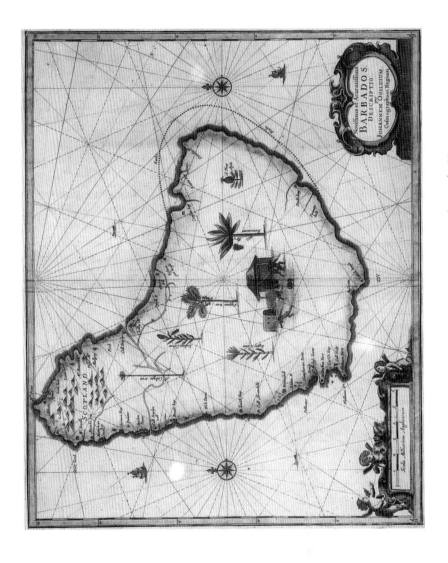

17 A new and accurate map of Barbados by John Ogilby, cartographer to the King

BIBLIOGRAPHY

Acosta, José de (1952) *De Procuranda Indorum Salute* (Trans. Francisco Matos), Madrid: Ediciones de la Biblioteca de Autores Españoles.

——, (1984) *Historia Natural y Moral de las Indias*, First edition, Vol. II, Madrid: Casa de Juan de León.

Acosta Saignes, Miguel (1967) *Vida de los esclavos negros en Venezuela*. Foreword by Roger Bastide, Caracas: Ediciones Hespérides.

Alba, Duke of (1951) *Mapas españoles de América, siglos XV–XVII*, Madrid.

Alegría, Ricardo E. (1978a) *Apuntes en torno a la mitología de los indios taínos de las Antillas mayores y sus orígenes suramericanos*, San Juan: Centro de Estudios Avanzados de Puerto Rico, and Santo Domingo: Museo del Hombre Dominicano.

——, (1978b) *Las primeras representaciones gráficas del indio americano, 1493–1523*, San Juan: Centro de Estudios Avanzados de Puerto Rico and the Institute of Puerto Rican Culture.

——, (1980) *Cristóbal Colón y el tesoro de los indios taínos de La Española*, Santo Domingo: Fundación García-Arévalo, Inc.

Allsopp, Richard, 'La influencia africana sobre el idioma en el Caribe' (Trans. from English by Arturo Ross Milton), in Moreno Fraginals, *Africa en América Latina*.

Alvarez Terán, Conceptión (1980) *Mapas, planos y dibujois* (from the Archivo General de Simancas), Valladolid.

Angulo Iñiquez, Diego (1942) *Bautista Antonelli*, Madrid.

Andrews, Kenneth R. (ed.) (1959) *English privateering Voyages to the West Indies, 1588–1595*.

——, (1978) *The Spanish Caribbean, Trade and Plunder, 1530–1630*.

——, (1979) *The Westward Enterprise: English Activities in Ireland, the Atlantic and America, 1480–1650*.

——, (1984) *Trade, Plunder and Settlement: Maritime Enterprise and the Genesis of the British Empire, 1480–1630*.

——, N.P. Canny and P.E.H. Hair, (eds) (1964) *Elizabethan Privateering. English Privateering during the Spanish War, 1585–1603*.

Arcila-Farias, E. (1946) Economía Colonial de Venezuela, Mexico City: Fondo de Cultura Económica.

——, (1957) El Régimen de la Encomienda en Venezuela, Seville: Escuela de Estudios Hispano-Americanos.

Arellano, Fernando (1987) *Una introducción a la Venezuela prehispánica: Culturas de las naciones indígenas venezolanas*, Caracas: Universidad Católica Andrés Bello.

ARISTOTLE (1976) *Anthropologie: textes choisis* (ed. and trans. Jean-Claude Fraisse), Paris: Presses Universitaires de France.

ARROM, JOSÉ JUAN (1975) *Mitología y artes prehispánicas de las Antillas*, Mexico City: Siglo XXI.

BACHMAN, VAN CLEAF (1969) *Peltries or Plantations. The Economic Policies of the Dutch West India Company in New Netherland, 1623–1639.*

BALANDIER, GEORGES (1975) *Antropo-lógicas*, Barcelona: Editorial Península.

BARNET, MIGUEL (1983) *La fuente viva*, Havana: Editorial Letras Cubanas.

BARRY, PHILIPPE *Mémoires et documents pour servire à l'histoire du commerce.*

BASSET-LOWKE, W.J. and GEORGE HOLLAND (1950) *Barcos y hombres*, Buenos Aires: Biblioteca Pleamar Conocimiento.

BASTIDE, ROGER (1969) *Las Américas negras*, Madrid: Alianza Editorial.

——, (1982) 'Los cultos afroamericanos', *Movimientos religiosos derivados de la aculturación*, Vol. 12: *Historia de las religiones*, Mexico City: Siglo XXI.

BATIE, ROBERT CARLYLE (1976) 'Why Sugar? Economic Cycles and the Changing of Staples on the English and French Antilles, 1624–54', *Journal of Caribbean History*, VIII–IX, pp. 1–41.

BENNET, J. HARRY (1967) 'The English Caribees in the Period of the Civil War, 1624–1646', *William and Mary Quarterly*, 3rd Ser., XXIV.

BENOIST, JEAN (1987) 'La organización social en las Antillas' (trans. from the French by Celia Antiga), in Moreno Fraginals, *Africa en América Latina.*

BENZONI, GIROLAMO (1857) *History of the New World*, London: Hakluyt Society.

BEROES, MANUEL (1982) 'Estructuración de los núcleos primeros y primarios de implantación', in CENDES, *Formación histórico-social de América Latina.*

BESTARD, JOAN and JESÚS CONTERAS (1987) *Bárbaros, paganos, salvajes y primitivos, una introducción a la antropología*, Barcelona: Editorial Barcanova (Temas Universitarios).

BIET, ANTOINE (1664) *Voyage de la France équinoxiale en l'isle de Cayenne.*

BLASQUEZ, ANTONIO (ed.) (1920) *Islario general de todas las islas del mundo*, by Alonso de Santa Cruz, 2 vols, Madrid.

BOITEUX, L.A. (1955) *Richelieu 'grand maître de la navigation et du commerce de France'.*

BOON, JAMES (1989) *Otras tribus, otros escribas: Antropología simbólica en el estudio comparativo de culturas, historias, religiones y textos*, Mexico City: Fondo de Cultura Económica. [English original: *Other Tribes, Other Scribes: Symbolic Anthropology in the Comparative Study of Cultures, Histories, Religions, and Texts*, New York: Cambridge UP, 1982.]

BOUCHER, PHILIP P. (1979) 'The Caribbean and the Caribs in the Thought of Seventeenth-Century Colonial Propagandists: The Missionaries', *Proceedings of the French Colonial History Society*, 4.

——, (1979) 'French Images of America and the Evolution of Colonial Theories, 1650–1700'. *Proceedings of the Annual Meeting of the Western Society for French History.*

——, (1989) *Les Nouvelles Frances, France in America, 1500–1815. An Imperial Perspective.*

——, (n.d.) 'A Colonial Company at the Time of the Fronde: The Company de la Terre Ferme de l'Amérique ou France équinoxiale', n.l.

BOUTON, JACQUES (1640) *Relation de l'établissement des François depuis 1635 dans l'isle de la Martinique.*

BOXER, C.R. (1965) *The Dutch Seaborne Empire, 1600–1800*, London.

——, (1969) *The Portuguese Seaborne Empire*, London.

BOYER DE PETIT PUY (1654) *Relation de tout ce qui s'est fait et passé au voyage que M. de Brétigny fit à l'Amerique occidentale.*

BRATHWAITE, EDWARD KAMAU (1987) 'Presencia africana en la literatura del Caribe' (trans. from the English by Feliciana Menocal), in Moreno Fraginals, *Africa en América Latina.*

BRAUDEL, FERNAND (1982) *The Perspective of the World. Civilization and Capitalism*, New York: Harper & Row.

——, (1982) *The Wheels of Commerce. Civilization and Capitalism*, New York: Harper & Row.

BRENNER, ROBERT (1972) 'The Social Basis of English Commercial Expansion, 1550–1650', *Journal of Economic History*, XXXII.

BRESSON, B. (JACQUES PETITJEAN ROGET (ed.)) (1975) *Histoire de l'Isle de Grenade en Amérique, 1649–1659*, (attributed to the religious Dominican Bénigne Bresson).

BRETON, RAYMOND (1647; rpt. 1978) *Relations de l'île de la Guadeloupe.*

——, (1923) 'The Voyages of Captain William Jackson (1642–1645)' in V.T. Harlow *et al.* (eds) *Camden Miscellany*, Vol. XIII.

——, (1925) 'A Breife (sic) Discription of the Islande of Barbados', in V.T. HARLOW *et al.* (eds) *Colonising Expeditions.*

BUCHER, BERNADETTE (1981) *Icon and Conquest*, Chicago.

BURG, B.R. (1983) *Sodomy and the Perception of Evil: English Sea Rovers in the Seventeenth Century.*

BUTEL, PAUL (1982) *Les Caraïbes au temps des flibustiers.*

——, (1982) 'Le temps des fondations: Les Antilles avant Colbert', *Histoire des Antilles et de la Guyane*, ch. III.

CALDERÓN QUIJANO, JOSÉ and LUIS NAVARRO GARCIA (1962) *Guía de los documentos, mapas y planos sobre historia de America … en la Biblioteca Nacional de Paris, Museo Britanico y Public Record Office de Londres*, Seville.

CAMUS, MICHEL (ed.) (1985) 'Correspondance de Bertrand Ogéron', *Revue de la Société haïtiene d'histoire et de géographie*, XLIII.

CANNY, NICOLAS and ANTHONY PAGDEN (1987) *Colonial Identity in the Atlantic World, 1500–1800.*

CARANDE, RAMON (1965) *Carlos V y sus Banqueros. La Vida Económica en Castilla (1516–1556)*, Madrid: Sociedad de Estudios y Publicaciones.

CARDOSO, CIRO F.S. and HÉCTOR PÉREZ B. (1981) *Historia económica de América Latina.* Vol. I: *Sistemas agrarios e historia colonial*, Second edition, Barcelona: Grijalbo (Editorial Crítica).

CARPENTIER, ALEJO (1970) *Tientos y diferencias*, Second edition, Montevideo: Editorial Arca (Colección Ensayo y Testimonio).

——, (1972) *La música en Cuba*, Mexico City: Fondo de Cultura Económica.

CARRERA DAMAS, GERMÁN (1985) 'Diez puntos sobre la enseñanza de la Historia de Venezuela', Caracas: *Revista Tierra Firme*, No. 11., 3.3 (July–September 1985).

——, (1987) 'Huida y enfrentamiento', in Moreno Fraginals, *Africa en América Latina.*

——, and JOSEFINA RÍOS DE HERNÁNDEZ (1982) 'Estructuración capitalista de las sociedades implantadas latinoamericanas', in CENDES, *Formación histórico-social de América Latina.*

CASSA, ROBERTO (1974) *Los taínos de la Española*, Santo Domingo: Editora de la Universidad Autónoma de Santo Domingo.

CDI (1864–84) *Colleción de Documentos Inéditos relativos al descubrimiento, conquista y colonización de las posesiones españolas en América y Oceanía*, 42 Vols, Madrid: Real Academia de la Historia.

CEHOPU (COMISIÓN DE ESTUDIOS HISTORICOS DE OBRAS PUBLICAS Y URBANISMO) (1985) *Puertos y fortificaciones en América y Filipinas*, Madrid.

CENDES (CENTRO DE ESTUDIOS DEL DESARROLLO) (1982) *Formación histórico-social de América Latina*, Caracas: Ediciones Biblioteca de la Universidad Central de Venezuela.

CÉSPEDES DEL CASTILLO, G. (1957) 'Las Indias en el Reinado de los Reyes Católicos', *Historia Social y Economica de España e Hispanoamèrica*, Vol. II., ed. Jaime Vicens-Vives, Barcelona: Editorial Teide.

——, (1987) 'Raíces peninsulares y asentamiento indiano, los hombres de la frontera', in Solano, *Proceso histórico del conquistador.*

CHATILLON, DR MARCEL and GABRIEL DEBIEN (n.d.) 'La propogande imprimée pour les Antilles et la Guyane au 17e siècle, recrutement ou racolage?', *Notes d'histoire coloniale*, 217.

CHAUNU, PIERRE (1969) *L'expansion européenne du XIII au XV siècle*, Paris.

——, (1969) *Conquête et exploitation des nouveaux mondes (XVIe siècle)*, Paris.

——, (1973) *Conquista y explotación de los nuevos mundos (siglo XVI)*, Barcelona: Editorial Labor (Colección Nueva Clio). [Original French edition: *Conquête et exploitation des nouxeaux mondes (XVIe siècle)*, Paris: Presses Universitaires de France, 1969].

——, and HUGUETTE (1955–8) *Seville et l'Atlantique*, Paris: Armand Colin.

CHEVILLARD, PÈRE (1659) *Les desseins de Son Eminance de Richelieu pour l'Amérique.*

CHUECA, GOITIA, FERNANDO and TORRES BALBAS, LEOPOLDO (1981) *Planos de ciudades iberoamericanas y filipinas*, 2 vols, Madrid.

CIVRIEUX, M. DE (1980) 'Los Cumanagoto y sus vecinos', in A. Butt Colson (ed.) *Los Aborigenes de Venezuela; Volumen I: Etnologiá Antigua*, pp. 27–240, Caracas: Fundacion La Salle.

CLENDINNEN, I. (1987) *Ambivalent Conquests; Maya and Spaniard in Yucatan, 1517–1570*, Cambridge: Cambridge University Press.

COLÓN, CRISTÓBAL (1982) *Textos y documentos completos* (Foreword and notes by Consuelo Varela), Madrid: Editorial Alianza.

COPPIER, GUILLAUME (1645) *Histoire et voyage des Indes occidentales.*

CORTESAO, ARMANDO and AVELINO TEIXEIRA DA MOTA (1960) *Portugaliae Monumenta Cartographica*, 6 vols, Lisbon.

CRAVEN, WESLEY FRANK (1930) 'The Earl of Warwick, A Speculator in Piracy', *Hispanic American Historical Review*, 10.

CUMMING, W.P., SKELTON, R.A., and D.B. QUINN (1971) *The discovery of North America*, London.

DE GOEJE, C.H. (1939) 'Nouvel Examen des langues des Antilles', *Journal de la Société des Américanistes*, 31, pp. 1–120.

DE JUAN, ADELAIDA (n.d.) 'Las artes plásticas en las Antillas, México y América Central', in Moreno Fraginals, *Africa en América Latina*.

DE LAET, IOANNES (1625) *De Nieuwe Wereldt ofte bechrijvinghe van West-Indien*; Sp. transl. *Mundo nuevo o descripción de las Indias occidentales* (1988).

DEBIEN, GABRIEL (1952) *Les engagés pour les Antilles. 1634–1715*, (1955) 'Les premiers trafics des Iles: flibuste, chasse et pêche', *Annales des Antilles*, 3.

DELAFOSSE, MARCEL (1949) 'La Rochelle et les Iles au XVIIe siècle', *Revue d'histoire des colonies françaises*, XXXVI.

DELGADO, P. (1970) 'La política española con los caribes durante el siglo XVI', in *Homenaje a Pérez-Bustamante*, pp. 73–122, Madrid: Instituto de Gonzalo Fernández de Oviedo.

DEL RÍO MORENO, JUSTO L. (1991) *Los Inicios de la Agricultura Europea en el Nuevo Mundo (1492–1552)*, Sevilla.

DENEVAN, W. (1992a) 'The Pristine Myth: The Landscape of the Americas in 1492', *Annals of the Association of American Geographers*, 82 (3), pp. 369–85.

——, (1992b) 'Stone vs Metal Axes: The Ambiguity of Shifting Cultivation in Prehistoric Amazonia', *Journal of the Steward Anthropological Society*, 20, pp. 153–65.

DEVEREUX, GEORGES (1974) *Etnopsicoanálisis complementarista*, Buenos Aires: Amorrortu.

DEVÈZE, MICHEL (1977) *Antilles, Guyanes, La mer des Caraïbes de 1492 à 1789.*

DOS SANTOS, JUANA ELBEIN and DOSCOREDES M. DOS SANTOS, 'Religión y cultura negra', in Moreno Fraginals, *Africa en América Latina*.

DUNN, RICHARD S. (1972) *Sugar and slaves. The Rise of the Planter Class in the English West Indies, 1624–1713.*

——, (n.d.) 'Experiments Holy and Unholy, 1630–1631', in K.R. ANDREWS, N.P. CANNY AND P.H. HAIR (eds) *The Westward Enterprise.*

——, (n.d.) 'Masters, Servants and Slaves in the Colonial Chesapeake and Caribbean', in DAVID BEERS QUINN (ed.) *Early Maryland in a Wider World.*

DU TERTRE, JEAN BAPTISTE (1667–71; rpt. 1973) *Histoire générale des Antilles*, 4 vols.

ECHAGOIAN, LICENCIADO (1941) 'Relación de la Isla Española Enviada al Rey Don Felipe II', *Boletín det Archivo General de la Nación*, XIX (Diciembre).

ELIOT, J.H. (1966) *Imperial Spain*, New York: Mentor Books.

ELLIOTT, J.H. (1970) *The Old World and the New 1492–1650*, New York: Cambridge University Press.

ESQUEMELING, JOHN (1684–85; rpt. 1951) *Buccaneers of America. A True Account of the Most Remarkable Assaults committed of Late Years upon the Coasts of the West*

Indies by the Buccaneers of Jamaica and Tortuga (both English and French)
(Eng. ed.).

FEIJOO, SAMUEL (1987) 'Influencia africana en Latinoamérica, literatura oral y escrita', in
Moreno Fraginals, *Africa en América Latina.*

FELIPE CARDOT, CARLOS (1973) *Curazao hispánico (antagonismo flamenco-español).*

FERGUSON, R.B. and N.L. WHITEHEAD (eds) (1992) *War in the Tribal Zone. Expanding
States and Indigenous Warfare*, Santa Fe (NM): School of American Research
Press.

FERNANDES-ARMESTO, F. (1992) *Columbus*, Oxford: Oxford University Press.

FERNÁNDEZ ALVAREZ, MANUEL (1947) 'Orígenes de la Rivalidad Naval Hispano-Inglesa en
él siglo XVI', *Revista de Indias*, XXVIII–XXIV, (Abril–Septiembre), pp. 311–69.

FERNÁNDEZ DE OVIEDO Y VALDÉS, GONZALO (1851) *Historia general y natural de las Indias*,
Vol. I., Madrid: Real Academia de la Historia; (1959) Madrid: Biblioteca de
Autores Españoles, 5 Vols.

FIGAROLA-CANEDA, DOMINGO (1910) *Cartografía cubana del British Museum*, Habana.

FRATI, CARLOS (1929) *El mapa más antiguo de la isla de Santo Domingo y Pedro Martyr
de Angleria*, Florence.

FROSTIN, CHARLES (1975) *Les révoltes blanches à Saint-Domingue aux XVIIe et XVIIIe
siècles.*

GAINER, KIM (1988) 'The cartographic evidence for the Columbus Landfall', *Terrae
Incognitae*, 20, pp. 43–68.

GALENSON, DAVID W. (1981) *White Servitude in Colonial America. An Economic
Analysis.*

——, (1986) *Traders, Planters and Slaves: Market Behavior in Early English
America.*

GARCÍA, JESÚS (1990) *Africa en Venezuela: Pieza de Indias*, Caracas: Cuadernos
Lagoven.

GASPARINI, GRAZIANO (1956) *El arte colonial en Venezuela*, Caracas: Ediciones
Armitano.

GEHRING, DR CHARLES T. and DR J.A. SCHILTKAMP (1987) *New Netherland Documents*,
Vol. XVII, *Curaçao papers, 1640–1665.*

GERBI, ANTONELLO (1982) *La disputa del Nuevo Mundo, historia de una polémica,
1750–1900*, Second edition, Mexico City: Fondo de Cultura Económica.

GIL, JUAN (1989) *Mitos y utopías del descubrimiento*, Vol. I: *Colón y su tiempo*, Madrid:
Alianza Universidad.

——, (1989) *Mitos y utopías del descubrimiento*, Vol. III: *El Dorado*, Madrid: Alianza
Universidad.

——, (ed.) (1987) *El libro de Marco Polo anotado por Cristóbal Colón/El libro de
Marco Polo de Rodrigo de Santaella*, Madrid: Alianza Universidad.

GIMÉNEZ FERNÁNDEZ, MANUEL (1960) *Bartolomé de Las Casas*, Vol. II:, Seville: Escuela de
Estudios Hispanoamericanos de Sevilla.

GONZALEZ, JULIO (1973) *Catálogo de mapas y planos de Santo Domingo*, Madrid.

GOSLINGA, CORNELIUS CH. (1971) *The Dutch in the Caribbean and on the Wild Coast,
1580–1680.*

GREENE, JACK P. (1987) 'Changing identity in the British Caribbean', in N. CANNY and A. PAGDEN (eds) *Colonial identity in the New World.*

——, (n.d.) and J.R. POLE (eds) *Colonial British America: Essays in the New History of the Early Modern Era.*

GUANCHE, JESÚS (1983) *Procesos etnoculturales de Cuba*, Havana: Editorial Letras Cubanas.

GUERRERO, JOSÉ G. and MARCIO VELOZ MAGGIOLO (1988) *Los inicios de la colonizacion en América (La arqueología como historia)*, San Pedro de Macorís, Dom. Rep.: Ediciones de la Universidad Central del Este.

GUILLÉN Y TATO, JULIO F. (1942) *Monumenta chartographica indiana*, Madrid.

HAMEL, FRED and MARTIN HÜRLIMANN (1984) *Enciclopedia de la música*, Vol. I:, Tenth edition, Barcelona: Grijalbo.

HAMELBERG, J.H.J. (1901–3; rpt. 1979) *De Nederlanders op de West-Indische eilanden.* 2 Vols.

——, (1901) *Documenten behoorende bij de Nederlanders op de West-Indische eilanden. I Curazao, Bonaire, Aruba.*

HARCOURT, R. (1613) *A Relation of a Voyage to Guiana*, London: W. Welby.

HARING, C.H. (1939) *El Comercio y la Navegacion entre España y las Indias en Epoca de los Habsburgos*, Paris-Brujas: Descléc, De Brouwer.

HARISSE, HENRY (1892) *The Discovery of North America*, London/Paris.

——, (1926) *A History of Barbados, 1625–1685.*

HARLOW, VINCENT T. (1925) 'The Voyage of Sir Henry Colt' in *Colonising Expeditions.*

——, (1926) *A History of Barbados, 1625–1685.*

——, *et al.* (eds) (1925) *Colonising Expeditions to the West Indies and Guiana, 1623–1667.*

HART, RICHARD (1984) *Esclavos que abolieron la esclavitud*, Havana: Casa de las Américas (Colección Nuestros Países, Serie Estudios), 1984. [English edition: *Slaves Who Abolished Slavery*, Kingston: Inst. of Social and Economic Research, Univ. of the West Indies, 1980.]

HARTOG, JOHANNES (1956–64) *Geschiedenis van de Nederlandse Antilles*, Vol. I, *Aruba*; Vol. II, *Bonaire*; Vols. III–IV, *Curaçao*; Vol. V. *De bovenwindse eilanden.*

HASSIG, R. (1992) 'Aztec and Spanish Conquest in Mesoamerica', in R.B. Ferguson and N.L. Whitehead (eds) *War in the Tribal Zone. Expanding States and Indigenous Warfare*, pp. 83–102, Santa Fe (NM): School of American Research Press.

HENKEL, WILLI (1984) *Die Konzilien in Lateinamerika. Teil I. Mexico 1555–1897*, Mit einer Einführung von Horst Pietschmann, Paderborn-München-Wien-Zürich.

HENRÍQUEZ UREÑA, PEDRO (1988) *Obra dominicana*, Santo Domingo: Sociedad Dominicana de Bibliófilos, Inc.

HILTON, J. (1925) 'Relation of the First Settlements of St Christopher and Nevis', in V.T. HARLOW, *et al.* (eds) *Colonising Expeditions.*

HOFFMAN, PAUL E. (1980) *The Spanish Crown and the defense of the Caribbean, 1535–1585*, Baton Rouge.

HULME, P. and N.L. WHITEHEAD (1992) *Wild Majesty. Encounters with Caribs from Columbus to the Present Day*, Oxford: Clarendon Press.

INCHÁUSTEGUI, J. MARINO (1958) *Reles Cédulas y Correspondencia de Gobernadores de Santo Domingo*, Vols. I–III, Madrid: Gráficas Reunidas.

INNES, F.C. (1970) 'The Pre-sugar Era of European Settlement in Barbados', *Journal of Caribbean History*, I.

IVES, VERNON A. (ed.) (1984) *The Rich Papers: Letters from Bermuda, 1615–1646: Eyewitness Accounts Sent by the Early Colonists to Sir Nathaniel Rich*.

JAHN, HANHEINZ (1970) *Muntú: las culturas de la negritud*, Madrid: Ediciones Guadarrama.

JEDIN, HUBERT (1972) *Manual de historia de la iglesia*, Barcelona: Biblioteca Herder (Sección de Historia).

JOURDIN, MICHEL MOLLAT DU and MONIQUE DE LA RONCIÉRE (1984) *Sea Charts of the early explorers*, London.

KEEGAN, W.F. (1993) *The People who Discovered Columbus. The Prehistory of the Bahamas*, University Press of Florida: Gainesville.

KI-ZERBO, JOSEPH (1980) *Historia del Africa negra: desde sus orígenes hasta el siglo XX*, Madrid: Alianza. [Original French edition: *Histoire de l'Afrique noir, d'hier a demain*, Paris: Hatier, 1972.]

KONETZKE, RICHARD (1953) *Colección de documentos para la Historia de la Formación Social de Hispanoamerica, 1493–1810*, Vol. I, Madrid: Instituto Jaime Valdés, Consejo Superior de Investigaciones Científicas.

——, (1963) *Entdecker und Eroberer Amerikas. Von Christoph Kolumbus bis Hernàn Cortés*, Frankfurt.

——, (1965) *Süd- und Mittelamerika I: Die Indianerkulturen Altamerikas und die spanisch-portugiesische Kolonialherrschaft*, Fischer Weltgeschichte, Bd 22: Frankfurt/M.

LABAT, JEAN BAPTISTE (1722; rpt. 1972) *Nouveau voyage aux isles de l'Amérique*.

LAFLEUR, GÉRARD (1985) 'Les Juifs aux Iles françaises du Vent (XVII–XVIIIe siècles)', *Bull, de la Société d'histoire de la Guadeloupe*, 65–66.

——, (1987) 'Les Protestants aux Iles françaises du Vent sous l'Ancien Régime', *Bull. de la Société d'histoire de la Guadeloupe*, 71–74.

LAMB, URSULA (1956) *Frey Nicolás de Ovando. Gobernador de Las Indias (1501–1509)*, Madrid: Consejo Superior de Investigaciones Científicas, Instituto 'Gonzalo Fernández de Oviedo'.

LAS CASAS, B. DE (1875) *Historia de las Indias*, Madrid: Real Academia de la Historia, reprint (1951) Mexico: Fondo de Cultura Economica, 3 vols.

——, and BERNARDO VARGAS (n.d.) *La destrucción de las Indias and Refutación de las Casas*, n.c.: Sociedad de Ediciones Louis Michaud.

LÁSCARIS, CONSTANTINO (1970) *Historia de la ideas en Centro América*, San José, Costa Rica: Editorial Universitaria Centroamericana.

LATORRE, GERMAN (1916) *La cartografía colonial americana*, Seville.

LÉVI-STRAUSS, CLAUDE (1970) *El pensamiento salvaje*, Mexico City: Fondo de Cultura Económica. [Original French edition: *Pensée sauvage*, Paris: Librairie Plon, 1962; English edition: *The Savage Mind*, Chicago: Univ. of Chicago Press (Phoenix), 1966.]

LIGON, RICHARD (1654; rpt. 1970) *A True and Exact History of the Island of Barbadoes*.

LING, ROTH H. (1889) *Bibliography and cartography of Hispaniola*, London.

LUGO, AMÉRICO (1952) *Historia de Santo Domingo, 1556–1608*, Ciudad Trujillo Librería Dominicana.

LY, ABDOULAYE (1957) 'La formation de l'économie sucrière et le développement du marché d'esclaves africains dans les Iles françaises d'Amérique au XVIIe siècle' *Présence africaine*, 13.

LYNCH, JOHN (1965) *Spain Under the Habsburgs, 1521–1598. Empire and Absolutism*, Vol. I., New York: Oxford University Press.

MAGUIDOVICH, IÓSIF P. (1979) *Historia del descubrimiento y exploración de Latinoamérica*, Havana: Casa de las Américas (Colección Nuestros Países, Serie Rumbos).

MATHEWS, THOMAS G. (1969) 'The Spanish Domination of Saint-martin, 1633–1648', *Caribbean Studies*, 9/1.

MAURO, FRÉDÉRIC (1984) *Die europäische Expansion*, Stuttgart.

MAY, LOUIS-PHILIPPE (1930) *Histoire économique de la Martinique, 1635–1763*.

——, (1932) 'La plus ancienne relation de voyage aux colonies françaises des Antilles', ('Anonyme de Saint-Christophe' c. 1640), *La Géographie*.

MENKMAN, W.R. (1942) *De Nederlanders in het Caraïbische zeegebied*.

——, (1947) *De West-Indische Compagnie*.

MERLE, DR L. and G. DEBIEN (1953–4) 'Colons, marchands et engagés à Nantes au XVIIe siècle', *Revue de la porte Océane*, December 1953–February 1954.

MILLER, W.H. (1945) 'The Colonization of the Bahamas, 1647–70', *William and Mary Quarterly*, January.

MORALES PADRÓN, FRANCISCO (1952) *Jamaica española*, Seville.

——, (1981) *Historia del descubrimiento y conquista de América*, Fourth edition, Madrid: Editorial Nacional.

MOREAU, JEAN-PIERRE (ed.) (1987) *Un flibustier français dans la mer des Antilles en 1618/20*.

MORENO FRAGINALS, MANUEL (1987) 'Aportes culturales y deculturación', in Moreno Fraginals, *Africa en América Latina*.

——, (ed.) (1987) *Africa en América Latina*, Second edition, Mexico City: Siglo XXI/UNESCO.

MÖRNER, MAGNUS (1969) *La mezcla de razas en la historia de América Latina*, Buenos Aires: Paidós. [English edition: *Race Mixture in the History of Latin America*, New York: Little, Brown, 1967.]

MOYA PONS, FRANK (1973) *Historia Colonial de Santo Domingo*, Santiago de los Caballeros: Universidad Catolica Madre y Maestra.

——, (1986) *Después de Colón. Trabajo Sociedad y Política en la Economía del Oro*, Madrid: Alianza Editorial.

——, (1995) *Azúcar y Plantaciones. Una Historia del Caribe*, Alianza Editorial, Madrid.

MUÑOZ, JUAN BAUTISTA (1981) *Santo Domingo en los manuscritos de Juan Bautista Muñoz*, transcription and notes by Roberto Marte, Santo Domingo: Ediciones de la Fundación García Arévalo.

NAGY, A.S. (1982) 'Las Rutas del Comercio Prehispanico de los Metales', *Cuadernos Prehispanicos*, 10, pp. 5–132.

NEWTON, ARTHUR PERCIVAL (1933) *The European Nations in the West Indies, 1493–1688*. London: A. & C Black.

——, (1967) *The European Nations in the West Indies 1493–1688*, New York: Barnes and Noble, Inc.

NÚÑEZ JIMENEZ, ANTONIO (ed.) (1980) *Mapas Antiguos de Cuba*, Havana.

OJER, P. (1966) *La Formacion del Oriente Venezolano; I, Creacion de las Gobernaciones*, Caracas: Universidad Catolica Andres Bello.

ORTIZ, FERNANDO (1983) *Contrapunteo cubano del tabaco y el azúcar*, Havana: Editorial de Ciencias Sociales.

OTERO, LISANDRO and FRANCISCO MARTÍNEZ HINOJOSA (1971) *Política cultural de Cuba*, Paris: UNESCO.

OTTE, ENRIQUE (1960) 'Carlos V y sus Vasallos Patrimoniales de América', *Clio*, CXVI (Enero-Junio), pp. 1–27.

——, (1977) *Las perlas del Caribe; Nueva Cadiz de Cubagua*, Caracas: Fundacion John Boulton.

OVIEDO Y BANOS, J. DE (1885) *Historia de la conquista y población de la provincia de Venezuela*, Madrid: Luis Navarro.

PAGDEN, A. (1982) *The Fall of Natural Man; The American Indian and the origins of comparative ethnology*, Cambridge: Cambridge University Press.

PALM, ERWIN WALTER (1955) *Los Monumentos Arquitectónicos de la Española*, 2 vols, Ciudad Trujillo: Universidad de Santo Domingo.

——, (1974) *Arquitectura y arte colonial en Santo Domingo*, Santo Domingo: Editora de la Universidad Autónoma de S.D.

PARES, RICHARD (1970) *Merchants and Planters*.

PARRY, J.H. (1964) *The Age of Reconnaissance. The Quest for Gold and the Service of God*, New York: Mentor Books.

——, (1966) *The Spanish Seaborne Empire*, New York: Alfred Knopf.

——, and R.G. KEITH (eds) (1984) *New Iberian world*, 5 vols, New York.

——, and PHILIP SHERLOCK (1976) *Historia de las Antillas*, Buenos Aires: Kapelusz.

PAWSON, MICHAEL and DAVID BUISSERET (1975) *Port Royal, Jamaica*.

PAZ, JULIAN (1933) *Catálogo de manuscritos de América existentes en la Biblioteca Nacional*, Madrid.

PELLEPRAT, PIERRE (1655) *Relation des mission des pères de la Compagnie de Jésus*.

PEÑA Y CAMARA, JOSÉ MARIA DE LA (1958) *Archivo general de Indias de Sevilla*, Madrid.

PÉREZ, FRAY JUAN MANUEL (1984) *Estos ¿no son hombres?*, Santo Domingo: Ediciones Fundación García Arévalo.

PÉREZ MEMÉN, FERNANDO (1987) *Estudios de historia de ideas en Santo Domingo y en América*, Santo Domingo: Academia de Ciencias de la Rep. Dom.

PÉROTIN-DUMON, ANNE (forthcoming) 'The Pirate and the emperor: Power and the Law on the Seas, 1450–1850', in JAMES D. TRACY (ed.) *The Political Economy of Merchant Empires*.

PETITJEAN ROGET, JACQUES (1955) 'Courants de migration et courants commerciaux vers la Martinique', *Annales des Antilles*, 2.

——, (1955) 'Les protestants à la Martinique sous l'Ancien Régime', *Revue d'histoire des Colonies*, 147.

——, (1956) 'Les juifs à la Martinique sous l'Ancien régime', *Revue d'histoire des Colonies*, 151.´

——, (1985) *La société d'habitation à la Martinique: Un demi-siècle de formation. 1635–1685*, 2 Vols.

Pichardo Moya, Felipe (1956) *Los aborígenes de las Antillas*, First edition, Mexico City: Fondo de Cultura Economica.

Pietschmann, Horst (1980) *Staat und staatliche Entwicklung am Beginn der spanischen Kolonisation Amerikas*, Münster.

Piffer Canabrava, Alice (1981) *A acúnar nas Antilhas, 1697–1755*.

Prem, Hanns J. (1989) *Geschichte Altamerikas*, München.

Provins, Pacifique de (1646) *Briève relation du voyage des isles de l'Amérique*.

Puis, Matthias du (1652) *Relation de l'establissement d'une colonie française dans la Gardeloupe*. Hilton, J. (1925), 'Relation of the First Settlements of St Christopher and Nevis, in V.T. Harlow, *et al.* (eds) *Colonising Expeditions*.

Rabb, Theodore K. (1967) *Enterprise and empire: Merchant and Gentry Investment in the Expansion of England, 1575–1630*.

Rafinesque, C.S. (1836) *The American Nations; or, Outlines of their General History, Ancient and Modern*, Philadelphia.

Ramos Pérez, Demetrio (1987) *El mito de Dorado, su génesis y proceso, con el 'Discovery' de Walter Raleigh y otros papeles doradistas*, Second edition, Caracas: Biblioteca de la Academia nacional de la Historia (Colección fuentes para la Historia Colonial de Venezuela).

Ratekin, Mervyn (1954) 'The Early Sugar Industry in Española', *Hispanic American Historical Review*, XXXIV (February), pp. 1–19.

Ríos de Hernández, Josefina (1982) see Carrera Damas, Germán.

Rivero de la Calle, Manuel (1966) *Las Culturas aborígenes de Cuba*, Havana: Editorial Universitaria.

Rochefort, César de (1658) *Histoire naturelle et morale des îles Antilles de l'Amérique*.

Rodríguez, Ileana (1984) *Primer inventario del invasor*, Managua: Editorial Nueva Nicaragua (Colección Quinto Aniversario).

Rodríguez Demorizi, Emilio (1945) *Relaciones Históricas de Santo Domingo*, Vol. II, Ciudad Trujillo: Archivo General de la Nación.

——, (1966) *España y los comienzos de la pintura y la escultura en América*, Madrid: Gráficas Reunidas.

——, (1979) *Mapas y planos de Santo Domingo*, Santo Domingo.

Romano, Ruggiero and Alberto Tenenti (1974) *Los fundamentos del mundo moderno: Edad media tardía, reforma, renacimiento*, Fourth edition, Vol. IV of *Historia Universal Siglo XXI*, Mexico City: Siglo XXI.

Rosenblat, Angel (1965) *La primera visión de América y otros estudios*, Caracas: Ediciones del Ministerio de Educación (Colección Vigilia).

Rossignol, Philippe and Bernadette (1985) 'A propos d'une liste d'habitants de la Guadeloupe datée de 30 octobre 1664', *Bull. de la Société d'histoire de la Guadeloupe.* 65–66.

Rouse, I. (1948a) 'The Arawak', in J. Steward (ed.) *Handbook of South American Indians (vol. 4)*, pp. 507–46, Washington: Smithsonian Institution.

——, (1948b) 'The Carib', in J. Steward (ed.) *Handbook of South American Indians (vol. 4)*, pp. 547–65, Washington: Smithsonian Institution.

——, (1986) *Migrations in Prehistory*, New Haven: Yale University Press.

SAINT-MICHEL, MAURILE DE (1652) *Voyage des isles Camercanes.*

SALAS, ALBERTO M. (1986) *Tres cronistas de Indias*, Second edition, Mexico City: Fondo de Cultura Económica.

SALAZAR BONDY, AUGUSTO (1969) *¿Existe una filosofía en Nuestra América?*, Mexico City: Siglo XXI.

SALER, B. (1988) 'Los Wayú (Guajiro)', in J. Lizot (ed.) *Los Aborigenes de Venezuela; Volumen III; Etnología Contemporánea*, pp. 25–146, Caracas: Fundacion La Salle/Monte Avila Editores.

SANDOVAL, ALONSO DE (1987) *Un tratado sobre la esclavitud*, Madrid: Alianza.

SANTA CRUZ, ALONSO DE: see BLASQUEZ (1920).

SANTIAGO PAEZ, ELENA (1984) *La historia en los mapas manuscritos de la Biblioteca Nacional*, Madrid.

SAUER, CARL ORTWIN (1966) *The Early Spanish Main*, Berkeley: University of California Press.

——, (1984) *Descubrimiento y dominación española del Caribe*, trans. Stella Mastrangelo, Mexico City: Fondo de Cultura Económica. [English edition: *The Early Spanish Main*, Berkeley: University of California Press, 1966.]

SCHMITT, EBERHARD (ed.) (1987) *Dokumente zur Geschichte der europäischen Expansion. Band 3: Der Aufbau der Kolonialreiche*, München.

SCHWARTZ, STUART B. (1985) *Sugar Plantations in the Formation of Brazilian Society. Bahia. 1550–1835*, Cambridge: Cambridge University Press.

SEPÚLVEDA, JUAN GINÉS DE (1988) *Historia del Nuevo Mundo*, Madrid: Alianza Universitaria.

SERVANT, GEORGES (1913) 'Les compagnies de Saint-Christophe et des Iles de l'Amérique (1626–1653)', *Revue de l'histoire des colonies françaises* I.

SIMPSON, LESLEY BYRD (1929) *The Encomienda in New Spain. Forced Labor in the Spanish Colonies, 1492–1559*, Berkeley: University of California Press.

SLUITER, ENGEL (1948) 'Dutch-Spanish Rivalry in the Caribbean Area, 1594–1609', *Hispanic American Historical Review*, XXVIII (February), pp. 165–96.

SOLANO, FRANCISCO DE, *et al.* (eds) (1987) *Proceso histórico del conquistador*, Madrid: Alianza Universitaria.

——, (1987) 'El conquistador hispano, señas de identidad', in Solano, *Proceso histórico del conquistador.*

SOUDEN, DAVID (1978) 'Rogues, Whores and Vagabonds? Indentured Servant Emigrants to North America, and the Case of Mid-Seventeenth Century Bristol', *Social History*, III.

STEVENS-ARROYO, A.M. (1988) *The Cave of the Jagua. The Mythological World of the Tainos*, Albuquerque: University of New Mexico Press.

STEVENSON, EDWARD L. (1903) *Maps illustrating early discovery and exploration in America 1502–1530*, New Brunswick.

——, (1909) *Early Spanish cartography of the New World*, (n.p.)

SUED-BADILLO, J. (1978) *Los Indios Caribes; Realidad o Fabula?*, Rio Pedras: Editorial Antillana.

——, (1994) 'The Island Caribs: New Approaches to the Question of Ethnicity in the Early Colonial Caribbean', in N. Whitehead (ed.) *Wolves from the Sea: Readings in the Anthropology of the Native Caribbean*, Leiden: KITLV Press.

TANNENBAUM, FRANK (1968) *El negro en las américas: Esclavo y ciudadano*, Buenos Aires: Paidós. [English edition: *Slave and Citizen: The Negro in the Americas*, New York: Vintage, 1946.]

TAYLOR, D. (1977) *Languages of the West Indies*, Baltimore: John Hopkins University Press.

TODOROV, TZVETAN (1987) *La conquista de América: la cuestión del otro*, Mexico City: Siglo XXI. [Original French edition: *Conquête de l'Amerique*, Paris: Seuil, 1982. English edition: *Conquest of America: The Question of the Other*, trans. Richard Howard, New York: Harper & Row, 1984.]

TOUSSAINT, MANUEL (1946) *Arte mudéjar en América*, Mexico City: Editorial Porrua.

TROCONIS DE VERACOECHEA, ERMILA (1984) 'Aspectos generales de la esclavitud en Venezuela', Caracas: *Revista Tierra Firme*, No. 8., 2.2 (October–December 1984).

TUDELA BUESO, JUAN PÉREZ DE (1955) 'Castilla ante los dos Comienzos de la Colonización de las Indias', *Revista de Indias*, LIX (Enero-Marzo), pp. 11–88.

——, (1955) 'Política de Poblamiento y Política de Contratación de las Indias', (1502–1505), *Revista de Indias*, LXI–LXII (Julio-Diciembre), pp. 311–420.

——, (1955) 'La Quiebra de la Factoría y el Nuevo Poblamiento de la Española', *Revista de Indias*, LX (Abril–Junio), pp. 197–252.

URFÉ, ODILIO (n.d.) 'La música y la danza en Cuba', in Moreno Fraginals, *Africa en América Latina*.

UTRERA, FRAY CIPRIANO DE (1951) *Historia Militar de Santo Domingo. Documentos y Noticias*, Vol. I, Ciudad Trujillo: Tipografía Franciscana.

VARELA, C. (ed.) (1982) *Cristóbal Colón. Textos y documentos completos*, Madrid: Alianza Universidad.

VARGAS, M. and BERNARDO VEGA (n.d.) *Refutación de Las Casas*, see LAS CASAS.

VÁSQUEZ DE ESPINOSA, ANTONIO *Compendio y Descripción de Las Indias Occidentales*.

VÁSQUEZ, FRANCISCO (1987) *El Dorado: crónica de la expedición de Pedro de Ursua y Lope de Aguirre*, Madrid: Alianza Editorial.

VEGA, BERNARDO (1980) *Los cacicazgos de la Hispaniola*, Santo Domingo: Ediciones del Museo del Hombre Dominicano.

VERLINDEN, CHARLES (1962) *Christoph Kolumbus. Vision und Ausdauer*, Göttingen-Berlin-Frankfurt.

VIGNERAS, L-A. (1976) *The Discovery of South America and the Andalusian Voyages*, Chicago: Chicago University Press.

VILAR, PIERRE (1987) *Historia de España*, Twenty-fourth edition, Barcelona: Grijalbo (Editorial Crítica).

VILLAPOL, NITZA (n.d.) 'Hábitos alimentarios africanos en América Latina', in Moreno Fraginals, *Africa en América Latina*.

VINDEL, FRANCISCO (1956) *Mapas de América en los libros españoles de los siglos XVI al XVIII*, Madrid.

WATTS, DAVID (1966) *Man's Influence on the Vegetation of Barbados, 1627 to 1800*, Hull University.

WHITEHEAD, N.L. (1988) *Lords of the Tiger Spirit; A History of the Caribs in Colonial Venezuela and Guyana, 1498–1820*, KITLV Caribbean Studies Series 10, Dordrecht: Foris Publications.

——, (1990a) 'The Snake Warriors – Sons of the Tiger's Teeth. A Descriptive Analysis of Carib Warfare, 1500–1820', in J. Haas (ed.) *The Anthropology of War*, pp. 146–70, Cambridge: Cambridge University Press.

——, (1990b) 'Carib Ethnic Soldiering in Venezuela, the Guianas, and the Antilles', *Ethnohistory*, 37 (4) pp. 357–85.

——, (1990c) 'The Mazaruni Pectoral: A Golden Artefact Discovered in Guyana and the Historical Sources Concerning Native Metallurgy in the Caribbean, Orinoco, and Northern Amazonia', *Journal of Archaeology and Anthropology*, 7, pp. 19–38.

——, (1992) 'Tribes Make States and States Make Tribes. Warfare and the Creation of Colonial State and Tribe in Northeastern South America', in R.B. Ferguson and N.L. Whitehead (eds) *War in the Tribal Zone. Expanding States and Indigenous Warfare*, pp. 127–50, Santa Fe (NM): School of American Research Press.

——, (1993b) 'El Dorado, Cannibalism and the Amazons. European Myth and Amerindian Praxis in the Conquest of South America', in W. Pansters and J. Weerdenburg, (eds) *Beeld en Verbeelding van Amerika*, Vol. I, pp. 53–70, Utrecht: Rijksuni-versiteit Utrecht.

——, (1994a) 'The Ancient Amerindian Polities of Orinoco, Amazon and the Atlantic Coast. A preliminary analysis of their passage from antiquity to extinction', in A. Roosevelt, (ed.) *Amazonian Indians from Prehistory to the Present. Anthropological Perspectives*, pp. 20–35, Tuscon: University of Arizona Press.

——, (1994b) *Wolves from the Sea: Readings in the Anthropology of the Native Caribbean*, Leiden: KITLV Press.

WILSON, S.M. (1990) *Hispaniola; Caribbean Chiefdoms in the Age of Columbus*, Tuscaloosa: University of Alabama Press.

WINSOR, JUSTIN (1889) *Narrative and critical history of America*, 6 vols, Cambridge.

WRIGHT, IRENE A. (1916) *The Early History of Cuba 1492–1586*, New York: The Macmillan Company, p. 390.

——, (1916) 'The Commencement of the Sugar Cane Sugar Industry in America, 1519–1538 (1563)', *American Historical Review*, XXI (July), pp. 755–80.

——, (ed.) (1928) *Spanish documents Concerning English Voyages to the Caribbean 1527–1568*, London: The Hakluyt Society.

——, (ed.) (1929) *Spanish Documents Concerning English Voyages to the Caribbean 1527–1568*. London: The Hakluyt Society.

——, (1930) *Historia Documentada de San Cristóbal de la Habana*, Havana.

——, (1932) *English Documents Concerning English Voyages to the Spanish Main 1569–1580*.

——, and CORNELIS F.A. VAN DAM (eds) (1934–5) *Nederlandsche zeevaarders op de eilanden in de Caraïbische Zee en aan de kust van Colombia en Venezuela gedurende de jaren 1621–1648. Documenten hoofdzakelijk uit het Archivo general de Indias*, Vol. I, 1621–1641 (1934); Vol. II, 1635–1648/9 (1935).

WYTFLIET, CORNELIUS (1597) *Descriptionis Ptolemaicae augmentum*, Louvain.

ZARAGOZA, JUSTO (1883) *Piraterías y agresiones de los ingleses y otros pueblos de Europa en la América Española desde el siglo XVI al XVIII, deducidas de las obras de Dionisio de Alsedo*, Madrid: Imprenta de Manuel Hernández.

absenteeism: of élite classes 225
acculturation 250, 273: antagonistic 301;
    linguistic 284; problem of 247
Acla, Panama 214, 219, 220; charter 220;
    founding of 44, 213
Acosta, Padre José de 257
adelantado (leader) 303 n.3
administrative systems: Indian communities
    95; Spanish in Caribbean 95, 96; Spanish
    municipalities 95
Africa: European traders in 11, 159; *see also*
    West African coast
Africans, black: ancestor cult 285–6;
    anthropology 284–5; beliefs and practices
    283–9; in Brazil 76; culture 247, 283–9;
    ethnic groups 160; legacy of 1, 281–9;
    numbers of 139; religious systems 287; as
    slaves 17, 67, 69, 105, 159–79: in Española
    69, 70, increased demand for 18, 57–8,
    population dominance 70; spirits 284–6,
    287–8; society, and slavery 160; witchcraft
    288
agriculture 268–9: changes to, in Caribbean
    20, 83, 193; and colonization 101, 193;
    importance of 65–6, 131, 154–5; labour,
    and gender 267–8; Taíno 33; *see also*
    conuco agriculture
Aguilar, Jerónimo de 52
Alanje, Isthmus of Panama 214
alarife (surveyor) 219, 235
Alcàçovas, Peace Treaty of, 1479 85–7
Alfinger, Ambrosio 186, 187
Amazon, River 13, 122; peoples of 196
America: biological isolation, end of 1;
    conquest of 2, 3; 'discovery' of 44;
    influence of viii; mainland, importance of
    98
'American Mediterranean' 3, 44, 57
Amerindians 12, 29; and African diseases
    168; 'barbarity' of 51, 53; behaviour
    towards 181; and Catholic faith 64;
    coexistence with Spaniards 94;
    crossbreeding, with slaves 169–70; cultures
    81, 247; decline in 35–8, 40, 78, 98, 101,
    115, 167; and Europeans 15–18 *passim*,
    120, 180, 182; expulsion of 15; extinction of
    15, 19, 57, 64–6, 97, 152, 183, 189, 212, 274,
    290; food resources 29–32, 36, 37; hostility
    of 143–4, 262; images of 257;
    intermarriage 194, 279; labour, forced
    64–6, 102, 104; metal tools, European 193;
    numbers of 15, 19, 35, 36, 65; occupations
    of 168; payment of tribute 92, 267;

physical characteristics 45; relationship
    with *conquistadores* 53–6, 290; rights of
    89; 'savagery' of 45, 53, 251; trading 12,
    13, 32; treaties 145; wars against 13, 81,
    144; *see also* Arawaks; Caribs; disease; meso-
    Indians; neo-Indians; palaeo-Indians; Taínos
Angola, coast of: slaves from 161
Anguila: settlement on 124
animal rearing, in Caribbean 38–9; effect of
    trampling 40; and trade 57
Antequera, Bolivia 219, 220
Antigua: fort on 144; settlement on 13, 124,
    154
Antilles: name derivation 43–4; slaves in 165;
    see also Greater Antilles; Lesser Antilles
Antonelli, Juan Bautista, engineer 231, 232,
    240, 245 n.65; and city maps 316, 317; and
    coral 'stone' 232–3; fortress construction
    234; and water supply 238
Arabs: Spanish attitude to 54; trading
    network 159
Arawakan language 32, 272
Arawaks 15, 31, 33, 267, 272, 275, 279;
    decline in 11; island 33; and sugar
    growing 17; *see also* Taínos
Araya, Punta de: saltpans at 121–2, 125
architects 291; arrival of 235
architecture 290–3 *passim*; religious 291
Arévalo, Rodrigo Sánchez de: and cities 209
areytos (festivals) 271, 274, 277; and music
    295–6
Aristotle: influence of 265–6
Armiñán, Cristóbal de, *alarife* 233, 240
arroyos 40
art: in Caribbean 298–9
Aruba 114: Dutch settlement on 13, 126,
    127; indigenous depopulation 38; slaves
    on 136
Asia: European traders in 11, 62; western sea
    route to 108
Atahualpa, 'king' 49, 50
Atlantic slave trade: *see under* slave trade
Audiencia (royal court of appeal) 89, 96,
    103; *see also under* Española
Avilés, Menéndez de 165
Azores: discovery of 85; slaves in 160
azoteas: see roofs, flat
Aztecs 194, 197, 198
Azua, Haiti 211, 213

Baeza, Spain 208, 209
Bahamas 114; *caciques* in 32; Columbus in
    63; Indians from 65; labour scarcity 212;

neo-Indians in 33: depopulation 38, 183; population of 271; San Andrés 149; settlement on 13, 127
Balbao, Vasco Nuñez de 104, 189, 213, 220, 225, 310
Baracoa, Cuba 214
Barbados 15, 18, 134, 142, 149, 154; African slaves in 139; Dutch in 138; English in 124, 140, 142, 185; forest on 39; Indian depopulation 38; map of 315; settlement on 13, 123, 129, 153, 154; state authority 151; tobacco in 135
Barbuda: Indian depopulation 38; settlement on 124
Barquisimiento, Venezuela: founding 187
barrancas 40
barrios 224
Bastidas, Rodrigo de, Bishop of Puerto Rico and Venezuela 188; and cattle 67
bastides, French: and city building 207–8
Bayamo, Cuba 214
Belize: Caribs in vii
Benzoni, Girolamo 70
Berrio, Antonio de 185
Béthencourt, Norman G. 3, 85
Bobadilla, Francisco de, Royal Governor 182, 210
bohíos (houses) 231, 250, 282; construction 270
Bonaire 114; Dutch settlement on 13, 125–7 *passim*; Indian depopulation 38; saltpans 136
Bonao, Haiti 210, 211
Borburata, Venezuela: founding 187
bozales 70, 166, 178 n.23
Brazil 121, 127; French in 116; Portuguese in 87; slaves from 18, 19; Spanish in 12; sugar in 17, 58, 74–6, 150
Bretendón, Orlando de 235
Breton, Father Raymond 146, 153
bridges: urban 239–40
Brodehaven, Christian 138
buccaneers: *see* pirates
Buenaventura, Haiti 211

cabildo (town hall) 219, 222, 223, 253, 283; stone 231, 232; wooden 230
Cabot, Sebastian, cartographer 313
cacao 57; trade in 116
cacicazgos 267
caciques (*curacas*) 31–2, 64, 100, 101, 181, 182, 267, 275, 305 n.23; rights of 92; and Taíno religion 275–7; white 253
Campeche wood: exploitation of 71
Canary Islands 2, 69, 84–6 *passim*; rediscovery of 3
cannibalism 6–7, 33, 45, 102, 182, 184, 251
Caparra, Puerto Rico 209, 213, 214, 239
Cape Verde Islands 87; Portuguese in 160
capitalism: in Europe 54; in Venezuela 59
capitulaciones (capitulations) 91, 221, 248
carabelas (caravels) 78

Caracas, Venezuela: founding of 59, 109, 187; slave imports 172; slaves in 165; stone bridges 239
Cardona, Nicolás de, cartographer 315
Cariban language 32, 33, 272, 300
Caribbean: and African culture influence 161; books from 298; definition of vi; economies 267–8: decline in 17, 98–9, 119; European luxury products 5; geography of 258–61; impact of African slavery 168; influence in development of colonial system 95–110; island maps 314–15; as 'laboratory' 2, 4, 8, 47–53, 59; role in Hispano-American empire 98; settlement colonization 87, 88–90; signification of 251–5; societies, and slavery 163; Spanish and non-Spanish 154; strategic importance 59–60, 97, 98, 109; as transit region 3; *see also* 'American Mediterranean'
Caribs (*caribes*) vii, 15, 33, 115, 124, 145, 181, 184, 186, 192–3, 267, 268, 271, 279; Black 169, 185, 189; and cannibalism 6–7, 102, 182, 185, 251; decline in 11, 151; elimination of 152; and northern Europeans 120; resistance by 123; wars 140, 143
Carlisle, Earl of 142, 151; and patents 130
carpenters: carving by 299; and latticework 230; in Panamá 230
Cartagena (de Indias), Colombia 97, 118, 154, 161, 188, 204; architecture 225; bridge 240–1; building layout 223; coral 'stone' 233; as *flota*-post 201; fortress at 58, 223, 234; Maroon uprisings 169; numbers of slaves in 168; plan of 316, 236; rectilinearity 216; and slave distribution 165; slave imports 166, 172, 173; water cisterns 237
Carta Puebla de Puerto Real 208, 217, 218
Cartas de Relación 212, 248, 250
Casa de Contratación (House of Trade): control by 165; and slave licences 164
Casas Reales, in cities 222, 243 n.38; stone 232; wooden 230, 231
Cassia fistula 71, 75, 78; fruit 66
Castilla del Oro 189, 217; gold from 56
Catholicism 117–18; and Africans 286; economic values of 10; and Indians 64
cattle 136; supplies of 154
cattle ranching 71, 75, 78, 127; development of 65–7 *passim*; in Española 211, 212; and European disease 83; in *llanos* 187; raids against 71
Cayman Islands 149
cemíes: and Christianity 277; and Taíno religion 276–7
Chagres, Isthmus of Panama: fortress 234
Christianity: in Caribbean 92, 103, 196–7, 198; in Europe 3–4; indigenous adaptation to 272; *see also* missionaries
churches: in cities 222; wooden 230

Ciguayos people 272
cimarrónes: see Maroons
Cisneros, Cardinal Jimenez de 105, 106
cities: architecture 215; assignment of space
    in 220; as capitals 221; central plaza 206,
    208; charters 207, 208, 220; coastal
    213–14; construction materials 223, 229–36,
    293; imports of 234; directives, for building
    211; ecological advantages 208; and
    English policy 202; as fortresses 207, 255;
    founding of 92, 101, 187, 201–41: process
    of 209–29; functions of 201, 202, 207, 222,
    223; government of 208; grid plan 202,
    204–6, 209, 215, 220; and Hispanic culture
    206, 207; infrastructure 236–41: bridges
    239–41, water supply 236–9; layout and
    design 215, 216, 220, 293: ideology of
    206–9 *passim*, 219, irregular 206; mapping
    of 316–17; as means of domination 201–4,
    207, 210; numbers of 209, 256; orthogonal
    plans 218; religious meaning of 207; sites
    of 314; social hierarchization, in urban
    space use 221, 224–9; Spanish 201–8: state
    planning 202; and spread of colonization
    203; stone buildings in 71, 231–4; walled
    227–8: social divide 228, 229
Claeszoon van Campen, Jan 130
climate 34; changes, and settlement 30;
    seasonal effects 34, 35
coastlands: for early settlement 34, 35
cochineal: trade in 59
Code of the Indies 221, 222, 225, 252, 316,
    317
cofradías (guilds) 161, 283
Colombia 96, 289; *see also Tierra Firme*
Colón, Diego, Columbus' son 89, 100–7
    passim, 183, 236, 256, 292
colonial system: administration 96; Caribbean
    influence on 95–110; and *conquistadores*
    96; and entrepreneurs 96; seizure of land
    96
colonization: and conquest 252–5; models
    7–8, 100, 105, 106, 253: Italian commercial
    105, *Reconquista* 105, seigneurial 107
Columbus, Bartolomeo 35, 64, 183, 272–3
Columbus, Christopher 184, 249; dismissal
    88, 99, 182; exploration 63, 85, 86; landing
    in Caribbean 1, 37, 45, 63, 182; and
    language 47; and maps 308; settlement
    colonization 87, 210, 255; spirit of
    adventure 255; writings 53
Colt, Sir Henry 126, 132, 134, 147, 148, 154
compadrazgo 279
Compagnie de Saint-Christophe 123, 128
Compagnie des Iles d'Amérique 129, 130, 139,
    142
Compagnie des Indes Occidentales 150
compaña 54; *Fuero de Cabalgadas* 54
Concepción, Isthmus of Panama 214, 215
Concepción de La Vega, Haiti 106, 210, 211,
    215, 299; and sugar production 67
concubinage 279

conquest: and colonization 252–5; military
    nature of 262–3
conquistadores 7, 44, 45, 47, 79, 90–3 *passim*;
    background of 90–2; and colonial rule 96,
    104; cultural influences 247, 303 n.7;
    independence of 254–5; loss of life 92;
    motives of 92, 253–5; and nudity of
    indigenous people 51; physical needs 213;
    relations with subject peoples 53–6; and
    the *Requerimiento* 48–50, 94; and
    settlements 217; in Venezuela, Gulf of
    186–7
Contarini, Giovanni Matteo, cartographer 310
contracts: of indentured labourers 16
conuco agriculture 36–40 *passim*, 64, 211,
    242 n.18, 267, 282; abandoned 39
Coppier, Guillaume 134, 143
coral 'stone': use of 232–3
Córdoba, Francisco Hernández de 190, 212
Coro, South America 256
Corselles, Pieter van 126
Cortés, Hernán 50, 52, 107, 148, 212, 219–21
    passim, 236
Cosa, Juan de la 188
cotton growing 33, 123, 126, 135, 136, 153, 269
Council of the Indias 95
Courteen, Sir William 124; Company 130
Cozumel, Isthmus of Panama 190
Creole: culture (*criolla*) 248, 303 n.4;
    societies vii
Cuba 6, 44, 58, 212, 272, 289; *caciques* in
    32; carpentry 230; conquest 89, 103, 184;
    decline in 99, 107; fish hatcheries 269;
    ginger in 73; gold in 7, 65; Indians from
    65; livestock trade 57; maps of 315;
    meso-Indians in 31; neo-Indians in 7, 33:
    depopulation 38, 115, 183; palaeo-Indians
    in 29–30; pigs in 39, 212; port cities 97;
    slaves in 164–5, 169; Spanish migrants 99;
    tobacco in 77; towns in 209, 214;
    vegetation 35; woods from 229
Cubagua, Venezuela: pearls from 58, 122,
    185, 187
Cuéllar, Diego Velázquez de 184
cultural reformulation 146–7, 198; with
    African slaves 146–7, 160–1; with Caribs
    146
culture, in Caribbean 20, 198; African 283;
    aspects of 247–302; conflict of 250;
    shaping 248–50
Cumaná, Venezuela 213, 256; missionaries in
    186; slave imports 172
Cuna ethnic group 189, 191, 195
Curaçao 114; Dutch trading station 13, 125–7
    passim, 137, 148, 151, 154; governors of
    130; indigenous population 38; saltpans
    136; slaving centre 163, 166; Spanish
    abandonment 58
curanderismo medicine 283

dances: African 288–9
Danish: in Caribbean 58, 60

Dantiscus, Johannes 4
Darién 187–9 *passim*, 213, 219, 261
Dávila, Pedrarias 104, 189, 220; and city
  building 208, 217–21 *passim*, 224, 225
De Laet, Johannes 121, 126
Delvas, Fernández 166
demographic changes: in Caribbean 70, 98–9;
  in north-west Europe 9
d'Esnambuc, Belin 123, 124
devastaciones (forced resettlement) 119
Dias, Bartolomeu 87
Dieppe school: of cartography 309, 312, 317
discovery, voyages of: and personal
  enrichment 91; provision of 91; reasons
  for 90
disease 139; and Europeans 19, 41, 275; and
  indigenous population 7, 19, 37, 38, 40–1,
  82, 101, 167, 168, 180–1, 183, 192, 274–5
Dominica 310; Amerindian opposition in 15,
  145, 151, 185, 193
doradistas 186, 187
Drake, Sir Francis 117, 216, 231
Du Parquet family, Martinique 142
Du Tertre, Father 134, 137, 154
Dudley, Robert, cartographer 313–14
Dutch: in Caribbean 58, 60, 114–56 *passim*;
  dominance, as traders 122, 125, 126,
  136–8; forts 125; mapping 313, 317;
  settlements in Caribbean 12–13; and slave
  trade 18, 163, 166; sugar technology 17;
  and tobacco growing 76, 77; wars against
  152
Dutch Leeward Islands 126
Dutch West India Company 128, 130
dyewood: growing 135; trade in 12, 116, 136

economy, Caribbean 267–8: decline in 17,
  98–9, 119; foreign domination of 20
education 257, 297–8; and schools 256
El Dorado: search for 186, 187, 198, 260–1,
  266
élites, social: absenteeism 225; in city walled
  enclave 228–9
Elmina slave station 20
encomienda (bonded labour) 4, 55–6, 64–6,
  93–5 *passim*, 104, 105, 211, 242 n.17, 253,
  264, 274
engagé (indentured labour) 16, 132, 137;
  treatment of 134
English 58, 60; in the Caribbean 9–12
  passim, 114–56 *passim*, 184–5; Civil War
  141; and Dutch traders 137; governors
  130; immigrants, numbers of 139, 140;
  mapping by 313, 317; population of 9;
  privateering raids 109; settlements, in
  Caribbean 12–13; and slave trade 163,
  166; and sugar production 17; and tobacco
  growing 76, 77: state monopoly 77
entrepreneurs: in Caribbean 91, 96; and
  proprietor patents 130
environment, Caribbean: effect of Spanish on
  37–41, 189; European changes to 154, 192,

193, 196; and first settlers 29–41; impact of
  46; influence on Europeans 19; influence
  on settlements 15–18 *passim*; new
  man-made 20–1, 39
Erasmus: influence of 264–5
Española (Hispaniola): African slaves in
  69–70, 107, 161; animal rearing 39;
  caciques in 31–2; cattle on 211, 212; city
  plans 215–16; colonization pattern 213;
  early settlements 167; emigration from 65,
  66; European influence 40; famine in 37;
  forts in 210; French in 152; ginger in 73,
  74; gold ornaments in 37; gold production
  65, 101; governor of 101, 182; isolation of
  75; maps of 314, 315; meso-Indians in 31;
  neo-Indians in 33, 35, 38, 167–8: decline in
  65, 115, 183; palaeo-Indians in 29–30;
  Spanish migrants 99; sugar: effect on social
  and political structure 68–9, estates 38,
  production 67, 68, 72, decline in 72–6;
  towns on 209; yucca plantations 78;
  see also Haiti; Santo Domingo
Espejo de Navegantes (sailing directions) 311
Esperanza, Haiti 210
Esquemeling, John, buccaneer 133, 134, 149
Esquivel, Juan de 183, 212, 213
ethnic groups 196; of Africans 160
ethnic intermixing 170
ethnic prejudice: in image of New World 248
Europe: Caribbean dependency on 155;
  Caribbean influence on 83; Christianity in
  3; economic stagnation in 62; luxury
  products from Caribbean 5; and need for
  gold 62–4; supplies from 152, 153; and
  trade with Lesser Antilles 155; trading
  goods 161
European expansion 2, 4; and
  entrepreneurial merchants 10; and
  intra-European trade 10; and investment
  capital 10; north-west, in Caribbean 9–21
European-ness: of *conquistadores* 248–50
Europeans: and Caribbean environment 19;
  effect of disease on 41, 275; effect on
  indigenous societies 180; legacy of, in
  Caribbean 1, 3; northern, in Caribbean 8,
  114–56; numbers of settlers in Caribbean
  16: decline 16, 19; and overseas
  colonization 128
exploitation, models of: in Caribbean 59, 60

factorías (feitorías), Portuguese trading
  settlements 63, 210, 253; collapse of 64
fauna, Caribbean 46, 192; loss of 154
Federmann, Nicolas 186, 187
Fernández de Oviedo y Valdés, Gonzalo 51,
  67, 189, 215, 220, 225, 235, 249, 257, 280,
  295, 298, 300, 312
Figueroa, Rodrigo de 181–2, 186
fishing 269
flora, Caribbean 39, 46, 192
Florida 96, 115, 118; 'discovery' of 183
flota-posts 201

flotas (fleet system): and privateering 12, 97, 109, 118, 143
Fonseca, Bishop Rodriguez de 88
Fonseca Dávila, Isthmus of Panama 219
food resources: of Amerindians 29, 30–2 *passim*, 36, 37, 267–9, 296–7; and conquest 212; European 296–7; importance of 213; syncretism 300
Fort Amsterdam 151
Fort Navidad, Haiti 86, 210, 240
Fort St Augustin 109
fortresses, in Caribbean 58, 144, 155; construction of 109, 292: stone 223; Dutch 125; on Española 210, 215
French: in the Caribbean 9–21 *passim*, 58, 60, 114–56 *passim*, 184; cartographers 309, 312, 317; and Dutch traders 137; Fronde 141; governors 130; immigrants, numbers of 139, 140; merchants 123; population of 9; settlements 12–13; and slave trade 163; and sugar production 17; and tobacco growing 76
Fuggers 23 n.8

Garay, Francisco de 183, 214, 221, 311
García Bravo, Alonso, *alarife* 219, 220
geography, of Caribbean 258–61; mythical 260–1
Geraldini, Bishop Alejandro 215, 235, 298, 300
Germany: and map printing 309; mining entrepreneurs, in Caribbean 4–5
ginger: growing 135; price of 73, 74; production, and decline in sugar 72–6 *passim*, 78; trade in 12, 59, 74, 116, 117: decline in 115
gold 7, 55, 58, 167, 186, 270; in Africa 159; as *cemí* 277; 'cycle' 56, 99, 213; discovery of 63; and *El Dorado* 198; in Española 64; exhaustion of 65, 66, 78, 97, 105; first settlers 271–2; forced Indian labour in 64–6; Indian ornaments 32, 37; and maps 310, 312; need for, in Europe 62–4; production of 65, 66, 102; slaves in 164, 165
Golden Age 45–6
governors: appointment of 130
Greater Antilles 152; *caciques* in 32; development of societies 167; economic decline 115; European effect on 180; gold ornaments 32; *Las Indias occidentales* 114; maps of 308–18 *passim*; meso-Indians in 30–1; neo-Indians in 31; and privateering 149; rapid conquest of 180–4; *see also* Antilles
Grenada 22; Carib resistance 145; settlement on 124, 125, 143–4, 155: and Caribs 145, 185
Grenadines: settlement on 125
Grijalba, Juan de 190, 212
Guadeloupe 310; African slaves in 139; Amerindians in 15, 120, 140, 145; Dutch in 138; French in 184; settlement on 13, 124, 129, 153, 154
Guanahacibibe tribe 31
Guanahani, Bahamas 86, 311
Guanajuato, Mexico: founding 202
Guarionex, native leader 182, 183
Guatemala: indigenous population in 168; slaves in 169
Gubenot, Laurent de 164
Guerrero, Gonzalo 52
Guiana (Guyana): coast of 13, 118, 122; development of societies in 167; European settlement in 127; *see also* Wild Coast
Guinea coast, Africa: slaves from 19, 150, 161
gully erosion: and animal trampling 40
Guyamí 189, 191, 195
Guyana 96; *see also* Guiana

Haiti 6, 109; Columbus' landing on 63, 86; decline on 87, 99, 107; gold in 7; indigenous population 7; port cities 97; *see also* Española
Hanseatic League 84
Havana, Cuba 214; architecture 225; carpentry in 230; coral 'stone' 233; dominant role of 75, 97, 98, 118, 154, 236; as *flota*-post 201; fortress at (La Fuerza) 58, 118, 215, 223, 234; founding 256; lumber trade 230; Maroon uprisings 169; number of slaves in 169; plan of 316; raids on 109; slave imports 172, 174; water supply 238; wood construction 229
Hawkins, Sir John 117, 119
Hawley, Henry 142
Henry the Navigator 3, 85
Heertjies, Cornelius 138
Herrera, Antonio de 313
Herrera, Juan de 235
hides: production of 6; trade in 12, 38, 116, 117, 127, 149, 187; uses of 66
Higüey, Dominican Republic 44, 214
Hispaniola: *see* Española
Hispano-American cities 201, 202
Hojeda, Alonso de 188, 224
Honduras 167; slaves in 169
horros (freed slaves) 283
Houel family, Guadeloupe 142
houses: in cities 225–6; clay-and-wattle 233; frontage widths 226, 227; indigenous 270–1; *see also* bohíos
Huguenots 118, 151
humidity: and health 260
hunting 269; tools 268
hurricanes 34, 47
Hutten, Philip von 186, 187

immigrants: from Europe 155; numbers of 138–9; slave 140, 150, 156, 163
Incas 197
indentured labourers: contracts 16, 132; European decrease 17; exploitation of 133; lack of 136; recruitment of 131–2;

wretched conditions 16, 131, 133, 134;
 see also engagé
indigenes: see Amerindians; Arawaks; Caribs;
 Taínos
indigo: decline in 115; growing 126, 153;
 trade in 59, 116
Indo-Americans: *see* Amerindians
influenza: effect on Indians 41
ingenios (sugar mills) 67–9 *passim*; in
 Española 72; in Puerto Rico 72; raids
 against 71; and tobacco use 77
interbreeding: practice of 51, 169–70, 194,
 279
interpreters: need for 52–3
investment capital 127; and European
 expansion 10, 14; in sugar, in Santo
 Domingo 68; in tobacco 125
iron: imported, for house construction 234
Isabela, Española 44, 210, 255, 256
Islas del Mar del Norte 115
Italians: and slave trade 162, 163
Italy 2; merchants 4

Jagüeyes 237
Jamaica 212, 289; animal rearing in 39;
 attacks on 149; *caciques* in 32; English in
 152; Indians from 65; isolation of 75;
 maps of 315; neo-Indians in 33;
 depopulation of 183; number of slaves in
 165, 169; occupation of 183; population of
 271; settlements on 214; as slave centre
 166; slave profits 166; Spanish
 abandonment 58
Jocheme, Albert 138
joint-stock companies 14, 115, 127, 136, 148

Kingston, Jamaica 214; planning of 202
kinship relations: African 289; indigenous
 278–9; mixed marriages 279

La Cosa, Juan de, cartographer 309–10
La Filipina, Isthmus of Panama 214
La Guayra, Venezuela: founding of 59
La Malinche: as interpreter 52
La Navidad, Haiti 44
Labat, Father 151
'laboratory': Caribbean as 2, 4, 8,
labour: scarcity 150, 212: in early settlements
 167, 183; sexual division of 278; *see also*
 indentured labourers *and under* Africans,
 black
ladinos 70, 178 n.23, 283
land lots: Columbus' distribution of 256; units
 of 135
Landa, Diego de 191
language 47, 300; colonial Spanish 50;
 see also Arawakan; Cariban; interpreters
Lares de Buahaba, Haiti 211
Las Casas, Bartolomé de 35, 38, 89, 100, 111
 n.4, 183, 184, 189, 249, 257, 265, 269, 298
Laws of Burgos, 1512 94, 100, 103–5
 passim

Le Grand, Pierre 126
Lesser Antilles: development of societies 167;
 French 154; French, English and Dutch in
 114–56 *passim*, 180, 184; Indians from 65;
 maps of 308–18 *passim*, population of
 138–9, 271; slower conquest of 180, 184–5;
 and trade with Europe 155; way stations in
 115, 116, 120; *see also* Antilles
Liendo, Rodrigo de, architect 291
Ligon, Richard 125, 134, 139, 140, 146–7,
 153
Lima, Peru 202; vice-royalty of 95, 97
literature, Caribbean 298
llanos, of Orinoco 187; ranches in 187
L'Olive, Captain Liénart de 124, 129
López de Velazco, Juan 209, 313
'Lords Proprietors' 14
Los Santos, Isthmus of Panama 214
Lucayans 186
Lucayas: *see* Bahamas

Macoryxes people 272
Madeira: discovery of 85; slaves in 160
maestros de azúcar 69
Magalhaes (Magellan), Fernâo de 108
Magdalena, Haiti 210
magic: practice of 263
Malcocello, Lancellotto 3
males, young: as African slaves 19; as
 indentured labourers 132; unmarried
 immigrants from Europe 9, 10, 16, 139–40,
 141, 146, 149
maps, of Caribbean 5, 308–18; Admiralty
 charts 313, 314; *padrón real*, master map
 309; *pinturas* 313; portolan 249, 310, 311;
 printed 309
Maracaibo, Venezuela: founding of 109
marble: in Africa 59
Margarita: early settlements 167; pearls from
 58, 122, 186, 192; slave imports 172; slaves
 in 165
Maroons (runaway slaves) 20, 70–1, 76, 147,
 148, 169, 170, 184, 185, 213, 281, 283, 286,
 288; African culture of 161; wars of 71,
 169, 283
Marquez, Pedro Menéndez 233
Martinique: Amerindians on 15, 120, 140,
 144, 145; Dutch in 138; French in 184;
 settlement on 13, 124, 154
Martyr, Peter 45, 50, 212, 255, 267, 303 n.5,7,
 304 n.20, 312, 314, 315
matrilineal filiation 278
Maya 190–1, 194, 197, 198; culture 191
Mayan: settlements, and European disease
 181; territories 44
Mediterranean: influence on Caribbean 3, 83;
 merchants, in Iberian Peninsula 5; *see also*
 'American Mediterranean'
Melilla, Jamaica 214
Menéndez de Avilés, Pedro 109
Mercator, Gerard, cartographer 313
mercedes de tierra (land ownership) 55

merchants, European: and Carib settlement
14, 136; charters for 128, 130;
entrepreneurial, and European expansion
10; investment 127
meso-Indians 30–1
mestizos 51, 80, 224, 279
Mexico 80, 107, 115, 118; emigration to 66;
Spanish in 12, 44, 81, 98, 99; trade with
57; vice-royalty of 95, 97, 108, 165
Mexico City 203; design 219
mezzanine-storey: in houses 225, 226, 231,
232
military: behaviour, and Tribal Zones 195;
nature of conquest 262–3
'Miller' atlas 310
Miskito 195
missionaries: in Caribbean 89, 186, 196–7;
and colonists 93–5; and towns 202; value
of 263; in Yucatán 191
missions: rule of, in Venezuela 186, 189
Modyford, Thomas 136
monasteries: architecture 291; in cities 222,
223
Montejo, Francisco de 190
Montemayor de Cuenca 315
Montesinos: sermon 1511 89, 94, 100, 103–5
passim, 264
Montezuma 'king' 49; palace 220
Montijo, Isthmus of Panama 214
Montserrat: Caribs in 120; settlement on 13,
123, 124, 129, 154
Morales, Andrés de 314
Moya, Luis de, master builder 235
mudéjar influence 230, 292, 305 n.25
mulattos 169, 179 n.31, 224; free-mulatto
companies 170; outside city walls 228
music 294–6; African 289, 295; compositions
295; and cultural reformulation 146–7;
instruments 295, 296; inter-racial groups
294; polyphonic 294
myths: indigenous 279–81

ñáñigos (secret societies), Cuba 286
Narváez, Pánfilo de 212
Natá, Isthmus of Panama 214, 215, 219;
charter 220
navigation: instruments 314; knowledge of
249
navíos (ships) 78
negroes: outside walled cities 228; *see also*
Africans, black
neo-Indians 31–3; extinction of 38; in
Greater Antilles 31; villages of 31–2
Netherlands, The: and the Caribbean 9–21
passim; population of 9; *see also* Dutch
Nevis: Caribs in 38, 120; northern Europeans
in 121, 123; settlement on 13, 124, 125,
129, 143, 154
New Spain: conquest of 50; vice-royalty of
97, 108
New World: idealization of 248
Nicuesa, Diego de 188, 212, 213, 224

Nombre de Dios, Isthmus of Panama 97,
214, 219; charter 220; wood construction
231
North Sea: merchants of, role in Caribbean 4,
5
nudity: of Amerindians, and Spanish 50–1
Nueva Córdoba: *see* Cumaná
Nuñez de Balboa, Vasco: *see under* Balboa

Ochoa, Hernando de 164
Ojeda, Alonso de, 212, 213
*Ordenanzas de Descubrimiento, Nueva
Población y Ocupación de las Indias*
(Ordinances for the Discovery, New
Settlement and Occupation of the Indies)
221–3 *passim*, 292
Order of Knights, German: in Baltic 4
Orinoco, River 13, 122, 192; region 185
orisha worship 273, 285, 287
Oristán, Jamaica 214
Orpín, Juan de 186
Ortelius, Abraham, cartographer 313
Ossorio, Antonio, governor of Santo Domingo
317
Ovando, Nicolás de, governor of Española
64, 100, 101, 184, 212, 279; and
city-building 210, 211, 217–19 *passim*,
221, 234, 253; and slave imports 164

padrinazgo 279
palaeo-Indians 29–30
Panamá 214; architecture 225, 226;
Audiencia 222; *cabildo* 219; carpenters in
230; charter 220; design 219; as *flota*-post
201; founding of 44, 225; freed slaves in
170; house frontage width 226–7; lumber
trade 230; map of 316; new, military
walled 219, 222, 227; numbers of slaves in
168; social groupings 226; stone bridges
239, 240; water cisterns 237, 238; wood
construction 229, 231; The Vaults 238
Panamá Viejo 219; monastery 223; plan of
317
Panama, Gulf of: pearls in 186
Panama, Isthmus of 71, 89, 96, 97, 104, 108,
116, 117; *Audiencia* of 189; Maroon
uprisings 169; settlement on 214, 218
Pané, Fray Ramón 275, 276, 298
Pánuco 213
paranaghiri 197, 198
Paria 85
patents: of proprietors 130; for settlements
128–9, 148
patroon system 130
Pearl Coast 185, 261; early settlements 167
pearls: and slaves 165; trade in 12, 55, 58,
116, 122, 186, 269
Pelleprat, Father Pierre 133
Pembroke, Earl of: and patents 130
Penonomé, Isthmus of Panama 214
Peru 107, 115; 'Gate of' 114; silver from
214, 240; Spanish in 12, 50, 97–9 *passim*

pigs: in Caribbean 39, 120, 154; in Española 211
Pineda, Alonso Avarez de 310, 311
piracy, in Caribbean 12, 14, 108, 117, 121, 148; English 148; French 119, 120; and Greater Antilles 149; as Spanish left 58, 97; and sugar decline 74–5
plantation: economy 7, 107; introduction 41; products, trade in 12; setting up 135
plazas: desacralization of 225; in towns 219, 220, 222, 224, 293
plunder and pillage: advantage of 55
poetry, Caribbean 298
political authority: on islands 142
political conflicts, in Europe: influence on Caribbean 141
polygamy: practice of 50
Ponce de Léon, Juan 213; and city-building 209, 215, 216, 218, 219; in Puerto Rico 183, 212
population: changes in north-west Europe 9; indigenous Indian 7, 35, 36; natural growth of 155; of settlers 271; size of early settlements 138–9, 140; social composition 10
Portobelo, Isthmus of Panama 71, 97, 214; Casa de la Negrería (slave house) 223; coral 'stone' construction 231–3; customs house 222, 233, 245 n.67; fortress at 58, 223, 234; founding 201, 219; layout 227; plan of 316; shipbuilding 230; slaves in 166; stone bridges 239, 240; topography of 222; water cisterns 238; water supply 236; wood construction 229, 231
Portugal 2, 3: sugar masters from 69
Portuguese: in Africa 59; in Asia 1; Atlantic exploration 63, 115, 116; maps by 309; slave monopoly 165, 166, 176 n.9; slave trading 20, 162, 163, 281; trading bases, in Africa 85
Potosí 202; founding 203
precious metals: trade in 12, 56
privateering: *see* piracy
proprietors 131, 150; absentee 130
proprietorship patents 130
Protestantism 117–18; and individual capitalism 10–11
Providence 149
pueblos (small Indian settlements) 256, 257, 270, 271, 293
Puerto Plata, Haiti 68, 211
Puerto Príncipe, Cuba 214
Puerto Real, Haiti 211; *Carta Puebla de Puerto Real* 208, 217, 218
Puerto Real, Spain 208, 209
Puerto Rico (San Juan) viii, 6, 44, 71, 86, 181, 183, 184, 212, 289, 310; animal rearing in 39; *caciques* in 32; conquest of 103; early settlements 167; ginger in 73; gold in 65; indigenous population 7: resistance by 183; isolation of 75; maps of 315; neo-Indians in 33: depopulated 38, 65, 183;

northern Europeans in 121; population 271; port cities 97; slave imports 172, 174; slaves in 164–6 *passim*: profits from 166; Spanish migrants 99; sugar production 72: decline in 72–6; tobacco in 77; towns in 209, 214: building 213, plans 216; yucca plantations 78

Quesada, Jimenez de 187
Quiñones, Losada 227
quotas, slave 164; proportion of women 170

raiding 116; *see also* piracy
Raleigh, Sir Walter 198
Reconquista 2, 4, 7, 84, 90, 91, 100–2 *passim*, 107, 204, 207, 209
Recopilación de Leyes de Indias: see Code of the Indies
relaciones geográficas 313
relationships: marriage and kinship 194, 196, 278–9
religions: indigenous 197–8; *see also* Catholicism; Christianity; Protestantism
religious: architecture 291; conflicts, from Europe 141; domination 263; life, and buildings 256; motivations, in Caribbean 117–18
Remedios, Isthmus of Panama 214
repartimiento 4, 55, 56, 93, 96, 101, 102, 104; *see also encomienda* 06, 181
Requerimiento, the 48–50, 94, 100, 104, 248
rescates (illicit exchange) 116, 117
Ribero, Diogo, cartographer 311
Richelieu, Cardinal 123, 128
Río de la Hacha: slave imports 172; slave profits in 166
Rojas, Cristóbal de, cartographer 316
roofs: flat 233, 245–6 n.70; tiles, materials for 233
runaway slaves 70–1; numbers of 70; raids by 71
Ruyters, Dierick 121

Saba: Dutch trading station 13, 126
St Augustine, Florida: church in 223; fortress 223, 234; founding of 201; lime in 233; stone construction 233; and topography 222
St Christopher: *see* St Kitts
St Croix 310; settlement on 125, 154
Saint-Domingue 152, 156: *see also* Haiti
St Eustatius: Dutch trading station 13, 126, 154; governors of 130; patroon system in 130
St Kitts 13, 119, 124, 126, 129, 140, 143, 154; Caribs in 38, 120, 144; decline of 150; French in 123; tobacco in 135
St Lucia: Caribs in 38: resistance by 145; English in 185; northern Europeans in 121, 122, 124

St Martin 143; Dutch trading station 13, 125, 126, 148; fort 125; governors of 130; northern Europeans in 121, 125; sea-salt in 126, 148
St Thomas Aquinas: and cities 206, 209, 219
St Vincent: Amerindian opposition in 15, 120, 145, 151, 169, 185; northern Europeans in 121, 125
salt 282; trade in 12, 121–2, 127, 269; gathering 125; sea- 126
saltpans 14, 122, 120–2, 126, 136,
Salvaleón de Higüey 211, 213
Salvatierra de la Sabana, Haiti 211, 213
San German, Puerto Rico 214
San José de Oruña, Trinidad 256
San Juan, Puerto Rico 67, 205, 214, 236, 256; church in 215; coral 'stone' 233; fortress at (La Fortaleza) 118, 215, 223, 234; founding 201; plan of 316; stone bridges 239–40; water supply 236–7; wood construction 229
San Juan de la Maguana, Haiti 211, 213
Sancti Spiritus 214
Sandoval, Alonso de 160
Santa Cruz, Alonso de, cosmographer 315
Santa Cruz, Haiti 121, 211
Santa Fe, Isthmus of Panama 215
Santa Fe, Spain 209, 218; influence, in city planning 205, 208
Santa María de la Antigua del Darién 189, 209, 213, 214, 219; plaza 220; slave imports 175; slaves in 165
santería 300
Santiago de Cuba 67, 214, 256; construction materials 234; water supply 237
Santiago de la Vega (Spanish Town), Jamaica 202, 214
Santo Domingo: *see also* Española
Santo Domingo 44, 56, 58, 64, 71, 97, 289; *Audiencia* 89, 97, 103, 105, 106, 108, 180, 313; and cattle trade 67; and ginger 73; Maroons in 281: uprisings 169; slaves 166, 169: acclimatization 164, imports of 172, 174, profits in 166, smuggling of 177–8, uprising by 164; and sugar 67, 68: decline in 75, investment in 68, 71; trade with 57, 75; vice-royalty 289
Santo Domingo (town) 98, 211; archbishopric 108; buildings construction 235–6; cathedral in 215, 235, 292; church in 235; coral 'stone' 233; decline of 118, 236; fortification plan 317; fortress (Homenaje Tower) 58, 215, 234, 292; founding of 210, 256; monastery 256; plan of 215, 316; as political centre 68, 69, 115; stone buildings in 71; university of 108, 109, 257, 297; and water supply 238–9
Santo Tomás, Haiti 210, 255
Sauvage, Jean le 106
Schouten, Pieter 126
sculpture, Caribbean 300
sea level: changes in, and settlement 29, 30

seigneurial-colonial structure 55
señores de ingenios 68, 69, 72, 73
Sephardic Jews: and European expansion 11
Sepúlveda, Juan Ginés 257, 265
servants: and slaves 147
settlement colonization 87, 91, 167; on American mainland 107; and Amerindians 15–18 *passim*; dispersed 155; and economic exploitation 215; fear of abandonment 152, 153; labour scarcity 88–90, 167; north-west European 12–13; numbers 271; pattern of 215; and piracy 148; and society 255–8; spread of 124; types of 13; and way stations 122
settlers: numbers in Caribbean, from Europe 16, 138–9, 140
Sevilla del Oro, Jamaica 214
Seville navigation school 308, 317, 318
sexes, disparity between: and labour 278; and population 19
sexuality: and Amerindians 50–2, 257; obsessiveness, and Africans 288
shamanism 197
shanty towns 225
shareholding companies 10
shipbuilding 230
Sieur du Bu 142
silver 198; in Mexico 97, 115; mining 8; in Peru 214; shipments, and piracy 117, 119
slash-and-burn agriculture 193, 267
slave rebellions 70–1, 164, 262, 283; *see also* Maroons
slaves, African: acclimatization of 163–4; as African wealth symbol 160; crossbreeding, with Indians 169; daily life of 282–3; demand for 17, 18; development of societies 167; freed 170; massive introduction of 140, 150, 156; numbers of 139, 165, 281; population dominance 69; resistance to status 169; and servants 147; and sugar 18, 67, 282; young males 19; *see also horros*
slave licences 163, 164
slave trade 19, 55, 117, 124, 159–79, 183, 281; administration 163; monopolies on 163
slavery: and European capitalism 162; ideology of 170; and legislation 170–1; and sustained development of colonies 171
smallpox epidemic 1518–19: and Indians 66, 73
smuggling: in Caribbean 75, 143, 149; raids 117, 119; of slaves 165, 177 n.22
social divisions 148
societies: development of 166–7; early, in Caribbean 38–49; fragmented 57; indigenous, and slavery 163; and settlement 255–8; structured 57; temporary character of 252; urban plans and hierarchy 224–9
Sores, Jacques de 109, 117
South America: 'Wild Coast' 13

Spain 3; Ferdinand and Isabella in 2, 44, 85, 87, 88–9, 101–5 *passim*, 249, 259, 291: and city planning 205, 208, 209; population of 9

Spanish: and Amerindians 31, 37, 95; in Asia 11; and Caribbean environment 37; colonial, language 50; colonial strategy 57–60; conquest, of American mainland 3, 98; decline in migrants 99; expansion 9–10, 79–110, 115; fear of black slaves 71; first expeditions 43–5; ideology of 254; influence, areas of 8; maps 308–9, 313, 315, 317; settlements, in Caribbean 12: raids on 13, 143; slave administration 163; state monopoly in tobacco 77; in *Tierra Firme* 186–91

spices: need for 62

Spira (Hohemut) Jorge 186, 187

spirit-worship 284–6: *see also orisha* worship

states: control on colonial settlements 128, 150: in Barbados 151

stone: for buildings 71, 231–4; carved 234; fortresses 234

stonecutters: scarcity of 231, 234

stonecutting: cost of 230

strategic position: of Caribbean 59–60, 97, 98, 109

Stuyvesant, Pieter 131, 136, 142

sugar: and African slaves 17, 67, 69; 'cycle' 99; Dutch technology 17; exports 67, 71; first plantations 67–70; price of 73; processing, and ginger 74; production 17, 66–8 *passim*, 71, 72, 78, 105, 135, 150: decline in 72–6, 115; and social and political structure 68; and taxes 68; trade in 12, 58, 116, 117; *see also ingenios; trapiches*

surveyors, naval 314

Taínos (*aruaca/guatiao*) 7, 33, 181, 186, 251; and *areytos* 274; diet of 268; myths 279; religious systems 275–8; tribal society 272; words 300

technical knowledge: European 296–7; indigenous 296, 297

Testu, Guillaume le, cartographer 312

Tierra Firme (Venezuela and Colombia) 'Spanish Main' 78, 114–18 *passim*, 121, 127; Caribs in 181; and changed ecology 189, 192; European occupation of 180, 185–99; export of slaves to 70, 151; number of slaves in 165, 168; tobacco in 122; towns in 209

tobacco 277; decline of 150; growing 33, 76–7, 123, 126, 127, 135–7 *passim*, 148, 268; investment 125; as medicine 76; price decline 17; in St Kitts 148; smuggling 76, 77; trade in 12, 14, 78, 122, 149: and Dutch 126

Tobago: Caribs in 38: resistance by 145; northern Europeans in 121, 125; settlement in 130

Toledo, Don Fadrique de 143

tools, metal: introduction to Amerindians 193

Tordesillas, Treaty of 87, 99, 309

tortoiseshells: trade in 116

Tortola: settlement on 124

Tortuga 49, 167; saltponds 125

trade: African 11, 159–79 *passim*; Asian 11, 62; in Caribbean products 12; European goods 161; importance of 155; inter-regional 56, 57; intra-European, and expansion 10, 84; local 56; monopolies 151; Spanish inter-settlement 12; transatlantic 56–7; *see also under* slave trade

trade routes: control of 58; influence of 155; and sugar decline 74–5

trading houses: in Seville 88

trading settlements: forts, Portuguese 85; *see also factorías*

transculturation 250

trapiches (sugar mills) 67, 68

Tribal Zones 192, 194, 195

tribalism: characteristics of 272

tribalization 194, 196

Trinidad 118, 122, 167, 181, 185, 261; colonial woodwork 230; first occupation of 185; meso-Indians in 30; neo-Indians in 32; northern Europeans in 121; number of slaves in 165; palaeo-Indians in 29–30

Trinidad, Cuba 214; wood construction 229

Trujillo: founding 187

Urabá, Venezuela, concession 188, 189, 213

Urabá, Gulf of 187, 188

urban concentrations: development of 155; *see also* cities

Valencia: founding of 187

Van Ulmen, Ferdinand 4

Vargas Machuca, Bernardo de 207

Vasco da Gama 87

vecinos (householders) 73, 253

vegetation 34, 35

Velázquez, Diego de, Governor 107, 212–14 *passim*, 256

Velázquez, Miguel 294

Vellosa, Gonzalo de, sugar producer 67

Venezuela 96, 181, 187, 289; coast, as source of slaves 59; cocoa from 57; missions in 186, 189; slave imports 184; slaves in 165; tobacco growing 77; Welsers in 59, 108

Venezuela, Gulf of: exploration 185–99

Veracruz 97, 118; fortress at 58; founding of 107; grid design 219, 220; plan 316; and slave distribution 165; slave imports 166, 172, 173

Veragua 213; concession 188, 189

Verapaz, Haiti 211, 213

Verlinden, Charles 3

Vespucci, Amerigo 44–6 *passim*, 53, 251, 312

Vignon, Nicolas 136
Villa Diego, Jamaica 214
Villanueva de Yaquino, Haiti 211
Virgin Gorda: northern Europeans in 121
Virgin Islands: Indian depopulation 38
Virginia: European settlement in 127
vodún 273, 287, 300

Walbeeck, Johannes van 126, 130
Warner, Captain Thomas: commission 129; in
    St Kitts 123, 129, 135
wars: Carib attacks 143–4; guerrilla 144; at
    La Vega Real 182; between Spanish and
    north Europeans 117, 118, 143
Warwick, Earl of 149
water supply: scarcity 239; urban 236–9
way stations 192; in Lesser Antilles 115, 116,
    122, 125
Wayú people 187, 191, 195
Welser company 5, 108, 186; failure in
    Venezuela 59; and slave imports 164
Weltanschauung 247, 252, 290, 304 n.11
West Africa coast 3, 85; *factorías* in 63
West India Company 121, 126, 151; *see also*
    Dutch West India Company
Westphalia, Treaty of 152

white population: freebooters 156; growth
    139; immigration 139; poor, minority 156;
    and slaves 70; socioeconomic profile 141
'Wild Coast': of South America 3, 122, 127
women: Indian, whitening 279; proportion of
    indentured labourers 133, 141; slaves,
    imported 170; white, shortage of 170
woods, rare: in building construction 229–31
    passim; carving 299; from Cuba 229;
    cutting 193; exhaustion of supplies 154;
    trade in 121, 127, 153, 270
work, concept: and Indians 274
writings: on Caribbean 298
Wytfliet, Cornelius 133

Ximénez de Cisneros, Cardinal 264

Yaquino, Haiti 213
Yucatán 96, 190–1, 193–4, 212, 213; Indian
    population of 58, 168, 181; peninsula 311;
    slave profits 166; Spanish abandonment
    191
yucca plantations 78

Zacatecas, Mexico: founding of 202
Zanja Real (Royal Canal): in Havana 238